PEELERS

— TO —

PANDAS

*An Illustrated History of
the Leicester City Police*

PEELERS TO PANDAS

An Illustrated History of the Leicester City Police

by Ben Beazley

Leicester Mercury

breedon **books** PUBLISHING

First published in Great Britain in 2001 by
The Breedon Books Publishing Company Limited
Breedon House, 3 The Parker Centre, Derby, DE21 4SZ.

Dedication:
for Elaine and Mark

ISBN 1 85983 231 8

Printed and bound by Butler & Tanner, Frome, Somerset
Cover printing by Greenshires, Leicester

Contents

Acknowledgements

The compilation and completion of this book has only been possible with the help and assistance of a large number of people. Some are professionals who have, in the course of their work, steered me in the right direction and fielded the myriad of queries which I have thrown at them. Others – usually old colleagues and retired officers – have given freely of their time and knowledge to identify many of the photographs which appear on these pages. A final group have – most trustingly – given me ready access to photographs and items in their personal possession, along with permission to reproduce them. It is most pleasing for me, now that the work is over, to be able to say a specific thanks to them all.

For permission to publish photographs from the Leicestershire Constabulary collection, lodged at the Leicestershire Records Office, I would like to thank the chief constable, David Wyrko QPM BSc. My thanks also go to Katrina Kemp of the Leicestershire Constabulary Registry Department, for her help in sorting through dusty shelves to recover documents and pictures.

Special thanks go to Carl Harrison, the county archivist of the Record Office for Leicestershire, Leicester and Rutland, for the assistance of his staff. I would particularly like to thank Lois Edwards for her efforts in searching out documents and retrieving heavy ledgers, and Clive Chapman for his invaluable contribution: tracing photographs buried in deep and often uncatalogued boxes. Similarly I am indebted to Alan Jeffreys of the Imperial War Museum, for his patience in solving the military questions that have arisen.

Without the photographs which have been so generously loaned, and the help given in identifying them, this book would be immeasurably diminished. In addition to the individual acknowledgements which appear throughout the book, I would like to make special mention of the following for their time and efforts: Philip and Joan Burt; the late Winston Goodman; Noel Haines; Norman Hull and Cliff Robinson. I would also like to thank Graham Hales of Breedon Books for his skills, and the time which he has spent in presenting the photographic work and other illustrations.

A further vote of thanks goes to John Peacock for his help in resolving queries over warrant numbers; to Steve Jeffrey for his help in researching the World War One Roll of Honour; to Geoff Williams for his help in preparing the draft copy; to Mike Ward for his numeracy skills; and to Ian Coutts for keeping my computer running, despite my best efforts to sabotage it.

My final thanks must go to four people, whose contributions have been especially relevant to the successful completion of this book. Jock Joiner, who has resolved so many issues by sharing his encyclopaedic first-hand knowledge of the Leicester City Police since 1935 with me, and identified so many people. David Simpson and Noel Haines, whose time spent identifying photographs, uniforms and badges, both police and military, has been indispensable. Lastly my wife Judy, for the dozens of hours which she has spent helping my research and working on the scanned images of damaged photographs in order to bring them up to a publishable level.

To all of these people, and any others whom I may have inadvertently overlooked – thank you.

Author's Note

The time spent researching this book has been particularly rewarding to me as an ex-officer of the Leicester City Police. It has also highlighted the need for certain explanations and clarifications in relation to some of the subject matter.

Probably the most basic point to clarify is the way in which the book has been set out. During the period 1836–1967, Leicester Borough Police and the subsequent City Police force was commanded by ten separate individuals. During the 19th century and the early part of the 20th century they were referred to as 'head constables', although this title later changed to 'chief constable', in order to fall into line with County Police forces. The work has therefore been presented following the chronological sequence of each of these men's period in office.

Historically the title of 'head constable' was taken by the officer in charge of a Borough or City force, while that of 'chief constable' was given to those commanding a county force. The apparent reason for this difference is that a head constable was responsible for his actions to the Watch Committee, which had been appointed by the local Corporation, while a chief constable was responsible to a county authority and perceived to have wider field of responsibility. In the case of Leicester Borough Police, the title appears to have been amended to chief constable early in World War One. In August 1914, Herbert Allen is referred to as 'the head constable', but from February 1915 onward he and his successors are given the rank of chief constable.

In respect of illustrations, it is an unfortunate fact that the further back one goes in history, the fewer photographs are available. For this reason, during the early chapters, there are relatively fewer illustrations than in later years. While this creates in places a numerical imbalance of photographs per chapter, it is I feel, preferable to reproducing matter out of context.

Either by research or by tapping into the personal recollections of various people, it has been possible to identify the subjects in a great number of the photographs – especially from 1931 onward. However, in some group photographs, there may be officers who have not been positively identified. While in some cases a blank space has been left in the captioning, in others it has been felt that it is better to leave out the identification of individuals in the picture altogether.

The object of this book is that it should be a good read for anyone with an interest in its subject, and at the same time be a serious research tool for the reader who is seeking specific information. It is for this reason that the section covering officers serving between January 1929 and April 1967 has been included. While every care has been taken to ensure that this section is as accurate as possible, there will, inevitably, with such a volume of entries, be some minor errors or omissions. Often people who were well known by one name are referred to in official documentation by a slightly different one. For instance, 'Hadyn' Bestwick is referred to using his first name, and appears as George Bestwick. Similarly, 'George' Brobyn is shown as Rowland Brobyn, 'Frank' Sandall as Thomas Sandall, and so on. Additionally, it is often difficult to track policewomen's history, as their warrant numbers are seldom quoted in records, and their names change with marriage.

Where I have thought it helpful to anyone using the book for research purposes, I have included in the captions of some of the older photographs the warrant numbers of officers, which while clear in the original picture, do not reproduce well. Although the names of the officers may not be known at the present time, this may be remedied by someone at a later date. Again, where appropriate I have pointed out and dated obvious changes in uniform, headgear and insignia, in the hope that this may assist a reader examining other photographs at a later date.

There are two tables produced as additions to the staff list section. One is of the force on the day that Oswald Cole became chief constable, in January 1929; the other of the force on the day that it ceased to exist in April 1967. Where there are gaps in the numerical lists of constables this is due either to the number being vacant, or to the fact that the identity of the holder of that number is unclear.

A particular area of difficulty has been in assigning the correct warrant numbers to sergeants. This arises from the practice of having a fixed establishment of sergeants at any one time. On promotion to sergeant, a constable lost his old number and took a new 'sergeant's number'. This

has caused some difficulty in drawing up the list of sergeants in the 'snapshot' of the force in April 1967. To circumvent the problem, I have arranged the list of sergeants serving in 1967 in alphabetical order, and listed their number where it is definitely known. The difficulty has been compounded by the fact that in the closing months of the force's history, some officers were promoted to the temporary rank of sergeant in preparation for the increased establishment which the amalgamated force would need. These men did not change their number at that time and after amalgamation the number-changing system was discontinued.

While some of the above may seem somewhat complicated, the explanations are given primarily for the benefit of any serious student who may wish to expand on the work in this book.

I hope that all who read the book will gain as much enjoyment from it as I did in writing it.

Ben Beazley

'I promise and swear that I will well and truly serve our Sovereign Lord the King in the Office of one of the Constables for the Borough of Leicester until I shall from thence be discharged by another being sworn in my room. During my continuance in the Office I will in all things well and faithfully demean and behave myself according to the best of my skill and judgement therein'.

The oath sworn before the Watch Committee and Mayor of Leicester Borough by Frederick Goodyer and the Constables appointed in January 1836.

CHAPTER ONE

Frederick Goodyer
(February 1836–December 1839)

In January 1836, Leicester, a medium-sized county town of around 60,000 inhabitants, situated in the heart of the English Midlands, was about to undergo a political and social metamorphosis which would take it well into the 20th century. Politically, an Act of Parliament – the Municipal Reform Act 1835 – replaced the existing scheme of local government in 179 boroughs throughout England and Wales with a completely new system. Socially, for the first time in Leicester a structured police force was established, which was to remain in place for the next 131 years.

These two changes, social and political, were immutably bound together, and it is therefore necessary to take a brief look at them, in order to understand what followed.

Law and order throughout the country was at a low ebb in the years following the Napoleonic Wars (1792-1815). Historically the responsibility for the policing of society had varied according to the time, but had rarely been satisfactory.

In the 16th century villages and towns were mainly administered by Justices of the Peace, who acted partly as magistrates and partly as influential landowners. An Act of Parliament, passed during the reign of Charles II in the late 17th century, enabled men to be employed as watchmen. Known as 'Charlies' after the monarch who had established them, the low standards maintained by those who undertook the work soon led to the name becoming a by-word for incompetence. As time passed, in an attempt to give some meaning to their efforts at preserving law and order, local authorities engaged parish constables to supervise and assist the watchmen.

The situation in London was no less difficult. Plagued by corrupt magistrates, including such men as the infamous Jonathan Wild, an attempt had been made during the 1740s to regularise matters with the establishment of the Bow Street Runners. Recruited by the magistrate Henry Fielding, the tasks undertaken by the Runners included serving court writs and acting as detectives.

Although the need for some form of professional police force to be established throughout the country was obvious, there were those in Government who felt that the political repercussions involved were too serious to risk. A select committee sitting to examine the proposal in 1822 concluded that the imposition of an effective police force would conflict too greatly with the nation's freedom. It was not until 1829 that the Home Secretary, Sir Robert Peel[1], succeeded in persuading the Government to form the Metropolitan Police force. Once a police force had been established in London, a model existed for the authorities in the provinces to follow.

Politically, there was a great deal of inequality in the manner in which local government functioned throughout the country. In boroughs this inequality derived from the fact that only a select few members of society were represented within the Corporations that managed local affairs.

Seeking to redress this situation, which had become a national scandal, a team of Com-

---

[1] Sir Robert Peel (5 February 1788 – 2 July 1850). Entered Parliament as a Tory MP in 1809. Home Secretary 1822–30. In addition to establishing the Metropolitan Police force in 1829, he was responsible for a revision of the penal code in which approximately 100 capital offences were removed. Peel was killed in a riding accident in Green Park, London on 2 July 1850.

missioners visited 246 towns in England and Wales in 1834, to conduct an audit of their affairs. The Corporation of Leicester was found to be particularly wanting.

The Leicester Corporation was a Tory stronghold which permitted no Whig or Dissenter to become a member, or have any say in its business. Because voting in general elections was restricted to those among the community who were freemen, the Corporation, once established, could maintain a tight control over who was entitled to vote by decreeing who became a freeman. In this manner they were able to exclude many wealthy and influential citizens from any voting rights. Given this absolute control, and virtually impregnable position, the members of the Corporation had for many years mismanaged – to the point of outright corruption – the finances of the town. Land deals had been struck which only benefited the Council members, and the affairs of charities of which they were executors had been mismanaged.

When the commissioners came to Leicester their investigations were blocked at every turn, by the Corporation in general and Thomas Burbidge the Town Clerk in particular. Burbidge had been a principal beneficiary of the Corporation's mismanagement.[2]

However, with an administration in London determined to bring to an end the lifestyle enjoyed by such Corporations, change was inevitable.

In September 1835 the Municipal Corporations Act came into force. Its requirements sealed the doom of the existing Corporations, including Leicester. New Councils were to be elected forthwith by a recently enfranchised section of the town's inhabitants. Being a ratepayer of three or more years standing in the town became the sole requirement for holding the vote. At a stroke, virtually every householder in the borough became a voter.

By January 1836, the old Tory Corporation had been removed and replaced by a new Liberal one, made up of Whigs and Radicals. An important characteristic of the new Corporation was that it largely comprised wealthy businessmen who were members of the same church, the 'Unitarian Great Meeting' in Bond Street. Men such as Thomas Paget, Joseph Whetstone and John and William Biggs – all future mayors[3] of the town – were all part of the congregation of this Dissenters church. Such was the influence of the Unitarian Great Meeting on local government in Leicester, that in future years it became known as 'the Mayor's Nest'.

Such political and social changes were a direct consequence of the Municipal Reform Act. The legislation also required each of the newly-formed Corporations throughout England and Wales to set up Watch Committees with an obligation to establish and manage a local police force.

Viewed from a modern standpoint, living conditions in Leicester in 1836 were abysmal, and less than ideal even by the standards of the day. A total lack of any form of sanitation – everyone, rich or poor, relied upon an outside privy, which in turn emptied into a cess pit that was usually situated only yards from the dwelling – combined with low-lying ground giving onto the River Soar on the outskirts of the town, fostered an unhealthy chemistry resulting in annual epidemics of disease. These varied from measles and smallpox to a form of summer diarrhoea that resulted in one of the highest infant mortality rates in the country. With no form of running water (it was not until the 1850s that water was piped from Thornton Reservoir), townspeople drew their supplies from wells, the town conduit in the Saturday Market Place near to Cheapside, or directly from the River Soar. The wells and the conduit were polluted by seepage from domestic middens and the Soar was contaminated with untreated sewage and refuse. The streets had only

---

[2] After his fall from grace under the new administration, Burbidge spent some years pursuing the Corporation for large sums of money, which he claimed were owed to him in compensation. He died in 1855 in a Debtors Prison.
[3] The term Lord Mayor was not taken into use in Leicester until 1927.

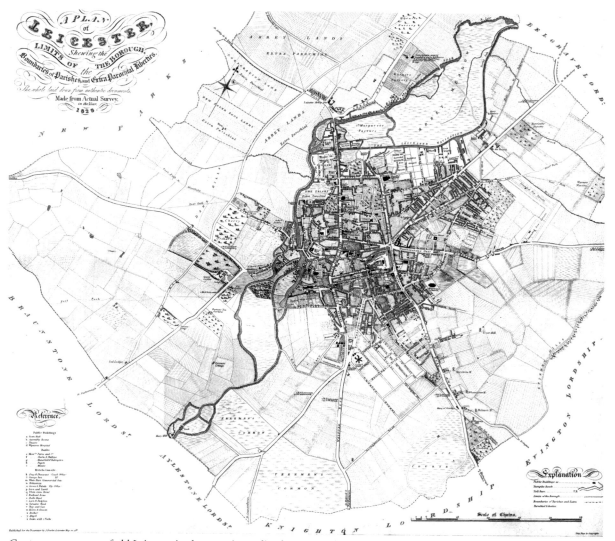

Contemporary map of old Leicester in the years immediately prior to the formation of the first police force in the borough.

been lighted by gas mantles within the last 15 years. Prior to 1821 the byways had – where feasible – been illuminated by burning oil lamps.[4]

Appointed in 1840, the borough's first Nuisance Inspector, George Bown, was to comment upon the accumulated filth in every corner of the town and the abundance of slaughter houses, pigsties and privies, all within a few feet of overcrowded dwellings.

There were, however, certain redeeming features present in the makeup of the town, through which it was entirely possible, given sufficient time, to remedy these defects.

Unlike many other towns, Leicester had retained at its extremities areas of land upon which it was possible to build, to allow expansion and alleviate many of the problems caused by overcrowding. Additionally, on the southern and eastern sides of the town there were a series of clay pits from which locally-produced red brick could

[4] The first street lighting was introduced in 1768-9 when the residents of Gallowtree Gate and Belgrave Gate joined together to purchase oil lamps.

Frederick Goodyer was the first head constable of Leicester Borough Police from 1836–39, when he left to become chief constable of the County Police force.

had grown up. Architecturally, the creation of the London Road area is in itself interesting. Large, almost opulent buildings with impressive façades are to be found along the main road, flanked by a network of lesser streets and avenues of comfortable, well-built palisaded and terraced houses occupied by middle class professionals and artisans.

Economically, in the middle part of the 19th century, the town relied heavily upon an industry based on framework knitting and stocking making. This trade was basically a cottage industry, and was firmly in the hands of a small number of wealthy businessmen (such as the Briggs brothers), who controlled matters by ensuring that they were responsible for leasing the frames for knitting and stocking-making to their own workforce. Inevitably this led to a tight economy, and for many years the average wage of a stocking maker remained at about 8s a week.

Depressing as this picture is, Leicester was not an isolated example, merely a snapshot of English society during the latter years of the pre-technological era. It was, however, time for things to alter.

Immediately after Christmas, on 4 January 1836, under the chairmanship of the borough's newly elected Mayor, Thomas Paget, the first meeting of the Watch Committee was held at the town hall in Town Hall Lane.[5] Advising the Committee on legal matters was the new Town Clerk, Samuel Stone, who was to become famous the length and breadth of the country for his legal skills.[6]

In order to set the scene for their proposed reforms, the Watch Committee first needed to ascertain what system of policing presently existed in the borough. To this end the former head constable, George Owston (who as part of the purging of the old regime had resigned his place in December of the previous year), appeared before the Committee.

be manufactured in great quantities. Since the turn of the century, a considerable amount of building work had been undertaken in order to widen the boundaries of the town. On the east side, from Humberstone Gate up towards High-cross Street and along by the river, an area of working-class houses had been developed. To the south, in the region of London Road, a better style of dwelling, aimed at the more affluent citizens,

---

[5] Later known as Guildhall Lane.

[6] Stone's Justices Manuals are still in use in the 21st century, as legal references used by Magistrate's Clerks throughout the United Kingdom.

Owston's report paints a woeful picture of disorganisation and potential corruption. There were a total of eight constables (known as policemen), within the town, each receiving a salary of £10 a year, plus expenses for attending at Quarter Sessions (5s a day for the first two days), fairs and functions.

Each of the 15 wards in the town had a ward constable, 13 of whom were assisted by a 'Headborough', who acted as his lieutenant. Given that for some reason, one of the wards had two constables, this made a total of 29 men. Additionally there were 45 constables who were sworn in generally for the borough, making a grand total of 74, plus the 'policemen' and Owston himself.

As the office of ward constable was unpaid, the men were obliged to make a living out of the expenses which they received. Such expenses derived from the executing of magistrates warrants, obtaining summonses, attendance at fairs, markets, and Quarter Sessions, the carrying of maces, waiting at Corporate feasts and the prosecutions they brought before the magistrates.

A further tier of policing existed in the form of five watchmen, employed by the parishes of St Mary and St Margaret, who also held the powers of a constable. Finally, two men were employed privately by St Margaret's parish as police constables, and there was also 'a private watchman or two, paid for by subscriptions raised in particular neighbourhoods.'

None of this information would have come as a surprise to those listening to Owston on that cold winter's evening in the town hall. The existing situation could not be allowed to continue. Men were eager to accept situations that attracted no payment but were funded by expenses derived from serving at table during municipal banquets, and obtaining of evidence leading to court convictions, and this had to stop. It cannot have escaped the Committee's attention

that if a constable earning £10 a year was paid 10s (or the equivalent of over a fortnight's wages), for two days ceremonial attendance at the Quarter Sessions, then there had to be other incentives that George Owston had neglected to mention.

The Watch Committee minutes are unequivocal:

…Your Committee cannot but deprecate such a mode of paying a body of men engaged in an arduous and important public duty, as extremely defective and imperfect. As fraught with temptation to generate disturbances in order to obtain or extort fees, as having a tendency to make officers unpopular and suspected and hateful to the people and thereby to destroy all that moral influence which a police force ought to have to be efficient. Your Committee consider the old system of paying fees as essentially bad and that whatever payment is made to public servants should be as far as practicable, regular and permanent.

Samuel Stone, in his office as the new Town Clerk, was instructed to 'insert an advertisement in the *Chronicle*, that 'persons desirous of [a] situation in the police make personal applications to this committee at the town hall on Thursday next at 10 o'clock with written testimonials as to character and fitness, and that none need apply except persons between the ages of 25 and 45 years…',[7] and also to '…prepare 16 ruled sheets to take down the names and qualifications of persons applying for situations in the police'. Thus the first steps were taken to provide Leicester with a 'New Police force.'

While it was felt that an adequate establishment of constables would be 50, it was decided that initially 40 men should be engaged, 35 as constables and five as sergeants. Following a request to the London Police for the services and advice of a reliable man, Frederick Goodyer was

[7] A minimum height limit of 5ft 8in was set in March 1841. This was, with occasional slight variation, to remain in place for the lifetime of the force.

despatched to the town and engaged (with the rank of inspector), as the new superintendent of Police and head constable.

With the mayor sitting as Chairman of the Watch Committee, it was likely that there would be little opposition to any proposals which the Committee should make, but it was nonetheless felt appropriate to lay down the responsibilities of all concerned. At its meeting of 19 January, the Committee formally stated the following terms of reference:

The first 'Peelers' appeared on the streets of London in 1828. Leicester was one of the early provincial towns to form its own 'New Police force' in January 1836.

Your Committee beg to remind the Council that though the expenses may at first sight appear considerable, they have ascertained from accurate calculation that a rate of two pence per quarter will be more than sufficient to defray it. They trust therefore that the Council will approve and ratify their arrangements. The Council must recollect that it is intended on the part of the Watch Committee to supersede private watchmen and public watchmen, the present Constables, policemen, Ward Constables, Headboroughs, Mace Bearers &c., That less expense will be incurred by the town in prosecutions, less expense in maintaining prisoners in gaol, that crime will be prevented by the activity and vigilance of the police. That property will be rendered more secure, public order more firmly maintained and public morals decidedly improved.

Your Committee beg further to remind the Council that if in the establishment of a New Police a sufficient number should not be engaged, [authorised by the Corporation], that if burglaries and robberies and street brawls take place as frequently under the new system as under the old, for want of engagement of sufficient men, complaints of dissatisfaction would necessarily arise and would to a certain extent be justified.

Your Committee being further under the necessity of reporting to the Secretary of State, it is indispensable that they should be able to make such a return as may be satisfactory to the Government and show that the police establishment in comparison with the relative amount of the population is in an efficient and satisfactory state.

A police force consisting of 40 Constables will not be equal in numerical amount to one half of the present Watch Constabulary force which it is intended entirely to supersede, and which however indirectly and variously and imperfectly it has been paid, has in the opinion of Your Committee cost the borough fully as much or more, than is proposed by the New Police.

Individually and collectively they therefore trust that the Council will concur with them in thinking that the number of police ought to be not less than the number recommended, and if so pledge themselves in their arrangements to use any economy that will be compatible with a faithful discharge of their duties and an attention to the public service.

The Corporation agreed in principle to the propositions, with the proviso that 'they would wish to appoint a number of special constables in October, and as a consequence reduce the number to 40.'

However, the number remained at 50. In addition to Inspector Goodyer, 45 constables and five sergeants constituted the initial body of the Leicester Borough Police force.

A constable's weekly rate of pay was set at 18s, a sergeant's at £1 1s 6d and Inspector Goodyer's salary was settled at £100 per annum. While the men were being fitted out with their uniforms, the new superintendent of Police was charged with examining the layout of the town in order to devise the best method of policing it.

Leicester borough, at this time and for the next few decades, was little different from most other Midlands towns. A down-turn in the economy after the Napoleonic Wars, which had ended less than a generation before, had seen a huge number of families wandering the roads and moving about the countryside. Vagrancy and petty crime committed by itinerants flourished.

The more intelligent elements of this fraternity were known as 'High Flyers', and developed their own hierarchy. 'Forney Squarers' made and sold imitation gold rings from brass buttons, which their female partners went about the town selling as family heirlooms. Wearing one ring and hiding others in her bodice, the woman would engage an unsuspecting (and ill-educated) servant girl in conversation, and then try and sell her what purported to be her wedding ring for between 2s and 4s. Other itinerants, pretending to be out of work lace makers (nearby Nottingham was a centre of the lace trade), set a different trap. Known as 'Dress Fencers', they would purchase a quantity of cheap lace and put it into a bag of sand, which after sufficient shaking about imparted a golden colour to the lace. This was then hawked from house to house as expensive pillow lace being disposed of to obtain food. Many of these criminals earned up to 12s a day.

Lower down the scale came the women who went from house to house, wearing widows weeds and pretending to be destitute. This particular enterprise was known as 'the Widows Lurk'. Bath bricks, bought for tuppence each by 'Paste Lurkers', were mixed with a farthing's worth of raddle and some turpentine to produce a mixture that was sold as a cleaning powder for brass and tin articles. At the lowest level, 'Griddlers' and 'Chanters', accompanied by 'Mumpers' (who collected the alms), sang maudlin songs in the streets and outside of public houses and beer shops, begging for a few pence.

Normally these vagrants would not remain more than about four to six weeks in any one place before moving on.

The town which Frederick Goodyer strolled through and around, tallying up drinking stews,[8] houses of ill-repute, dwellings and lodging houses, was a very different one to that which, 131 years later, the last chief constable, Robert Mark, would relinquish guardianship of. The best way in which to appraise the town and its needs, is to join Goodyer on his survey of the borough.

---

[8] The Beer Act of 1830 provided that anyone with a room, and the money for a licence (usually about 8s), could sell beer. Unlike public houses, the beer houses were not subject to police control and thus their proliferation was virtually uncontrolled.

Officers of the Leicester Borough Police Force January 1836

Inspector & Head Constable   Frederick Goodyer.

Serjeant

1	George Atkins	Highcross Street.	4	Samuel Russell	Margaret Street.
2	William Betts	Belgrave Gate.	5	John Withers	Navigation Street.
3	James Hutchinson	Woodboy Street.			

Constable

6	George Broughton	Mansfield Street.	29	John Hutchin	Sanvey Gate.
7	Thomas Brown	London Road.	30	Samuel Hawley	Friar's Place.
8	James Bowater	Welford Road.	31	John Jelley	Regent Street.
9	William Baum	Frog Island.	32	Thomas Jackson	Northampton Street.
10	George Burdett	Redcross Street.	33	Samuel Johnson	High Street.
11	William Brown	Yeoman Street.	34	Samuel Kenney	New Market Street.
12	John Beales	Sanvey Gate.	35	Leeson	Bakehouse Lane.
13	John Cooper	Oxford Street.	36	William Lole	Infirmary Square.
14	William Chamberlain (1st)	Highcross Street.	37	Edward Morton	Humberstone Road.
15	George Cammack	Burley's Lane.	38	Joseph Marvill	Braunstone Gate.
16	John Cox	Wharf Street.	39	Henry Mitchell	Braunstone Gate.
17	Edward Cosby	Churchgate.	40	Edward Rastall	Colton Street.
18	William Clarke	Nicholas Square.	41	Thomas Scotton	London Road.
19	William Chamberlain (2nd)	Archdeacon lane.	42	Samuel Simpkin	
20	Joseph Cox	Conduit Street.	43	James Smith	Southgate Street.
21	John Clarke	Brown Street.	44	William Sharpe	Eldon Street.
22	John Deakins	Duke Street.	45	Benjamin Tatlow	Belvoir Street.
23	Robert Deacon	Northgate Street.	46	James Taylor	Eldon Street.
24	John Drakely	Green's Lane.	47	Thomas Tilston	Wheat Street.
25	William Bevans	Belgrave Gate.	48	Henry Wade	Belgrave Gate.
26	Abraham Evans	Town Hall Lane.	49	George Wale	St. Peter's Lane.
27	Joseph Fitchett	Russell Street.	50	William Young	Bazaar Street.
28	Thomas Hollins	Belgrave Gate.			

Taken from the Watch Committee minutes of January 1836, this list shows the names and addresses of the original Leicester Borough Police officers.

Ambling at a sedate pace along Highcross Street, away from the centre of the town on the morning of his review, Goodyer was passing Sanvey Gate on his right and entering into Northgate Street within a few minutes. Crossing over the bridge spanning the Leicester Navigation by North Mill and Marston's tan yard, another few hundred yards brought him to the North Bridge over the infamous River Soar, reeking of pollution and decay. A further 15 minutes gentle stroll brought him into the open fields of the Abbey Lands.

Retracing his steps along Northgate Street the new head constable turned first down Sanvey Gate, then up into Churchgate, returning to the town centre near to the Haymarket.

To his left was Humberstone Gate, with its regular cavalcade of fairs and entertainments. He mused on how many of his new men would be needed to keep order and watch out for pick pockets at these events. Turning his gaze a little further to the left he studied Belgrave Gate – the poorer part of the town. Abbey Street, with its lodging houses and rookeries, was home to an itinerant population of migrant workers.[9] This would be where he would need to ensure that the men on the beat were well-briefed and never isolated.

Had he but known it, within a few years this tiny cluster of streets would be witness to Leicester's first racist disturbances, when Irish immigrants, seeking refuge from the ruined economy of their homeland, came into conflict with the local English community.

Quietly contemplating his responsibilities, the new superintendent made his way down Gallowtree Gate, into Granby Street and thence to London Road. Gazing up the hill along the old turnpike road, Frederick Goodyer knew that this would be the respectable end of the town. Experience told him that even if his patrols were less busy here than in Belgrave Gate, there would still be law enforcement pressures emanating

from this affluent suburb. A notably respectable district would house the more articulate and well-connected denizens of the town. They would have high expectations of his new police force, and the voice to make them heard.

There being little point in trudging all of the way up London Road to look at fields and a smattering of new houses, Goodyer turned sharply to his right down Waterloo Street and Hastings Street, to its junction with Cavalry Road.[10] Here he stopped and surveyed the expanse of fields away to the south, as far up as Occupation Road. Then, directing his attention back towards the town, his eye settled upon the recently opened prison, its massive red brick walls and turrets dominating the southern edge of the borough.

An hour and a half of walking had taken Goodyer in a full circle. As he sauntered back past the Infirmary and the Bridewell along Oxford Street, the head constable was feeling relatively pleased with himself. His brief had been to explore the town and examine its policing needs. This he had done. During his perambulations he had reviewed his situation and arrived at several conclusions, not least of which was the prime location for his new police station.

The Watch Committee agreed that the decision concerning the whereabouts of a Central Station House was a matter of some urgency. After discussing and rejecting several alternatives (including the lower part of the Exchange, the Engine House, the Old Guard House, and the Bridewell), it was resolved to utilise that part of the town hall, previously assigned to the storage of the Corporation's dishes and crockery, along with the adjacent outbuildings and kitchens, currently occupied by the town fire engines.

This was the place which to Frederick Goodyer, during his morning's deliberations, seemed the obvious location. It was within a few minutes walk of any part of the town and in a building well

---

[9] Twenty years later in 1855, figures showed that there were 38 common lodging houses in the borough, accommodating between 550 and 600 persons on a nightly basis.

[10] Later Lancaster Road.

After 1839, when the County Police was formed, their first headquarters was situated (within the borough) at 4 The Market Place.

known to every resident. It also had the advantage of putting him in daily contact with his political masters, thus ensuring short and easy lines of communication.

With the town divided into 31 beats, it was only a short time before the newly appointed constables were patrolling the streets wearing a uniform (modelled on the Metropolitan Police style), of top hat, blue lapelled coat adorned with white buttons and the town arms on the collar, buff waistcoat, drab kerseymere breeches, gaiters and gloves.

Additionally, each officer carried a rattle with which to summon assistance and a stave with which to defend himself. The men, chosen mainly for their appearance and stature (the only other requisite being an ability to read and write), were received by the populace as a mixed blessing. There were those among the respectable middle classes who saw the advent of law and order as something to be welcomed, while others, mainly among the criminal fraternity, viewed matters from a different perspective. The common denominator was that one and all, they considered that the new police were essentially spies, and if to be tolerated, were certainly not to be trusted.

Policing of the town was under the direction of Goodyer from the outset, and, thanks to his experience gained in London, well organised. The officers' working routine was split into three distinct phases: daytime, night time and reserve.

During the day, 10 constables and a sergeant worked from five in the morning until nine in the evening. Four men patrolled from 5 a.m. until 8 a.m. They were then relieved by the remainder, who patrolled until midday, when the first group returned to relieve them until 5 p.m. At this point the original group returned to duty until 9 p.m. when the night shift took over.[11]

Twenty-five constables and three sergeants paraded for the night shift, along with a reserve of two constables and a sergeant, who remained at the police station to handle prisoners and assist officers who encountered difficulties or disturbances on their respective beats.

Inspector Goodyer, for his part, was to supervise the whole of the force and be responsible for discipline and good order. One of the stated reasons for his engagement was that apart from his expertise in setting up the new force of men, he was an outsider:

> …from the excellent recommendation which the police officer from London brought with him, as well as from the consideration that in introducing the new system, it was indispensable to have some person thoroughly acquainted with it to initiate the men and beyond this from the conviction that an intelligent stranger, free from any local bias or feeling would have more admitted and allowed moral influence than any townsman however well respected.

Goodyer was ordered to report to the Watch Committee on a regular basis and keep an occurrence book in which to record every [disciplinary] case that came before him. Finally, he was charged with apprising his men of their duties and furnishing every constable with a printed copy of his instructions, with which the officer was expected to be thoroughly conversant.

In practice Goodyer's discipline book was to become – certainly in the early stages – a well-used document, by both sergeants and constables.

Watchmen were fore-runners of the new police force. Established during the reign of King Charles II (1660–85), the poor quality of these men was well known, and the modern term 'charlie', meaning someone who is incompetent, originates from them.

This is hardly surprising when the criteria for engaging officers is examined. It was a simpler age, as yet untouched by the complexities of improved living conditions or the expectancies inherent in career structures. Men were invited to present themselves, along with a written testimonial, at a given time at the town hall. They were to be between 25 and 45 years of age, literate, in good health, of good character and suitable stature. After all of those who were suitable had been engaged, an arbitrary decision was made as to which of them should be given supervisory roles carrying the rank of sergeant. These were

---

[11] Split shift working was employed until the 1960s, although in a less drastic form.

men with absolutely no previous experience and – more importantly – no role model or bench mark to work to. Their predecessors had been corrupt and lazy individuals. They themselves were totally untrained and came from a number of completely unrelated occupations. Goodyer alone knew from experience what was needed.

Not unexpectedly, the discipline offences committed were commensurate with the times. During the first year, among the 50 men, there were 29 instances of constables and sergeants being found in varying states of intoxication or arriving for duty incapable through drink. Another common offence was that of men being found asleep on doorsteps or in warm outhouses and privies on night duty. The punishments imposed by the chief constable and ratified by the Watch Committee were proportionate to the circumstances. First offences usually drew a reprimand, loss of pay, or a reduction in rank. Subsequent lapses resulted in the man's dismissal. A 'reserve list' of applicants for the job of constable evolved surprisingly quickly, allowing a deal of freedom to dismiss those who transgressed.

Not all misdemeanours were quite so mundane. On taking Sergeant William Betts before the Committee on 31 October 1836, an indignant Goodyer gave evidence to the members that he had made a late night visit to the town hall police station, resulting in his having the necessity of putting the sergeant on report for '…having a female closeted with him in the Inspectors' Room, on the night of Tuesday last, and taking improper liberties with her…' The gentlemen of the Committee, apparently seeing a degree of humour in this situation which eluded the head constable, declined the option to reduce Betts in rank, choosing instead to fine him one week's pay.

Just after Christmas – in February 1837 – the inspector reported that '…Constable Brown has been suspended from duty for having been found in an house of ill-repute with a prostitute on his

knee…' At the same hearing, constable Thomas Hogg was reprimanded for selling meat from a stall in the market.

Conversely, rewards for good work in the form of gratuities were also available, thus establishing an early pattern of incentives. For instance, in September Sergeant Betts and Constable William Brown were awarded 5s each, 'being a gratuity from a gentleman for looking after his watch while in a state of intoxication'. (There is a degree of irony in this, given that these are the same two officers disciplined at another time for salacious behaviour.) A shilling was awarded to Constable Edward Crossley for recovering a smock belonging to a pauper at St Margaret's Poor House; and a gratuity of 2s 6d from Dr Moore (Surgeon) to Sergeant Withers for 'getting the money for damage to his bell'. A rather dubious allowance of between 1 shilling and 10s continued to be made to individuals for court appearances where the prosecution was successful.

At the end of the first year of its existence, the general feeling among those responsible for the administration of the borough's affairs was that the new venture was a singularly successful one, and the salary of the head constable should be increased forthwith to £130 per year, with a house rent free, and coals to be provided.

Despite their genuine commitment to the concept of the new police, the town council also kept certain options open in case the venture was not a complete success. During the summer of 1836, 20 special constables were appointed in each ward, their sole item of equipment being a stave bearing the words, 'Special Constable'. From the outset, four 'General Constables' were appointed (outside of the new police), at a salary of £20 per annum. Their responsibilities included attendance at Corporation meetings, assisting the constables in keeping the peace, and acting as firemen.

The decision made at this stage, that the organisation should be responsible for both law enforcement and firefighting, was one which, during the next 35 years, would prove to be problematic and at times controversial. After the Great Fire of London, 170 years before, fire insurance offices had begun to open all over the country.

These were accompanied by various private fire brigades, funded through the insurance companies. In Leicester the first one to open an agency was the Sun Fire Office in 1738. During 1834 the Leicestershire and Midland Counties Fire and Life Insurance Company opened offices in Market Street. This company maintained two private fire engines.

Three of the general constables were appointed to be captains of teams of volunteer firemen, whose role in the event of a fire in the town was to man the three fire appliances belonging to the Corporation. Payment was made to the volunteers for practice times and turning out to fires. The fourth general constable, Henry Scott, was appointed 'Inspector of Fire Engines' and put in charge of the maintenance of the tiny Brigade. In October 1836, these general constables were given notice that their services would not be required after the end of the year. Scott, in order to continue in his position as inspector of fire engines, was absorbed into the police force.

Over the next two years, the constables walking their beats became an accepted part of town life and a pattern of general law enforcement began to emerge. The days of a detective department and out-stations had not yet arrived. Life was conducted at a leisurely pace and, other than for the occasional serious crime – which would be dealt with personally by Inspector Goodyer – the demands placed upon a constable were relatively simple. During the day he was occupied with 'the suppression of vagrancy and mendacity', which offended the proprieties of the rate-paying citizens. After dark the brawls and drunken disturbances in the streets of the town were his prime employment. Physical abuse, such as when

The old town hall in Town Hall Lane was the original Leicester Borough Police station from 1836 until 1876, when it moved to the new town hall in Horsefair Street. In later years the building became the Guildhall Museum and Town Hall Lane was renamed Guildhall Lane.

'Constable Thomas Ward was severely injured in the Newarkes', during the winter of 1838–39, was accepted as an on-going fact of life. In accordance with the Corporation's wishes, during the first two years – between 1836 and 1838 – 128 special constables were enrolled. Although the agreement was that they be paid 3s 6d a day if called out, their services were not required.

As the presence of the new police became commonplace in the town, so some of the more influential citizens began to vie for preferential treatment. A prime example came in January 1838, when Goodyer reported that he had detailed a constable to patrol the wharf of the Leicester and Swannington Railway, provided that the company pay all expenses for the man.

With landowners such as Messrs Hutchinson and Bell complaining that their land near to Willow Bridge Street was not sufficiently protected, 10 rural constables were engaged on a part-time basis. Paid 2s 6d on those days when they were employed, the authority of these rural constables was denoted by the wearing of an armlet. At the beginning of 1839 John Peberdy was sworn in as a constable, 'in place of Patrick - deceased', to patrol the towpath and protect the property of the Leicester Union Canal Company. Not all of the rural constables were totally reliable. In April 1839, John Drakely, who was engaged at 10s 6d a week on the direct instructions of the mayor, 'to guard the Corporation lands near to Cows Lane, against damage and depredations', was dismissed for stealing manure.

The rural constables were at best merely watchmen. In May 1840, the somewhat less than enthusiastic assessment of these men by Goodyer's successor, Robert Charters, was:

William Smith	Inactive – not intelligent
Joseph Powell	Timid – anxious to do his duty
John Cowell	Unhealthy – asthmatical
John Gordon	Tolerable
James Gunn	Rather dull
William Bass	Young – rather sleepy
William Hubbard	Heavy
Samuel Manning	Fair – improvable

Smith, Cowell, Bass, Gunn and Hubbard to be laid off.

After holding office as head constable[12] for just under three years, Frederick Goodyer resigned his position in December 1839, to take office as the first chief constable of the newly formed Leicestershire County force. Despite the shortness of his period of tenure as head constable of Leicester Borough, Goodyer's achievements should not be underestimated. Having started with literally nothing, at the end of three short years he left the town with the basis of a functioning, disciplined police force that would take it into the second half of the next century.

---

[12] Until after the turn of the century it was customary to refer to the chief officer of a Borough force as the 'head constable' and that of a county force as a 'chief constable' This was based upon the perceived differences in their responsibilities to a Watch Committee in a borough and a Police Authority in a county (see Author's Note, p 7).

CHAPTER TWO

Robert Charters
(January 1840–October 1871)

Goodyer's successor, Robert Charters, was another Metropolitan policeman, summoned from London by the Watch Committee to take over the reins of command. Destined to be the Borough force's longest-serving chief officer, Charters remained in Leicester for the next 31 years. His period in office was punctuated by a series of historic landmarks during the middle years of the 19th century.

By 1851–2 there were 7,381 policemen employed in forces throughout England and Wales, of which the Leicester Borough force counted 51 officers. (Forty-three constables, seven sergeants, and the inspector, who was also head constable.)

The great famine in Ireland between 1845 and 1851 resulted in a significant increase in the Irish population of Leicester. Combined with the depressed economic situation throughout the country, and a particular shortage of work in the town, relationships between the indigenous population and these immigrants from Ireland flared into disorder on more than one occasion. At the same time chartist groups seeking governmental reform were organising activities both locally and nationally.

Abroad, the Crimean War (1853–6), the Austro-Prussian War in the summer of 1866, and the Franco-Prussian War of 1870–1, fought over the disputed territories of Alsace and Lorraine, set the scene for future global conflict.

One of Robert Charters' early innovations was to split his officers into groups according to service and merit. During his first year of service a man was retained in the 'C' class, at 17s a week. Thereafter he moved up into the 'B' class at 18s and, if deserving of further reward, could be advanced into the 'A' class (which was restricted to between 10 and 15 men), at 19s.

This early re-structuring was probably due to the fact that from the original body of men sworn in as constables four years previously, only two constables and one sergeant remained. There were many reasons for this, not the least of which was that Goodyer had enticed several borough men to join him in forming the new County Police force, on the promise of instant promotion. Other factors included the nature of the work, which was often less than popular, unsociable hours, and a high risk of injury through assault.

Where a man fell foul of the discipline code, the Watch Committee now had the option to exercise the sanction of reassigning him to a lower group, thus imposing an ongoing fine in the form of a reduction in pay. After March 1840 each officer wore the badge of his class on his tunic collar. Some years later this was extended by a system of service stripes and related pay increments. In July 1863, for instance, one stripe denoted five years service and two stripes 10 years. The stripes brought with them a penny a day pay increase for the holder. A silver stripe was awarded at 15 years, and a gold stripe at 20, with a good conduct enhancement at 25.

The problem of maintaining discipline was a constant challenge in the management of the

Robert Charters, head constable of the Leicester Borough Police force 1840–71.

force. Modern chief constables regularly fall back upon the assertion that, along with any other organisation, the police force reflects the society which it serves. This premise was equally valid in the 19th century and is reflected in the misdeeds of policemen and the manner in which they were dealt with.

Offences of a minor nature took the form of idling and avoiding arduous duties. In June 1840, PC (Police Constable) 7 Cook was reported by the night duty sergeant to have 'been found laying down on his beat asleep at 2.30 a.m. – Cook stated that he was not asleep, he had fallen over and was recovering.' During the same month, PC 13 Thomas Johnson was found asleep, sitting on a privy at 4.15 a.m. Johnson asserted that, 'he was not asleep but resting as he was wearied out by the constant exertions that night – it being a holiday time'. Such matters habitually drew a reprimand for the miscreant.

Drunkenness was tolerated more in an age when ale was the staple drink of the working classes than in later years. In March 1842, the dismissal of Sergeant John Bladon for repeated drunkenness resulted in Bladon writing a conciliatory letter to the Chairman of the Watch Committee.

To Wm Biggs Esq.
Burgess Street,
25 March 1842
Sir,
Pardon the liberty I take in addressing you on the subject, but in consequence of my dismissal I am at present shut out from employment and the possibility of again engaging as an officer, for in the counties the chief constable is prohibited by Act of Parliament from engaging any man dismissed from a police force, and to apply in a borough would be useless as a reference to you Sir as Chairman of the Watch Committee or to the superintendent would be unavoidable.

Therefore, I hope you Sir, and the Gentlemen of the Watch Committee will take it in consideration and allow me again to enter the ranks and I will prove to you by my future conduct I am not unworthy of the trust you again repose in me.

Hoping this will have a little influence and attention from yourself and colleagues.
I remain Sir,
Your Obedient Humble Servant
John Bladon

Bladon was reinstated with the rank of constable and appears to have kept his word. The next time that he comes to notice is in December of that year, when he was awarded a gratuity of 10s for arresting a man later convicted of stealing 13 dozen pairs of stockings.

Around this time, provisions begin to be made for police officers to earn extra money through

Signs and Marks placed on door posts and other places by vagrants - mid 1800's

✗   *'No Good' - too poor and know too much*

   'Stop' - if you have what they want they will buy. They are pretty 'fly' (knowing)

   'Go in this direction' - it is better than the other road. Nothing that way.

◇   *'Bone' - (good). Safe for a cold 'tatur'*

▽   *'Cooper'd' - spoilt by too many tramps*

▣   *'Gammy' (unfavourable)- likely to have you taken up*

⊙   *'Flummoxed' (dangerous) - mind the dog*

⊕   *'Religious'- but on the whole, 'tidy'*

During the middle of the 19th century one of the predominant criminal classes was vagrants. Rarely staying in one place for more than a few weeks, they left signs for each other on gateposts and trees along the way.

overtime, and concerns are shown for conditions of work.

Late in 1841 (in November), three pence an hour was set aside for those constables who had performed extra duties at the theatre and at the Cricket Ground (which at the time was situated in Wharf Street). Sergeants Wright and Sheffield had been awarded a gratuity of one guinea each in September 1841, for keeping the force books in good order. Sergeant Agar was paid an extra guinea for drilling the men.

That same year, Reverend Brown complained that 'the police are unable to attend a place of Religious Service on Sundays'. The basis of this protest could have originated from the reverend himself, in his concern for the religious welfare of the police, or it could have been a grievance which had been subtly fed to him by the police officers themselves. The truth of the matter was that, at that time and for many years to come, the police did not have any rest days. Full employment meant exactly that – seven days a week. (Over the years, nationally, each force made *ad hoc* arrangements for annual and weekly leave. It was not until 1910, with the passing of the Police (Weekly Rest Day) Act, that all police officers up to the rank of Inspector were granted one day's leave in seven.) The reply to the Reverend Brown is singularly unhelpful '…only the night police are unable to attend, and that falls by rotation to each policeman to serve on the day force about every third Sunday only, and the Committee do not see that any alteration of the regulation can be made.'

In the early years the organisation of police forces throughout the country was still in an embryonic state. Each Police Authority and Watch Committee was left to its own devices when determining the pay and conditions of its employees – a situation which was to prevail until after World War One.

With no formal representative body, the means of negotiation between members of the force and the Watch Committee was conducted through testimonials, submitted for consideration by the committee. The matter of annual leave was considered on a yearly basis. In June 1859, four days leave of absence for the year was granted to the officers of the Borough force. This was reiterated three years later in June 1862, with the postscript that the absences are to be granted at the discretion of the head constable.

The virtual autonomy of local authorities is underlined by the refusal of the Leicester Watch Committee in 1851, and again in 1856, to implement the terms of the Police Superannuation Fund Act. The basis of their refusal was that, '…[the provisions of the Act], should not be adopted by the council, and that they will await until a further Act, which they feel is fairer to the ratepayer.'

The mid-Victorian negotiating process is nicely illustrated in the following memorial, submitted by the constables and sergeants in April 1866:

> To the Chairman of the Watch
> Committee
> of the Borough of Leicester.
> 24 April 1866

We the undersigned sergeants and Police constables of this Borough beg most respectfully to submit to you the following memorial for a small advance of wages, and we are induced to doing so for the following reasons.

Namely that the wages of the artisans and all other branches of labour in this town within the last few years have risen fully 25 per cent for 5 ½ days labour, while our own wages for the last 25 years have not been advanced more than 12 ½ per cent for 7 days labour.

In addition to the above, house rent is more than one fourth higher than it was some time ago with every probability of still becoming higher, while at the same time, coals and provisions of nearly all kinds have very considerably advanced in prices and added very much to the crippling of our resources. Under these circumstances we have come to the conclusion to solicit your Committee for an advance of 2s per week which would be a means of keeping our position in the scale of society and enable us to provide for ourselves and our families more of the common necessities.

[Signed]

As a result of this plea, a pay increase of 1s 6d a week was granted to the men.

—oOo—

One of the earliest documented crimes dealt with by the Borough Police force was the murder of Mary Waring, during the spring of 1842.

Superintendent John Chapman served under Robert Charters. The only date recorded for his career is of his promotion to sergeant in May 1852, which would indicate that he probably served from the 1840s to the 1860s. A later, undated annotation to this photograph reads 'Deputy Chief Constable.'

Waring, who worked as a frame work knitter, went to lodge at the home of Stephen Barnes and his family in Grange Lane (off Oxford Street) at the beginning of March 1842. Given the fact that this was a small house, in one of the poorer districts, the number of occupants is also an indication of living conditions at the time.

The household comprised Barnes; his wife Ann; their children, 15-year-old Isaac and 18-year-old Mary; and two other lodgers, Charlotte Barnacle, who was 20, and an old woman known as Suky Mees. In view of the number of people living in the house it was inevitable that rooms had to be shared, and Mary Waring and Charlotte Barnacle slept together in the parlour.

It is apparent that Mary Waring did not get

along with the other two young women in the household, Barnacle and Mary Barnes. On the afternoon of Wednesday 6 April, which was only four days after Barnacle had taken up lodgings in the house, the two girls visited a neighbour, Ann Johnson, at her house in Jones' Yard just off Grange Lane, and asked her what she knew about poison. Johnson told them that 'as much arsenic as would lay on a shilling', could undoubtedly kill a person.

Later that same day, Barnes and Barnacle were identified as having visited three chemists in the town, attempting to purchase arsenic. The first two (both of whom made positive identifications the following day at the police station), William Wales Simpson of Hotel Street and Thomas Palmer of Market Street, refused to serve them. On visiting the third, Joseph Hooley Lockyer, in the Market Place, they were successful. Having told him that they wished to kill bugs and fleas, he sold them a penny worth of arsenic.

At about eight o'clock that evening, Mary Waring returned home from work and made herself a meal of bread and butter, with tea made in a tea kettle which she always used. Later in the evening she complained to Mrs Barnes of feeling unwell and took herself off to bed.

At this time, both Mary Barnes and Charlotte Barnacle were out of the house. As darkness fell, Waring's condition became worse, and Mrs Barnacle fetched her husband down from the upstairs room where he was working as a stocking maker. It was decided that nothing should be done for a while, and he returned to his work leaving his wife to look after Mary Waring, along with the other two girls, who had now returned home.

Later, at around 11 o'clock, Barnes came back downstairs to find that Mary Waring's condition was unchanged and his wife was now vomiting in the chimney corner. Stephen Barnes put his wife to bed, then made a pot of tea in Waring's tea kettle, giving Ann Barnes a cup and taking one for himself. Significantly, the two young women refused to drink any of the tea.

At about two o'clock in the morning, because his wife and Mary Waring were so ill, Stephen Barnes went to the house of Dr John Stanford Pell in New Street. On his arrival there, he was violently ill in the street. Dr Stanford Pell was sufficiently perturbed by Barnes's story and his condition to summon Constable John Biddles from his beat nearby, to accompany him to Grange Lane. It is possible that the doctor was also nervous about going into this area of the town at night alone.

On their arrival at the house, the doctor and the constable found Mary Waring dead and Ann Barnes seriously ill. On the doctor's instructions, PC Biddles took possession of the teapot and kettle, which on later analysis were found to contain large quantities of arsenic. A post mortem revealed quantities of arsenic in Waring's body.

Next morning, (Thursday 7 April) at about 9 a.m., PC Goddard was sent to the house to arrest the two women. As they were being walked to the station house a large crowd of onlookers joined the constable and his prisoners. Along the way one of the crowd, Sarah Boulter, who was also a resident of Grange Lane, called to Barnes, 'Mary, what can you think of doing so? What could you do it for?' Barnes called back to the effect that she 'had only fetched the stuff', that she and Charlotte had previously, 'had words' with Waring and she (Barnes), 'had wanted to give her some jalap'. Charlotte, she said, had 'said to give her a little arsenic to give her some pain…'

Once lodged at the station house, Charlotte Barnacle refused to be interviewed. Mary Barnes, however, told the police that Mary Waring had complained that sleeping with Charlotte had given her fleas, and wanted to know how to be rid of them. 'Old Suky Mees' (the other lodger), she said had told them to sprinkle arsenic, which they had bought and put on Waring's chair.

At their subsequent trial at Leicester Assizes for the murder of Mary Waring, both women were found guilty of manslaughter and transported for life to the penal colonies.

A comment made in the *Leicester Journal* at the time of the trial provides an interesting insight into how the activities of the new police were regarded by the popular press of the day.

> …we have been told on good authority that on the day of the killing, when apprehended, they both made confessions to a constable admitting their guilt to the fullest extent. We always look with much disgust upon declarations of this kind, and there is generally a degree of sympathy for the parties when guilt is proved by conversations with a policeman or turnkey. It savours too much of the French system for an English taste.

—oOo—

With the passage of time police work became more clearly defined, and areas of specific responsibility began to emerge.

In September 1843, the magistrates asked that the coroner 'address his precepts to Sergeant Wright', who, on payment of 2s 6d for each inquest, was the first of a long line of police coroner's officers. Wright, who had joined the Borough Police on 23 August 1837, was a well-known figure in the town. In 1841 he had led a party of constables dealing with a riot at the workhouse, during which he sustained an injury to his head from a missile thrown at the police. Later, in 1849, Sergeant Wright was appointed Inspector of Nuisances,[1] a post which he held until his retirement, after 35 years service, in March 1873.

1847 stands out as a year when Charters implemented several changes to the force. The first was the creation of a detective department.

Four years earlier, in November 1843, Constables Francis Smith, Thomas Haynes and Thomas Sibson were each given 5s by the Watch Committee for good work. There is no indication of what this good work entailed, but it is significant that Smith and Haynes were the officers who later formed the nucleus of the detective force. The first specific reference to them being detectives comes in February 1847, when it is mentioned that the two sergeants of the detective police force have silver badges. They had probably been promoted from constables to sergeants, and given responsibility for dealing with crime. Subsequent mention is made on several occasions of officers patrolling the town centre watching for thieves and pick-pockets at the fairs held in Humberstone Gate, under the direction of Detective Sergeants Haynes and Smith.

Around this time the perceived seniority of the detective branch over uniform becomes apparent for the first time. During a week's absence from the town in the spring of 1853, Charters informed the Watch Committee that his duties would be taken over by Sergeant Haynes. Later that year, both Haynes and Smith were given the unpaid rank of inspector.

In September 1856, both the inspectors sought – unsuccessfully – a 54 per cent increase in salary, from 25s a week (£65 per year), to £100 a year. Their claim was based on the fact that £100 was the salary on appointment of a superintendent in a County Police force. In view of the fact that at this time the head constable of the borough's salary was only £175, their request was turned down. They were, however, awarded an extra 4s a week.[2]

A minor change of responsibilities in 1847 again established a role which was to become central to the structure of the police. During the summer of that year, Sergeant Sheffield was told that he would in future be employed in the station house 'for the taking of charges'. Thus the first charge sergeant for

---

[1] Under a Home Office Instruction, after 31 December 1873, police officers were debarred from acting as Inspectors under the Nuisances Removal and Public Health Acts.

[2] Five years later, in 1861, a further application by Smith and Haynes was successful, and their salaries were increased to £100 per year. One proviso was that as the local authority had now accepted the concept of superannuation, they paid their own subscriptions.

the force was appointed. Six months later plans were submitted for an improvement to be made in the cells for the accommodation of overnight prisoners and those detained on warrants. At the same time, a plan was prepared for a residence for Charters at the police station.[3] The plans included a new cell, 10ft by 9ft by 5ft 2in, at a cost of £17. The existing cells were to be equipped with water closets and pipes costing £24, with an extra £10 for the plumbing work.

In October 1846, the Corporation appointed the first two medical officers in the country, Mr John Buck, Surgeon and Dr John Barclay. Buck appears for the first time in police circles five months later, in March 1847, when he is described as the 'Medical Inspector'. As the first official police surgeon, he made it his early duty to produce a standard form, which he submitted to the local authority to be used for prospective candidates for the police force. The form itself is indicative of the general expectations of a medical practitioner at that time, examining an average working man:

Medical Examination for the Leicester Police force

Name:

Age:

Height:

Trade:

I have examined the above named candidate for admission to the Police force and find him to be in perfectly good health. He is free from rupture, varicose veins of the legs, or marks of old ulcers adhering to the bone. He has free use of all of his limbs and his sight and hearing are good. I consider him to be capable of undergoing the fatigue to which a policeman is necessarily exposed.[4]

Dated at Leicester, this............day of......................18...

Signed..........................

In June 1853, John Buck resigned from his position as police surgeon when he accepted the post of superintendent of the County Lunatic Asylum.

One further change to the existing order which Robert Charters made was the discontinuance of employing rural constables, now referred to as 'supernumaries'. The organisation, never particularly efficient, had by the 1850s outlived its usefulness. Incidents such as the conviction, in the summer of 1848, of one of its members, William Deakin, along with Special Constable Wallace, for stealing cherries from Dr Noble's orchard, brought the office into complete disrepute. A proposal by the head constable in November 1855 that the supernumary force be disbanded and its members put into the Borough Police 'D' Division (probationary constables), was readily accepted. Doubtless Charters felt that from that point on it was a simple matter to lose the men through natural wastage.

The position of clerk was created in February 1870 in acknowledgement of the fact that it was not practicable to expect one of the existing sergeants to be responsible for all of the administrative work involved in the organisation of the force. An advertisement offering the rank of sergeant to the successful candidate drew 48 applications for the post, which was filled in April by Charles Pole, a county policeman. The chief clerk's position quickly became central to the smooth running and efficiency of the force. It also became, both in Leicester and elsewhere, a training situation for prospective chief constables. Pole remained with the Borough force for three years, until in March 1873 he accepted an appointment as the head constable of Grantham Police.

By the mid-1850s the Government had decided that some form of overall control of provincial police forces needed to be exercised. (The Metropolitan Police force was exempt from this, and remained directly responsible to the Home

---

[3] In April 1851 Charters asked for an extension to his living accommodation as he had a large family and only three bedrooms. At some future date he moved to live on London Road.

[4] The popular idea that policemen in the 1800s were massive, hulking figures is largely misplaced. In any society there are exceptions, and on old photographs there is evidence of extremely large men. (Interestingly, these are often among those who have been promoted to sergeant and above, begging questions about the criteria for selecting supervisory officers). However, the majority of men were around middle height – hence in March 1841 the introduction of a minimum height limit of 5ft 8in – and of average build. (This is evidence of the relatively poor diet of most working-class men.)

An old photograph of the officers and men of the Borough force in the courtyard of the old town hall police station sometime between 1840 and 1871. The figure in the centre of the front row is Robert Charters.

Secretary.) In 1856 the County and Borough Police Act was passed by Parliament, which for the first time created an Inspectorate of Constabulary. Two inspectors were appointed initially. Lieutenant-Colonel John Woodford, the chief constable of Lancashire, was given responsibility for the northern part of the country, while Major-General W. Cartwright took the southern area, including Leicester.[5] They were joined in 1857 by a third inspector of constabulary, Captain Edward Willis, the retired chief constable of the Manchester Police. The inspectors brief was to visit the various police forces to assess their efficiency. Once a force had been certified by the inspector as efficient, both in numbers and discipline, a monetary grant was made, defraying one quarter of the force's expenditure on pay and clothing.

General Cartwright paid his first visit to the Leicester Borough Police in March 1857. He made several 'suggestions' to the Corporation for the improved efficiency of the force. Some were minor, such as a revision of the beats which the men patrolled, and the appointment of a relieving officer, to assist the Board of Guardians, both in their dealings with destitute wayfarers, and as a deterrent to vagrancy. (Where the line was to be drawn between the two categories is a matter for surmise). The issue (at 3s 10d a pair from Messrs Parsons & Brown), of handcuffs to every officer became a common practice.

Other recommendations, such as an increase in the number of officers, were further reaching. Cartwright recommended that as the present inspectors (Smith and Haynes) were detective officers, they should now officially be classed as such – effectively endorsing the creation of a specialist department. A reluctant Watch Committee was strongly advised that the time had come for its members to accept the previously avoided superannuation scheme for the force.

[5] Prior to this, every force had submitted a quarterly return to the Secretary of State, outlining its manpower situation. Cartwright, who was a veteran of the Peninsular War, had no previous experience of police matters.

Inevitably, the functioning of any police force is driven by the social circumstances in which it operates. The years between 1842 and 1848 were particularly difficult for the head constable and his men, because of the activities of the chartist movement. Although they had had experience over the years in dealing with disturbances, this was the first time that the men of the Borough force were at the centre of political conflict.

Chartism was a movement begun in the mid–1830s[6] by men such as William Lovett and Francis Place, whose aim was to secure political change in the country. The chartists[t] were so named because they had drawn up a six-point charter, demanding universal suffrage with vote by secret ballot; annual parliaments; an abolition of the property qualification of Members of Parliament; payment of Members of Parliament; and equality of electoral districts. Following the refusal by Parliament of a petition in 1839, chartist activities resulted in riots in Birmingham, the north of England and Newport in Wales. In 1842 they presented a second petition to Parliament, re-defining the reforms that they were demanding. This also was refused, resulting in various outbreaks of civil disorder in the name of chartism over the following years.

At the time that the chartist movement was active, conditions in Leicester were particularly bad. Trade was at a record low and the worst affected section of the workforce – the hosiery workers – was also the largest in the town. The result was a deep financial depression, which lasted several years. An unfortunate corollary to the workers circumstances was that their employers, the manufacturers themselves, were also sustaining heavy losses and were unable to ameliorate the situation. (In 1837 around 7,000 men were out of work and receiving poor relief in Leicester, and the situation did not improve quickly.) In October 1838 the Leicester and Leicestershire Political Union was inaugurated. The

following month, under the leadership of John Markham, the union affiliated itself to the charter. The chartist leaders in the Leicester district advocated a moderate and non-violent approach to the achievement of the movement's ends.

Radical chartism came to the fore in Leicester following the particularly severe winter of 1839–40, and the arrival in the town of Thomas Cooper, a journalist. Cooper ousted Markham as the chartist leader and began to move the local union toward undertaking more drastic measures. Early disturbances broke out during the first week of May 1842, necessitating the assistance of some County Police officers. The situation was quickly dealt with, and a grateful Corporation awarded the head constable two guineas and each of his men an extra day's pay.

Cooper, the central chartist figure, was absent from Leicester in late 1842, when in the middle of a series of strikes, rioting broke out. The rioters marched out of town on 19 August, intending to join forces with other rioters. Intercepted by the local yeomanry on Mowmacre Hill, the rioters were halted and dispersed in what has come to be known as the 'Battle of Mowmacre Hill'. Further disturbances in Loughborough prompted Robert Charters, at the request of Frederick Goodyer (the chief constable of the County Police), to send four officers to the town to supplement the county strength.

Later that day pockets of disorder broke out in and around Leicester town centre. In the evening a mob stoned police officers in Churchgate, several prisoners were taken and a running battle ensued as the prisoners were hauled off to the station house. At the same time a mob carrying a large flag appeared in Welford Road. As the regular police were fully engaged in the town centre, the mayor, Thomas Stokes, led a party of special constables to disperse this gathering. After some further disorder, several men were arrested in Welford Road and taken to the station house in Town Hall Lane. Until late that night the police

[6] Initially known as the London Working Men's Association.

station and surrounding streets were virtually besieged by the chartist demonstrators. Any police officers attempting to take a prisoner into the station house were forced to run a gauntlet of stones and missiles. The disturbances continued into the following week, with the Riot Act being read to a gathering in the Market Place on Thursday, 25 August.

One week to the day after the Battle of Mowmacre Hill, two police officers from Staffordshire – Superintendents Rhodes and Cottrill – arrived in Leicester with a warrant for the arrest of the chartist leader, Thomas Cooper. Obviously pre-warned of the Staffordshire officers arrival, Charters sent Sergeant Wright and a constable to Cooper's shop in Churchgate, where they arrested him. Although it was only a five-minute walk to take their prisoner back to the station house, news of Cooper's arrest spread quickly and a large crowd soon gathered outside the police station.

At the town hall, a special magistrates court, chaired by the mayor, had been convened. The terms of the warrant were read to the Court by the Staffordshire officers, alleging that, while at a chartist meeting at Hanley in Staffordshire, Cooper had 'used inflammatory and exciting language, leading the mob to acts of violence'. The prisoner was handed over to the two Staffordshire superintendents, and with an escort of eight constables, bundled into a waiting horse-drawn omnibus, which took the party to the railway station and off to Stafford.

With the departure of Cooper, chartist activities in the town effectively ceased. Cooper never returned to pursue his activities in Leicester after his release from Stafford gaol.

One final bout of chartist-inspired agitation flared up in February 1848, as a protest against the way in which poor relief was being administered. For a period of just under six weeks, in September and October of that year, while this concluding spasm of disturbances in Leicester was taking place, a reserve of constables was permanently held at the town hall. Constables slept on improvised beds made of wooden trestles.

Probably hoping to raise the morale of the people in the Midlands during this depressed period, in December 1843 Queen Victoria, along with Prince Albert, the Duke of Wellington and the Dowager Queen Mother, spent a week touring the region. Leaving Windsor by train on Tuesday 5 December, the royal party travelled first to Birmingham, then across to Derby and Chatsworth, before arriving at Belvoir Castle for a stay with the Duke of Rutland.

The journey back to Windsor included a stopover in Leicester, on the morning of Thursday 7 December. From the standpoint of a royal visit, this is probably the shortest in the history of the town. Arriving at the Great Northern Railway Station at 11 o'clock in the morning, the Queen and Prince Albert, accompanied by an escort of the Leicestershire Yeomanry, drove by carriage directly from Belgrave Gate to the Midland Railway Station on London Road, and departed for home.

None the less, the town prepared for the visit as a major event. Mock arches were constructed along the route and every building was decked out with flags and bunting. Robert Charters and his men were on duty from 6 a.m., to control the gathering crowds and man the barriers erected along the route. Policemen were stationed along the streets, with instructions not to allow any carriages or horses to enter any highway through which the procession was to pass. The arrangements for the visit clearly show that the office of head constable had not as yet become one to which a degree of social standing was attached. Charters is specifically instructed to be mounted and accompanied by two constables at the bottom end of Belgrave Gate, whereas in later years the chief constable would have been included in the party of dignitaries receiving the guests at the railway station.

—oOo—

After the dark years of the 1840s, affairs began to pick up in the borough. By the 1860s new commercial ventures, in the form of boot and shoe manufacture and light industry, had to an extent replaced the hosiery trade as the town's main source of income.

In the middle and later decades of the 19th century there was a general economic upturn, which would continue uninterrupted for some 50 years, until the outbreak of the World War One in 1914. Evidence of this is shown by the Corporation's decision, in the summer of 1851, to allow any member of the police force to visit the Great Exhibition at the Crystal Palace in Hyde Park, one weeks leave of absence being granted in order for them to do so. That those who travelled to London found their stay enjoyable is apparent from the letter sent to Charters in September by Inspector Fairbrass of the Metropolitan Police, thanking his men for their gift to him of a silver snuff box in return for looking after them.

The Borough Police was coming of age by the middle and late 1850s, inasmuch that men who had joined the force at an early age and remained with it were coming to the end of their useful working lives. Decisions had to be taken about retirement.

John Clarke, who eight years previously had been given 5s 'for his courage in apprehending a man for stealing sheep' was deemed to be too old to continue as a constable in October 1852. It was decided that 'the sum of £20 be awarded as an allowance [to Clarke], who is now unable to discharge the duties of a Police constable, in consideration of his length of service, and that he receive 5s a week until this resolution has been submitted to the Council'.

A more detailed comment upon the life and prospects of anyone serving as a police officer in these early years is demonstrated in this report by the incumbent police surgeon, on Sergeant Francis Tarratt of the Borough force.

To the Gentlemen and Members
of the Watch Committee
30 October 1855
Gentlemen,
By the direction of your Chairman, I have enquired and examined the health of Sergeant Tarratt.

I find that he is 52 years of age and that he entered the Police force in May 1836, and has consequently been therein above 19 years.

About 10 years ago he received an injury which occasioned a rupture and from which he will always be liable. In an Irish row about six years ago he had his teeth knocked out, which materially affects mastication and consequently his general health.

He has also been on several other occasions more or less injured.

Upon examining his present state of health I beg to report that he is evidently much reduced in strength, not only by his increased age but by the injuries he has received, and that he is now unequal to the regular arduous duties of a Police sergeant.

I think his is a case in which some relief from the regular night duties during the winter season might be allowed.

I remain Gentlemen,
Your Obedient Servant,
John Moore, Surgeon.

For the next nine years, until he was 61, Sergeant Tarratt was allowed to perform light duties on a wage reduced to 20s a week. In March 1864 he retired on a pension of 8s a week.

The 1850s and 1860s were not a particularly

happy time for the Leicester Borough Police. Many things seemed to go amiss, both for the men and for the head constable. Charters's report on the condition of the force at the end of 1850 was a matter of some concern for the Watch Committee. Over the summer period that year, four officers had been dismissed from the force and a further five fined for offences of drunkenness. Two had been fined for being absent from their beats, one for using abusive language to a sergeant, and another was under suspension for associating with a prostitute.

Charters himself was the subject of a complaint in May 1853 by Mr James Kirby, to the effect that he was employing policemen at his home in London Road as gardeners at the rate-payers' expense. Charters, while apologising to the Committee for this indiscretion, put forward the rather lame excuse that, 'he had not – except to a very trivial extent – employed any members of the Police force in his garden…' The Committee, in very clear terms, instructed the head constable that in future, no police officer, whether on or off-duty, was to be so employed.

In 1856, Samuel Stone, the Town Clerk, voiced a disquiet about the payment to police officers of small sums of money, which were viewed as perquisites. Historically, an allowance claimed through the court had always been paid to constables for their attendance at Quarter Sessions and Assizes. Whatever sum was granted, the officer was allowed to keep between 2s 6d and 5s for himself, 'as an encouragement to activity'. It was also commonplace for residents to make gifts to constables who found their premises insecure. A fee of three pence was paid to an officer each time he served a warrant by going into the county.

Stone was so troubled by these practices that he wrote to the Home Office seeking guidance as the town's legal advisor. The reply which came back was unequivocal – all such payments should cease forthwith.[7]

The force continued to be dogged by misfortune into 1863. In January, Constable Daniel Basford was involved in a brawl with a man named Benjamin Pallet, during which Pallet received injuries from which he subsequently

Known as 'D' cuffs because of their shape, this type of handcuff was the only type ever issued to officers in the Leicester Borough and City Police forces. The locking mechanism was operated by the removable screw, which can be seen in the right-hand cuff. Although it was possible in theory to 'snap' the cuffs into the locked position, this was inadvisable as it usually cut a small piece of flesh out of the wearer's wrist. Because of the weight and unwieldy nature of these handcuffs, officers found them difficult to carry on their person and preferred to use them solely for escort purposes.

died. Despite complaints from the dead man's family, the Watch Committee chose to deal with the incident as an internal matter, and found that Basford had, in their opinion, not behaved improperly. It was not an auspicious beginning to the new year. At the end of the summer, Constable John Marston, having been found guilty by the magistrates of assaulting a person found sleeping in a brick yard, was dismissed from the force.

Evidence of an internal dispute came to public notice in October 1863, when one of the Detective Inspectors, Francis 'Tankey' Smith, gave six months notice of his intention to retire. Although the reason which he gave for his retirement was, 'failing eyesight and bodily strength', this was patently untrue, as after leaving the force he

[7] Despite Stone's warnings, the practice of rewarding officers continued well into the mid-1870s. In March 1875, Messrs Faire Bros, in token of their gratitude for the conviction of persons who had stolen elastic web from their factory, insisted that Inspector Wilkinson receive three guineas reward and Detectives Elton, Preston, and Taylor £2 10s each. Constable Sturgess was given two guineas. Four months later Inspector Wilkinson was presented with £3 10s, and Detective Gee with £1 10s, for recovering property stolen from the Revd Davys.

immediately established himself as a successful private detective. Smith, who had been a serving officer for over 20 years (he joined the force in February 1840), was a colourful and charismatic character, highly regarded for his professional abilities. His most celebrated case had been the previous year in 1862, involving the disappearance of James Beaumont Winstanley, the high sheriff of Leicestershire. Winstanley had disappeared in July and Smith was given the job of finding him. With careful detective work, Smith traced the high sheriff to Coblenz in Germany, where he had in fact been drowned in a ferry boat accident.

During January 1864, halfway through his period of notice, Francis Smith was put on a disciplinary report by Robert Charters for, 'leaving the station house on Saturday evening [last], without reporting in as instructed, and failing to report to the town hall the following day at 1 p.m.'

For the head constable to take such a course of action against a senior officer clearly indicates that there was much more involved than can now be discovered. An embarrassed Watch Committee reprimanded Smith.

Tankey Smith in his turn immediately lodged a complaint against Charters, claiming that despite warnings from the Committee, he was still employing a police officer as his gardener, and that others were having to cover the man's duties. Allegations and counter allegations of misconduct now began to abound, with constables and sergeants appearing for both sides. To the Watch Committee, and any other informed observer, it was apparent that the police force was divided into two camps – one for Smith, and one for the head constable. With a very limited course of action open to them, they once more severely censured Charters for his misuse of a police officer, and allowed Smith to retire.

Soon after this, Charters found himself in another unenviable situation, for which on this occasion he was not to blame. At the time the police force and fire brigade were still bound together as a joint organisation. In March 1864, Henry Scott, the head of the fire brigade, had retired. His position was taken by Sub-Engineer George Clamp, of the London Fire Brigade. Clamp was engaged by the Watch Committee with the rank of police inspector, and designated superintendent of fire engines. There were serious reservations within the force from the outset, and George Clamp's appointment was not a popular one. The first official complaint against Clamp was made in January 1866 by Constables Barker and Hutt, who alleged that the inspector had been drinking in a public house while on night duty. Clamp made a case for his defence and the complaint was dismissed. Later, in November 1869, Charters himself put Clamp on report for falsifying his duties, and behaving improperly in the Eclipse public house and later at the police station. Again, because of conflicting evidence, the Watch Committee dismissed the case, but expressed deep concern at 'the ill-feeling now existing between Inspector Clamp and the officers of the force'. Over the next few months, a series of allegations and counter allegations were made, including a complaint that Clamp had arrived at the scene of a fire in a drunken state and used abusive language.

Matters came to a head during the month before Charters resigned from office, in September 1871, when Clamp was charged before the magistrates with larceny. Although found not guilty by the court, the Corporation, now desperate to rid themselves of the embarrassment which he was causing, demanded his resignation. Clamp applied for the job of superintendent of the fire brigade at Stockport – and asked that the Corporation supply a suitable character reference. The Watch Committee agreed to his request, on the condition that he first resigned his post as an officer of the Leicester Police. Although a copy of the character reference which they eventually supplied no longer exists, the note in the Committee minutes states that, 'a character should be supplied [based], on the entries in the report book…' A few days prior to Christmas Clamp, realising that his situation was desperate, withdrew his notice. The action had little effect. His immediate dismissal from the police force was confirmed and his fire brigade appointment, which was renewable yearly, was ended a few months later in April 1872.

There is no doubt that the Clamp affair was the catalyst for the creation of the Borough Fire Brigade as an organisation independent of the police force.

As from 19 December 1871, the Leicester Borough Police ceased to have any further responsibility for fire fighting and the Leicester Borough Fire Brigade became a separate entity.

After a total of 41 years in the police force (he had joined the London Police in 1840), 31 of which had been spent as the head constable of the Leicester force, Robert Charters retired.

In 1830 his appointment had been made by the simple process of asking the Metropolitan Police to send to Leicester a suitable officer. Four decades on, there were sufficient candidates available for the vacancy to be advertised and the best applicant appointed.

CHAPTER THREE

Joseph Farndale
(October 1871–February 1882)

The advertisement for a new superintendent of police for the borough, placed in the Leicester papers, *The Times*, the *Police Gazette*, and the *Naval and Military Gazette* resulted in applications from 56 prospective candidates. Their occupations and qualifications were many and diverse. The chief constables of Barnstable, Kidderminster, Aylesbury, Margate and Salford, along with the ex-chief constables of Castleford and Plymouth, applied. Other hopefuls, who had no previous police experience, included 32 military officers; two school masters; a book keeper; three coastguards and the superintendent of a lunatic asylum.

From an eventual short list of five, Joseph Farndale, the head constable of Chesterfield, was selected. A married man of 30, with one child, Farndale had spent seven years in the Middlesbrough Police force before, in 1869, becoming head of the 15-man force at Chesterfield. It was agreed that the new head constable's salary should be £220 per year, rising over five years to £250, with a house included.

The comparison chart below shows that, given the size of the force, the wage offered to the new head constable was extremely fair. Following a recommendation by the inspector of constabulary, Colonel Cobb (which coincided with Farndale's appointment), a target was set to achieve a ratio of one police officer per thousand head of population. This figure was attained in September 1872, when the establishment reached 98 men for a populace of 95,084. (Ratio of 1:970).

Town	Est. of Force	Salary of Ch. Cons	Salary in £s in relation to no of officers	House provided
Birmingham	338	£500	1.48	Yes
Bristol	303	£450	1.48	No
Leeds	301	£360	1.20	No
Sheffield	270	£500	1.85	No
Newcastle-upon-Tyne	174	£400	2.30	No
Hull	172	£300	1.74	No
Bradford	157	£300	1.91	No
Nottingham	106	£300	2.83	No
Norwich	97	£250	2.58	No
Leicester*	98	£220	2.24	Yes
York	44	£175	3.98	No

*based upon Sept.1872 establishment.

Farndale took office on 27 October 1871. As expected, he began at an early stage to make alterations and reorganise the force in an attempt to reconcile differences and re-establish efficient working conditions.

One of his first, and given the recent events, most sensible moves was to give the Borough force a new image. The high silk hat was replaced by a more practical army style helmet, and light caps were ordered for the senior officers. A tunic, held at the waist by a heavy leather belt, replaced the long frock coat. The cumbersome rattle, long outmoded, was replaced by a whistle and chain.

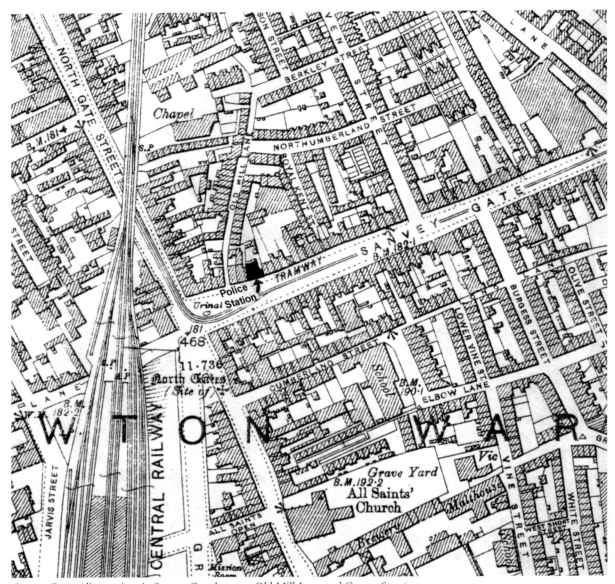

Sanvey Gate police station, in Sanvey Gate between Old Mill Lane and Craven Street.

For the first time, the wyverns which were to become the most celebrated emblem of the force, appeared on the men's tunics.[1] A further step taken early in his period of office was to regulate the time during which a constable was to be regarded as 'on probation'. It was decided that any candidate for the office of constable would be allowed a period, not exceeding five weeks, during which to apprise himself of the duties of his office. At the end of that time, the head constable was empowered to dismiss the man if, in his opinion he would not make a suitable officer.

With Detective Inspectors Smith and Haynes now retired, Sergeant George Langdale was

[1] The exact date that the helmet replaced the top hat is not certain. It is definitely between January and November 1872. The first officer to be seen on the streets of the borough in a helmet was Constable John White, who resigned from the force to become the town hall keeper on 19 November 1872. The wearing of caps by officers was deferred until the spring of 1873. The bill for the new uniforms was: 100 helmets @ 10s 3d = £51 5s 0d; 100 whistles and chains @ 2s = £10; 100 leather belts @ 5s 6d = £27 10s 0d

Inspector George Langdale (January 1854–April 1886)

the force for a further eight months before he obtained the position of head constable at Colchester in November 1873.

Farndale, in an effort to minimise sickness levels, ensured that every member of the Borough force who had not been vaccinated since he was 15 (or in fact never), was vaccinated against smallpox at the expense of the Corporation.

In October 1872, at the end of his first year in office, Farndale was instrumental in the publication of the Borough force's first chief constable's report. An extract from this report gives an indication of the levels of crime and disruption over the decade from 1863 to 1872.

Year	Indictable	Arrests	Arrests for Drunkenness	Assaults
1863	159	110	274	546
1864	200	121	350	623
1865	202	147	422	676
1866	156	98	386	597
1867	153	105	315	592
1868	193	108	304	625
1869	149	123	349	622
1870	132	88	348	575
1871	214	143	402	526
1872	185	113	490	523

The head constable took the opportunity in his report to make the comment that:

…many of these cases are undetected through want of funds. When a robbery is reported and the offender has left the town, the person robbed is asked if he is prepared to pay the cost of the prisoner being apprehended and brought back. If he is not, no further steps are taken, but the robbery is entered on the books and shows against the efficiency of the police as an undetected crime, though they have not had the remotest chance of detecting it.

In another observation made at this time, Farndale makes the point that:

promoted to detective inspector, given £2 wages a week and made head of the detective department. He was now assisted by three detective constables, Elton, Preston and Taylor, who received a salary of 27s a week plus £5 a year clothing allowance.

The chief clerk, Charles Pole, was also promoted to inspector and given an assistant – Sergeant George Mercer. It cannot be a coincidence that the 32-year-old Mercer resigned his position as clerk at Chesterfield – Farndale's old force – in order to take the job.

In March 1873, George Mercer was promoted to chief clerk when Pole left to become the head constable of Grantham. Mercer remained with

…in consequence of numerous complaints relating to disorderly houses, I have taken proceedings against several, and succeeded in closing down one which has been a nuisance for several years. However, 28 remain, all of which are common brothels of the lowest class.

Under the new leadership of Joseph Farndale, the Leicester Borough force appears to have quickly regained its former stability. In February 1873 a brass band was formed, which over the succeeding years gave concerts in the town's public parks, and at various functions. As an added incentive to good conduct and industry, a Merit Class was created, promotion into which carried an extra shilling a week pay for constables and an enhanced wage of 32s a week for sergeants.

When making an application for an increase in salary in the autumn of 1874, Farndale reveals an understanding of local politics, which, almost a century later, was to be developed into a fine art by a later chief constable, Robert Mark.

As Farndale explains:

…[I] will here point out how my salary may be increased without costing the Borough any more than when I was appointed. In January 1872 an Act of Parliament known as the Pedlars Act came into operation which enables me to earn and pay over to the Borough Fund about £80 a year. Now whatever increase you decide to give, one half of the amount will be paid by the Treasury and the £80 referred to will do more than cover the other half…

Apparently convinced by the argument, the Corporation granted the head constable an increase in salary from £250 to £350 a year.

Over the years the accommodation at the town hall had become inadequate. The Borough force had doubled in size since 1836 and it was time for a move to more suitable premises. Plans for a new town hall had been under discussion for some time. The site agreed upon for the new municipal buildings was an area of land variously referred to as 'the sheep market', 'the cattle market', and 'the old horse fair'. Situated between Horsefair Street and Bishop Street, it provided an ideal location for a town hall, fire station and police station.

Designed by F.J. Hames of Lincoln's Inn Court, and built by Messrs Brass and Company, also of London, the construction took exactly two years from the laying of the foundation stone by William Kempson (a previous mayor of the borough) to being ready for occupation. At an eventual cost of £53,000, the new town hall was completed in August 1876.

Provision was made on the Bowling Green Street side of the premises for the Fire Brigade. The Fire Service benefited greatly from the move. Their new headquarters included sleeping space for 30 men, a large muster room, a workshop for repairing the fire engines, trucks and hand reels which were based there and a hose drying room.[2] Included in the Fire Brigade section of the building was a commodious house for the Brigade superintendent.

The new police station and cells were located at the Horsefair Street and Town Hall Square corner of the building. Compared with the space allocated to them in the old town hall, the new police station must have appeared enormous.

The new station consisted of a muster room 56ft by 32ft, a waiting room and store rooms. A chief clerk's office was provided, along with offices for the inspectors, detectives and nuisance inspectors. At the rear (probably shared by both police and firemen), a drill square was laid out. Additionally, there was a charge room and 13 cells (eight for males and five for females), for the holding of prisoners, who could be taken directly from the cell block up into the court rooms above.[3] The chief constable's office was near to the

---

[2] In August 1892 the Fire Brigade moved into the central fire station in Rutland Street.

[3] After the police moved to Charles Street police station in the early 1930s, this cell block was still used on a daily basis for the reception and holding of prisoners due to be brought before the courts. For the next 100 years, prisoners arriving at the town hall were taken through the rear entrance in Bowling Green Street into the old drill yard, from where they were led down a steep flight of steps into the cells. The magistrates courts sitting daily on the ground floor of the town hall gave way, at the appropriate times of the year, to either Assize or Quarter Session courts.

(top) Detective Sergeant Daniel Preston. He served in the Leicester Borough Police from 1 August 1865 until 14 November 1875, when he left to become head constable of Banbury Police.

(left) PC John White, believed to be the first constable to have worn a helmet in the borough in 1872. White left the police force in November 1872 to become the town hall keeper.

the town centre were decorated with flags and bunting, and church bells began to ring from seven o'clock in the morning. At 10.30 a.m. sharp, the final sitting of the magistrates court in the old town hall was commenced. This was later followed by a final and wholly symbolic meeting of the Corporation, during which speeches were made and the history of the old town hall recounted.

The mayor and Corporation, led by mounted policemen and the bands of the Volunteer Rifles and the Yeomanry cavalry, formed a procession through the town streets to the new town hall. Among those in the cavalcade were representatives of local branches of the Foresters and Nottingham Oddfellows, the Royal Antediluvian Order of Buffaloes, and the most important tradesmen of the borough. Farndale, on horseback, led the magistrates and their clerks. Decorated fire engines, en route to their new station, preceded the lamplighters, who carried festooned poles.

There was, in all of this, a cost to the rate payers. The opening of the new town hall was a civic occasion of major importance, with huge crowds of local people gathering to witness the spectacle. Over a hundred extra police were drafted in from the County force, Derby Borough and Nottingham Police. Saddle horses were hired from a local hack master, at a cost of £3 7s 6d, as mounts for Farndale and a dozen of his officers. In an obvious anticipation of itinerant criminals, attracted by the crowds drifting into the town, detective officers were brought in from London, Manchester, Sheffield, Birmingham and Nottingham. The cost of policing the entire event added up to £80 14s 7d.

That the Borough Police had, under Joseph Farndale, recovered from the difficulties experienced in the latter years of Charters's term

Bowling Green entrance. As with the Fire Brigade superintendent, Farndale was provided with quarters in which to live.

Rooms were allocated elsewhere in the town hall for the Corporation lamplighters to report for duty and to prepare and mend lamps.

The date set for the grand opening was 7 August 1876 – Bank Holiday Monday. Shops in

Sergeant (later Inspector) John Pemberton was chief clerk of the Leicester Borough Police until October 1876, when he was appointed head constable of Grantham Police.

in office was shown in April 1876, when a further member of the force, Joseph Wilkinson – head of the detective department – was appointed chief constable of the Kendal Police.[4] This was followed, two months after the move to the new headquarters, by the departure of Inspector John Pemberton to become head constable at Grantham. He had been with the force as chief clerk since November 1873 (when Mercer left).

Along with the move to the new town hall came an awareness on the part of the Watch Committee that, with the boundaries of the town beginning to spread, there was now a need to consider the establishment of one or more branch stations on the outskirts of the borough. In late 1875, Aldermen Barfoot and Winterton journeyed to Oldham, Salford and the Bootle division of the Liverpool Police to make enquiries as to what arrangements applied in those police districts. As a result of their enquiries it was proposed that premises should either be acquired or built on the outskirts of the town, to include a large muster room, where men could be briefed and charges received, and at least three cells for the detention of prisoners. The branch station should be equipped with a telegraph, and have living quarters attached for the officer in charge.

Various suggestions were made for the location of the new branch station. The old Weigh House on Welford Road could be converted, or it could be built on some land which was being cleared in Bath Lane, near to West Bridge. At the other side of the town, locations in the Belgrave Gate and Wharf Street districts were considered. Eventually, two cottages in Sanvey Gate were purchased for a total of £525, and the construction of a branch station commenced. Work was completed by September 1878, and George Langdale, as the force's senior inspector, was appointed officer in charge. One of the requirements placed upon Langdale – and later inspectors and sergeants who lived at similar branch stations – was that in return for free accommodation, he would be supplied with coals for 2s 6d a week, and his wife would be expected to keep the station and cell block clean.

Later, in August 1879, 423 square yards of land was purchased just off of Belgrave Gate, in Woodboy Street, which was to be the site for the force's second branch station.[5] The land cost the Corporation £730. A further £1,000 was set aside for building the police station. Inspector Hickinbottom took up residence at the Woodboy Street branch station in September 1880.

With three stations in different parts of the town, Joseph Farndale needed to consider the question of communications, which until now had been conducted by messenger. A contract was signed between the Corporation and the Postmaster General, and for an annual rental of £25 10s 0d, a year, 'telephonic communications' were installed between the central and branch stations.

Alongside these improvements to the

[4] Wilkinson's position was left open for several months until John Tempest Clarkson, the recent chief constable of Halifax, was appointed detective inspector in the Leicester Borough force at 40s a week plus £10 a year clothing allowance.
[5] Although the Watch Committee notes are clear that 'an area of land' was purchased, there is an anomaly. A note in October 1879 indicates that the tenant of a property in Woodboy Street was paid £10 by the Committee, 'to compensate for her loss of tenancy'.

As part of the review of uniforms which Joseph Farndale undertook, the wearing of a heavy leather belt with a metal interlocking clasp fixing was introduced in January 1872.
(Courtesy N.Haines)

organisation, life within the force continued, uninterrupted by any major national events, such as those that had punctuated the middle years of Robert Charters's term of office. With an improvement in the economic state of the borough during the second half of the 19th century, public attention turned to matters affecting life in the community. Complaints began to be made concerning traffic using the thoroughfares of the town. A recommendation was made as early as 1870 by the Highways and Sewerage Committee that the constables should take action 'to compel all drivers of vehicles [and] persons with trucks, bicycles or perambulators to keep on their left side of the road'.

This concern over traffic regulation (which mainly centred upon market days), also brought into being the first form of waiting restrictions in the borough. One of the areas where provision was made for carts to stand in 1881 was in Rupert Street. Conflicting commercial interests immediately became apparent. A complaint was lodged by one of the property owners in Millstone Lane, alleging that obstructions to his premises were being caused. This was countered by Mr Pagett, licensee of the Marlborough Head Inn, and supported by his neighbours, who

asked that carts be allowed to stand near to their premises in Marlborough and Duke Street. In support of this proposal, Pagett pointed out that he had stabling for 30 to 40 horses, and that the streets in question were conveniently placed for country folk coming into the town, whose presence was good for local business.

In an era when noise levels were, by later standards, maintained at an extraordinarily low level, the term, 'disruption of the peace', was often taken quite literally. A letter from the Reverend Ingram of St Matthews vicarage at Christmas 1879 complains:

> …on Sunday last, during the one hour period from 11 a.m. to noon, no less than 16 coal carts passed my house, the drivers on each, furiously ringing on a bell. On Tuesday at 11.15 a.m. standing at the corner of Brunswick Street, close to the school room door, I saw no less than six of these carts, the drivers ringing their six bells simultaneously.

A bye-law introduced the following April imposed a fine of 40s for causing an undue nuisance by ringing bells, blowing horns, or using any other noisy instrument – the Town Crier excepted.

The unpredictable and often violent conditions of a Victorian policeman's working life did not appear to lessen with the passage of time, as shown in this letter of resignation from Joseph Langton.

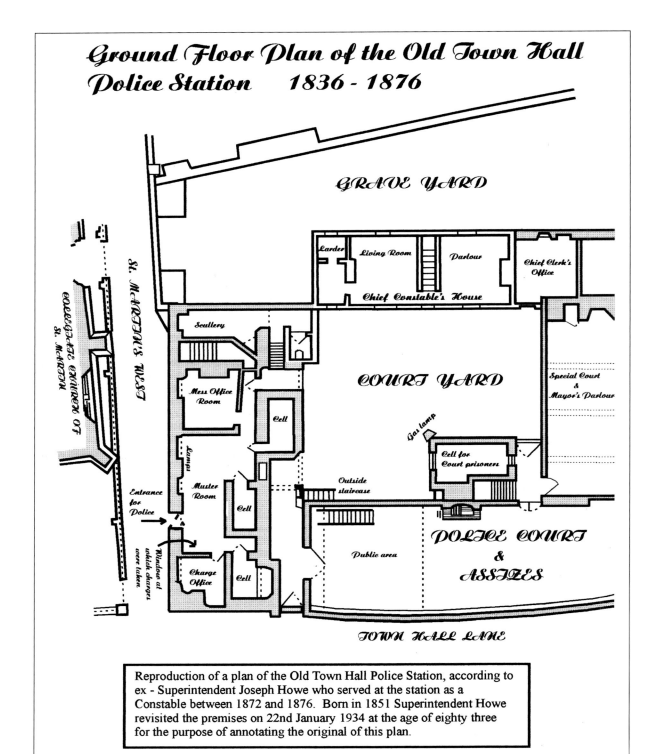

Ground Floor Plan of the Old Town Hall Police Station   1836 - 1876

GRAVE YARD

Larder   Living Room   Parlour   Chief Clerk's Office

Chief Constable's House

St. MARTIN'S WEST

COLLEGIATE CHURCH OF ST. MARTIN

Scullery

COURT YARD

Special Court & Mayor's Parlour

Mess Office Room

Cell

Gas lamp

Cell for Court prisoners

Lamps

Outside staircase

Muster Room

Entrance for Police

Cell

Public area

POLICE COURT & ASSIZES

Window at which charges were taken

Charge Office

Cell

TOWN HALL LANE

Reproduction of a plan of the Old Town Hall Police Station, according to ex - Superintendent Joseph Howe who served at the station as a Constable between 1872 and 1876. Born in 1851 Superintendent Howe revisited the premises on 22nd January 1934 at the age of eighty three for the purpose of annotating the original of this plan.

To the Watch Committee
of the Borough of Leicester
17 October 1876

Gentlemen,

I very much regret having to resign my post as constable after a service of nearly 16 years, from the following causes – namely in the year 1868 I was attacked by two brothers named Hook, who it will be remembered garotted Mr Pegg in King Street, when I was severely bruised by them, the effects of which will cause me wearing a truss.

On the morning of 17 August 1874 when trying the security of the doors of Messrs Roberts and Co., warehouse in the Market Place, through the greasy state of the causeway I fell down and fractured my leg and was confined to my bed for seven months. Since that time I have had an ulcer forming on my heel which prevents my standing for any length of time. Having received these injuries while in the execution of my police duties I sincerely hope that my long term of service will entitle me to the satisfactory and liberal consideration of the Committee, and I beg to leave myself in their hands, hoping that they will deal with me liberally as possible, as the means left to me of getting a living for my wife and four children are very poor.

I beg to remain Gentlemen,
Your Obedient Servant,
John Langton. PC60

There is no record of the Watch Committee's response to John Langton's letter.

In spring 1878, the sergeants of the Borough force wrote to Farndale, asking that he discuss with the lighting authorities their practice of turning off the street lights during the summer months.

Inspector Joseph Wilkinson. A married man with four children, Wilkinson came to Leicester as head of the detective department (with the rank of inspector) in November 1873. Prior to this he had been a detective with the Sheffield Police. His salary at Leicester was £104 a year with an allowance of £10 for uniform. In April 1876, Wilkinson left Leicester having been appointed head constable of the borough of Kendal. He is pictured in the uniform of the Kendal force.

…the extinguishing of street lights one hour before daylight, and sometimes at midnight, this we find to be of great detriment to the constables in the performance of their duties, while at the same time it affords an opportunity to thieves to commit depredations and escape with any property they may have in their possession without detection.

An unfortunate incident in 1878 caused the head constable a deal of embarrassment.

The new town hall, built on the site of the old cattle market in 1872. The police station entrance was at the far right of the building. Note the width of the doorway. All police stations in the borough at this time had an extra wide doorway in order to allow the 'drunks handbarrow' to be brought into the station, where its occupant would be discharged into the cells.

Inspector Pemberton's replacement as chief clerk was one Thomas Allen, previously of Addlestone in Surrey, where he had been employed as a sanitary inspector. In the middle of the summer, on Wednesday 31 July, Allen set off to the bank with £230 in various forms of cash and cheques, including the force wages for the week, all the incoming petty cash and, as was later discovered, the contents of the tea fund. Allen never arrived at the bank, and by the time suspicions were aroused he had caught a train out of the town and was never seen again.

In the 10 years during which he was head constable of Leicester Borough Police force,

Joseph Farndale achieved a great deal. Having taken over a force which was experiencing a period of exceptionally low morale, by changing its physical appearance and improving working conditions, he quickly restored it to an efficient working unit. In altering the overall structure and embarking on an expansion of the organisation, he ensured that the force remained on an equal footing with other forces throughout the country.

A crucial factor in this process of development and consolidation was the overall improvement in living conditions in the town. From the 1860s onward, Leicester moved away from its dependence on the hosiery and stocking trade,

Joseph Farndale, head constable of Leicester police 1871–82.

and became a major centre of the boot and shoe industry. This trend was accompanied by a proliferation of other enterprises, all of which added to the growing economic stability of the town. From Christmas 1874, horse-drawn trams began to operate a regular public transport system within the borough. Although education did not become compulsory until 1880, Board Schools were opened earlier (1874), in King Richard's Road and Syston Street. Between 1876 and 1891 an ambitious flood prevention scheme, which involved the widening of the River Soar and the rebuilding of West Bridge, did much to improve the general health of the town.

It was against this background of overall progress that the Leicester Borough Police force was able to consolidate its position and expand its activities. Joseph Farndale's success as head constable was confirmed when he was appointed chief constable of Birmingham in February 1882.

CHAPTER FOUR

James Duns
(March 1882–June 1894)

The position of head constable was advertised with a salary of £300 per annum, plus house rent, rates paid, free coals, and uniform supplied. On this occasion, the advertisement drew 46 applications, including several serving chief constables from locations as far away as the Isle of Man. Among these were George Mercer, now head constable at Colchester, and John Pemberton, head constable of Grantham, both of whom had previously served in the Leicester Borough Police.[1] A local aspirant was Edward Holmes, super-intendent and chief clerk of the Leicestershire County Police. Holmes, who was 34 at the time, was unsuccessful in his bid and later went on to become chief constable of the County Police.

Interestingly, neither of the ex-borough men were considered for the job, although Holmes, the county man, was included in the eventual short-list of three. Following a final interview at the town hall, James Duns, the 36-year-old chief constable of Durham, was appointed as the fourth head constable of the Leicester Borough Police.

Taking up his position almost immediately, the new head constable's first task was to organise the policing arrangements for the visit of the Prince and Princess of Wales in May 1882, for the opening of the Abbey Park in Leicester.

Three hundred and seventy-four police officers, including several detectives and 20 mounted men (from the Metropolitan Police), were drafted in from neighbouring forces. On the day of the visit, Prince Albert Edward (later Edward VII) and Princess Alexandra were greeted by tumultuous crowds at the Midland Railway Station when the royal train arrived from St Pancras at just after one o'clock in the afternoon. Although it was not a particularly hot day, the sun was shining brightly, and the crowds were in a festive mood. Several hundred people had arrived in the town from outlying districts by excursion trains. These were augmented by large numbers of sightseers who had travelled in by diverse means from the outlying villages and county district. The royal party and local dignitaries, in a procession of 27 coaches, made their way first to the Market Place. There they were greeted by a crowd of several thousand people, including an estimated 6,000 school children. After hearing a loyal address, delivered on behalf of Leicester's Masonic Brethren by their Grand Master Earl Ferrers, the Prince and Princess continued along Belgrave Gate and into the park. Here, after the appropriate speeches before an invited audience, Prince Edward declared the park open. (The public were not yet admitted to the grounds, due to fears that damage might be caused to the shrubbery and gardens by a large influx of visitors.)

Following lunch in the park's new pavilion, the royal party made its way back to the railway station, and departed late in the afternoon on the return journey to London. Despite the vast crowds and the large police presence, there was no trouble.

One of the first major issues for Duns to

[1] Charles Pole and John Pemberton left Leicester Borough Police in close succession to become head constable of Grantham. Pole cannot have remained at Grantham for very long.

Inspector James Allen (22 February 1876–5 May 1903).

service stripes meant that it was possible (and totally undesirable), for some officers in the lower divisions to be earning more than a man in the top division. The rates of pay which the Home Office suggested should be adopted were simpler, and while retaining the service stripes, moved men through the divisions on the basis of length of service.

Detective Sergeant David Stewart (November 1887–November 1894).

resolve in his new role was that of the classes into which constables were divided, along with the matter of service increments. For the last nine years, the scales had remained constant, with the top pay of a constable in 'A' Division, which was the Merit Class, standing at 27s 6d a week. Admission to 'A' Division was by recommendation for good work and discipline. The divisions were complicated by a system of service stripes, which were awarded at five year intervals – one stripe at five years, two stripes at 10, a silver stripe at 15 and a gold one at 20 – on receipt of which a man's pay was increased by a penny a day for each stripe.

In an effort to standardise matters, the Home Office first criticised the Leicester pay scales, then made their own suggestions. The government comments were quite legitimate. In their view, the process of paying a penny a day in respect of

Constable:	on joining 'C' division, 22s 9d, moving through 'B' division into 'A' division after 8 years, to receive 28s 7d a week.
Sergeant:	29s 2d on appointment, rising to 32s 8d after 8 years.
3rd Class Inspector:	32s
2nd Class Inspector:	42s
1st Class Inspector:	46s
Detective Inspector:	48s

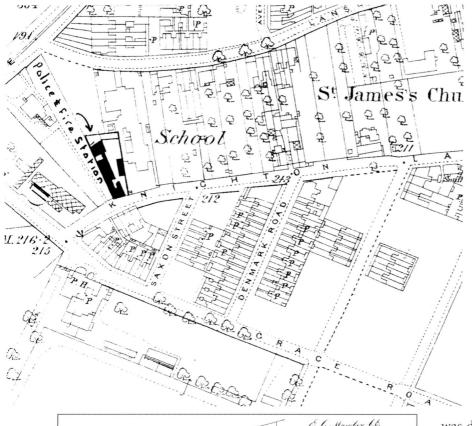

The first police station in the Aylestone District (October 1892–January 1896). It was situated between Lansdowne Road and Knighton Lane (also sometimes referred to as Knighton Road).

mission of the Watch Committee he arranged that members of the force and their families, in two separate parties, should spend a day enjoying the seaside at Skegness.[2]

James Duns' first experience of civil disorder in the town was the result of his having to obliquely enforce an unpopular piece of legislation.

Historically, the town had, prior to the completion of the flood prevention scheme, an extremely poor public health record. This was due, among other causes, to the annual flooding of parts of the town, when the River Soar, polluted by effluent, burst its banks. A result of this flooding was that the borough was prone to outbreaks of diseases and infections such as 'summer diarrhoea' (which was particularly deadly to young children), typhoid and smallpox.

Despite legislation which required all infants to be vaccinated against smallpox, there was a strong anti-vaccination lobby in the borough. It was considered by many that the process of vaccination was flawed, and that it in fact often caused skin complaints. (There was some medical evidence to support this theory.) In 1869 the 'Anti-Vaccination League' had

This review of pay differentials was an important move for improving the morale of the force. Aware that a further contentious issue related to the lack of rest days, during the summer of 1883 Duns arranged the first instance of what was to become an annual event. With the per-

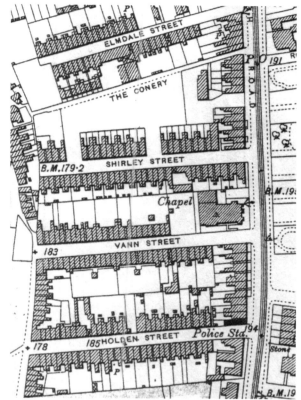

Belgrave police station, situated at the junction of Holden Street and Loughborough Road.

been formed in Leicester, and the town quickly became a centre for campaigners nationwide.

The Board of Guardians (responsible for the administration of the Poor Laws), was responsible for enforcing the law requiring children to be vaccinated, and those who refused to comply were prosecuted. In November 1882, a distress warrant was issued by the magistrates against Thomas Pratt, of 45 Wellington Street, for non-payment of a 10s 'vaccination fine'.

On Thursday 16 November, armed with the warrant, Constables Mardlin, Brightmore and Thirlby visited the address in Wellington Street and seized a bookcase worth between two and three pounds. Eight days later, on Friday 24 November, Sergeant Keeling and several officers took the bookcase to the Nags Head yard in Millstone Lane, where it was sold at auction. A huge and disorderly crowd attended the sale. The bookcase realised sufficient money for Pratt to be given three guineas after the amount of the outstanding fine had been deducted. Immediately the business had been completed, general disorder broke out and Duns, with a detachment of 20 men plus Sergeant Keeling and his officers, was required to disperse the crowd.

The first major setback for James Duns came in the spring of 1885, when a safe-breaking at the premises of William Colton in Belgrave Gate caused the police considerable embarrassment. The letter of grievance, sent to the Watch Committee by the complainant, outlines the circumstances of the robbery.

Chairman and Gentlemen
of the Watch Committee
43 Belgrave Gate,
Leicester.
18 May 1885

Gentlemen,

In consequence of the robbery which occurred at my warehouse on the night of the 7 inst., by the removal bodily of the iron safe weighing with the books, 3 cwt., 3 qtr., or more and containing cash amounting to £40 or thereabouts with many other articles.

I am anxious that the Committee should investigate the conduct of the sergeants and the Constables upon the various beats that night through which the property is supposed to have been conveyed.

A lighted candle must have been burning in the warehouse for several hours and which ought to have been observed from without.

And supposing the robbery to have been effected as late as three o'clock in the morning, the gates which were left unfastened could not have been touched by the police, otherwise the theft would have been discovered many hours earlier.

As a rate payer contributing over £100 per year for my property in the borough I have a right to expect a supervision of a more perfect kind.

Immediately on the discovery of the burglary I should have offered a reward of £50 or £100 but was overruled by the chief constable, now I feel it is so far gone that the responsibility rests with the Committee, but still I am not unwilling in any way to help them to bring the perpetrators to justice for the reputation of the force is at stake, the public generally are condemning the blindness of those who should have eyes to see and ears to hear.

Mr Duns and the chief of Detective department have rendered every possible assistance but (up to the present), of no avail.

The force outside of this department in my humble judgement are responsible and other means must be tried.

I would therefore suggest that the Committee employ an expert, independent altogether of the local force.

So far as my own employees are concerned I have given the police every assistance, both as to their conduct and movements and nothing has transpired to lead them or myself to think they are any way connected with the robbery.

If I can render any further assistance to the Committee or the police I shall be most happy to do so.

I am Gentlemen,
Your obedient servant,
William Colton.

The Watch Committee took Colton's complaint seriously, and instructed Duns to prepare a review of how the incident had occur-

Detective Sergeant Joel Palmer (31 December 1867–3 July 1894).

red. As an indication of their displeasure, the committee deferred their deliberations about a pay increase for the head constable from £300 to £350 until the matter was resolved. The irony of their action at this particular time seems to have escaped the committee. Duns had personally performed his duties satisfactorily, and in asking for an increase in pay was actually seeking to redress a short-fall between his current wage and his predecessor's salary, who on leaving the force to go to Birmingham, was earning £450 a year. Duns was originally engaged at £300 – which was only two thirds of the appropriate rate.[3]

The head constable's report into the incident addressed several issues, which in retrospect should have been dealt with before this incident occurred. His immediate and predictable reaction was that the officers on the three beats in the immediate vicinity on the night in question had been neglectful of their duty and should be disciplined.[4] As a corollary, all officers would henceforth alternate the direction in which a beat was walked, in order to break up any discernible working pattern.

A serious criticism was made of the detective department, to the effect that its officers had insufficient contacts within the criminal fraternity.

Not unexpectedly, Duns took the opportunity to make a plea for an increase in the number of officers. His final comment, although not intended as such, is a criticism of his own lack of forward planning:

[3] Duns's struggle for parity was destined to be ongoing. Two years later, in December 1888, while seeking a further increase of £50, he pointed out to the Watch Committee that he was, 'still earning £100 a year less than his predecessor seven years earlier, and he [Farndale], additionally received £50 for the upkeep of a horse!'.

[4] For many years prior to this when a burglary was not discovered by an officer on his beat during his tour of duty, he was required to appear at the next meeting of the Watch Committee to explain why.

Superintendent Charles Hickinbottom was the first superintendent of Belgrave police station. A native of Long Whatton near Loughborough, Charles Hickinbottom served in the Leicester Borough Police force from 17 January 1871 until his retirement at the age of 51 on 10 March 1896.

…there is no doubt that even with the present staff, an improvement could be made by dividing the town into divisions and an Inspector placed in charge of each with a sufficient number of sergeants and Constables who would parade at their divisional station for duty and be thereby enabled to reach their beats much quicker than they do at present, having in many cases fully a mile to walk before they reach those situate on the outskirts of the town, which as a matter of course necessitates at each relief those beats being wholly unprotected for a considerable time, and were an Inspector to be placed in charge of each division that officer would feel the undivided responsibility of his position…

At this point Detective Sergeant Robert Dexter is mentioned for the first time. Dexter, at 34 years of age, had been a serving officer in the Leicester Borough Police for 12 years, the last five of which had been spent in the detective department. An extremely able detective, in September Dexter arrested a man named Sharpe who lived at Belgrave, and charged him with the safe-breaking at Colton's. While being interviewed by Dexter, Sharpe also admitted a further safe robbery at the premises of Messrs Gimson and Company, and a third burglary at a private house for which a man named William Kirby had been convicted, and was serving a prison sentence. Dexter's work on this last offence resulted in Kirby being pardoned and released from prison just before Christmas 1885.

Inspector (Drill Instructor) William Keeling (5 October 1875–18 December 1900).

James Duns, head constable of the Leicester Borough Police force, March 1882–June 1894

Robert Dexter remained with the Borough Police force as a detective for the next 15 years until his retirement as a superintendent in March 1900.

Duns' reorganisation of the force's working practices were complicated and at best a clumsy muddle. By the autumn of 1889 the men were being divided equally between day and night shifts. However, in order to achieve this, one third of the night men were recalled during the day to perform an extra four hours duty. At the weekends, resources were even more stretched, and half the night men were recalled during the day. The consequence was that, each night, some of the officers were allowed to go home early, in order to take a few hours sleep before returning to the day shift.

A particularly time consuming, and inefficient practice grew up during these years, which was to be the bane of every beat officer's life for the next 80 years. In the time since Thomas Cook had organised his first excursion train from Leicester to Loughborough in 1841, the average householder's lifestyle had changed. Now, each year, during the summer months, Leicester families packed their suitcases, locked up their houses, and went off to the coast for an annual holiday. Before going away, the majority called in at the police station and left details of

Sergeant William Bottrill (16 May 1873–4 July 1899).

their address and how long they would be absent for. This information was duly logged in a small book for each beat, which became known as 'the unoccupied house book'. Every constable going out on patrol took with him the book for his area, and it was his duty to visit every unoccupied house at least once during his shift, to ensure that all was in order, and record the fact in the book.

While it can legitimately be argued that this 'protection of property' was part and parcel of the policeman's routine, it was (and always remained), an impractical proposition. The main reason for this was that the vast majority of people were away at virtually the same time. This resulted in up to 60 or 70 houses in any one area being empty during the summer months. The beat man's position was unenviable. He could not physically check each house, especially when other matters required his attention. Therefore he either did not visit the houses and risked being disciplined for failing to work his beat properly, or he filled in fictitious visits, which if the house was broken into placed him in a serious position.

One particular event relating to the routine checking of property on night duty occurred in late 1886, when PC Frederick Coleman discovered that a factory premises in Erskine Street off of Humberstone Road had been broken into. The head constable's report on the matter clearly indicates the precarious circumstances in which a lone constable could find himself.

…I beg most respectfully to call your attention to the case of PC no.48 Frederick Coleman, and as the facts are already pretty well known to your Committee, I will content myself by saying that, early on the morning of Wednesday the 29th of September last, [1886], while PC Coleman was in the act of examining the interior of the warehouse of Messrs Leavesley and North, in Erskine Street, he discovered on the premises the notorious burglar named 'Nutting', whom he at once closed with when a most desperate and terrific struggle ensued which lasted about an hour and a half before he, [Coleman], succeeded in making him a prisoner, and whom he immediately afterwards conveyed to the central police station unaided.

During the struggle Coleman received no less than 28 wounds on his right hand and 12 on his left, together with three or four other wounds of a superficial character on his right arm and head. Thus it will be seen that notwithstanding the severe injuries that were inflicted on the constable, yet he appears to have most manfully stuck to his prisoner throughout and in fact exhibited that dogged courage and determination which I have very rarely seen equalled and never excelled.

It is therefore with very great pleasure that I recommend PC Coleman to your favourable consideration, feeling assured that you will be unanimously of the opinion that such bravery as he has undoubtedly shown himself to be possessed of merits some suitable and substantial recognition at your hands.

PC Coleman I might say joined this force on the 31 January 1871, consequently he has served for a period of 15 years and nearly two months without a single report for misconduct or otherwise having been recorded against him.

Nutting I might add was tried at the last Assizes on a charge of warehouse breaking and with unlawful wounding PC Coleman

with intent to resist his lawful apprehension. The Judge, Mr Justice Grantham sentenced him to 20 years penal servitude, thus ridding the town for some considerable time of a most dangerous and desperate character.

The Judge also awarded the sum of £10 to PC Coleman for the exceptional bravery displayed by him…

Frederick Coleman was promoted forthwith to the rank of first class sergeant, with a wage of 32s a week. Sadly, he died in January 1895. A year later his wife was given a special award by the Watch Committee of £187 4s 0d, being the equivalent of one months pay for each of his 24 years of service.

Although regular weekly rest days were still a thing of the future, the Police Act of 1890 finally regularised the situation in relation to police officers retiring. As from this time a police authority could make regulations fixing the age at which a police officer, after completing 25 years service, would be entitled to retire on a pension. (Prior to this individuals had negotiated a retirement settlement with the local authority, which was a very precarious business for the person retiring.) The terms were that the officer could retire, without a medical certificate, at not less than 50 and not more than 55 years of age. One of the first officers to leave under these provisions, in July 1891, was Detective Sergeant John Elton, who having served in the Borough Police for 33 years and 85 days, was 63 years old.

Ever cautious, the businessmen who made up the Watch Committee quickly deemed it prudent to define exactly what constituted a man's period of service. With the assistance of Doctor Henry Tomkins, the police surgeon for the Borough force, a set of guidelines were drawn up.

In reckoning the length of a man's service and his pension payment, the inclusive dates of his joining and leaving would stand, less: all days absent through sickness (in which case – other than where injured on duty – a shilling a day

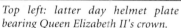

Top left: latter day helmet plate bearing Queen Elizabeth II's crown.

Top right: from the turn of the century until World War One helmet plates carried the officer's warrant number in the centre.

Bottom: bearing the King's crown and without the lion rampant supporters, this plate bearing the legend 'Leicester Borough Police' was taken into use during the First World War and worn until 1919. (Courtesy N.Haines)

would be deducted from his final settlement); his entire pay for any period of sickness brought about through his own misconduct; all days during which he had been suspended from duty by disciplinary matters; and all days absent without the consent of the Watch Committee. Within these parameters an officer was at liberty to retire, provided that he tendered one month's notice.

—oOo—

During the height of the summer, in August 1893, a major problem came to light in respect of the usage of part of the town hall buildings as a mortuary. On the 3 May that year, the neighbours of Eliza Clarke, a 50-year-old woman who lived alone at 7 Oxford Street, near to the Magazine, became concerned that she had not been seen for some time. They reported their disquiet to the local beat officer, Constable 134 George, who visited the house. Breaking a back kitchen window to gain access, George found the woman fully clothed, dead in bed. From the condition of the body it was apparent that she had been dead for some days. After Doctor Crossley, a local physician, had attended, the body was removed to

Details of a report drawn up by James Duns during 1882, at the request of the Watch Committee. It outlines exisiting pay scales, prior to the implementation of the Home Office rates. The report was presented on 18 July 1882.

Leicester Borough Police

Inspector Detective	48/-	1/- per week advance during each year up to 50/-
Inspector 1st Class	46/-	
Inspector 2nd Class	42/-	The Second Class Inspectors to continue such for two years before promotion to First Class.
Inspector 3rd Class	38/-	The Third Class Inspectors to continue such for two years before promotion to Second Class.
Chief Clerk	35/-	
Detectives	32/-	
Sergeants Merit Class	33/-	Promoted by the Watch Committee for meritorious conduct only.
Sergeants First Class	32/-	
Sergeants Second Class	30/-	The Second Class Sergeants to continue such for three years before promotion to First Class.
Merit Class Constable	28/6	Promoted by the Watch Committee for meritorious conduct only.
1st Class Do.	27/6	
2nd Class Do.	25/6	The Second Class Constables to continue such for twelve months without complaint or punishment before promotion to First Class.
3rd Class Do	24/-	The Third Class Constables to continue such for six months without complaint or punishment before promotion to Second Class.
4th Class Do	23/-	The Fourth Class Constables to continue such for four months without complaint or punishment before promotion to the Third Class.

the room used as a mortuary at the town hall. The science of refrigeration was at this time in its infancy, and certainly did not extend to the preservation of corpses. For several days, both prior to and after a post mortem had been conducted, the body remained in a closed room adjacent to the police offices.

The reaction from those working at the town hall was not unexpected. In what was obviously a concerted campaign, a total of 12 reports, signed by every supervisory officer of any consequence, landed on the head constable's desk within a period of 48 hours. Objections varied from the inability to have any windows open and being unable to use the muster room, to the abandoning of drill out in the yard. Indications are that the mortuary was at the rear of the building, near to Duns living quarters. That this was an ongoing situation is shown in a reference made by Inspector John Watkinson, the chief clerk, to the fact that on two other occasions, the bodies of men killed on the railway had caused similar problems.

It is probable that the use of the town hall police station for mortuary purposes was a relatively new thing. The seasons of the year at this time were fairly consistent – long hard winters with heavy falls of snow, giving way to hot summers punctuated by violent rain storms. The new town hall had by now been open for 17 years,

during which time it would have been reasonable to have expected some prior form of complaint. The intensity of the reaction to the circumstances, would indicate that this was in fact a new innovation. One contemporary reference in a letter from a Mr A. Hall talks about, 'your new [mortuary], building' and alludes to the appointment of a caretaker.

On balance, it is probable that, the Fire Brigade having vacated part of the building the previous August, this was the first summer when accommodation had been available for the experimental use of a room for mortuary purposes.

Whatever the inconvenience to those based in the town hall or the merits of their argument, nothing was done for a further 10 years, until in 1903, the Borough Medical Officer of Health Charles Killick Millard added his weight to the complaints.

—oOo—

From 1885 onwards, tentative moves were made to extend the boundaries of the borough to incorporate some of the surrounding suburbs such as Aylestone and Knighton. With improved amenities in the town, including an efficient sewage disposal system and running water, incorporation of these small villages made administrative sense. A Bill authorising the extension of the town boundaries passed through Parliament on 3 July 1891, and resulted in the absorption of West Humberstone, Belgrave, Knighton and Aylestone. Leicester Borough now contained approximately 42 per cent more inhabitants than it had 10 years before.

These boundary changes meant that the police responsibilities were also altered. It was agreed that eight constables of the County Police force stationed within the district to be incorporated should be allowed to transfer into the Borough Police force, bringing with them their appropriate periods of service. Additionally a further 20 new men were recruited. For the first time in his nine years with the force, Duns with an increase of salary to £500 a year, in accordance with his increased responsibilities, managed to achieve a higher salary than his predecessor.

Now that the Borough Police force was accountable for the policing of Knighton and Aylestone districts, it was necessary to find a suitable police station on the south side of the town. On the 15 December 1891 a lease was negotiated with Mr Hunt, the owner of the property at 139 Queen's Road, to use the premises as a police station, and Superintendent Joseph Howe was installed as the first superintendent of Knighton District.

On the northern side of the town, after a degree of wrangling over property values, the County Council handed over possession of their

Sergeant 20 Frederick Coleman. He joined the Leicester Police on 31 January 1871 as constable 48. During the night of 29 September 1886, while checking premises in Erskine Street, he disturbed a burglar named Nutting, with whom he fought for an hour and a half before making the arrest. In recognition of his conduct he was immediately promoted to sergeant first class at a salary of 32s 8d a week. He died nine years later in 1895. After his death his widow was granted a payment of £187 4s 0d – one month's pay for each of Coleman's 24 years of service.

Inspector John Vann, chief clerk. He joined the Borough Police in 1886 and retired in September 1911. He died on 15 February 1946.

Inspector James Hickinbottom joined the Leicester Borough Police on 22 August 1854, and served for 29 years before retiring on 22 July 1883. At this time most officers served for only 25 years.

police station at Belgrave, on the corner of Loughborough Road and Holden Street to the Borough Police force. Command of this district was given to Superintendent Charles Hickinbottom.

The following year, in March, Duns negotiated a contract with Messrs Gent and Company, a local firm based in St Saviours Road, to install a 'double line telephone system with interchangeable switchboard', at the central police station at a cost of £225 10s 0d. Thereafter for a rental (payable to the Post Office), of £74 per year for the next seven years, the central and branch stations were provided with an up to date telephone system. In February 1893 the National Telephone Company installed 'an instrument', at the town hall in the central police station at a rental of £10 per annum, thereby connecting Leicester Police to the national network.

—oOo—

The Cruelty to, and Protection of Children Act 1889 began to address the issue of child abuse both nationally and locally. Previously, in the winter of 1892, Mr Robert Harvey, the Leicester Coroner had expressed concern about the number of bodies of newly-born children that were being found in the town. Specifically, in December that year, he alluded to a case with which he was currently dealing, of a child's body found wrapped in newspaper in a public thoroughfare. This, he pointed out, was the sixth case during that year, and the matter was becoming a scandal.

Under the Protection of Children Act, no person was allowed to employ any child in the streets for profit between the hours of 10 at night and five in the morning. A local authority could extend these hours as they felt appropriate. While the Borough Police set two plain clothes officers the task of enforcing the Act, the sanctions taken

This group of Borough Police officers dates from between 1882 and 1885. Seated third from the right in the front row is Sergeant Joseph Howe, who later became a superintendent. He is wearing 10-year service stripes. Four other older officers in the picture are wearing silver stripes (15 years) or gold stripes (20 years).

in respect of offenders seem to have been less than punitive. A senior officer's report early in the next decade states that

> …a large number of children found hawking in the streets have been brought to the station and their parents sent for, who generally plead ignorance of the law and promise not to offend in future… A number of persons have been charged before the Magistrates for causing or procuring children to be in the streets for the purpose of inducing the giving of alms, the majority of whom were convicted and this class of offence has greatly decreased during the last year or two…

In 1892, the most recently appointed police surgeon, Doctor Arthur Barlow, of 2 Melbourne Road, was given a clear definition of what his duties comprised. He was to attend on casualties at the police station and elsewhere when requested by the police. He was to issue certificates in cases where children were ordered to be detained in Industrial Schools or Reformatories, and he was to give relevant medical evidence in the police court.

Additionally, the police surgeon was responsible for the health of the officers of the Borough Police force. Generally, this involved his taking a sick parade at 12 noon each day at the central police station, or visiting those officers too sick to attend the parade. The doctor's duties

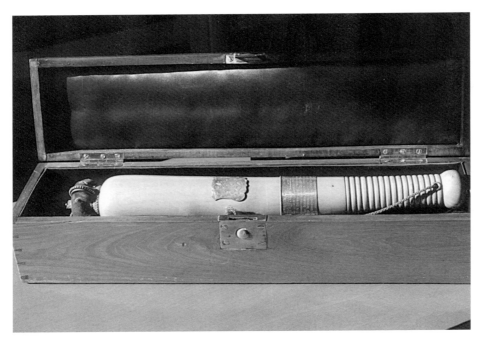

'PRESENTED TO: PC FREDERICK COLEMAN

Of the Leicester Borough Police force by a few Belgrave & Leicester Admirers in recognition of his gallant conduct on the occasion of his apprehending the notorious burglar "Nutting" on the morning of 29th September 1886.
  Oliver Burton. Hon. Sec.'

also required him to report on officers whose health no longer permitted them to carry out their work.

In the summer of 1893, at the age of 47, James Duns' health began to show signs of serious deterioration. At first Doctor Barlow ascribed Duns' physical condition to nervous prostration, and advised that he be given a month's leave to recuperate. The head constable returned to his home at Hawick near the Scottish border, where, during a period of convalescence, he was treated by a local practitioner.

Although he returned to duty after his period of leave, over the next 18 months his condition deteriorated rapidly, and it became obvious to both his own medical adviser, Doctor Bremner, and to the police surgeon, that he was suffering from a form of cancer.

On 24 May 1894, by mutual agreement with the members of the Watch Committee, James

Duns submitted his resignation, and ceased to be the head constable of the Leicester Borough Police force the following month.

James Duns returned to Hawick, where he died at the age of 49 on 11 November 1895. He had served as a police officer in Newcastle-upon-Tyne from May 1868 until November 1876, when he transferred to the Durham Police force. Having served in Durham for a further five and a half years, he moved to Leicester, where he remained until his retirement in 1894 – a total of 26 years. One week after his death a petition was submitted to the Leicester Watch Committee by a group of his friends, endeavouring to obtain a pension for his wife and four children. The reply was unequivocal. '…No pension is allowed for Constables wives where the officer dies 12 months after leaving the force'.

CHAPTER FIVE

Thomas Wilkinson Lumley
(July 1894–June 1907)

With the departure on ill-health of James Duns, it was necessary to secure another head constable as a matter of some urgency. In the interim period (which as things transpired was just under two months), Superintendent William Hawkins was given charge of the force. Once again, of the 28 applications for the position, two were from serving officers within the force – Superintendents Joseph Howe and Robert Dexter. As was the case when Duns was appointed, neither of the local men were short-listed. In the circumstances, this appears somewhat strange. Both men were well qualified, and given the need to find a speedy resolution to the situation, either would have been suitable.[1]

The position went to Thomas Wilkinson Lumley, whose appointment was confirmed on 18 July 1894. An imposing man, standing six feet tall, the 40-year-old Superintendent Lumley was divisional commander of the Smalley Division of the Derbyshire Police, a position which he had held since 1889. For the first time since 1836, the Corporation decided that the appointment (at £400 a year), would not include accommodation.[2] A decision to incorporate the chief constable's living quarters at the new town hall into the administration offices had been taken immediately after Duns retired. Duns' resignation took effect from 24 May, and four days later the magistrates clerk R.R. Backwell made a request that the head constable's vacant accommodation be added to the Magistrates Clerks department. This could, he explained, 'be most easily effected

Chief Superintendent William Hawkins (1 June 1875–13 November 1906). Hawkins was the first senior officer to be appointed chief superintendent. There were in fact only two other chief superintendents after Hawkins, Geary and Judd. After 1929 no one else was appointed to the rank.

by blocking up the door into the house'. A counter proposition was that the quarters would provide suitable space for the police surgeon to carry out his duties. Lumley, on his arrival in Leicester, moved into 'Weathersfield' at 167 Hinckley Road. Six months later, 'telephonic lines' were installed between the central station and his house.

[1] Dexter and Howe were the same age, 43, and had both served in the Borough Police force for 22 years. The Borough Extension Act in 1891 had resulted in their promotion from inspector to superintendent. Although unsuccessful in their applications, both were content to serve under Lumley for several years. Howe retired at the end of 1899, and was followed a few months later in 1900 by Dexter. In 1934, at the age of 83, Joseph Howe returned to the old town hall police station and assisted in annotating a plan of the premises, a copy of which is reproduced elsewhere as an illustration. (see p. 46)

[2] Wilkinson's salary was increased to £500 in January 1896

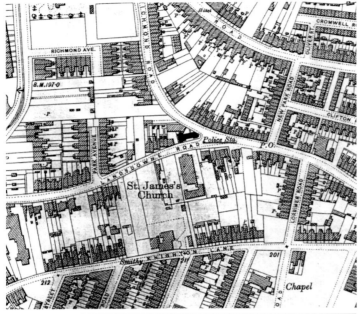

The location of the Aylestone Police station after 1896, at the junction of Lansdowne Road and Richmond Road.

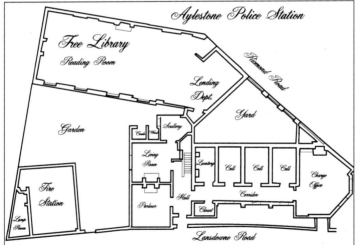

much to be desired. Situated on the piece of ground between Knighton Lane and Lansdowne Road, next to the school, the police station itself lay at the back of the house.

In April 1893 the owners were pointedly required by the Watch Committee to, 'put into reasonable and proper repair the premises occupied by Sergeant Arnold, failing which other accommodation would be obtained and the tenancy terminated'. A further complication was that the upper storey of the police station was being rented out to a group of Wesleyan Methodists. The owners response, through their agent, Mr Burgess, was to enquire if the Corporation would not consider purchasing the property, and then it could do with it as it wished. Immediately after Christmas 1893, just after a new lease had been signed by the Corporation, the owners disposed of a large part of the ground adjoining the police station to the Education Committee, in order that the abutting school playground could be enlarged. As a temporary solution the Watch Committee negotiated a rent reduction from £25 to £23 a year, and set about finding a new site entirely.

An early problem for Lumley to apply his mind to arose over the branch station at Aylestone Park. The extension of the borough a year or two earlier had demanded that premises be acquired for a police station in the suburb. A house and buildings were rented for the sum of £25 on Knighton Lane, near to the junction of Grace Road. The location and condition of the property (opposite Saxon Street, which later became Harold Street), left

On 8 December 1894, the Corporation bought from a Mr Moore, for the sum of 9s a square yard, 744 square yards of land at the junction of Lansdowne Road and Richmond Road, for the purpose of erecting a combined police station and public lending library. Plans were drawn up by Messrs Harding and Topott, and in July 1895 a building tender submitted by Herbert Carrington for £1,747 was accepted. When the lease on the old

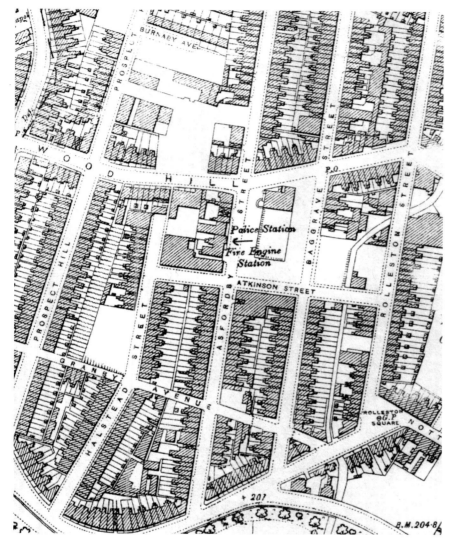

North Evington Police station, situated in Asfordby Street opposite the Market Square.

which was being offered at 14s a square foot, in order that a combined police and fire station could be built. In the meantime, part of the nearby market hall was leased from the architect Arthur Wakerley for use as a temporary police station. During the following summer, plans for the new building were approved at an estimated £3,696, and John Jewsbury, a builder at 40 Oxford Street, was given the contract to build the station. As part of the overall plan, Wakerley offered to sell the Corporation 524 square yards of land at the rear of the building in Halstead Street for £324. After due consideration, the Watch Committee turned down this offer on the grounds

premises expired, an extension of a few weeks into early 1896 was granted prior to the police moving into their newly commissioned branch station.

While policing of the southern part of the borough's newly-acquired territory had been resolved, it was becoming apparent that the rapidly growing suburb of North Evington, on the eastern side of the town was also in need of a branch station.

In December 1896, proposals were made for the purchase of a piece of land in Asfordby Street,

that Wakerley wanted to put clauses into the sale which they found unacceptable. In March 1899 the Corporation gave nine months notice of their intention to quit the market hall premises as from the 25 December, when they took up residency in the North Evington branch station .[3]

—oOo—

The subject of rest days for the police continued to be a bone of contention. As far back as August 1893, members of the force had lobbied

[3] The final bill for work on the North Evington branch station, submitted in April 1900, exceeded the original estimates by £607

Detective Inspector (later Superintendent) Robert Dexter. He joined the Leicester Borough Police force in February 1872, and was described as 6ft 1in tall, and a labourer by occupation. Dexter proved himself an outstanding detective and was promoted to superintendent in 1891. He retired in April 1900 at the age of 49, having served for 28 years.

Superintendent James Nicholson (October 1877–July 1901) was the second superintendent at Knighton.

for what appeared to be a reasonable allocation of annual and weekly leave. At that time, their memorial to the Watch Committee pointed out that, '…present leave of absence amounts to 11 days a year. Seven days at [any], one time, and one Sunday every 13 weeks.' To bring the Leicester Police into line with other forces they asked for, '…23 days in a year. Ten days at one time, and one day – a weekday or a Sunday – every 28 days'.

The problem of rest days and leave was not confined to the police. It is apparent that by late 1896 pressure was being brought to bear by all the Leicester Corporation employees, to secure what they felt to be a fair resolution to the problem. At a council meeting held on 17 November, it was proposed that as from Wednesday 16 December 1896 Corporation employees from all departments (including the police), were to be granted one day's rest in seven without loss of pay. The relevant committees were charged with examining the recommendation and reporting back with the budgetary implications. Lumley's reaction was that to implement such a resolution would require an extra 28 men, and incur a cost of £2,200. Other departments returned similar projections and on the 1 December the motion was quietly deferred.

As far as the Borough Police force was concerned, a compromise was reached two months later, in February 1897. By appointing a further 12 officers to the force, and allowing an extra £1,000 on the budget, extra leave days could be allocated. Officers would be allowed one

Sunday off in every six, which in real terms gave them an extra four days leave a year, making 10 days annual leave and a further eight rest days. Even at this point, not everyone was included in the agreement. A hurriedly-drafted letter to the committee from the sergeants of the force, dated 20 March, makes the point.

> We the uniformed and detective sergeants request that as you have granted an extra four days leave of absence to the constables of the force, the privilege may be extended to us. Inspectors get one Sunday off in four, whereas sergeants get one Sunday off in seven…

At the beginning of 1899, the year that Great Britain went to war with the Boers in South Africa, Leicester saw it's first motorised taxicabs. In a letter dated 10 January, the newly formed Leicester Motor Car Company sought permission from the authorities to begin plying for hire in the streets of the town.[4]

> Rose Bank,
> Freemen's Common,
> Leicester.
> 10 January 1899
> Councillor Royce,
> Chairman of the Watch Committee.
>
> Dear Sir,
> A Company is now in consideration for running motor cars in this town as wagonettes on the Aylestone and Belgrave Roads, and before anything further is settled, the Company (which would consist of tradesmen of the Town), wish to ask the Watch Committee whether they are agreeable to license these motor cars, and if so what the licence would be for each car and driver.
> The number suggested at first is two, and the Company is of [the] opinion that the fare for each passenger should be two pence.
> The Company wish me to say for further information to your Committee that the makers of the motor cars send with each new car a practical and experienced man for one week, so that the intended driver may have every benefit of knowing how to manage them. The cars would be kept continually running all day, and therefore no difficulty would arise in having standing positions for same. Any further information the Company will be pleased to send on to you.
>
> Awaiting your favourable reply,
> Believe me to remain on behalf of the Company,
> Yours faithfully,
> J.E. Lester.

The Watch Committee raised no objections and endorsed the new venture, which commenced operations a few months later in June.[5] It cannot be coincidental, in view of the routes proposed by the taxicab operators (along the main roads leading to the cattle market on Aylestone Road), that a bye-law was passed in March – two months after the application – relating to the driving of animals to market. On penalty of a five pound fine, it was declared that

> …no person shall drive any bull, ox, cow, sheep [or], pig through or along any street or road in this borough between the hours of 12 o'clock midday and two o'clock in the afternoon on Wednesdays, [market day], or after the hour of nine o'clock in the morning on Sundays. And that no person shall at any time take or cause to be taken any bull through or along any street within this borough unless it be thoroughly secure to a staff or a rope and led by a person capable of controlling it…

---

[4] A report by Charles Bennion, MIME in October 1899 states that he had examined a 'Lifu' motor car, which the Leicester Motor Car Co., intended to use, and found it to be safe. However, he recommended that a screen be placed at the bottom of the boiler in order to more effectively shield the brilliant light of the furnace.

[5] James Ernest Lester was an electrical engineer with business premises at 2 Cank Street.

Despite the growing presence of motor vehicles in the town, the legislation remained in effect for many years. In late 1914, William John Turner, a farmer, and dairyman William Howgill, were each fined 2s 6d by the magistrates for allowing their cows to stray in Walnut Street and Aylestone Road.

As a further token of their good intentions, the Leicester Car Company, in September wrote to the head constable:

> We have given the enclosed printed instructions to our drivers. We have also given to them further instructions not to exceed, in crowded areas, six miles an hour. I may say that we have travelled 20,000 miles during the four months that we have been running cars, carried 28,000 passengers and without a single accident. We should be obliged if your officers would kindly report to us any case where a driver refuses to stop when meeting a restive horse…

An inevitable conflict between the old legislation and new technology arose in various applications of the law. One illustration of this related to the displaying of lights on vehicles. On a horse-drawn cart the absence of a lamp was an inconvenience, on a motor vehicle it constituted a danger. Consequently, police throughout the country began to enforce legislation which was in dire need of reappraisal. A letter was sent to all chief officers of police forces from the Home Office in April 1900, which illustrated the problem. A recent case brought under a local bye-law, which required that every person in charge of a vehicle ensure that lighted lamps were adequately displayed, had resulted in a young lad driving a cart being sent to prison. The Home Office circular urgently asked that local authorities review any such local legislation, and ensure that it was rephrased to apportion liability to the owner of the vehicle.

Thomas Wilkinson Lumley was head constable of Leicester Borough Police from July 1894–June 1907.

As the concept of the new form of locomotion slowly began to be accepted, so the local authority and the police adapted their practices and procedures. The head constable asked at the beginning of 1904 for 20 new officers, in order that he might regulate traffic at the town's junctions and tramway points. (This is where the practice of referring to a policeman on traffic duty as a 'pointsman' probably originates.) Later that year, during mid-summer, the first direction boards in the town for the information of motorists and cyclists made an appearance at the corners of Hinckley and Narborough Roads, and Welford and Aylestone Road.

Another new prospect which was raised for the first time in 1899 was that of the employment of females by the police in Leicester. It is obvious that, in preceding years, when women prisoners were brought to the police station, a female was needed to deal with such matters as searching her and attending to her needs. It is almost certain that this type of work was undertaken on an *ad*

increase in accommodation has been arranged...'

One of the reasons why a female member of staff was needed was for dealing with female drunks, whose care in custody required an attendant of the same sex. With excessive drinking still being perceived as a social problem, in 1898 the government passed an Inebriates Act, which allowed local magistrates to consign those identified as hopeless drunks to specified reformatories for treatment. (The Borough Police force had its own problems with drink. Disciplines for drinking on duty continued, although at a lesser rate than in previous years. Senior officers were not immune to the problem. As far back as 1875 Inspector Newell was suspended from duty for chronic drunkenness, and reduced in rank. In December 1892 Inspector Keeling had been 'severely reprimanded for appearing before the Watch Committee in a state of drunkenness... and further conducting himself in a disrespectful manner...' The incident obviously did not blight the inspector's career, as he served for another eight years, until his retirement in November 1900. Inspector John Arnold was not so fortunate. After 25 and a half years service, he was required to resign in March 1900, 'for drunkenness on duty'.)

hoc basis by any available female – either a policeman's wife, or a station employee. The proposal to formally employ a female attendant at the central police station was received with a degree of caution. Raised in May 1899, the question was deferred 'until such time as an

In order to comply with the requirements of

PC 92 Thomas Simpson. 23 January 1877 to 7 April 1903. His grandson, David Walter Simpson, later joined the force in October 1957 as PC 115. (Courtesy D.W. Simpson)

the Inebriates Act, in March 1900, Leicester's Watch Committee entered into an agreement with the Royal Victoria Home For Inebriates at Weston-on-Trym, near Bristol. For a flat rate of 6d per day per bed, seven places were kept for committals from the Leicester courts. At this time the hospital was in a position to accept at any one time 44 men and 176 women from various parts of the country. In April 1902 the establishment found itself in financial difficulties and this arrangement was superseded by a yearly subscription of £250 from each of the contributing authorities. Under the revised scheme, bed space in the home was thereafter allocated on an admissions basis.

Whether or not the treatment available at Brentby was effective is open to question. The Watch Committee, apparently perturbed that the

Leicester magistrates were, in their view, not fully utilising the reformatory, rather pointedly reminded them of the existence of the facility in the summer of 1907. Unappreciative of this apparent rebuke, the magistrates responded by furnishing details of the history of recent committals:

Elizabeth Hughes; sent to [the], Inebriates Home in September 1901. She went on her discharge to Salford where on 18 January 1904 she was sentenced to one months imprisonment for being drunk and disorderly. Nothing more known other than she has not since returned to Leicester. Ada Hallam; sent to Inebriates Home in January 1901. Since her release she has been convicted eight times for soliciting for prostitution, twice as a riotous prostitute, once for committing an act of indecency in the street with a man and five times for drunkenness. Sarah Bland and Minnie Orson; sent to the Inebriates Home in 1903, have since been convicted of drunkenness.

Locally, a Home for Inebriates was established on Glenfield Road at its junction with Franche Road. The 'Dane Hills', 1 -2 Franche Road, was licensed as a retreat under the Habitual Drunkards Act 1879. This establishment, under the supervision of Dr Henry Riley, provided 19 bedrooms, two closets and two bathrooms for the care of alcoholics.

The Licensing Act of 1902, which came into operation on 1 January 1903, set out to address the problem of drunkenness by attempting to exclude offenders from licensed premises. Under the provisions of the Act, courts convicting those deemed to be 'habitual drunkards', were obliged to supply to the chief constable of the district the person's description and a portrait. This the head constable was required to have printed and circulated to all licensed premises and clubs in his

Founded in 1873 by Sergeant William Poultney, the Leicester Borough Police Band played in local parks and at civic functions for 33 years until its dissolution in 1906. In this photograph the band master (wearing top hat) is John Smith, formerly band master of the Leicester Volunteer Regiment.

police area. The subject of the notice committed an offence if, within three years of a conviction, he or she attempted to purchase any intoxicants in a licensed premises. Penalties for contravention of the Act were high from the outset. The fine for the drunkard was 20s for a first offence and 40s for any subsequent offence.[6] A licensee contravening the law by supplying any drink to the man or woman was liable to a fine of between £10 and £20.

For his part, Lumley instigated a licensing department within the Borough Police force, comprising one inspector and four plain clothes constables. In a paper published in March 1905, he reported that since the Act had come into

PC 111 Albert Sims, bassoonist in the Borough Police band. This photgraph dates from around 1906, just before the band ceased to exist. Albert Sims joined the force in 1904, and retired as an inspector in June 1929. (Courtesy N. Haines)

[6]Fines for simple drunkenness at this time were usually around 2s 6d.

Horsefair Street in the middle of the 1890s, looking towards the new town hall. The police station was housed in the corner of the building which is shown in the picture.(Courtesy N. Haines)

The men of the North Evington Police station in Asfordby Street, probably photographed soon after the opening of the station in December 1899. The pill box cap worn by the senior officer in the front row, J.T. Norton, was replaced after January 1908 by a more modern version. (Norton became superintendent at Belgrave Police station in the early years of the century.) The fact that none of the men are wearing Boer War medals would indicate that the war in South Africa was still in progress. (Courtesy S. Jeffrey)

force, there had been in the borough 353 prosecutions for drunkenness, 27 of persons being drunk in charge of a child apparently under the age of seven, and four licensees dealt with for permitting drunkenness on their premises.

—oOo—

War in the South African Transvaal was declared on 12 October 1899, and all army reservists were recalled to join the colours. Five members of the Leicester Borough Police on the reserve list left to join their units and five replacements were engaged, with a stipulation

that at the end of the war they would be permanently engaged.

Provision for the families of officers called away to serve in the army was in place by December. Where an officer on active service left a wife and family, 12s a week was allowed to his wife and 2s for each of his children under 15 years of age. In the case of an unmarried man who had responsibility for supporting his parents, a sum not exceeding 8s a week was allowed.[7]

It was during this wartime period that the promotion was made, on 15 October 1901, of Superintendent William Hawkins to chief superintendent. This move, which created the

[7] In the case of a married man it was assumed that his army pay and allowances would make up the difference in his wages.

LEICESTER BOROUGH POLICE.

SHOPBREAKING.

WANTED

In this Borough on a charge of breaking and entering a Pawnshop, on the 16th April, 1904, and Stealing therefrom Jewellery to the value of £200,

A MAN

Name unknown, age about 30 years, height 5ft. 7 to 9in. fairly well built, dark hair, short dark brown moustache, rather pale face, scowling appearance, and looks under his eyebrows. Wearing at the time of the Robbery, **A CAP, JOCKEY PATTERN, WHICH HE PULLED CLOSE OVER HIS HEAD,** a blue serge suit, a light overcoat, and a small white silk handkerchief, 12in. square, with a lilac striped border one inch deep, which he took from the Pawnshop in the place of his own, which he left behind. Was wearing pyjamas instead of an undershirt and drawers. Will be found in the company of low prostitutes, and told two here that he had undergone 12 months' imprisonment for Shopbreaking. He stays at low Public Houses. Had a revolver in his possession, and also another which he stole from the Pawnshop. The thief obtained access to the shop by climbing over the wall, and removing the stanchions of the back window by drilling and sawing out the woodwork.

Please cause immediate enquiry to be made for this man, and if found, arrest and wire, when an officer shall be sent to fetch him, or should he be recognised by this description, kindly forward photograph for identification to

T. W. LUMLEY,

HEAD CONSTABLE, LEICESTER.

Detective Department, Central Police Station,
23rd April, 1904.

ALFRED TACEY, PRINTER AND LITHOGRAPHER, 17 TOWN HALL LANE, LEICESTER.

Leicester Motor Car Co., Ltd.

INSTRUCTIONS TO DRIVERS

The Cars must **not be driven above 8 miles an hour** in the Town, and **12 miles an hour** in the Country.

The Cars to be **steadied down** when turning corners and when passing through busy or crowded thoroughfares.

No Car to be **over loaded** with passengers beyond the number it is licensed to carry.

The advertised time of running to be **strictly kept.**

The Rule of the Road must be strictly followed thus :—
In meeting keep to the left.
In overtaking pass on the right.

In meeting **restive horses** speed must be immediately **slackened** and, if necessary, the Car to be instantly stopped.

In case of any accident, no matter how trivial, the names and addresses of **two witnesses** at least must be taken.

Tickets for all fares **must be given** to each passenger before starting the journey, and the number of passengers **marked off** on the way sheet.

Drivers being **intemperate or uncivil** to passengers will be liable to instant dismissal.

By order of the

April 24, 1899. **LEICESTER MOTOR CAR Co., Ltd.**

Superintendent Charles Crisp, a native of Derby, joined Leicester Borough Police on 23 September 1873 at the age of 22. Before retiring on 26 June 1906 he had been superintendent at Belgrave police station.

post of chief superintendent for the first time in the force's history, was taken in order to prevent Hawkins retiring at a time when his experience was needed. Over the next few years the rank of chief superintendent was to be a transient one, appearing and disappearing according to the requirements of the day. An example of this occurs when, in October 1906, Hawkins retired. Considerable difficulty was experienced in finding a replacement, and Inspector Theodore John Geary was eventually created chief superintendent in his place.

On the 15 July 1902, a few weeks after the coronation of Edward VII, the first of the police reservists, William Bradford and George Wiggins, returned from the war to resume their places as constables. Under a new piece of legislation, the Police Reservists Act 1902, they were allowed to count the time they had spent on active service as pensionable police service.

—oOo—

During the first decade of the 20th century, the Leicester Borough Police became involved for the first time in a social welfare project. The Police

Charles Pole joined the Borough Police on 4 April 1870 as chief clerk, having previously held the position in the county force. He remained with the Borough Police for three years, until he was appointed head constable of Grantham Police in March 1873.

Aided Association was formed to provide clothing for destitute children in the town. A collection of cast-off clothes and boots was made by the police (doubtless augmented by local manufacturers), and was set aside for needy cases. Anyone who was in dire financial straits, and unable to adequately clothe their children, could make an application to the local police station for assistance from the association. Alternatively, any police officer seeing a destitute child in the street was instructed to go to his or her home and undertake some enquiries. The next stage was that a visit would be made to the home of the child, either by the local beat policeman, or an approved, 'visitor'. Having made an assessment of the family's circumstances, an allocation was made, of items such as boots and clothing. Measures were built into the scheme

Inspector Henry Richards joined the force on 28 February 1883, and retired on 19 October 1909.

Thomas Wilkinson Lumley, head constable of Leicester Borough Police 1894–1907.

Members of the Leicester Police band at the inauguration of the city's electric tramway system in July 1904. (Courtesy N. Haines)

to protect the child in question. On receipt of the clothing (which was identifiably marked), the parents had to sign an undertaking that in principle the items were 'on loan to them'. In this way, if the items were subsequently sold or offered for pawn, the police could, and would, prosecute the parent for the theft of the goods. Conversely, all pawnbrokers and second-hand dealers in the borough were well aware that for them to accept any such clothing was an offence. Where a needy child had been clothed by the association, the local beat man was charged with keeping an eye out to ensure that they were wearing the clothes or shoes provided. The earliest receipts relating to the Police Aided Association date from the beginning of 1897. The scheme was certainly still

in being in 1911, when it supplied 4,574 items of clothing and 915 pairs of boots to 936 children in the town.

—oOo—

Over the years, the question of what to do with the remains of those unfortunates who had met with sudden death in the borough had been a moot issue.

In November 1903, the subject of the mortuary at the town hall was again brought to the attention of the Corporation – this time by the newly-appointed Medical Officer of Health for the borough, Doctor Charles Killick Millard, whose description, on taking over his duties, of

Superintendent Joseph Howe (10 August 1872–12 September 1899). One of the last officers to work at both the old and new town hall police stations, Joseph Howe returned to the old station in 1934 to annotate the original layout of the building on a plan. A slight man, only 5ft 10in tall, Howe was born in 1851 and was employed as a railway porter before joining the police force. He retired on 12 September 1899, having been the first superintendent in charge of Queen's Road police station in Knighton.

the available facilities with which he was expected to conduct pathology work, leave a deal to be desired even by the standards of the time.

> The Chairman and Members
> of the Watch Committee
> Town Hall, Leicester
> 28 October 1903
> Gentlemen,
>
> In compliance with your request I beg to make the following report on the Public Mortuary at the Town Hall.
>
> From a structural point of view, the mortuary appears to be satisfactory and equal to the requirements of the town.
>
> It is however, somewhat devoid of conveniences. It is desirable that warm water should be provided and as this will only be required occasionally I would suggest that a small geyser would be a suitable arrangement.
>
> It would be reasonable I think, to provide a case of post mortem instruments, costing three or four guineas.
>
> There is no cupboard in the mortuary, hence, sponges, bottles of disinfectant and other requisites cannot be put tidily away.
>
> It has been suggested that some means should be provided for minimising the nuisance arising from bodies recovered after decomposition has commenced.
>
> I have ascertained at Battersea where a new mortuary has recently been erected [that] they have an iron tank on wheels, about the size and shape of a coffin, fitted with an airtight lid. A portion of this lid is glazed so that bodies can be identified without disturbing them. The tank is filled with a solution of formalin – the lid of which is heavy, [and] is raised by a chain and counter poise.
>
> Such an arrangement must be desirable where decomposed bodies have frequently to be dealt with, especially in hot weather. In Battersea a considerable number of bodies are recovered from the Thames – It is a question for your Committee to decide whether there would be a sufficient use to justify a similar provision in Leicester. – I am informed by the chief constable that during the present year (10 months), only four bodies have been brought to the mortuary in a decomposed state. Last year the number was only two.
>
> In conclusion I would suggest that the

The old horse-drawn prison van, at the rear of the town hall. The Edwardian coat of arms on the vehicle dates it to between 1901 and 1910.

mortuary, might with advantage, be 'done up' and some different arrangement be made for keeping it clean and tidy. There seems room for some improvement in this latter respect.

I am Gentlemen,
Your obedient servant,
C.Killick Millard[8]
Medical Officer of Health.

The matter was to remain unresolved for the next two decades. In February 1905 the St John's Ambulance Brigade made a complaint about what they considered a misuse of their horse-drawn ambulance – it being used for the conveyance of decomposing bodies to the police mortuary. The hapless Lumley promised to make alternative arrangements, although what they were exactly is not clear.

In 1923, structural alterations to the town hall required that the mortuary be removed from the building once and for all. A temporary mortuary was established in the disused Fire Brigade premises at the Aylestone police station. Despite protests from the nearby residents, it was not until four years later, in November 1927, that a purpose-built mortuary was taken into use on Welford Road near to the Cattle Market. The mortuary remained at that location until November 1960, when it moved to the Leicester Royal Infirmary complex. From that time, police constables were also relieved of the unpalatable task of acting as mortuary attendants and washing down bodies.

Despite the interlude of the Boer War, the seven years during which Thomas Wilkinson Lumley served in Leicester as the chief constable of the borough were remarkably uneventful. The day-to-day life of the force was disturbed by just one tragic event, which was never satisfactorily resolved. It related to the death, just before Christmas 1906, of Constable 208 William Henry Wells.

Wells, a married man, had joined the Borough Police in 1902 at the age of 27, and at the beginning of August 1906, three months prior to his death, had been transferred to the Belgrave section. On Tuesday 20 November, in the evening, PC Wells, having reported for duty at the Belgrave branch station, went out alone on his beat, which covered the Marjorie Street and Dundonald Road area.

At 2.30 a.m., PC James Slater, the reserve man at Belgrave station, made up some bottles of hot coffee for the night men, and went on his rounds, ensuring that each man had a warm drink. Having given PC Wells his bottle in Cossington Street, he went to PC Clarke on the next beat, spoke with him and then returned to collect Wells' empty flask. An hour and a half later, Constables Clarke and Wells, avoiding the night sergeant, met up for a chat and a smoke in Law Street. Seeking shelter from the weather, the officers bemoaned the soaking rain, which had been falling for the last two hours.

Sometime between three and six o'clock in the morning, Jane Butler, an elderly 74-year-old

[8]Charles Killick Millard, who lived at 'The Gilroes', Groby Road, served as Medical Officer of Health for Leicester from 1901 until 1935.

Sergeant 9 Vincent Shaw. A member of the Borough force from 22 February 1876 until 10 April 1906, he spent the latter part of his service as the sergeant at North Evington police station in Asfordby Street.

On his application to join the Leicester Borough Police in June 1887, Richard Smith Cole was described as being 6ft 1in tall, a drayman, aged 23. As an inspector he applied unsuccessfully for the position of head constable in 1907, when T.W. Lumley retired. Cole served for a further six years and retired in November 1913.

woman, was asleep in her bedroom at 84 Marjorie Street, when she was awakened by the sound of moaning. Thinking that it was her granddaughter in the next room, she got up to check, but the child was sound asleep. As she returned to her bed, Jane Butler heard the moaning again, but his time from further away and she realised that it was coming from someone outside, moving down the street. Because the street lamps were not illuminated, she was unable to make out what was happening outside.

The last person to see PC Wells alive was a grocer's delivery man, William Platts, who on his way to work at a quarter to five passed the policeman in Belgrave Road near to Olphin Street. Platts was struck by the fact that PC Wells was examining something in his hand, and

appeared to be very preoccupied. The delivery man spoke to Wells, saying ' Good morning, there has been a lot of wet in the night…' Wells replied, 'Yes there has', and continued to walk on.

When PC Wells failed to sign off from duty at 6 a.m. Superintendent J.T. Noton, who lived at Belgrave police station was awoken, and a search was instigated. After four hours, when nothing had been found, Noton himself was searching some waste ground near to the canal, when he found Wells' helmet floating in the water at the back of Dundonald Road. Focussing the search on this area, he brought in a local boatman, and ordered that the canal be dragged. Noton was

Sergeant William Henry Major (8 January 1878–24 July 1906).

puzzled, because in order to get down to the canal at this point, PC Wells must have gone off his beat onto Abbey Park Road, to climb down onto the towpath.

William Wells' body was recovered from the canal near to Marjorie Street. Except for his helmet, which had floated away, he was fully dressed, including his greatcoat, which was belted up. His lamp was still attached to his belt and had not been broken. His truncheon, whistle and handcuffs were all intact. In his pocket were his note book, pipe and tobacco. His watch had stopped at 4.55 a.m. – 10 minutes after he had spoken to William Platts. Other than a small post-mortem mark on his temple, the body bore no signs of injury.

No explanation was ever forthcoming for how William Wells came to be in the canal, or off his beat. An inquest, held by the borough coroner, Robert Harvey, at the Municipal Buildings on the 29 November 1906 found that:

William Henry Wells… he being 31 years old and a Police constable, was found dead in the Leicester canal near to Marjorie Street in the Borough of Leicester on Wednesday, 21 November 1906, and that death was due to suffocation by drowning. The Jurors do further say that there is no evidence to show how [the], deceased came into the water.

—oOo—

As in the case of his predecessor, Thomas Lumley, after six and a half years in office, found his health to be deteriorating. In March 1907, the police surgeon, Dr Arthur Barlow, certified that, having undergone a serious operation, the head constable had suffered a nervous breakdown and would be unfit for duty for some time. His situation did not improve. In May, Dr Shaw, a Harley Street specialist, declared that if given three months of total rest, Lumley might be fit to return to duty, but this was by no means certain. After mutual discussion between the Watch Committee and the head constable, it was decided that he should resign at the beginning of June 1907.

CHAPTER SIX

John Hall-Dalwood
(September 1907–February 1913)

The arrival of John Hall-Dalwood as chief constable was accompanied by the usual plethora of applications from a wide range of candidates. The 71 aspirants included 25 retired or serving army officers, 15 serving chief constables, and one internal candidate – Inspector Richard Smith Cole.

The 38-year-old Hall-Dalwood was well qualified for the position at Leicester. A barrister-at-law, he had for the past five years been the deputy chief constable of Kent. Prior to that he had served as a major in the Connaught Rangers,[1] and had some experience in the Royal Irish Constabulary. Hall-Dalwood took office at Leicester on 2 September 1907. In the time which elapsed between Thomas Lumley's departure and John Hall-Dalwood's arrival, Chief Superintendent Theodore Geary had managed the force, in gratitude for which the Watch Committee awarded him the sum of £50.

The practice of employing men with military experience directly into the ranks of the police service at chief officer level was long established, and not about to become a defunct practice. A prime example is Percy (later Sir Percy) Sillitoe. In 1923, at the age of 35, Sillitoe applied for, and obtained, the post of chief constable of Chesterfield. His experience prior to this had been in Africa, where he served for a while in the Rhodesian Police (a large proportion of which had been war service), and later – still in Africa – as a civil servant. Of the British Police Service, on his own admission, he knew nothing. During the following 23 years Sillitoe served as chief constable of no fewer than four police forces, including Sheffield and Glasgow – where he attained a reputation as a 'gang-buster'– before being appointed director-general of MI5 in 1946.

The uniform worn by the officers and men of the force had not changed since the days of Joseph Farndale. In January 1908, the new chief constable, no doubt influenced by his military background, withdrew the old-fashioned round pillbox cap with a slashed peak, worn by senior officers since the beginning of 1873, and issued a more modern style, with a peak which stood off the face. The style of greatcoat worn by sergeants and constables was altered slightly, and later (in September 1913), black buttons and a heavy leather belt, worn outside of the coat instead of through a slit in the back, were added. The belted tunic was retained, along with the service stripes and merit badge on the lower right forearm. The St John Ambulance badge continued to be worn on the upper right sleeve.[2]

—oOo—

Early in 1908, on the morning of Saturday 4 April, one of Leicester's best known characters, PC 83 John 'Tubby' Stephens died. Weighing in at 24 stone, Stephens was reputed to be the heaviest policeman in England. In 1879, the British Army in Africa under Lord Chelmsford

---

[1] John Hall-Dalwood is variously referred to in the early stages as both captain and major. The correct title appears to be major.

[2] From 2 August 1881, in common with other Forces throughout the country, Leicester Borough Police constables were required to pass a St John Ambulance examination. Success in this examination qualified them to wear the St John Ambulance badge. The qualification appears to have been allowed to lapse during the early 1930s.

was defeated at the Battle of Isandhlwana by the Zulu Chieftain, Cetawayo. Serving as a Gunner in the Royal Artillery John Stephens went to Africa as part of the reinforcement expedition. Following the Battle of Ulundi in August that year, and the subsequent capture of Cetawayo, Stephens was awarded the Zulu War Campaign Medal and clasp. At the end of the campaign he remained in Africa as part of the garrison force for the next seven years, before returning to England in 1886, when he joined the Leicester Borough Police force.

Tubby Stephens served in the Borough Police for 22 years and became a household figure. His death, after an illness of a few weeks, was the result (doubtless attributable to his excessive weight), of heart disease. Huge crowds gathered outside his home address at 84 Cobden Street to pay their respects. The funeral cortège was flanked by an escort of 20 uniformed Borough Police officers, led by Inspector Richard Smith Cole. At the rear, following Stephens's wife and children, were the chief constable and Chief Superintendent Geary in a carriage. The route through the town centre and along Welford Road to the cemetery was lined with thousands of townspeople.

Several postcards were later produced to commemorate Tubby Stephens's passing, one of which, with his picture

Helmet plate in use during the first decade of the 20th century. (Courtesy N. Haines)

The details of this officer are not known. The style of the badge on the helmet plate, which carries Queen Victoria's crown, would indicate that the picture dates to around the turn of the century.

Superintendent Tom Batt (30th May 1883–5th July 1910), first superintendent of the bye-laws department.

Inspector John Arnold (3 November 1874–6 March 1900).

superimposed on a backdrop of the clock tower, read;

> Poor old Stephens, how we'll miss him
> From his customary beat;
> Never more his stalwart figure
> Or stern, but kindly face we'll greet!

—oOo—

A month after Stephens's death, the burgeoning taxi-cab industry in the town received a sobering challenge from an unexpected quarter. Realising the potential of the motor car, the Watch Committee began to consider applications from London-based firms who were trying to establish themselves in the provinces. One such application, from the 'Mass Motor Cabs Company', of New Oxford Street, London, sought licences for 50 cabs to stand in Leicester. Horrified, the local motor-taxi operators, petitioned the Watch Committee in the middle of May not to entertain applications from outside of the borough. '…We beg to draw your attention to the very depressed state of the cab and hack business… we ask you to restrict the issue of new licences for either cabs or brakes…'

Having consulted with the Hackney Carriage Department at the central police station, the businessmen of the Watch Committee decided that a ready compromise would not be a bad thing for the borough. In June, 20 licences were granted to the Provincial Motor Cab Co. of London to run metered taxis in Leicester. The charges were set at 1s for any distance not exceeding a mile, 3d for every extra quarter of a mile, plus 1s for every 15 minutes of waiting time.

—oOo—

Although it was not at this time being utilised in Leicester, the science of identifying suspects by their fingerprints was now in its early stages.

Town Hall Square, September 1912. The presentation of medals commemorating the coronation of King George V. Those members of the Leicester Borough Police who received the medal were: Chief Superintendent Geary; Superintendent Hircock; Inspectors Sturgess, Carson, Cole and Batt; Sergeants Hart, Smith and Unwin and Constables Atkins, Grant, Short and Mason. Former inspector Vann and former sergeant Lobley are also present. The most identifiable figures in the picture are Superintendent Challis Hircock in the front row looking directly at the camera, and in the back row, the large figure of Inspector Richard Smith Cole.

Since the end of the 19th century, police officers had been seeking improved means of identifying criminals. In 1882, Alphonse Bertillon of the Paris Police introduced a system of identification, known as the 'Bertillon System', for identifying people based upon their bodily measurements. Other methods which were being developed were based upon fingerprints and photography.

The knowledge that a person could be identified by their fingerprints dated back to the Babylonians and the ancient Chinese. Modern interest in fingerprint identification sprang from the work of Sir Francis Galton and Sir Edward Henry. The latter became commissioner of the Metropolitan Police, and together the two men developed a procedure of fingerprint identification, based on grouping the patterns of arches, loops and whorls. Taken into use in 1901 by the Metropolitan Police at Scotland Yard, this became known as the Galton-Henry System. Although well respected, the system required expert

knowledge combined with sophisticated techniques to make its use effective. To achieve its full potential, in the absence of a specific subject to compare a print against, a large database was essential. For this reason, the use of fingerprints in the provinces was a refinement which was still a few years away.

The second scientific innovation – the camera – was, as far as the Leicester Borough Police was concerned, more readily accessible. By the turn of the century, photography was a well-established practice, both on a professional and a hobbyist level. While only as sophisticated as the technology of the time permitted, cameras were still by later standards very restricted.

An example is in the common police practice of photographing bodies in the mortuary. It had been found that there were practical difficulties in deflecting a camera on a tripod down to a suitable angle to photograph a corpse without losing some degree of clarity. A solution was to strap the body onto a stretcher, then stand the stretcher against a

Knighton Police station, situated in Queens Road between Clarendon Park Road and Bulwer Road. The building immediately adjacent is the Salvation Army barracks.

wall in order to take a photograph. The result was, on occasion, quite macabre. After the Houndsditch shootings in 1910, which culminated in the Siege of Sydney Street, the dead police officers were photographed in this manner, having first been dressed in their uniforms, with greatcoats buttoned to the neck and helmets tied onto their heads. At the central police station in the town hall, photography work, when required, was carried out by Constable Barnes, a hobbyist (there were professional photographers in the town, and although their services were utilised in later years, at this time, what was obviously a cheap option was taken) using his own camera equipment. In December 1908, two weeks before Christmas, Barnes's camera developed a fault, for which the Watch Committee authorised a repair at their expense...' the camera belonging to PC

Barnes, [which], has been used for a considerable time by the Detective Department, be put in order, and a £1 be paid to PC Barnes for the use of it'.

—oOo—

Unlike the Army and the Royal Navy, no official decoration or award existed which specifically related to the Police Service. In October 1909, seven months before his death, King Edward VII gave his consent for the striking of the King's Police Medal.

Dark blue, with a narrow silver strip either side, 120 medals were to be awarded each year.[3] A broad list of qualifications for the award was drawn up. Included were: conspicuous acts of gallantry in saving life and property, or preventing crime and arresting criminals; an especially distinguished record as an administrator or detective officer; success in the organising of police or fire services and special services rendered in dealing with serious outbreaks of crime or public disorder. A further area of merit concerned valuable political and 'secret' services and special services to royalty and heads of state. Lastly, an all-embracing proviso covered prolonged and distinguished service.

The first recipient of the decoration in the Leicester Borough Police was Constable 218 John George Stafford, for bravery 'in rescuing William Peberdy from drowning on the 9th August 1909'. The next officer to be awarded the decoration was in 1912, when PC 207 William Henry Gray was presented with it for, '...bravery in stopping a runaway horse attached to a heavy van in a crowded street at great risk to himself'.

—oOo—

Another landmark event came the following year, with the passing of the Police (Weekly Rest Day), Act 1910, which gave all police officers from the rank of constable to inspector, the right to one day's rest in seven. An immediate consequence in

[3] 40 in the UK, Ireland, the Channel Islands and the Isle of Man; 30 for service in the Dominions; 50 for service in the Indian Empire.

Officers of Knighton sub-division, pictured at Queen's Road police station in 1911.
From left to right, back row: -?-, PC 251, PC 249, PC 236. Front row: PC 76, PC 122, Sgt 26, PC 114, PC 107. Two of the constables
and the sergeant are wearing service stripes on the right forearm, indicating that each has between ten and fifteen years service.
The officers first and second from left in the front row and the officer on the far right are wearing 'on-duty' bands on their right
wrists. These bands dated back to the time when policemen were required to wear uniform at all times, and its presence indicated
whether or not an officer was on duty. The bands are not mentioned anywhere in the force records so it is not known exactly when
they were worn or under what circumstances. Officers are not seen wearing them after 1930.

Leicester (as in most other forces in the country), was that a further 10 officers had to be engaged before the new regulations could be implemented.

The new rest day provisions were followed two years later by the acceptance of the recommendations of the National Health Insurance Commission to pay constables and firemen 10s a week for a period of six months, while they were on sick leave.

—oOo—

The early summer of 1911 saw the final winding up of what had in the latter years of the 19th century come to be regarded by the citizens of the town as an institution. The Leicester Borough Police Brass Band had been formed during Joseph Farndale's time, in 1873. For the next 33 years, the police band was a regular feature at weekends and during the summer evenings, playing selections of popular music in the Town Hall Square and on the parks and recreation grounds around the town.

Led by their band master, John Smith (formerly band master of the Leicester Volunteer Regiment), the players embodied a representative cross section of the force. Chief Superintendent

Theodore Geary played clarinet; two future superintendents – Sergeant Daniel Choyce and Inspector Cornelius Carson played the double bass and the French horn respectively, while Inspector Sturgess, five sergeants and 13 constables made up the remainder of the 22 man ensemble.

The Police Band, along with the 'Police Holiday Fund', came under scrutiny in June 1906, due to the fact that it was funded by public subscription. The practice of policemen and their families being allowed to take annual trips to the coast had been instituted in the early 1880s by James Duns, and was paid for by donations from the townspeople. During 1905 the Fund received £307. 4s 6d from 948 subscribers – 357 of whom were local licensees. Similarly, the band also existed on charitable donations, something which, along with the working hours lost through practice and concert times, was seen as undesirable.

The committee decided that it was time for both of these activities to cease. In respect of the Police Band, the committee's resolution was that, 'as the outcome of their investigation [the Watch Committee], find that the Police Band militates against the efficiency of the Police force and cannot sanction it's continuation in its present form beyond the season ending the 30th September 1906'. It was not, however, until May 1911 that Chief Superintendent Geary finally provided an audit of the instruments and equipment for disposal. Possibly, as a former member of the band and a senior officer of the force, he had hoped that by prolonging the disposal of the band's equipment the decision might be rescinded. If so, he was to be disappointed, and it would be over 30 years before another musical section (the Special Constabulary Band), was instituted in the years after World War Two.

As an expression of their appreciation of the

The Three Cranes public house in Humberstone Gate, where Annie Stevens' drinking session caused the argument which resulted in the Argyle Street shooting and the killing of Frederick Greaves in May 1911. Seen standing in the doorway is the licensee at the time, Tom Pratt

bandsmen's efforts, four of its members, Theodore Geary, Inspectors Sturgess and Carson, and Constable Mason, were among the 15 Borough Police officers presented with the King's Coronation Medal[4] before the assembled crowds in Leicester Market Place in September 1912.

—oOo—

Two noteworthy incidents, both involving sudden deaths, occurred during the years immediately prior to the outbreak of World War One.

The first, referred to in the local press as 'the Argyle Street Shooting', relates to the killing of Frederick Greaves by James Thomas Stevens, in May 1911. James Stevens and his wife Annie, after only two years of marriage, separated in April 1911. Annie, taking with her the couple's eight-week-old baby, went to live in lodgings with George King – a pedlar – and his wife at 21 Bow Street. Her husband, now unemployed, moved away to live in Kettering.

On Saturday 13 May, James Stevens cycled over from Kettering to pay a visit to his wife and child. Arriving at Annie Stevens' lodgings around five o'clock in the afternoon, he was told by Mrs King that Annie had left the baby with her (Mrs King), as usual when she went out to work – at Hill's factory in Wharf Street – at 8 o'clock that morning, since when she had not returned. James Stevens then went to the Three Cranes public house at the corner of Wharf Street and Humberstone Gate. There he found his wife, who had been drinking since lunchtime (when she finished work), with her sister Alice Maude Greaves.

After an argument between the couple in the bar of the pub, Stevens left and returned to his wife's lodgings. During the early evening he returned several times to the Three Cranes, each time attempting to persuade Annie to go back and look after her child. It is obvious that on each occasion a dispute ensued. On one of his visits he

Superintendent Henry William Hazeldine (November 1881–December 1908)

encountered his brother-in-law, Frederick Greaves, (Alice's husband) in the bar. Greaves, an ex-boxer, who was supposedly on friendly terms with James Stevens, offered to buy him a drink. Stevens refused, and bought himself a drink. The fact that there was apparent bad feeling between the two men was not commented on at Stevens' subsequent trial.

Around seven o'clock, Annie Stevens and her sister, both of whom were by now extremely drunk (before either could leave the public house, they had to be given soda water in an attempt to sober them up), left the Three Cranes along with a third woman, Gertrude Makepeace, to go to Annie's lodgings in Bow Street. At Bow Street, still in a drunken state, they collected the baby and set off with it in what is variously described as a perambulator or a mail cart.

[4]Coronation of King George V.

Leicester Borough Police Football Team in 1910. From left to right, back row: PC Bingham, PC Morton, PC Payne, PC Morris. Third row: PC Underwood, PC Lucas, PC Clowes, Mr J.Blessington, PC Cookman, PC Grant, PC Staines, PC Stafford. Second row: PC Bradshaw, Insp. Hircock, Chief Constable Major Hall-Dalwood, Sgt Arnold, PC Bassett. Front row: PC Middleton, PC Dobney, PC Scott. (Courtesy N.Haines)

James Stevens joined the women as they made their way down Wharf Street towards Russell Square, en route to the Greaves's home address in Argyle Street. A dispute broke out between the couple, in which Annie's sister became involved, resulting in Stevens violently attacking the two women. Although later charged with unlawfully wounding his wife, the charges were not proceeded with, and at the trial, no evidence was given as to exactly what occurred. However, the injuries that Stevens inflicted on the women were sufficient for both to be taken to the Leicester Royal Infirmary by ambulance for treatment.

While the women were at the hospital, Stevens went to the address of an acquaintance named Norman at 70 Mansfield Street. There he borrowed a small bore 'rook rifle' and a quantity of ammunition, telling Mr Norman that he was going shooting the following day.

At 10.50 that night, James Stevens turned up

Group of officers on the steps of St George's Church (at the rear of what was later Charles Street police station) after the dedication of the church's new electric clock, 22 February 1911.

again at 21 Bow Street. He showed the rifle to George King, stating that he was going to kill Annie, 'and someone else'. Stevens then left the house on foot to go to Argyle Street, where his wife and her sister had arrived home shortly after 11 o'clock. Immediately Stevens had departed, King went to the nearby police station in Woodboy Street to alert the police.

News of the incident in Wharf Street and the injuries to the two women had spread through the Belgrave district, and a large group of people were gathered in the Greaves's house by the time that they arrived home soon after 11 o'clock. Frederick Greaves, who had gone with the women to the hospital, returned with them.

While everyone was congregated in the front room, people became aware that James Stevens was in the house with the rifle. At one point he was seen with the rifle to his shoulder, aiming into the crowded room. After a short while, he moved out of the house into the street.

Not fully appreciating the danger of the situation, people left the house to find out what was happening. Among them was Frederick Greaves, who, rolling up his sleeves, went towards Stevens with the obvious intention of hitting him. Stevens fired the single shot weapon at Greaves, hitting him in the heart and killing him instantly.

Stevens then fled from the scene and was detained by two men in Gresham Street, who handed him over to Constable Clarke, one of the police officers from Woodboy Street who had been out looking for him.

At his trial, no mention was made of why James and Annie Stevens' marriage had broken down within weeks of the birth of their first child, or of

Leicester Borough Police tug-of-war team, 8 August 1908. From left to right, back row: PC Palmer, PC Preston, PC Matthews, PC Grey. Front row: PC Hankinson, PC Davies, Inspector Cole (Captain), PC Bingham, PC York.

Leicester Borough Police force cricket team, 1908. From left to right, back row (all standing on verandah): PC Warrington, PC Lucas, PC Able, PC Dobney. Middle row: PC Mason Jnr, PC Buckby (wearing boater hat), PC Mason (seated), PC Whyman (arms folded), PC Clarke (seated), PC Green (wearing panama hat), PC Preston. Front row (all seated): PC Woodward, Sgt Major Dix, PC Adkinson, Supt Hazeldine, Insp. Boyle, Insp. Hircock, -?-. The role of Sgt Major Alexander Dix within the Borough Police is nowhere explained. He joined the force in December 1900 with the rank of sergeant. Thereafter he is referred to as 'Sgt Major', and in this photograph clearly has a warrant officer's insignia on his right forearm. In October 1914 Dix was given the rank of police inspector. A possible explanation is that he was engaged – and served as – a drill instructor.

Chief Superintendent Theodore John Geary was born in 1860 and was a professional musician before joining the Leicester Borough Police force in August 1883. Rising through the ranks, he was promoted from inspector to chief superintendent in November 1906, and was responsible for the management of the force during the period between the retirement of Thomas Lumley and the arrival of John Hall-Dalwood in September 1907. For this service he was awarded an ex-gratia payment of £50.

why Stevens had refused to accept a drink from the deceased in the Three Cranes, preferring to buy his own, despite the fact that they were supposedly friends. Even more strangely, the prosecution did not pursue Stevens's comment to George King that he was going to kill Annie 'and someone else'.

The defence entered a plea of not guilty to murder, and made a play upon the deceased being

Leicester Borough Police rifle team, 1910. From left to right, back row: PC 100 Bacon, PC 81 Pemberton, PC 254 Stanborough, PC 123 Wells, PC 238 Matthews, PC 128 Bradshaw, PC 94 Bassett. Middle row: PC 87 Robertson, PC 224 Bingham, PC 215 Porter, Sgt 27 Coleman, Sgt 18 Smith, PC 235 Brooksbank, PC 148 Brightty, PC 55 Reeves. Front row: Insp. C. Carson, Insp. C. Hircock, Ch. Supt T. Geary, Ch. Cons. J. Hall-Dalwood, Supt J.T. Noton, Insp R. Smith Cole, Insp Warner. Although the headgear of senior officers had now changed to a cap with the peak set off the face, the badge of the inspectors remained as a wyvern. It was not until later that the wyvern was combined with the king's crown. (Superintendents had already begun to wear the heavy collar insignia and cap badge with wreath.)

an ex-boxer, claiming that Stevens had at the last moment been in fear of him. A further defence point was that when he killed Greaves, Stevens had not raised the rifle to his shoulder to aim, but had fired it from the hip. The prosecution failed to counter this with the fact that the accused had been seen with the rifle to his shoulder in the house immediately before the killing.

The Judge, Mr Justice Pickford, summed up very strongly for a verdict of guilty to wilful murder, and on the evidence, must have been disappointed and puzzled when the jury found Stevens not guilty of murder but guilty of manslaughter. James Thomas Stevens was sentenced to seven years penal servitude.

The second incident related to the murder of a middle aged prostitute by the name of Annie Jennings. On Wednesday 3 January 1912, the woman's partially clothed body was found in the upper room of her lodgings at No.1 Court 'C' in Archdeacon Lane. Her throat had been cut, and from the marks found at the scene of the crime, it was apparent that her body had been dragged across the bedroom floor and propped up against the bed to make it look as if she had committed suicide. A knife lay beside the body. The most

In Affectionate Remembrance
OF
P.C. Stephens,
Who passed away on April 4th, 1908,
Aged 48 years.

He did 22 years' Service on the Leicester Police Force,
and was acknowledged to be England's Heaviest
Constable, his weight being over 24 stone.
He also served his Country in the Zulu War, 1879.

Poor old Stephens, how we'll miss him
From his customary beat;
Never more his stalwart figure
Or stern, but kindly face we'll greet!

"REQUIESCAT IN PACE."

*Memorial card to PC 83 John William Stephens, who died on Saturday 4
April 1908 following a short illness, at the age of 48. Reputed to be, at 24
stones, the heaviest policeman in England, Stephens had served in the Royal
Artillery in Africa prior to joining the Leicester Borough Police in 1886.*

*Major John Hall-Dalwood, chief constable
September 1907–February 1913.*

unusual feature was that her neck bore a livid bite mark.

About 10 o'clock that evening, Archie Johnson, a 26-year-old rubber worker, was arrested on suspicion of her murder and later charged with the offence. The evidence against

Johnson at this stage was that he had been a known associate of Annie Jennings and had been seen in company with her during the afternoon of the 2 January – the day she died. Johnson admitted being with her in the Crown and Cushion public house, and stated that he had introduced her to a soldier who had gone off with her as a client. (The soldier was later traced and agreed that this was correct.) Later that afternoon, Johnson himself had gone to Jennings' lodgings with her, and on this occasion a neighbour had observed the woman drawing the curtains of her room. Archie Johnson maintained

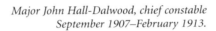

*The funeral of PC 83 'Tubby' Stephens
making its way to Welford Road
Cemetery.*

that he had left Annie at 4.50 p.m. and returned to his own lodgings, where he had remained for the rest of the evening. This point was disputed by the prosecution, who brought in a witness to swear that he had seen Johnson in another public house later that evening.

At the trial at the end of January, the evidence, which was extremely tenuous, took on a macabre aspect. Initially, the judge instructed that the court be cleared of all ladies. Once that had been done, a section of the deceased woman's neck, pinned to a board and displaying the bite mark, was produced and entered as evidence. Next a pad of blotting paper, which the police had used to obtain a sample of Johnson's teeth (by dint of

getting him to bite it), was brought before the court. A protracted wrangle then took place between various medical men, who gave evidence as to whether or not the bite in the woman's neck was identical to that in the blotting paper. The end result was that the jury decided that the two did not match, and a verdict of 'not guilty' was quickly recorded.

John Hall-Dalwood was to be the last chief constable for the next 40 years whose period in office was to pass without national events dictating at least a part of his actions and policies. After a period of just under six years in Leicester, Hall-Dalwood resigned his position when he was appointed chief constable of Sheffield Police.

Belgrave police station c.1908. The notice on the wall refers to the Dogs Act 1906, and the pill box cap worn by the officer in the front row was discontinued after 1908. From left to right, back row: PC 176, PC 99, PC 195, PC 41, PC 126. Middle row: PC 185, PC 63, PC 78, PC 58, PC 73, PC 187, PC 177. Front row: PC 82, PC 64, Sgt 18, Insp. J.T. Noton, Sgt 23, PC 154, PC 174.

CHAPTER SEVEN

Herbert Allen
(February 1913–December 1928)

The World War One Years

The appointment in February 1913 of Herbert Allen as chief constable of Leicester Borough Police force was, to all intents and purposes, a complete deviation from the policy of the previous 77 years. Whereas historically the position had been advertised, and almost as a matter of procedure any local candidates ignored, on this occasion the process was reversed.

Following John Hall-Dalwood's appointment as head of the Sheffield Police, a decision was taken by the Watch Committee to appoint the head of the Borough detective department, Herbert Allen, without advertising the post. Why the matter was dealt with in this way is open to speculation. It is possible that with a European war imminent, the Watch Committee wanted someone in place who was familiar with the force. A more likely alternative is that an internal promotion could be effected for less cost to the corporation than the existing chief constable's salary. In 1912, Hall-Dalwood was earning £600 a year, but Herbert Allen was engaged as his replacement at £500. Irrespective of the reasoning, the selection of Allen for the job was sound. He had been with the force for a number of years, having been appointed detective inspector just after the turn of the century, and promoted to detective superintendent in 1904.

The new chief constable was fortunate in that he inherited a well-run force, with which he was personally familiar. One of the alterations to procedures which he made during his first year in office was to introduce a system for cautioning juvenile offenders. During his previous experience as head of the detective department, it had doubtless become apparent to him that in certain cases an alternative to prosecution was desirable. Between Allen taking office in February 1913 and January 1914, 78 juveniles who had offended for the first time were cautioned by a superintendent as an alternative to putting them before a court.

January 1914 saw two alterations to the status quo within the force. The first was that the minimum height limit for future recruits was set at five feet nine inches. The second and more complex change addressed the perennial question of retirements and pensions.

Under the terms of the Police Pension Fund, which had been established in 1890, a police officer in the borough was entitled to retire after 26 years service, with a pension of two thirds of his pay. This had been varied two years later by a ruling that, irrespective of service, a constable must retire at 50 years of age, and a sergeant at 60. The officers and men of the force now applied to the Watch Committee for the compulsory retirement age to be discontinued, and retirement to be based solely upon length of service. On the advice of the borough treasurer, W. Penn-Lewis, a compromise was arrived at. Based on the existing age limits, which required that a man joining the force must be between 21 and 25 years of age, a maximum term of 28 years service was set. On this basis, as from April 1914, all constables and sergeants would in future retire at between 49 and 53 years of age.

Along with every other institution in the country, when Great Britain declared war on Germany in August 1914, the Leicester Borough Police force underwent fundamental changes. Despite the gathering war clouds, the reality of being at war seems to have taken most local authorities, Leicester Corporation included, by surprise. Based on the supposition that any war with Germany would be fought on foreign soil and quickly resolved, the authorities during the early days of hostilities made two decisions which they were later to regret.

Initially, 19 serving members of the Leicester Borough Police force, all constables, were recalled with immediate effect to the colours as military reservists.[1] Believing that the war would be over within a few months, the Corporation then took the decision to release from the workplace any man who wished to volunteer for service in His Majesty's Forces. The result was that, in the opening days of the war, a large number of men employed by the Corporation left to join up. Within a matter of weeks, the Police, Fire Brigade, Tramways, Gas and Electricity Departments all found themselves seriously short of staff.

The second commitment made by the Corporation was that those employees away on active service would be treated as being temporarily absent and still in the pay of the Corporation. On 10 October 1914, the Watch Committee declared that 'no obstacle be placed in the way of the Borough Police joining the colours, that they be not asked to resign and that they be reinstated on their return from the war…' By the end of 1915, in addition to the reservists who had been recalled, a further 70 members of the Borough Police force had enlisted in the armed forces. From an authorised establishment of 295 men, Herbert Allen had an actual force of 208. Almost a third of his men were away at the war.[2]

The name of the sergeant seen wearing No.11 is unknown. The helmet plate which he is wearing does not have side supporters, which dates the picture to between World War One and the mid-1920s (possibly as early as 1921). Unfortunately, there is no mention in the available research material of the significance of the crown worn by some sergeants over their chevrons. The practice appears to have ceased during the mid-to-late 1930s.

[1] Even this obvious event had not been properly prepared for. On 11 August, one week after war was declared, the Watch Committee resolved that PCs 255 James Sheppard, 33 William Dickinson and 34 Charles Cattell should be subject to discipline on their return from the war for rejoining the reserves without the prior consent of the head constable.

[2] The situation did not improve. In his Annual Report for 1917, Herbert Allen states that by the end of the year, 8 men had been killed in action, one had died while serving with the colours and 83 were away with HM Forces.

The identity of this officer, wearing No.24, is unknown. From his uniform and the Boer War medals, the picture appears to date from around the beginning of World War One. The bright white metal helmet plate replaced the older wreath with the officers number in the centre at around this time.

(Courtesy N.Haines)

An alarmed Watch Committee, now fully appreciative of the difficulties that its open policy had created, issued an instruction in October 1915 '...that no further application for permission to join the army or navy from members of the force be considered'.[3] The other logical step to be taken was that no officer was now allowed to retire from the force, other than on medical grounds, for the duration of the war.[4]

Although with hindsight it is obvious that to permit such large numbers of men to enlist was an error of judgement, it should not be presumed that Leicester Corporation was alone in this miscalculation. In November 1915, with the prospect of conscription now an imminent reality, the police service throughout England was severely depleted.

Police officers serving in HM Forces on 1 November 1915

Police force	Establishment	Number of men enlisted	Percentage of force
Liverpool	2,262	576	25.06
Manchester	1,394	436	31.27
Leeds	721	218	30.23
Bristol	617	218	35.33
Sheffield	587	94	16.01
Hull	463	116	25.05
Bradford	453	87	19.20
Newcastle-on-Tyne	400	106	26.50
Nottingham	370	130	35.13
Salford	330	79	23.93
Portsmouth	300	120	40.00
Leicester	295	91*	30.85
Cardiff	294	75	25.51
Plymouth	262	71	27.09
Stoke-on-Trent	233	60	25.75
Birkenhead	229	24	10.48
Sunderland	227	46	20.26
Brighton	208	86	41.34
Bolton	202	60	29.70
Oldham	172	36	20.93
Middlesbrough	168	51	30.35
Southampton	163	49	30.06
Swansea	161	54	33.54
Derby	153	36	23.52
Blackburn	159	42	26.35

* In addition to those on active service, four officers were 'on loan' to the military.

[3] This was amended the following month (October 1915) by the Committee consenting to a 'further six officers being released, provided that they were single men'

[4] Under the Police Emergency Act 1915, constables who wished to retire and were compulsorily retained in a police force were granted a non-pensionable allowance of 10s per week, over and above their pay.

During September and October 1914, the Leicester Police took on 40 new recruits, and increased the number of special constables in the borough from 96 to 200.

Throughout the next four years, the special constabulary worked alongside the remaining regular officers in the borough. Each special constable performed a four hour tour of duty once every two weeks. As they did not have a uniform at this time, these part-time officers wore a brassard on their arm declaring their role. At one point, in May 1915, some 608 special constables were listed as sworn in for the borough, of whom 382 were regularly performing duties. This large number is probably due to an offer by the Citizens Training League to enrol their members *en masse* as specials. Members of the special constabulary paraded for the last time in the town hall muster room at 10 p.m. on Saturday 2 January 1919. After singing *Auld Lang Syne,* they disbanded, for the time being.

In March 1920 the services of the special constabulary were officially recognised with the introduction of the Special Constabulary Long Service Medal.[5] In order to qualify for this award the recipient needed to have served as a special constable during the recent war for not less than three years, during which time he must have performed not less than 150 hours of duty. In order to encompass those who would serve during peacetime, a further provision was made that – other than during the recent war – a person must have served in the special constabulary for not less than nine years, have taken a course in police training and have performed such duties as required by the chief constable.

The commitment made by the Corporation, to regard employees who were serving in the armed forces as being temporarily absent, presented the local authority, as time went by, with a massive financial obligation. As an early measure, a decision was taken to pay the wives of married

PC Charles Cox. He joined the force in around 1897 and retired on 26 December 1922. The first of three generations to serve in the Leicester Police, he was succeeded by his sons Ernest (PC 227) in 1924 and Norman (PC 148, Det. Ch. Insp. in 1967), and his grandson Brian (PC 155) in 1950.

(Courtesy J. and E. Ward)

men who had joined up half of the man's weekly salary. The dependents of single men (usually widowed mothers), were given an allowance of 7s 6d a week.

Six months into the war, in March 1915, the question of allowances was reviewed and put on a more formal footing. Married men would have the Separation Allowance paid to them by the army made up to equal their police pay. (In practice these payments were received by their wives.) Single men were to have a sum equivalent to one third of their police pay.

[5] Ribbon one and three eights inches wide; central part (one third of the whole), red; remainder black and white longitudinal stripes. Name of the holder to be engraved around the rim. Where awarded for service during the war (World War One), an additional clasp was awarded with the words, 'The Great War 1914-1918.'

rest day. In June 1915 this was replaced by the payment of a War Bonus to constables, between 1 shilling and 2s a week. It is an indication of the rise in the cost of living over the next four years that in October 1918 a flat rate War Bonus of 16s a week was being paid to all sergeants and constables.

As the war progressed, so the economy of the nation in general became more strained. Resources which were being poured into financing the war effort had to be found from somewhere, and inevitably one of the areas to suffer was the public sector. Other than the payment of War Bonuses, the wages of groups such as the police and fire services were effectively frozen for the duration of the war.

Another financial aspect which had to be addressed, both locally and nationally, was the fact that with the strength of the police being drastically depleted, the remaining officers were working longer hours and rest days to cover the deficiencies. An interim measure, taken by the Corporation in August 1914, was to pay constables between 5s and 6s in lieu of each lost

For the police force and fire brigade in Leicester (along with other Borough Corporation employees), this created a particularly difficult situation. With its various industries and central geographic location, Leicester rapidly became a focus for munitions production. Local factories manufactured everything, from artillery shells to boots and uniforms. This meant that the men and

Certificate of Service issued to Sergeant 14 Herbert Greaves on his retirement from the force. (Courtesy S. Jeffrey)

PCs 151 Harry Preston and 62 Horace Udale. The helmet plates date this picture to the years immediately prior to World War One. Horace Udale joined the Leicester Borough Police in March 1912 and left to serve with the colours in March 1915. PC 151 Harry Preston joined the force in 1904 and served for 25 years, retiring in 1929.

women employed in these factories were earning high wages and overtime payments, with the attendant improved living standards.[6] Combined with increases in the cost of living, the overall effect was to dramatically drive down the value of public sector wages, which were fixed.

In May 1916, a deputation of inspectors, sergeants and constables appeared before the Watch Committee and presented a petition on behalf of all ranks, asking for some increase in pay on the grounds that: 'the cost of living was becoming unbearable; workers in other sectors could improve their wages by working overtime; and the rates in the Leicester force were lower than in most other police forces of a comparable size.'

The example was given that a constable joining the force earned 27s a week. By supplementing this with 3s a week War Bonus, and payment for one rest day which he was obliged to work, his salary amounted to £1. 15s 8d a week.

Refusing the petition, the Watch Committee, as a gesture, agreed to increase the officers boot allowance from six pence to a shilling a week.

The comparisons for February 1915, given below, bear out the assertion that police pay in Leicester (where there had not been a pay increase since 1912), was particularly low. They are also very relevant in the context of the negotiations forced upon the government in 1919.

[6] Managers and white collar workers, on fixed salaries, were also adversely affected by this imbalance.

Force	Strength	Pay	
		on appointment	after 20 yrs
Liverpool	2,261	30s	40s (after 15 years)
Glasgow	1,996	27s 5d	37s 4d (after 10 years)
Birmingham	1,431	29s	39s
Manchester	1,394	28s	40s
Leeds	720	28s 6d	37s 6d
Bristol	617	28s	40s
Sheffield	583	28s	39s
Hull	463	28s	38s
Bradford	448	28s	39s
Newcastle-on-Tyne	400	28s	39s
Nottingham	343	28s	39s (after 16 years)
Salford	330	27s	36s
Leicester	295	27s	36s
Cardiff	294	30s	40s (after 15 years)
Portsmouth	283	28s	38s
Dundee	256	27s	37s 4d (after 10 years)
Birkenhead	247	30s	40s (after 15years)
Stoke-on-Trent	233	28s	39s
Bolton	202	28s	38s
Aberdeen	200	27s 5d	37s 11d (after15 years)
Oldham	172	28s	38s
Middlesbrough	168	28s	36s
Swansea	161	28s	37s (after 15 years)
Blackburn	158	27s	36s
Derby	153	28s	38s (after 18 years)
Huddersfield	138	29s	39s (after 15 years)
Coventry	137	29s	39s
Burnley	135	26s 6d	35s
Northampton	134	25s	35s (after 11 years)
St Helens	134	30s	41s
Stockport	133	27s	39s 2d
Preston	130	27s	35s (after 15 years)
Halifax	126	28s	38s

Acts of Parliament and regulations, brought in as wartime expedients, placed new responsibilities upon the police. The Aliens Restriction Act 1914 was one of the first pieces of legislation to be passed. This required all German, Austrian, and Hungarian nationals (of whom there were approximately 20 in the Leicester Borough), to register immediately with the police in the district in which they lived. Every householder renting accommodation to a German had to report the fact to the police. No German was allowed to travel a distance of more than five miles from their place of residence without a police permit, and had to return there within 24 hours. Germans were prohibited from possessing any firearm or ammunition, any explosive substance, petroleum spirit, benzol, or any inflammable liquid in excess of three gallons. They were also prohibited from possessing a motor car or motorcycle. Finally, it was an offence for any German to possess homing pigeons, signalling apparatus, cypher or code books, or any other means of conducting secret correspondence.

In the confusion of the moment, during the first week after the declaration of hostilities, some 50 suspected aliens were taken into custody and held prisoner at the Corn Exchange, most of whom were subsequently released. Eventually, six of the detainees were classed as military reservists and taken to York under escort. One month later, in September 1914, a further dozen suspected reservists were arrested and handed over to the army.[7]

From September 1914 onward, Belgian refugees began to settle in the town and surrounding district, and they also were required to register as aliens. (By the beginning of 1918, the number of registered aliens living in the town had risen to 3,019). As the situation became more settled, toward the middle of 1915, the police were able to make more detailed checks, which resulted in a further group of suspects being detained. On 28 July, in a series of raids, 24 men and six women were arrested as hostile aliens. The men were sent to Handforth and Lofthouse Internment Camps, while the women were deported.

Aerial attacks by Zeppelin airships and later by Gotha bombers, along the south and east coasts into the Home Counties and the Midlands,

[7] They were later released on parole, on condition that they would not to take up arms against Great Britain.

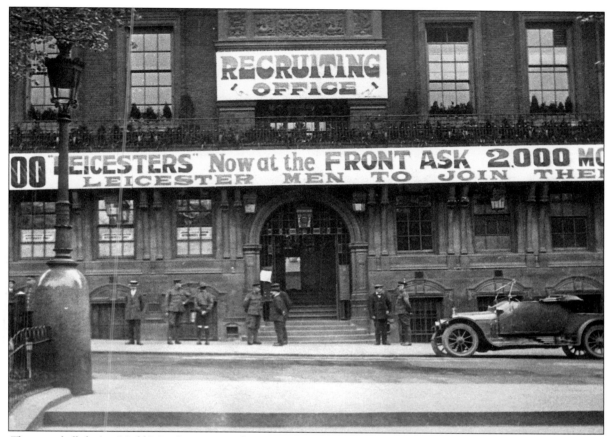

The town hall during World War One. Among those near to the steps is a Boy Scout messenger, who would act as a runner delivering messages for the police and town hall officials.

prompted the taking of precautions against aerial attack.

The first and most obvious provision was the passing of regulations imposing what became known as 'the blackout'. The requirements of the blackout were drawn up and promulgated by the military, to be enforced by the civilian police.

Military Order re Zeppelin Raids issued by Officer Commanding 11th Northern Division.

I, Major General F. Hammersley being a competent Military Authority in exercise of the powers vested in me by Regulation 12 of the Defence of the Realm Consolidation Regulations 1914, do hereby order and direct as follows:

That all lights other than light not visible from the outside of any house shall be kept extinguished between the hours of sunset and sunrise in all places mentioned in the Schedule hereto; except such lights as are not contrary to the following Regulations:-
(1) In all streets and public places and on bridges, a portion of the lights must be extinguished in such a manner as the chief Officers of the Police shall direct so as to break up all groups or rows of lights, and the lights which are not so extinguished must be made invisible from above by shading or by

COUNTY BOROUGH OF LEICESTER.

POLICE NOTICE.
AIR RAIDS.

The public are requested to make themselves acquainted with the following instructions with regard to the steps that will be taken in case of raids by hostile aircraft. They are earnestly asked to assist the Authorities by remaining calm, and by willingly and strictly complying with these instructions. They can greatly assist in safeguarding the Town by always strictly observing the Lighting Orders, and using the darkest curtains they can obtain.

Should it become known that hostile aircraft are approaching the neighbourhood, the following steps will be taken:

HOOTERS.– Steam hooters will be blown for a period of five minutes (if safe to do so). This warning will consist of a succession of five blasts - four short ones, followed by one long one.

As no steam hooters are now sounded after 4-0 p.m., the alarm may be recognised when a hooter is heard in the evening.

TRAMS.– The electric trams will be stopped immediately, and remain stationary until all danger is believed to be passed.

GAS.– The gas will be reduced to a minimum, and householders are earnestly requested to extinguish what light remains, taking great care to turn off the taps at the gas jets and the meter, to avoid danger in case of fire, or of explosion or suffocation after the pressure is restored.

ELECTRIC LIGHT.– The electric light will be gradually reduced to a minimum, and in this case also the public are requested to switch off what light remains.

FLASHLIGHTS.– The use of flashlights at such a time is strictly prohibited.

MOTORS AND OTHER VEHICLES.– Drivers must reduce their lights as low as possible, and proceed at a walking pace, and with the greatest caution. They must stop if requested. Motor horns must not be sounded unless absolutely necessary to avoid accident.

The Police have had strict instructions to report any driver who disobeys this Order.

If the drivers of vehicles are not bound to proceed they are requested to draw into side streets, extinguish their lights, and remain stationary. It should be borne in mind that the position of a town is likely to be located by the noise of traffic.

PUBLIC.– The public are strongly advised to remain at home. The windows and doors of the lower floors should be closed to prevent the admission of noxious gases in case of poisonous bombs being dropped etc. A supply of water or wet sand should be kept ready so that a small fire could be promptly and effectively dealt with.

FIRE ALARMS. Inhabitants should ascertain the position of the nearest Fire Alarm.

STREET LAMPS.– Householders opposite street lamps that are lit are requested to assist by turning them out.

SPECIAL CONSTABLES, Auxiliary Firemen, St. John's V.A.D., Citizens Training League, and other bodies, should assemble according to arrangements in force.

H. ALLEN,
14th February 1916   **Chief Constable**

Although Leicester Borough was never the subject of an air raid during World War One, the sirens were sounded regularly when enemy aircraft were in the vicinity.

painting over the tops and upper portions of the globes.

(2) Sky signs, illuminated fascias, and lights used for outside advertising or illuminating of shops must be extinguished.

(3) All interior lights (except in factories), must be partially shaded by blinds being half pulled down.

(4) In factories in which night shifts are working the upper windows must be shaded so that no lights are visible from outside, and such of the lower windows must be similarly shaded as may be settled in conjunction with chief Officers of the Police.

(5) The lighting of Railway Stations, sidings, and goods yards, must be reduced to the intensity sufficient for the safe and prompt conduct of business.

(6) The sides of lights along the water front must be painted or obscured so as to prevent the reflection of the light upon water.

(7) The aggregation of flares in the street markets is prohibited.

(8) The interior lights of tram cars and omnibuses must be so obscured by curtains or otherwise as to be invisible from the outside, or if not obscured no more than one light shall be used.

No outside lights shall be carried except a red tail light and a head light of moderate intensity.

(9) All public lamps under the control of the local Lighting Authority shall be extinguished and kept extinguished from 10 o'clock until sunrise.

Schedule

Leicester

The Police and Military Patrols have received orders to enforce the above Regulations. Any person contravening the Regulations commits an offence and becomes liable to be tried by a Court of Summary Jurisdiction or by Court Martial.

Made and published at Grantham
on the 15 March 1915.
(Signed), F. Hammersley.
Major General.

…The Order must be enforced at once. Shopkeepers whose lights shine into the street must be warned to cover them and any refusal to do so must be reported so that

Photographed during World War One, this group of soldiers on an outing from the 5th Northern General Hospital are seen in Belgrave Gate outside the Pavilion Theatre of Varieties. The constable in the foreground is wearing a helmet which is often referred to as 'colonial style', the plate of which does not have the lion rampant supporter (plates with the side supporters came into use during the 1920s). The merit badge and two service stripes on the forearm of his right sleeve indicate between ten and fifteen years of service.

the information may be forwarded to the Military Authorities for any action they choose to take.
(Signed) H. Allen
Chief Constable

The orders were not well received by many members of the public, who considered them to be an unnecessary infringement of their liberties. One month after the restrictions became law, Thomas Mortimer, a confectioner of 5 Applegate Street, when reported for showing a light at his premises by Inspector Clark and PC Matthews, told the officers that; '…he hoped the Germans would come and shoot Major General Hammersley'. Taking a serious view of his comments, the magistrates at the town hall made it clear to Mortimer that they were in a position to send him for court martial, fine him £100 or send him to prison for six months. Having stated their

During the General Strike of 1926, officers from Leicester city were sent to other parts of the Midlands to assist surrounding forces. Seen here at Moira, with a sample of 1920s transport are Inspector Walter Allen (far right), and Sergeant 9 Samuel Bonnett (centre). The sergeant on the far left is from the Leicestershire County Constabulary.   *(Courtesy N. Haines)*

options, because this was the first prosecution under the regulations to be brought before them, the bench fined him 15s plus costs.

Similarly, in June, John Henry Burbidge of 42 Gwendolen Road was fined 10s for showing a light, which he had left on to illuminate his wife's way home – and for being abusive to a constable.

The effects of the threat of aerial bombardment were quite profound and resulted on occasion in some startling evaluations. One such was made in a government communication to the Lord Lieutenant of Leicestershire, advising him to expect as a result of Zeppelin attacks on Lincolnshire; 134,000 refugees, accompanied by 27,000 horses and 19,000 vehicles.

Although the air raid warnings were sounded with regularity (12 times in 1916, seven in 1917 and five in 1918), Leicester itself was never the

subject of a raid. The nearest town to be attacked was Loughborough. During the early evening of Monday 31 January 1916, a force of six Zeppelins arrived over the Midlands, dropping 220 bombs across a wide area of several counties, including Derbyshire and Leicestershire.

The airships appeared over Loughborough at around seven o'clock, and dropped several bombs onto the town. Shops, houses and a pub were damaged and 10 people killed, as well as several others being injured.

In the borough of Leicester hooters were installed in locations such as the Midland railway station, the power station and the Co-operative Society's 'Wheatsheaf' boot and shoe factory in Knighton Fields Road East. The use of other steam hooters in the town was then prohibited for the duration of the war.

During World War One a large number of special constables were recruited to assist the regular police. The metal brassard was worn to denote their position as a special constable.

(Courtesy N. Haines)

The signal for an approaching Zeppelin or enemy aircraft was four short blasts and one long blast. After September 1916, if an alert was initiated during the late evening or early hours of the morning, one short blast was given in order to 'alert police officers who were on duty, but not disturb the slumbering citizenry'.

Once the alarm had been raised, all off-duty police, special constables, St John's Ambulance

Pictured prior to leaving for France during World War One, this group of Borough officers had enlisted in the Army Service Corps. All those on the front row are wearing spurs, denoting that this was a horse-drawn section. That they did not all remain in this unit is shown by the fact that PC 48 Briggs was killed in action in France on 18 December 1917, while serving in the Mounted Military Police, and Arthur Hall (later Superintendent), was always known as 'Gunner' Hall, indicating that he transferred to an artillery regiment. From left to right, back row: PC 254 A. Hubbard, PC G. Drake, PC 152 R.B. Willis, PC 282 W. Needham. Middle row: PC 33 C. Hardesty, PC 48 J. Briggs, PC W. Harris, PC 41 A. Lockwood, PC 46 W. Cowley. Front row: Det. Cons. 253 A.R. Hall, PC 249 J. Rouse, Det Sgt (Cpl) R. Clowes, Sgt (Instructor) T. Moore, PC 51 W. Rosevear, PC 88 W. Fairey, PC 89 W. Fieldsend.

men and women and volunteer corps personnel were required to report to their stations. Volunteer motorists reported for duty and parked their cars outside the central police station at the town hall, in readiness either to transport police officers to strategic points or to be used as ambulances. Vehicles at the 5th Northern General Hospital and the War Hospital were put on stand-by. Police and volunteers went to high buildings to

PC 95 George Cookman (later Sargeant).

listen for the engines of the approaching dirigibles. All on and off-duty firemen (plus those of private brigades), reported to their respective stations and a gas engineer in a motor car toured the streets.

At the end of 1914, the government took the opportunity to pass through Parliament the Intoxicating Liquor (Temporary Restriction) Act 1914. The Act, which was most unpopular from

the outset, aimed at curtailing the drinking habits of the population by restricting the opening hours of licensed premises.[8]

With a population of around 228,000 inhabitants, Leicester had a total of 711 premises licensed to sell intoxicating liquor. These comprised 256 fully-licensed premises, 104 beer houses and 351 beer and wine off-licences. This was not an unusual number for the size of the town. Unfortunately, during the previous year there had been 630 convictions for drunkenness, the highest rate in the borough for two decades. Although difficult to substantiate, this was probably due to the fact that the nearby Glen Parva Depot was a staging point for troops in transit and as such Leicester had become almost a garrison town, with a large number of soldiers in transit swelling the population.

One argument which the government put forward in support of its licensing campaign was that, nationwide, the wives of men away at the front were spending their army allowances in public houses. While there would undoubtedly be instances where this was true, the general assertion did not stand up to examination. Apart from the fact that the majority of these were married women, living in straitened circumstances with families to bring up, there was absolutely no demographic information to support the allegation.

Despite pressure from the local temperance organisations, the Watch Committee and licensing justices were by no means convinced, and they were sceptical of the thin arguments put forward to justify the hastily-passed legislation.

Although immediate action was postponed, the government kept to its position, and on 30 December 1914 Leicester Licensing Justices were forced to announce that, in direct compliance with a Military Order issued under the Defence of the Realm Act and effective from that day, all public houses in the borough would close at 9

[8] Another provision of the Act prevented 'treating' and decreed that a man would only purchase his own drink.

This photograph, taken just before World War One, is endorsed: 'Presented to Superintendent Carson by the Officers and Men of the Knighton Division on his promotion to Superintendent and removal to Central Division. 6th March 1913.' Cornelius Daniel Horace Carson (front row, centre) joined the Leicester Borough Police in August 1888, at which time he was described as being 21-years old, 5ft 10in tall and a soldier. He retired in January 1919 at the age of 52, having served for 31 years. (The presence and identity of the small child seated between Carson's legs is unexplained.)

p.m. In an obvious gesture of hostility they added that 'in order to comply with the spirit of the Act they had agreed to close all clubs under the Intoxicating Liquors,(Temporary Restrictions) Act at 9 p.m. as from 1 January 1915'.

Across the country there was little parity. In York, as in Leicester, public houses closed at 9 p.m., in Sheffield they shut at 9.30 p.m. during the week and 10 p.m. on Sundays. In Leeds and Northampton licensed premises closed at 11 p.m. during the week and 10 p.m. on a Sunday.

—oOo—

While major issues such as pay and conditions, along with the restrictions imposed by the war,

exerted a major influence over the force, day to day events and life within the town continued much as before.

In July 1914, a particularly horrific murder took place on the outskirts of the town, at Western Park. At 34 years of age, Arnold Warren, an engineer by trade, was a compulsive gambler. His unsuccessful gambling and violence toward his wife led to the couple separating in May 1914. Their two-year-old son James remained with his mother. On Friday 10 July, Warren's estranged wife left the child with his grandmother, Elizabeth Warren, at 48 Gaul Street, while she went off to work. In the early evening, at about half past five, a young girl by the name of Elizabeth Skidmore

PC 134 William Dickinson (1910–1936). The photograph was probably taken in the stable yard at Belgrave police station between 1919 and 1921.

called at Mrs Warren's house to collect James and return him to his mother. As she was walking with the child, Elizabeth Skidmore encountered Arnold Warren on a nearby recreation ground. Warren asked her to return to his mother's house with a note, while he looked after his son.

When the girl returned from her errand, Warren and the child had disappeared. Shortly before eight o'clock that evening, Stanley Hackney, a shoe hand, was walking across the fields near to Western Park when he found Warren unconscious on the ground, a bottle of laudanum in his hand, and a cut-throat razor nearby. Beneath him lay the body of James Warren with his throat cut.

Hackney summoned the assistance of PC 267 Ashburner, who managed to revive Arnold Warren, whom he then arrested for the murder of his son.

At his trial at Leicester Assizes, before Mr Justice Avery, Warren told the court that on the day of the murder he was depressed, having lost heavily on a horse called Early Hope at Haydock Park race track. His plea of not guilty was dismissed by the jury and he was hanged at Leicester Prison at 8 a.m on Thursday 12 November 1914.

The constable who arrested Warren, PC Harry (Snowy) Ashburner, later became a distinguished figure in the Leicester Police. Ashburner joined the Leicester Borough Police force on 15 May 1912. After serving a short spell in the army during the latter months of 1918[9], he returned to the force, where he spent the majority of his

[9] In April 1918, Ashburner, along with 17 other Borough Police officers, was conscripted into the army. It is believed that he served in a Guards Regiment while in France.

Herbert Allen, chief constable of Leicester Borough Police force February 1913–December 1928.

service in the detective department. Superintendent Snowy Ashburner retired in January 1946.

—oOo—

In September 1914, the branch station in Sanvey Gate was closed down, and the premises sold off to Mr Scott, the owner of an adjacent wood yard, for £535. This loss was partly offset at the beginning of the following year, when negotiations were commenced to purchase 834 square yards of ground at the corner of Hinckley Road and Carlisle Street, with a view to building a new station on the west side of the town.[10]

Throughout the next four years, all manner of organisations made their individual contributions to the war effort and in assisting the depleted police force. One such was the Boy Scouts Association, which in October 1914 was granted £10 by the Corporation, toward their expenses in guarding the Knighton Railway tunnel.[11] Boy Scouts were also used by the police as runners, to take messages between police stations and to other parts of the town.

A further innovation, which was to become a permanent feature, was the shared use by the police of the on-street fire alarms belonging to the fire brigade, at night. Connected to the switchboard at the central fire station in Rutland Street, these were used by members of the public to summon assistance in emergencies.

One of the questions which presented itself in late 1915 was the establishment of a home for the detention of '…lads between 14 and 21 years (who are all wage earners) who have been committed under the Probation Act'. Initially the Church Army home in Grasmere Street and a house at 3 DeMontfort Square were proposed, neither of which were considered by the Home Office to be suitable. Twelve months later, in December 1916, a five year lease, at £35 per year, was signed with Mrs Clara Bramley, the owner of 134 Highcross Street, for the premises to be utilised as a detention home for boys. The police probation officer, Gilbert Ellwood, was appointed superintendent at an annual salary of £25 plus accommodation.

An arrangement made in July 1915 provided for the home address of PC Harold Jenney, at 23 Larch Street, to be used as a detention home for girls. In respect of each of these girls, Jenney and his wife received 2s 6d a week (this sum was increased to 5s in March 1917), plus incidental expenses. This arrangement continued until September 1919, when Jenney, now a detective sergeant (later coroner's officer), relinquished the responsibility and the girls were transferred to the home address of PC Rhodes Parkin, at 26 Prospect Hill.

[10] This station was in fact never built. Later, a site at the junction of Hinckley Road and Tyndale Street was deemed to be more suitable.

[11] The Boy Scouts Association was utilised by local authorities and police forces across England to guard railway lines and tunnels against possible sabotage.

Officers of North Evington outside Asfordby Street police station, December 1928. From left to right, back row: PC 55 Sheppard, PC 225 Garfield, PC 228 Bailey, PC 221 Fraser, PC 242 Warner. Middle row: PC 81 Merriken, PC 157 Perkins, PC 236 Newberry, PC 114 Meese, PC 86 Ecob, PC 39 Kirby, PC 82 Leeson, PC 156 Vines, PC 49 Cross. Front row: PC 93 Burton, -?-, Sgt 16 Staines, Div. Insp. Faulkner, Sgt 26 Buckby, PC 202 Nutting, PC 37 Matthews.

During its first year in operation, the boys home in Highcross Street received a total of 77 cases. Of these 7 were detained; 17 put on probation; 10 bound over; 20 sent to industrial schools; 14 sent to reformatories; 6 birched and 3 returned to their parents. Additionally, the Watch Committee agreed to pay 1 shilling a head per week for the maintenance of boys sent to the Northamptonshire and Warwickshire Reformatories.

—oOo—

As the first year of the war saw the murder of James Warren by his father, so the final year was marked by the trial of Thomas Taylor for the murder of his wife Elizabeth.

Thomas and Elizabeth Taylor married in 1908. They had two daughters, Edith Jessie who was born in 1910 and Frances Edna, who was born in 1912, a year after the couple emigrated to Canada. When war broke out, Thomas Taylor, who had been a regular soldier in the Dublin Fusiliers and had seen service in South Africa during the Boer War, enlisted in the Canadian Expeditionary Force. With her husband posted back to England for training, Elizabeth returned with the children to live in Leicester. During his training period, Thomas Taylor was severely burnt in an accident when some

This mid-morning photograph from between the wars shows the low volume of traffic in the city centre during the 1920s. The pointsman had to move his position at regular intervals to accommodate the passage of tramcars.

billets caught fire on Salisbury Plain, and although he later served in France, he was repatriated to Canada in 1916 to be medically discharged.

Elizabeth refused to join Taylor in Canada, so he later returned to England, where he found that during his absence she had begun an affair with a foreman at the factory where she was working. At this point they decided to end their marriage and Elizabeth moved to live in Beeston, taking with her their youngest child. The eldest girl, Jessie, went to live with her father in Leicester at 28 Raglan Street.

Elizabeth Taylor spent Christmas 1917 in Leicester, with her sister at 139 Sheridan Street. During that time, her husband made approaches to her to return home and resume the marriage.

On Boxing Day Jessie Taylor spent the day with her mother and Thomas went to collect her from the house around 6.30 that evening. The couple went out into the back yard of 139 Sheridan Street to discuss their marital situation. A heated dispute developed and Taylor, pulling an open razor from his pocket, slashed his wife across the throat with it. While relatives took the woman into the house, where she died shortly afterward, Thomas Taylor quietly took his daughter back to their lodgings in Raglan Street, where he was later arrested.

At his trial at Leicester Assizes, before Mr Justice Horridge, evidence was given that in the moments prior to the murder, Taylor had been severely provoked by his wife. The jury found Thomas Taylor guilty of murder with a strong

Traffic pointsman on West Bridge, c.1920s. Traffic at this time flowed two ways across the bridge, and this particular point would only have been manned at peak periods.

Regular point duty officers after October 1927 wore white helmets and sleeves along with white gloves. Although the helmets were later discontinued, white cuffs continued to be worn on point duty until the late 1960s. Cuffs consisted of a detachable cotton or nylon sleeve, and constables carried a pair in their inside pocket at all times, in order to be able to direct traffic on a point or at an incident. White gloves – cotton in summer and woollen in winter – were part of a constable and sergeant's regular daytime dress. The officers in these two pictures are PC 106 Fred Marshall and PC 89 'Gilbert' Fieldsend.

recommendation for mercy. Taylor's situation evoked a great deal of public sympathy and on the 12th February 1918 his sentence, as the result of a 12,000 signature petition, was commuted to penal servitude for life.

—oOo—

During the early months of 1919, the members of the Borough force who had served in World War One began to return in small groups as they were demobilised. Not all of those who went away returned to serve. Eleven had been killed in action or died of wounds. 35 were wounded, some of

A view of Charles Street prior to the building of the new police headquarters in September 1933.

whom were no longer able to perform police duties. Apart from campaign medals, three officers had been awarded the Distinguished Conduct Medal; five the Military Medal and two the Meritorious Service Medal. Three men received foreign decorations for valour: one French and one Belgian Croix de Guerre, and one Medaille d'Honneur. Additionally, four officers were given Divisional Command Certificates.

Military service was to count as pensionable for police purposes. As a necessary measure, each man who returned to duties was sworn in anew as a constable.

As regards to Corporation employees (including policemen), who had been disabled in

PC 180 F. Hutson, Royal Marine Artillery. Killed in action, 9 November 1917.

PC 199 Albert W. Osborn, Leicestershire Regiment. Killed in action, July 1917.

the war, every effort was made to re-employ them in a variety of posts. The Watch Committee laid down a specific policy of employing ex-policemen as cleaners, gaolers, telephone operators, clerks and court or coroner's officers.

On Tuesday 10 June 1919, huge crowds gathered in the town and on Victoria Park to welcome HM King George V and Queen Mary when the king granted the town city status. Probably the largest public event seen in Leicester either before or since, the visit was accompanied by a huge procession, which included a military march past of regiments from all parts of the region, accompanied by units of demobilised men and regimental brass bands. The assembled crowds were controlled by 200 men of the Borough Police – henceforth to be known as the Leicester City Police – assisted by 680 officers drafted in from surrounding forces.

The years after World War One
Economic constraints dictated that the wages of the police, along with other public

service employees, were seriously eroded during the war. The government was well aware that as soon as an armistice was signed the matter would have to be addressed. In February 1918 the Home Secretary wrote to police authorities throughout the country stating that '…It is clear that after the war there will be a general call for the pay of the police to be increased… Until such time as a pay agreement has been reached, it is imperative that any local pay awards be non-pensionable in the form of War Bonuses or short term allowances'.

In the same month, Herbert Allen attended a conference in Sheffield to discuss the matter with other chief officers. As a part of the re-appraisal of the police structure nationally, a proposition was also made at this conference that the Leicester Borough Police and the County Police, along with Derby, the West Riding of Yorkshire, Nottingham and Lincolnshire become affiliated to form a Number 3 Police District.

What was not appreciated at government level was the depth of feeling

PC 55 A.E. Reeves, Leicestershire Regiment. Killed in action, February 1916.

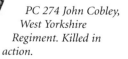

PC 274 John Cobley, West Yorkshire Regiment. Killed in action.

PC 48 John H. Briggs,
Mounted Military Police.
Died of wounds,
December 1917.

PC 259 E. Maddock MM,
Royal Horse Artillery.
Killed in action, 13
November 1917.

evoked by the situation, or the vehemence and degree of militancy with which the police would press their claims.

As early as August 1918, strike action was being mooted by the Metropolitan and City of London Police. The result, accompanied by the resignation of the Commissioner of the Metropolitan Police Sir Edward Henry, was that an increase of 10s per week for all ranks (in those two forces), was granted and a non-contributory widows pension fund was instigated. One of the prime objectives – recognition of the newly-formed National Union of Police and Prison Officers – was refused.

Panicked by this display of militancy in the capital, within the next two months individual local authorities offered hastily prepared packages to the provincial police forces. In December 1918, following a series of negotiations, Leicester, along with most other provincial authorities, accepted the new rates of pay being implemented in London. Constables were to be paid from 43s to 51s a week, sergeants from 56s to 60s and inspectors would receive £230 a year, rising to £260 after six years.[12]

At eight o'clock in the morning of Thursday 2 January 1919, under the Chairmanship of

Inspector Daniel Choyce, a meeting of members of the Borough Police was held in the muster room of the town hall police station. A unanimous decision was taken by those present to become members of the National Union of Police and Prison Officers, and to invite an executive member of the union to come to Leicester to address the force.

Fully aware of events taking place elsewhere in the country, the Watch Committee dared not dismiss the declaration outright. The same day, having met representatives of the force, a temporary compromise was agreed. While membership of the union would not be countenanced, a representative committee could be formed to present and discuss grievances with the Watch Committee.[13]

Such was the level of feeling within the police service, that irrespective of the Watch Committee's resistance, at a meeting of county, borough and railway police held at Shaftesbury Hall on Friday 7 March 1919, the Leicester branch of the National Union of Police

PC 261 William Alfred Bailey, Royal
Horse Artillery. Killed in action,
November 1916.

[12] These scales were interim and were adjusted in 1919 by the provisions of the Desborough Report.

[13] It is apparent that early members of this group were not later penalised for their activities. Three inaugural members went on to become senior officers of the force. Daniel Choyce retired as a superintendent, George Keen as an inspector, and John Gabbitas as deputy chief constable.

PC 89 Richard Hazelwood, Grenadier Guards. Killed in action, 25 July 1917.

and Prison Officers was founded.

During the early summer, prior to the Police Act 1919 being passed by Parliament, feeling among police officers nationally about pay and working conditions was running at such a level that strike action was being openly discussed. The Leicester Watch Committee, deeply concerned about the implications of any participation in industrial action by Borough Police officers, issued a statement that:

> …any police officer connected with the Leicester force, quite regardless of his rank, length of service, or any other consideration, who fails to report for duty in the ordinary course of his service, without the express knowledge and sanction or approval of the chief constable, will be forthwith dismissed. Any police officer, of any rank, dismissed from the force under the conditions aforesaid described, will under no circumstances be permitted to re-join the Leicester Police force, and his dismissal will result in the loss of all service counting towards his pension and of all payments he has contributed to the pension fund.

In the event, on 31 July 1919, while the Police Act was still being debated in Parliament, 2,364 men from seven police forces went on strike. The strike was short-lived and officers returned to work very quickly. All of those who went on strike

were dismissed, and none were ever reinstated. Men of the Leicester City Police were not among those who went on strike.

A direct result of the unrest was the setting up of a committee under the chairmanship of Lord Desborough, whose remit was to examine the pay and conditions of the police forces throughout the country and to formulate a comprehensive pay and negotiating strategy.

The implementation of the subsequent Desborough Report made sweeping changes in the organisation and management of the police. For the first time, an overall pay scale was arrived at, and agreement was reached on representation. Local arrangements were still to be arrived at in relation to the scale of rent allowances paid to officers by the local authorities.

A Police Federation, representing all ranks below superintendent, with a brief to consider and represent its members on matters affecting welfare and efficiency, was established. Three levels of boards were to be inaugurated in each police force, one for constables, one for sergeants and one for inspectors. With the creation of the Police Federation, the Police Act of 1919, among its various clauses, also declared it to be an offence for a police officer to be or seek to become a member of any trades union.

—oOo—

While there was not a formal mounted section within the Leicester force, horses were used at various times, and a section of officers who served as mounted police certainly did exist. Prior to

PC 232 George Arthur Manton, Coldstream Guards. Killed in action, April 1916.

World War Two photographs exist of ceremonial occasions where City Police officers such as Inspector Peter Gray and Sergeant Arthur Medhurst are leading parades along with the chief constable.[14] Others mentioned over a period of time, who had duties in respect of a mounted section, were PC 134 William Dickenson, PC 182 Leslie Green, PC 263 Samuel Whitfield, PC 143 'Sam' Jones, PC 82 Cyril 'Tich' Leeson, PC 188 Bernard Wilson, and PC 102 Joseph Henry 'Jockey' Shingler.

Documentation of the Leicester Police's equine associations is extremely sparse. In June 1919 the Watch Committee is recorded as having paid a sum of £25 to the 'NCOs and men of the Army Remount Department, in recognition of their assistance to the Mounted Police Detachment on the occasion of the royal visit'. At the same time a formal arrangement was entered into with the military to acquire the loan of two horses for police use at a yearly fee of £7 10s 0d – the horses to become the property of the Watch Committee after six years – in 1925. This agreement was amended in May 1922 when the Corporation bought the horses for £22 10s 0d each from Northern Army command. From references in October 1924 to repairs being carried out to the stables floor at Belgrave police station, it

is most likely that this is where they were kept.

—oOo—

Although the employment of the first policewoman was still a decade away, two women who were employed as probation officers had close links with the City Police in the period immediately after World War One. These probation officers, Mrs Kenyon and Sister Nellie Jones, were not in the pay of or under the authority of the Watch Committee. Both women attended the police court at the town hall each morning, to attend to the needs of female prisoners. Dividing the women and girls by age, Sister Jones dealt with those over 21, while Mrs Kenyon took care of those under that age. When a female received a custodial sentence, one of the two probation officers accompanied her to the institution. Sister Jones also undertook to visit women prisoners in Nottingham gaol. With a sense of propriety typical of the age, Sister Jones went into the witness box with any female who was required to give evidence, in order to give her moral support. The remit of these two women appears to have been very wide. Any constable encountering a girl or woman in the streets, whom he felt was in need of assistance, called upon their services. As particular mention is made of Victoria Park, which was a notorious haunt of prostitutes, there is a strong indication that guidance was probably of a moral nature. In April 1925 the status of Mrs Kenyon, now referred to as the 'Police Court Missionary', in relation to her police work, was

---

[14] Both of these were primarily foot patrol officers.

employed on a more formal basis by the Watch Committee, which paid her £26 a year for her services.

Female attendants at the central police station had a completely different role. Their job was seen quite clearly as that of female gaolers, responsible for searching and guarding prisoners. There appear (certainly at the beginning of World War One), to have been two ladies employed in this work, and their salaries are something of a barometer of the rises in cost of living and wages during the war. In June 1913, Miss Ada Hart was engaged as the 'second matron', at 16s a week. During November 1918, the weekly wage of the female attendants and searchers was increased from 20s to 25s a week. Fifteen months after the end of the war, in February 1920, the pay of the two matrons then employed by the force, Elizabeth Warwick and Marian Brooker, was raised from 33s to 36s a week.[15]

That thought was being given, by the public if not the police, to the question of women police officers is shown by an approach to the Watch Committee at the beginning of 1921.

On Wednesday 26 January, a deputation from various social and political groups presented themselves before the Committee and urged that the employment of women as police officers be considered by the City Police. Having debated the matter for some three weeks, the Watch Committee delivered a resounding 'no' to the proposal. After deliberating, they had arrived at their decision based on the premise that work that could be better performed by women than men

PC 183 W. Woodward, Royal Marine Artillery. Killed in action, 9 November 1917.

was already in hand. Patrol duties, which it was being suggested could best be carried out by women, were purely social and rescue work, and would be far better performed on an unofficial voluntary basis.

—oOo—

The early 1920s saw the beginning of what was to become a disastrous world-wide depression. In Leicester as elsewhere, by 1921 work was short, and the number of unemployed men was rising daily.

During the morning of Friday 30 September 1921, a group of around 600 unemployed men gathered outside the Trade Hall in St James's Street, with the intention of using the building to hold a protest meeting against the plight of the unemployed in the town. The meeting, organised by Bertram Charles Ley, who at 25 was himself unemployed, had been widely advertised by handbills and posters. Unfortunately for Ley, due to an oversight the venue had not been properly booked for the gathering.

Because information had leaked out at an early stage that Ley and his followers intended to either hold a meeting in the hall or burn it down should they not be granted access, there had been sufficient time for the police to prepare for possible disorder.

On their arrival at the Trade Hall, Ley's group was refused access. Any thoughts of firing the building were thwarted by the presence of

[15] In December 1926 a third matron was engaged at £3 per week.

Inspector Keene and a group of 14 constables. Keen was soon joined (at about 10.15 a.m.), by Superintendent Daniel Choyce – who ironically, when an inspector in 1919, had been one of the spokesmen for the Borough Police when they were endeavouring to better their own position by forming a trades union. Choyce had with him a further 35 men, whom he positioned in the Haymarket. After being spoken to by Councillor Adnitt and Alderman Hill, the demonstrators allowed themselves to be moved away by the police into the Haymarket, where the two police contingents were in a better position to control them.

After holding a meeting accompanied by some inflammatory speeches, mainly directed at the police presence, the crowd moved off, with the declared intention of going to the Poor Law Offices in Rupert Street. Once it was confirmed where the crowd was heading, Choyce detached 25 officers and sent them directly to the Poor Law Offices, with instructions to position themselves inside the establishment, out of sight.

As the crowd started to move off from the Hay-market along Gallowtree Gate and Granby Street, Inspector Keene and the remaining 24 policemen cut through Vestry Street and the wholesale market, heading the crowd off at Horsefair Street. In this manner the demonstrators arrived in Rupert Street under a loose police escort.

PC 276 T. Percival, Leicestershire Regiment. Killed in action.

Choyce, meanwhile, had gone ahead of Keene to the town hall police station, in order to muster what few extra men were available. Some of these he deployed into the Poor Law Offices, raising the number inside the building to 28.

On arrival at the Poor Law Offices, the crowd found the doors closed against them. They then held a further meeting in the street, which, according to one witness in a nearby factory, lasted for about an hour. Eventually, becoming frustrated at their inability to gain access, someone in the crowd threw a stone which broke a fanlight in the front door of the building. Superintendent Choyce at this point took the decision to deal with what he felt had now become a mob.

The doors to the Poor Law Offices were opened from the inside and Choyce gave the order for the mob to be dispersed. The crowd, having had no prior indication of the police presence in the building, was taken completely by surprise. A baton charge was made against the assembly, as a result of which 10 of the demonstrators in the front ranks were injured and had to be taken by ambulance to the Royal Infirmary for treatment. (No police officers appear to have been hurt.) The crowd disintegrated quickly. After a series of short running battles in the nearby streets, good order was soon restored.

Although the police action in breaking up the demonstration with a baton charge drew a deal of criticism from many trade unionists and other bodies, there is no doubt that Choyce's planning

George 'Fred' Marshall joined the Leicester Borough Police in December 1921 as PC 106, having served in the army throughout World War One. After the Armistice in 1918 he went to Russia with the British Expeditionary Force, where he saw action fighting with the White Russian army against the Bolshevik forces. In July 1936 he was promoted to sergeant. He retired in December 1946, having completed 25 years service.

and execution of the operation, from a police standpoint, was immaculate. With a relatively small number of officers he first controlled the march from the city centre to the Poor Law Offices. In Rupert Street, having waited until he was satisfied that the demonstrators were not going to leave of their own volition, at the first signs of disorder he used a reserve of men to clear the street.[16] Unfortunately, in a time of general hardship, the incident did not endear the police to the public.

—oOo—

After World War One the role of the motor car in society became ever more important. Herbert Allen was the first of the city's chief constables to have to address the problems of congestion and traffic nuisance caused by motor vehicles.

In October 1922, he drew the attention of the City Council to the problems as he perceived them. The roads within the city were too narrow to facilitate the free passage of motor cars and vans. This was complicated by tramcars travelling through and stopping in thoroughfares, a problem which was further exacerbated by shopkeepers blocking the roads with their goods. Bad cambers, combined with the speed of vehicles, made motoring in the city centre unsafe.

His proposed solutions were radical for the time, but with hindsight, eminently sensible. In

[16] Superintendent Daniel Choyce retired in June 1929. He died on 2 October 1959, aged 85.

Members of Leicester City Police outside the town hall police station between September 1926 and February 1928, possibly on the occasion of Staff-Inspector Palmer's retirement.

From left to right, back row: PC 174 E. Pym, PC James, PC 195 A. Higgins, PC 182 L. Green, PC 96 H. Nichols, PC 106 G.F. Marshall, PC 200 G. Parrott, PC G. H. Smith, PC Joyce, PC 161 C. Alborn, PC 66 J. Weston, PC 219 A. Medhurst. Middle row: Sgt 5 G. Newberry, PC 146 A. Hillman, PC 194 J. Capps, PC 72 M. Adkinson, PC 84 F. Scott, PC 189 W. Bates, PC 33 H. Hardesty, Sgt 25 W. Grey, Sgt 17 L. Shepherdson, Det. Sgt 24 H. Jenney. Front row: Det. 198 E.C. Turner, Det. Sgt 18 A. Hall, Det. Insp. H. Ashburner, Insp. C. Cooper, Insp Keen, Supt. D. Choyce, Staff Insp. Palmer, Insp. W. Allen, Insp. J. Gabbitas, Sgt. 24 C. King.

later years some were implemented. Allen's first suggestion was that the course of some of the tram lines should be altered to curve in towards the kerb, taking the halting trams out of the centre of the road, and allowing traffic to pass by them. Next he advocated that the footways around the Clock Tower should be reduced in favour of road widening, as in his opinion, the wide footways were '…mostly used by idlers'. (The traffic flow at the Clock Tower was greatly improved in 1926 by the imposition of a rotary system around it.)

Herbert Allen's final and most drastic proposal was that the slums along the line from Colton Street and Upper Charles Street to Belgrave Gate should be demolished and a new road cut through which would '…alleviate the traffic problems for generations to come'. With commendable foresight the chief constable commented that '…there is every prospect of the increase of vehicles continuing and if so it is clear that in the near future some of the central streets will become practically impassable at certain times of the day unless alternative routes are provided'.

In the short term, the local authority made an order preventing the driving of cattle along Welford Place and through Belvoir Street into the city centre as far as the Clock Tower between nine o'clock in the morning and seven o'clock in the evening. For his part, Allen placed his traffic pointsmen on pedestal-type boxes, in order that they should be more visible, and instituted a motorcycle patrol to deal with '…reckless and dangerous driving and excessive speed'.

While the unemployment position in Leicester, as elsewhere during the 1920s, was extremely serious, in his annual report for 1926 – the year of the General Strike – the chief constable comments on the good order which was maintained in the city. Other than to send police officers from the city to assist in strike duties at the Leicestershire coalfields, '…the General Strike passed off without a single incident requiring police action.' Along with other public sector groups during this period, the police were subject to cut-backs. Allen was required to reduce his establishment (presumably through natural wastage), by five per cent, bringing the force's strength down to 252 officers.

At the beginning of 1928, Herbert Allen's general health began to fail, and in September he informed the Watch Committee of his intention to retire with effect from December of that year.

CHAPTER EIGHT

Oswald John Buxton Cole
(January 1929–December 1955)

The years prior to World War Two

Born on 17 December 1890 into a well-to-do police family (his father was chief constable of Oxford), Oswald John Buxton Cole joined the Brighton Police in 1909. In common with many of his contemporaries he served in the British Army (as a gunner), during World War One, being taken prisoner during the Battle of Cambrai in 1917. Upon his return to the police service after the war, Cole, still a relatively young man at the age of 33, became the chief constable of Worcester, a position he held until moving to Leicester.

Engaged at an annual salary of £800, and destined to be the second longest-serving chief constable in the history of the Leicester City Police, Oswald John Buxton Cole took office on Tuesday 1 January 1929.

The new chief constable came to the force at a time when the first of a series of major transitions was taking place in the police service throughout the country. Along with other chief officers, Cole had to address the question of employing women as police officers.

Exactly two years previously, in January 1927, a Home Office memorandum had clearly stated:

…the [Home] Secretary recognises that the need for the employment of police women depends in the main upon the local conditions of each force, and in particular, the question of whether there is a sufficient volume of work of a kind which can most appropriately be performed by women, to justify the appointment of whole time police women in addition to the regular police establishment. The Secretary of State hopes however that the Police Authority will not lose sight of the desirability of appointing one or more police women where the circumstances justify that course…

As early as April 1929, Councillor Emily Fortey had raised the question of employing women police officers. The situation at this time was that Mrs Kenyon (the court probation officer), was employed at 10s a week for the purpose of taking statements from, and looking after, young girls and women who were involved in sex cases or otherwise came to police notice.[1]

Miss Fortey, in view of the impending changes in the law, considered this arrangement to be hardly adequate, and moved that a woman should be employed full-time as a police officer. Substance was given to the resolution by the recent decision of a Royal Commission on police powers and procedure, which had endorsed the employment of female officers.

Such a radical proposition was not one to be accepted lightly by an organisation which had, for almost a hundred years, been exclusively a man's domain.

A sub-committee was formed and the chief constable charged with making enquires in other police districts. Three representatives of the Leicester branch of the National Council of Women were invited to participate in the

[1] Mrs Kenyon retired in September 1929. She was replaced by Miss Gertrude Emma Hill, 14 Park Avenue, Aylestone, at a salary of £26 per annum.

During the 1930s many outer beats were worked by officers on cycle patrol. The officer pictured is PC 123 Isaac James Webster. His son Kenneth Webster later served in the city force as PC 393.

deliberations. While these ladies, in line with the findings of the sub-committee, firmly endorsed the engagement of women officers, their inclusion in the discussions should not be regarded as being in any way dramatic. All three, Mrs C.J. Bond, the wife of a retired local surgeon, Mrs Astley V. Clarke, also the wife of a well-known medical practitioner in the town, and Mrs Parsons, whose husband was a member of the City Council, were well and truly part of the establishment.

At the end of September 1929 it was decided, on an experimental basis, to advertise for a trained policewoman, to commence work at a salary of £3 a week. The successful applicant was to receive an allowance of 10s a week for rent and clothing, and was not to be counted in the establishment of the force. On 12 November 1929, Eileen St Claire Sloane, who had spent a short time as a policewoman in Liverpool, was given a temporary appointment. An example of the reluctance to accept the inevitability of change is evident when, rather than incur the expense of

having a uniform tailored for the new recruit, her old one was purchased for £8 11s 0d – one third of the original cost – from the police at Liverpool.

Because she was not included in the establishment of the force, nor actually sworn as a constable (and as such did not have a warrant number), Eileen Sloane's position was quite tenuous. For two and a half years her duties were various, but always on the periphery of police work. Having attended the magistrates courts at the town hall on a daily basis, she was then responsible for escorting any female prisoners to the local Midlands gaols at places such as Birmingham. From time to time she would work with the detective department, mainly taking statements, examining indecent letters and assisting with female complainants and witnesses. Other than this, her duties comprised dealing with women who were found to be wandering the streets at night and patrolling local parks during the daytime, looking for young people behaving in an indecent manner.

Laying of the foundation stone of Charles Street police station by Alderman W.J. Lovell on 2 May 1932.

After three and a half years with the city force, Eileen Sloane resigned in May 1933. It was then decided to advertise for '...a woman social worker, age not to exceed 35. To be advertised for at the rate applicable to the police force, it being understood that, subject to satisfactory service she will eventually become a member of the Police force'. Due to high unemployment and low wages, an unusually large number of applicants presented themselves for the post. A total of 51 women, the oldest aged 50 and the youngest aged 21, applied.

From a short list of six, the successful candidate was Barbara Denis de Vitré, who took up her appointment on 28 June 1933. A serving officer with the Sheffield Police, she had been a policewoman for just under three years. Prior to this she had been with the police service in Cairo. Probably the most successful woman officer in the force's history, Barbara de Vitré went on to become an assistant inspector of constabulary. Six months after joining, in December 1933, it was recommended that her wage be increased to 62s a week and that she be sworn in as a constable – 'so that she can make arrests.'

Between April and July 1936, two more posts were advertised in the London newspapers. Additionally, 24 universities and 143 different

Vehicles of the transport fleet, Charles Street yard c.1936.

girl's schools were contacted in a search for suitable female candidates. The first advertisement drew 60 applications, the second took the figure to 98.

As a result Miss Dora Hay Constable and her sister Miss Anne Briggs Constable MA, from West Lothian, were engaged on probation for two years. As senior policewoman, Barbara de Vitré was promoted to sergeant four months later in November 1936.

—oOo—

In the latter months of his incumbency, Herbert Allen was instrumental in setting in motion a plan for the removal of the police force from the town hall, to a new purpose-built headquarters in the city centre.

With the redevelopment of Charles Street, which created a new main thoroughfare running from one side of the city to the other, the opportunity presented itself to move the police from their now overcrowded accommodation in the town hall to somewhere more suitable.

In consultation with Herbert Allen, the city surveyor, Arthur Gooseman, had by late November 1928 identified a site of some 2,790 square yards at the south end of the development, which was eminently suitable for a new police headquarters.

Gooseman described the location as, 'an island bounded by Northampton Street, George Street, Colton Street and Church Street.' After January 1929, working with the newly arrived chief constable, the city surveyor set to work preparing estimates for what was to be one of the most modern provincial police headquarters in the country. By April 1930 a draft proposal for the purchase of land at a cost of £18,135 and an

Future assistant chief constable, PC 179 Eric Lacy, is pictured alongside an early 1930s patrol car.

estimate for building work which brought the total cost to of the project to between £61,000 and £65,000, was lodged with the Home Office.

Along with the prospect of moving to a new headquarters, Cole decided that the time was right to re-appraise the manner in which the city was patrolled and served by his newly-acquired force.

During the 1930s the force had several talented musicians, some of whom gathered together to form a small orchestra. From left to right, back row: Sgt 37 Len Vines. Front row: PC 45 Walter Garner, W. Sgt Barbara Denis de Vitré, Det. Insp. Thomas 'Bill' Hayward.

In October 1929, the city was, for policing purposes, divided into four areas. Central, with 23 day and 45 night beats constituted the city centre. Belgrave, under an inspector and two sergeants comprised five day and eight night beats. These operated from stations at Woodboy Street and Loughborough Road. North Evington, under the management of two sergeants, had five day and nine night beats, worked from the police station in Asfordby Street. Finally, on the south side of the town was the Queens Road police station, run by an inspector and two sergeants who also had responsibility for a sub-area at Aylestone, which was worked from one police station on Lansdowne Road and another on Wentworth Road. This area encompassed seven day beats and 10 night beats.

As always, the hours during which the various stations should be open to the public was a matter for debate. The common practice was for the station at the town hall to be open 24 hours a day, while the remainder opened selectively between eight in the morning and midnight. In the absence of those sophisticated surveys, which in later years would supply empirical data upon which to base staffing levels, the simplistic consideration was that 10 officers were required to man the stations – and that was 10 men who were not patrolling beats.

With all the police cover provided by foot patrols, officers paraded at their respective stations in shifts, along with a duty sergeant, to be briefed by an inspector. They then marched out to their beat and commenced patrol duties. Halfway through his tour of duty each man returned to the station for a half-hour meal break, before returning to his designated area. By staggering meal times it was possible for constables to cover adjacent beats during these meal breaks.

In other parts of the country a new innovation was being implemented which allowed for a better usage of manpower. Generally known as the 'box

PC 89 Fieldsend, pictured in 1936 putting an injured child into the fire brigade ambulance following an accident in the High Street. (The fire brigade in Leicester were responsible for maintaining an ambulance service until World War Two.) The officer is wearing a white traffic helmet, indicating that he was permanently engaged on traffic duties.   *(Courtesy N. Haines)*

system' it was based upon a series of small cabins – which quickly became famous as 'police boxes'- placed at strategic locations for officers to use as a base from which to work.[2]

Painted a distinctive shade of dark blue and constructed of timber, the box, measuring just over 7ft high by 5½ft square, had a single door in the front through which the policeman gained access. (Some were slightly larger to accommodate a bicycle.) Inside, illuminated by a small electric light bulb, was a deal table, bolted to the wall, a wooden stool and a tiny electric fire. A telephone directly linked to the police station and situated on a shelf at one side was accessible to the public by lifting a flap on the outside of the box. Every officer carried a Yale key (known as a 'box

key', and attached to his whistle chain), which gave access to all boxes and police stations in the force area).

O.J.B. Cole argued that, if he were allowed to set up 39 of these boxes throughout the force area, he could at a stroke improve policing in the city. Areas would be patrolled more effectively and men released back onto the streets from office duty.

A constable would commence his tour of duty at the box by 'ringing in' on a direct line to a switchboard at the central police station, and receiving his instructions and messages. A copy of 'daily orders' would be posted each morning in the box. Instead of leaving his beat to walk in for refreshments, he would simply eat a packed meal

[2] A police box system was in use in the Chapeltown area of Leeds by January 1931.

Recruit group, June 1935. From left to right, back row: PC 207 S. Straitham, PC 255 A. Wickham, PC 174 W.E. Morris, PC 254 J.K. Jones, PC 240 S. Page, PC 222 S.F. Smith. Front row: PC 144 M. Ellsworth, PC 256 W. Jarvis, PC 139 W. Joiner, PC 219 A. Samson.

(Courtesy J. Joiner)

(provided by himself), in the box. (No longer were bottles of hot coffee to be taken out to men on cold winters nights, to be drunk in shop doorways.) Members of the public would, by opening a hatch in the side of the box, be able to pick up the same telephone as the policeman, and be immediately in contact with the police switchboard.

Strategic locations throughout the city were selected at varying ground rents. While the average

This photograph of PC 214 Adams directing traffic in the inter-war years is dominated by the ornately decorated carriers lorry which is passing.

was 2s 6d a year, some owners required more – such as the London and North Eastern and the London Midland and Scottish Railway Companies, who required 10s a year for their sites at Belgrave Road and Narborough Road. With extra supervisory responsibilities, an allowance of 1s 6d a week was made to sergeants in order that they might use their own pedal cycles to travel from box to box. Once erected, not all of the boxes were particularly well received. The owner of the land of the one on Cavendish Road asked that the box be removed to the library site on Lansdowne Road, and the box at the junction of Ratcliffe Road and London Road was declared by a prospective house vendor to be 'a deterrent to the sale of property in the area'. In a different vein a request by the army recruiting office to affix posters to the sides of the boxes was summarily dismissed.

While the box system undoubtedly ensured that the public received an improved level of policing, it also served to deepen the existing gulf between the ranks. Constables were required to work a beat for the duration of their tour of duty – usually eight hours. During that time the officer was required to be at certain points on the beat (including the box), at appointed times. Time spent at the box – including that taken for the consumption of meals – was regulated to the minute. For their part, sergeants were required to visit each officer twice during the shift, once before and once after the meal. The duty inspector would visit a constable once during his shift in order to ensure that the sergeant had made his required visits. Socialisation within the hierarchy was non-existent (a curious phenomena considering that every supervisory officer, of whatever rank, had to begin his career as a constable), and discipline extreme. To be late at a point, spend a few minutes too long at a box, or be caught speaking with an officer on the next beat was a disciplinary offence. In between dealing with police matters, the box system afforded the perfect opportunity for supervisors and supervised to play a serious game of hide and seek. At night, PCs would signal with torches to each other as a warning of the approach of a duty officer. Sergeants and inspectors would hide in doorways or wait, concealed, just in sight of a box, in order to time how long the beat man was inside. Being caught resulted in an appearance before the chief constable, accompanied by an admonition or official caution for a first offence, and a fine or loss of pay on any subsequent occasion.

A further consideration was the increased workload which would be imposed upon the telephone system at the central police station. The two war-disabled male telephonists who were

The first home of the traffic department was in the converted police station at Woodboy Street in the Belgrave district. This picture was taken between the setting up of the section in January 1930 and the promotion of PC Jack Shipman to sergeant in November 1935. From left to right: PC 183 Cyril Betts, PC 163 Alfred Foulds, PC 61 Harry Watkins, PC 54 Roy Gill, PC 34 William Holden, PC 203 William Welch, PC 199 J. Shipman, Insp. Shirley Wicks, Ch. Cons. O.J.B. Cole.

Cap badge worn by constables and sergeants prior to 1957.

currently employed would not cope with the anticipated influx of calls from members of the public ringing in on the direct lines from the boxes. It was decided that in readiness for the proposed launch of the scheme on 31 December 1930 two additional operators would be employed. In order to keep costs down, the candidates had to be young men of 18 years of age who were suitable for later employment as police officers. (Applicants who did not fill this criteria were rejected.) At a salary of 25s per week, rising to 37s 6d when they were 20, one was to work full time on the switchboard, while the other was employed in the staff office, relieving on the telephones as necessary.

—oOo—

In order for the new strategy to be effective, the force's transport system would have to be reviewed and upgraded. There were five vehicles in use by the City Police: a Humber motor car which was kept at the fire station; a Morris van for the conveyance of prisoners; two solo motorcycles and a motorcycle combination. Depending on circumstances these were all housed in and around the town hall yard and the central police station. Compared with the fire brigade, which had possessed a motorised fleet of vehicles since before World War One, this was an abysmal situation. Cole took the opportunity to combine the implementation of the box scheme with persuading the Local Authority to re-think its vehicular policy.

The agreement reached was that, having purchased an extra motorcycle combination for £90 and a four-seater motor car at £300, the old

station cottages at Woodboy Street in Belgrave should form a transport depot.

Having stripped out the ground floor to create garage space, the upper storey was converted into accommodation for an officer and his family to live in. A staff of six constables was designated to form this first transport section. The next step was to appoint someone to supervise the depot and maintain the vehicles. The basis of this choice seems to have been a little bizarre. It was decided that an advertisement should be placed, 'with other Forces and the Fire Brigade to ascertain a suitable candidate and promote him to the rank of sergeant'. As it transpired PC 183 Cyril Betts, a Leicester City policeman, was appointed on 16 September 1930.

In O.J.B. Cole's own words:

…even had the police box system not been mooted, the provision of police transport in this city was inevitable in order to keep pace with the present day tendency on the part of the criminal population to remove themselves as quickly as possible from the scene of their depredations. To deal effectively with this type of criminal the police must be given equal or greater mobility.

Certainly during the initial years, the transport section focussed primarily on using motorcycles for both patrol and despatch work. Later, the old Zenith motor cycles and Triumph combination were disposed of. Between March 1933 and April 1934 three new Royal Enfield combinations made an appearance, each bought from H.P. Lavender's. (With the new ones purchased for between £90 and £97 each, the trade-in prices for two of the old ones were £20 and £8 respectively.) The purchase, during the summer of 1932, of 12 'special heavy weight rubber cloth Macintoshes', at two guineas each, indicates that there were at that time a dozen officers engaged on motor cycle patrol duties.

Members of the Leicester City Police force on the parade ground of the magazine barracks in 1931.

By the end of 1936, the motor transport department numbered one inspector and 16 constables. The force vehicle fleet comprised four cars, 'for road patrol'; two cars for general use; two general purpose vans and one for the conveyance of prisoners and two motorcycle combinations which were used mainly in conjunction with the police box system.

Masterminded by Superintendent John Gabbitas (whose reward was a promotion to deputy chief constable on the retirement of Dugard Robertson in 1936), the box system was declared to be fully operational by April 1931. (There was an isolated addition in July 1934, with the erection of a small box on the clock tower, near to Churchgate, on land owned by Montague Burton.) This allowed Cole to move along to the next phase of his modernisation plans, namely the closing of some of the police stations on the boundaries of the city.

On 21 January 1930 a decision was taken to close the sub-station at Aylestone, and transfer ownership of the property on Lansdowne Road to the libraries department. The tenancy of the old Knighton station was relinquished on 24 June 1930. On 30 December 1930 work from the Belgrave police station ceased and, four months later on 21 April 1931, the property was sold.

It was decided that North Evington police station in Asfordby Street, which had opened at the dawn of the new century, was to be closed down, and Inspector Shepherdson – who lived in the accommodation at the station – re-housed.[3]

In July 1933 the 936 square yard site, purchased 18 years earlier in 1915 for the proposed police station at the corner of Hinckley Road and Carlisle Street, was deemed to be unsuitable and sold to Mr Ireland for £397.

The closure of Belgrave police station saw the end of an era. It had, apart from anything else, been the only station in the force area which had stabling for horses. Although there was never formally a regular mounted section, one constable, Ernest Boyles (PC 78), who joined the force in 1926 and lived at Belgrave station, patrolled regularly on horseback. Described in the *Charles Street Clarion* of July 1950 as, 'Leicester's only mounted policeman… the public will remember him patrolling the city boundaries on his horse. Often performing traffic duty at Groby Road, and on crossing patrol at Hinckley Road…' Ernest Boyles's mounted days ended in 1931 with the disposal of Belgrave police station and the consequent sale of his horse.

[3] Due to co-ownership with the fire brigade, the disposal of the North Evington station proved impracticable and it was later re-opened as a police station in late 1958.

This drastic reorganisation of the basic structure of things, while not well received by all concerned, was absolutely necessary. In order to move forward, a degree of surgery was required, and the closure and disposal of these now outmoded buildings presaged a move into the future. The changes made would influence the workings of the force until the end of its independent existence in 1967.

—oOo—

The latter part of 1933 saw the completion of the construction of the City Police force's new headquarters in Charles Street. With the depression affecting public spending, in September 1931 the Home Office made a formal request to the local authority to put a moratorium on the project, due to the prevailing financial climate. The City Council refused on the grounds that it was:

…absolutely necessary in view of the very unsatisfactory condition of the police quarters [at the Town Hall] and [they] are further of the opinion that delay is impossible owing to the fact that the completion of the alterations to the Town Hall, which are already in progress, is contingent upon the removal of the police department from the building.

Built by Messrs W. & H.

Horsefair Street, October or November 1935. The parade is led by Inspector Richard Braithwaite Willis, flanked on his left by Sergeant 33 'Jack' Shipman, and on his right by Sergeant 25 Frank Cross. The three identifiable officers marching behind Sergeant Cross are PCs 136 J.F. Chesterton, 62 Dick Burley and 106 Fred Marshall.

The annual inspection of the force on Victoria Park. The photograph can be dated to between 1937 and 1940. Prior to 1937 the chief constable wore a cocked hat, not the ornate helmet that Oswald Cole is wearing. The pavilion in the background was destroyed by a parachute mine in November 1940. (From 1937–39 government inspections of the force were carried out by Col J. de Coke.)

Foulds Ltd, of Eastern Boulevard, the building work and commissioning of the new headquarters in Charles Street was completed in September 1933 at a cost of £49,441. The three-storey façade looking out across Charles Street, 18 inches thick and faced with gleaming Portland stone, was broken in the middle by high wrought-iron gates closing off the imposing archway leading through into the main drill yard. Looking at the front of the building, the left-hand wing accommodated the parade room and offices for sergeants, inspectors and operational staff. To the right of the archway on the ground floor was the public enquiry office, with the charge office and cell block at the rear. The first floor was occupied by the administration offices, detective department, chief constable's suite, and the Watch Committee chamber.

A system of lights and bells mounted along corridor walls could be employed from the

telephone switchboard to page the various members of staff around the complex.[4] An effective internal telephone system was not installed until several years later.

Almost 16 months to the day after the foundation stone was laid by Alderman W.J. Lovell, with the work and commissioning completed, the opening ceremony was held on 4 September 1933.

Following a luncheon given at the Lord Mayor's rooms in New Walk, the honoured guests – who included His Majesty's Inspector of Constabulary, Major General Sir Llewellyn Atcherley, a bevy of chief constables and politicians from around the region and members of the Leicester City Council and its appointed officers – were taken to the new police headquarters. There in the parade room, promptly at a quarter to three, the Right Honourable Douglas Hacking, Parliamentary Under Secretary of State, declared the building

[4] This system, although not often used, remained in situ until the 1960s.

Leicester City Police football team, December 1937–April 1938, taken outside the charge office in the Charles Street yard. From left to right, back row: A. Collins, C. Smith, W. Peberdy, D. Snape, J. Pomfret, A.W. Read, R. Eadie. Middle row: D. Fraser, F. Smith, F. Sawford, A. Taylor, F. Wright, J.W. May, A. Moore, L. Norman, R. Onions. Front row: Sgt G.H. Smith, C. Bleackley, A. Ch. Cons J. Gabbitas, Ch. Cons. O.J.B. Cole, Sgt B. Ecob, D. Carstairs, C. Clements. Seated cross legged: S.F. Smith, J. Todd.

Two of the officers pictured were later killed during the war. Det. Cons. (later Det. Sgt) 109 Leonard Norman died in November 1940 in a bombing raid on the city. PC 72 Charles Bleackley was killed in late 1941 while serving as a sergeant in the RAF.

open. After the speech making and the presentation to Mr Hacking of a silver cigarette box as a memento of the occasion, Charles Street police station was opened to the public.

During this period of reorganisation O.J.B. Cole also took time out to make adjustments to his own position within the framework of things. During the interim period between the end of Herbert Allen's tenure and the appointment of Cole, the force had been managed by Superintendent Dugard Robertson, whose policing experience extended back to the 1900s. Nine months after taking office, Cole, in need of a lieutenant, persuaded the Home Office to appoint Robertson as deputy chief constable, with the continuing rank of superintendent. (A previous application to upgrade the position to chief superintendent had been refused).

At the same time, in August 1929, he engaged in the role of 'short-hand typist' Margaret Nowell Atter, at an annual salary of £130. In doing this he

established a new and powerful institution within the organisation. 'Miss Atter' as she was always known, was the first 'chief constable's secretary'. In just over three years, by December 1933, 'due to the nature of her work', Margaret Atter's salary had risen to £182 10s 0d a year, which was marginally less than the wage of an experienced constable, who could expect to draw around four pounds a week.[5] Miss Atter remained as chief constable's secretary and civilian administrative assistant for the next 30 years, until ill health forced her retirement in June 1959.

In May 1932 the chief constable and the head of the detective department, Superintendent Joseph Boon, made a visit to the West Riding police headquarters at Wakefield. The purpose of the trip was to appraise the Yorkshire force's photographic and fingerprint facilities.

As a result of their findings, an in-house studio department was established as an adjunct to the detective department.[6] Detective Constable 174 (later inspector) Eric Pym, who had recently passed the promotion examination to sergeant with some distinction, was sent away to Wakefield on a five week training course in fingerprinting and photography.

On his return with a shopping list in September 1932 the following items were purchased and the studio department was created:

1 Kodak View camera with wide angle lens	
two stands and two special shutters	£3 16s 6d
1 Developing tank and loading fixture	£5 18s 6d
1 Filter	15s 0d
1 Sashalite outfit for flashlight photographs	£2 5s 0d
Dusting powder and brushes etc.	£1 0s 0d

[5] It is obvious that her role was never intended to be solely a short-hand typist. Other civilian salaries in 1929 do not compare:- J. Coleman, the storekeeper, earned 55s a week, while the station charwoman was paid 12s a week for two hours a day – equivalent to 1s 0d an hour.
[6] Although such departments were usually referred to by other forces as the 'scenes of crime department', in Leicester it remained 'the studio' throughout its existence.

PC 104 Frederick John Staniforth (December 1922–January 1948).

Superintendent Shirley Arthur Wicks. The photograph was taken between March 1939 and the retirement of Superintendent Wicks just after the war, and gives rare close-up view of the ornate collar insignia worn by superintendents before open-neck tunics were adopted.

These were augmented 10 months later by the purchase, for £20, of a second-hand 'auto-focus' enlarger (a new one being £45), to be used for enlarging fingerprints, as 'presently the work is being done by an outside photographer at a high cost'.

A section of the organisation which had been allowed to fall into decline during the recent years was the special constabulary. Since the last shift of wartime specials had paraded at the town hall in January 1919, little call had been made on their services and few accounts of their numbers maintained.

Following the annual inspection of the force in 1932, when a total of 33 special constables paraded, it was decided that a review was overdue. By December it had been ascertained that '…due to the lack of records, the state of the Special Constabulary is not now clear…not many of them respond to calls for duty when required'. A survey of the 170 whose names remained on the active list revealed that 81 of them were over 60 years of age,

and had no further interest, while 71 (most of whom had been special constables during the war), still wished to continue in the role.

With a view to reorganising the Special Constabulary as an operational part of the force it was proposed that:

All those under 60 who wished to remain, should be re-sworn under the Special Constables Order 1923.

As the special constables at present only have an armband, they should also be issued with a cap.

A letter of thanks for their previous services be sent to those who are discontinuing.

Those who qualify should be given their long service medal.

Recruiting of more special constables should be commenced.

Class of probationary constables photographed in December 1937. From left to right, back row: PC 285 W.J. Urquhart, PC 286 F.D. Watson, PC 43 G.H.W. Bestwick, PC F.K. Llewellyn, PC 284 S. Smith, PC 281 G. Lott, PC 65 W.D. Barlow. Front row: PC 279 A. Storey, PC 172 J. Briggs, PC 262 J.H. Chambers, PC 283 T.F. Sandall, PC 289 W.A. Roberts.

It cannot be coincidental that this renewed interest in the state of the special constabulary was evinced at a time of particular hardship in the country at large. Only six short years had elapsed since the General Strike of 1926. The world-wide depression of the 1930s was rendering more and more men jobless. An all-time high in the unemployment figures equated with a distinct possibility of civil unrest, and the need for extra vigilance on the part of the authorities.

A typical example of the commercial difficulties in the town is shown in a letter sent to the chairman of the Watch Committee, Alderman Lovell, by a group of men who felt that the provisions of the law were being unfairly applied to them in the course of their attempting to gain a living.

17 Fayrhurst Road,
Leicester.
Nov 21 1932
Sir,

We the undersigned desire on behalf of the Street Traders Association, to register protest against the restrictions imposed on men selling from hand trucks in Leicester.

Most of us are men with wives and families and we are only trying to get an honest living.

We have little chance in these days of getting a livelihood by regular employment.

We do not want to defy the Law and the Police and all that we ask is to have an opportunity of discussing the matter with the Watch Committee so that we can put our point of view.

If you could arrange for the Watch Committee to receive a deputation we should be greatly obliged.

We are Sir,
Yours faithfully,
S.P.Lewitt, Chairman
W.Bailey
A.Ford

The request for a meeting, lying on the table next to a minute from the owners and occupiers of business premises in Cheapside and Silver Street asking the police to enforce the law in such hard times for all, could not be acceded to.

Many men unable to obtain work in other parts of the country sought jobs in Leicester, particularly in the police force. Between September 1929 and October 1935, of a total of

104 new recruits to the Leicester City Police force, 83 were from other parts of the country, from areas as far apart as Scotland and Somerset, Wales and Scarborough.

While the men of the police were considered to be relatively safe in their employment, they also were the subject of government constraints. In September 1931, along with other economies, the government reduced police pay in the forthcoming year by six and a quarter per cent, with a further cut of the same amount in the following year. This meant that by the end of 1933, police pay nationally would be reduced by 12½ per cent. (Although the Government proposals were projected into 1933 the cuts, at varying levels, continued beyond that. During the summer of 1934, as a result of pressure from both the police federation and various local authorities, the adjustment was brought down from 10 per cent to five. Pay was not restored to it's full level until July 1935.)

There was a small respite to the financial

Class of probationary constables photographed in December 1937. From left to right, back row: PC 212 H.J. Snell, PC 248 J.F. Sutton, PC 165 A.J. Pomfret, PC 106 A.W. Easson, PC 151 R. Pert, PC 246 M.J. Woolley, PC 72 C.J. Bleackley. Front row: PC 77 J. Cassie, PC 56 R.H. Aldridge, PC 143 H. Green, PC 258 J. Todd, PC 262 A. Sharpe.

Class of probationary constables photographed in March 1935. From left to right, back row: PC 250 S.T. Branson, PC 224 A.E. Sheard, PC 245 W.R. Beaumont, PC 247 J.E. Norris, PC 246 J. Artless, PC 171 M. Davie. Front row: PC 248 W.G. Hamilton, PC 96 N. Pickles, PC 64 S. Berry, PC 249 W.F. Gee.

hardship which these subtractions made when in May 1933 pay scales moved up marginally to allow a new entrant to the force to receive 62s 0d

Led by Inspector Lancelot Shepherdson, this contingent of City Police officers, photographed in February 1936, is part of a parade celebrating the force's 100th anniversary.

a week instead of 55s 0d – the eventual pay scale rising after 12 years service to 90s 0d.

—oOo—

The enactment of the Children and Young Persons Act in October 1933 was to be of particular importance as far as the police service

throughout the country was concerned. The Act aimed to safeguard the well-being of children from a very young age until they became adults. In reality, from this point onward there was a particular function within the police service for female officers. While the role of the policewoman has never been constrained to this relatively narrow field, the 1933 Act focussed upon an area which made the widespread employment of female officers inevitable.

A corollary to the Act was that certain obligations within local government departments were subject to change. Among these were the provisions relating to the responsibility for the long-term detention of young offenders.

The institution with which the Leicester City Police were primarily concerned was the boys detention home at 134 Highcross Street. Under an agreement with the owner, Mrs Bramley, signed in 1916, the County Council paid half of the rent and upkeep, plus £155 10s 0d for adapting the

New Walk box, situated at the town end of New Walk near to Welford Place, sandbagged against bomb blast and flying debris. The site was later cleared as part of the construction for the New Walk Centre.

premises. In 1933 a flat rate of 10s for the first day and 3s for each subsequent day of a boy's detention was being paid. The original superintendent, Gilbert Ellwood, left late in 1927, following a dispute with the local authority, and thereafter staffing and supervision of the home was an obligation of the chief constable and Watch Committee. In July 1932 the superintendent of the home, ex-constable Charles Turner, had resigned, and the post passed to another latter-day policeman, George Sidney Windmill. Windmill, having been a constable prior to 1914, had lost an eye in the war and after rejoining the force following the Armistice, had been forced to retire when it was found that he was suffering from tuberculosis. Described as 'having now fallen upon very hard times', he was pleased to accept the job along with a salary of £25 a year and accommodation.

There is little doubt that the opportunity, under the new provisions, to pass the responsibility for this particular establishment over to F.P. Armitage, the director of education, was one which was welcomed.

—oOo—

An extension to the city boundaries in April 1935 proved the efficacy of the existing policing system. While the boundary changes prompted a major reassessment of policing needs, any readjustment was relatively easy to achieve.

By including in the city the parishes of Evington, Humberstone, Thurmaston, Birstall, Beaumont Leys, Gilroes, New Parks, Braunstone and Lubbesthorpe, the policing area was increased by 8,397 acres and 19,552 residents. Some of the newly acquired areas, such as Evington and Humberstone villages, Gilroes, New Parks and Braunstone Estate, were suitable for a resident constable. The case for a resident man was actually slightly biased insomuch as it was felt that '…the resident constable will be able during off

duty periods to attend emergencies which may occur on his area thus obviating the need to despatch a vehicle from headquarters'.

Inevitably, such changes would involve cost. Resident officers would require houses to live in. From the outset it was agreed that property should be bought rather than rented. (In much later years, during the 1980s when the preference of most officers was for home ownership, this policy led to the police authority having to dispose of a large number of these houses.) A decision was taken that it was essential that the police houses should be on or near to main roads or at particular points (such as in the middle of housing estates), bearing in mind the area being policed.

Some properties were readily available. A house previously within the domain of the county authority at 58 St Peter's Drive in Humberstone was deemed to be suitable for a city inspector. The premises at 5 Waltham Avenue, Braunstone were transferred to the city to be occupied by a constable. Other suitable properties were then sought in various parts of the city.

Most importantly, the remainder of the districts were well suited to an extension of the box system. For instance, it was felt that the newly-acquired Saffron Lane housing estate could be dealt with quite adequately by installing a police box on Saffron Lane near to Stonesby Avenue.

With the enlargement of the force's responsibility came the obvious need to seek from the Home Office an increase in manpower. For supervision purposes, two areas of the city – one to the extreme east and one to the extreme west – required the presence of a resident inspector assisted by a sergeant. Posts for two extra uniformed sergeants and one detective sergeant were applied for. A new post for a full-time constable as a coroner's officer was also created.

Loath to miss a golden opportunity, the senior

officers of the force presented a memorandum to the local authority, reminding them that more responsibility equates with higher remuneration. Under the terms of the Desborough Report the inspectors and superintendents had for some time been entitled, by virtue of the city's population being in excess of 200,000, to an increase in pay. An inspector's starting salary moved up from £310 to £320, and a superintendent's from £400 to £450.

—oOo—

Fifteen months later, in July 1936, by superimposing the 'on-call system' on to the existing method of working beats from police boxes, a final pre-war refinement was possible.

There were at that time 42 telephone lines out from the police headquarters switchboard to the various police boxes. With the expansion of the city limits it was obvious that further telephone points were going to be necessary. However, erecting more police boxes would involve unnecessary expenditure when all that was needed were 'speaking points'.

Coincidentally, an offer came from the GPO (General Post Office) to install an on-street 'Police Telephone and Signal System' (the on-call system), which had already been adopted by 40 other police authorities up and down the country. The system was primarily aimed at making the use of a police telephone by the public much easier. A telephone 'post' with a light on the top was installed at various locations 'on-street'. The simple process of opening a flap and lifting the handset established a direct line to the police station switchboard. An added attraction from the police perspective was that the GPO would install a new switchboard at Charles Street headquarters, and also a number of new internal lines within the headquarters building. As for cost, including the installation of the new call points, the proposed system was, at £893, £242 per

year more expensive than the existing one, but with great advantages.

War Years

The middle years of the 1930s represented a busy time for the police in England and Wales, nowhere more so than in Leicester.

February 1936 saw the centenary celebrations of the force's inauguration. The chief constable had sent a Christmas card to all members of the force, the Watch Committee, magistrates and councillors, and the main festivities commenced on the ninth day of the February, with a parade of officers through the town centre followed by a commemorative service held at the cathedral in St Martin's, which was attended by the Lord Mayor and members of the City Council. For the evenings of the 10 and 11 February, Lancaster Hall was hired and celebratory dinners given. All members of the force were invited, along with the high court recorder, Mr P.E. Sandlands, and Watch Committee members. In addition to the meal the evening's entertainments included policemen dressed in period costume from the 1800s and music played by the City Police orchestra.

Two months later, in mid-May, Charles Street police station was decked out – at a cost of £15 – with bunting and flags for the silver jubilee of King George V and Queen Mary. Seventeen officers, including the chief constable and three superintendents, were presented with Jubilee Medals by Alderman Wilford in a ceremony at the Granby Halls on Wednesday 8 May, and a contingent comprising an inspector, one sergeant and 21 constables was despatched to represent the force at a national review in Hyde Park.

A sad footnote to this event is that the following year one inspector from each police force in the country was sent to London to constitute a police representation at the old king's funeral.

Having served as a police officer in Bristol during the war years, Winifred Hope Winter joined Leicester City Police as W. Sgt 1 in June 1944. She left the force to marry in April 1946. Unlike her male counterparts, she wore an open-neck tunic, with the king's crown and insignia on her shoulder in place of a warrant number.   *(Courtesy J. Joiner)*

which unlike its contemporary at Birmingham was to remain a minor player in the world of aviation, Leicester now had its own aerodrome. A snapshot of the cost of living at this time is provided by the police catering arrangements. It was decided that each man should be allowed 1s 6d 'meal allowance' for the day, and that the police would supply everyone with a cold main meal, which would add an extra £7 10s to the overall budget.

It was during 1935 that one of the first really important technological innovations of the 20th century was taken on board by the police. The Home Office – and consequently chief officers of police – were now beginning to appreciate the potential

Small enamelled lapel badge worn by special constables at a time when uniforms were at a premium.
(Courtesy N. Haines)

benefits of wireless communication.[7] In the Midlands region, Nottingham Police were at the forefront of wireless technology, having established a transmitting station of their own. Thus Nottingham was the logical venue for an exploratory seminar, attended by O.J.B. Cole and 13 other chief constables, on 1 July 1935. The interests of the Home Office were represented by His Majesty's Inspector of Constabulary Major-General Sir Llewellyn Atcherley. The work already carried out by Nottingham was discussed at length and General Atcherley impressed upon the gathering

...the extreme desirability of wireless being introduced into Police Forces as soon as was practicable... although it could not admittedly be foreseen to what effective use the system might be put yet, it was felt that a beginning must be made, even if it was only of an experimental nature[8].

With the opening of the new municipal aerodrome in July 1935, 60 men from the city force were sent out assist county officers dealing with the traffic and controlling the eager sightseers who swarmed to Stoughton to witness the event. Although it was a very small airfield,

---

[7] In 1932, in the US, the New York Police Department pioneered the use of radio patrol cars with messages received and transmitted in morse code.
[8] Robert Mark, who as a Special Branch officer worked with Atcherley during the early part of the war, described him as, 'a dear old man, the father of the RAF's famous flying twins'.

The Police Auxiliary Messenger Service was established early in the war, soon after the Battle of Britain. members of this organisation were usually young men who were not old enough to fight. The uniform initially consisted of a boiler suit with a white lanyard and steel helmet. Pictured outside Charles Street police station, the contingent is marching in the old style of 'four abreast', which was later replaced in all branches of the force by 'three abreast'. Marching in the foreground is Messenger No.4 Clifford Wilfrid Robinson, who left shortly after this picture was taken to serve in the Royal Navy. After demobilisation in 1946 Cliff Robinson joined the Leicester City Police as PC 152.
(Courtesy C. Robinson)

A regional area made up of Lincolnshire, Rutland, Northampton, Leicester, Derby and Nottingham was agreed upon. Leicester's financial contribution to the scheme was set at £200 per annum. Radio sets for vehicles would be supplied by the Nottingham Police at £200 each, while a teleprinter was installed at Charles Street police headquarters at a cost of £275 a year, in order that messages could be passed to the Nottingham control room for re-transmission by wireless.[9]

Twelve months later, in July 1936, Cole was able to state that, 'during the past three weeks experiments have been made with the Philco

Wireless receiver which has been fitted to an Austin 10 patrol car by the chief officer of the Fire Service. Very clear audible speech has been received as far south as Northampton'. A further two Philco radios were purchased forthwith for £20 each. In May 1938 two vehicles – a Morris 12hp (costing £215), and a Wolseley 12hp, were purchased specifically to be used as wireless patrol cars. During the winter of 1938 a regular radio patrol vehicle was put into operation, crewed during the day by two uniformed constables and after dark by plain clothes officers.

It was not until February 1942 that, sharing a

[9]Earliest radio transmissions in the Region were by Morse Code.

PC 166 Jim Muir engaged on switchboard duties at Charles Street police station.

transmitter based at Lancaster Place, the City police and fire services moved to the use of a VHF radio band. The new equipment cost £1,000, of which the police authority bore half. In April 1946, the City and County Police forces became, along with Rutland, Northamptonshire, and Peterborough, part of the No.5 Area Regional Wireless System.

Since the beginning of the decade, the populace of Leicester had become quite accustomed to the sight of policemen riding motor cycles and patrolling in tiny MG sports cars. The Road Traffic Act of 1934 imposed for the first time a speed limit of 30 miles per hour within the city. In 1935 a system of unilateral waiting was implemented in the city centre, to deal with what was, at the time, considered to be major traffic congestion. The regulations were brought into force in Belvoir Street, Halford Street and Churchgate, and during the 10 months between August 1935 and June 1936 a grand total of 334 motorists were reported for contraventions. In real terms, this amounts to an average of between eight and nine motorists dealt with per week in the entire city centre. The restrictions were extended in late 1936 to include other parts of the town, with the comment that

> …the congestion in Gallowtree Gate is caused primarily by motorists leaving their cars for an undue length of time while shopping, and when both sides of the roadway are lined with parked cars, it is impossible to clear traffic away quickly owing to the frequent passage of tramcars in the space remaining…

At the same time, Cole, who was involved with the National Safety First Association, started to post figures of road traffic accident casualties in the windows of police boxes as part of an early road safety campaign.

By the mid-1930s it was becoming apparent that the transport accommodation at Woodboy Street was both physically inadequate and geographically unsuitable. Since 1930 the vehicle fleet had expanded to include an emergency van, a prison van, two cars for the detective department, and a further two cars for road patrol work.

Two houses, 48 and 50 Colton Street, at the rear of the police headquarters, came up for sale in late 1935. Standing on a piece of land, 264 yards square, the site was admirably suited for the building of a garage annexe and gymnasium. The owner of the property, Mr J.H. King, was approached and the site purchased for a total of £1,200 in March 1936. The proviso was also made that on completion of the work, Woodboy Street should be put up for auction with a reserve price of £1,000.

There is a popular misconception that despite the events taking place in Europe during the early part of the decade, Great Britain, in September 1939, entered into a state of war with Germany totally unprepared, and generally overtaken by, circumstances beyond her control. It is true to say that the implications of happenings during the early years of the rise of National Socialism and

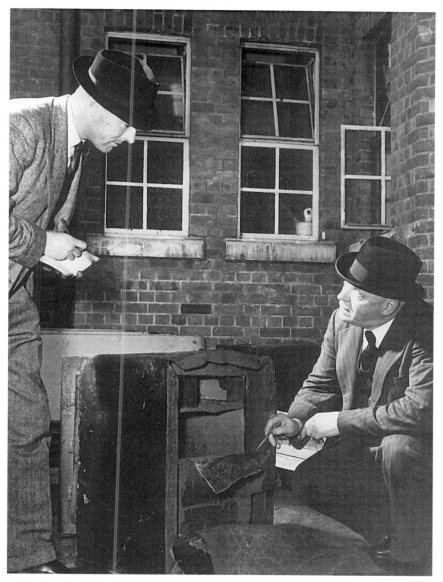

Detective Inspector Douglas McMurdo and Superintendent Harry Ashburner, in the yard at Charles Street police station, examining a safe which has been broken open.

In spring 1936, a full three and a half years before the outbreak of war, police officers were being trained at the Home Office (Air Raid Precautions Department), training school at Gloucester. In May Inspector Harold Poole was the first city officer to attend a course at the centre, with a view to organising in-force training in war duties. He was later followed in 1938 by Sergeant Walter Broadhurst and Inspector Frederic Shelvey.

Inspector Shelvey was given a brief, in April 1938, to set up an air raid precautions department. Having attended a two week, 'anti-gas' course at Falfield in Gloucester, with the assistance of a constable – who worked as storekeeper – Frederic Shelvey began the task of training the huge number of air raid wardens who were soon to be required. Shelvey was later joined by Sergeant Bernard Ecob, who in February 1939 attended a 17-day course at the civilian air raid precautions school at Easingwold in Yorkshire.

Hitler's Third Reich were often underestimated and to an extent ignored. Working to the old adage of, 'storm in the Channel – Europe cut off!', there was a deal of disassociation by many sections of British society with Hitler's activities. However, at government level there was recognition of what was happening and the inescapable consequences for Great Britain at a relatively early stage.

The activities of Sir Oswald Mosley were also causing concern among the establishment. Oswald Ernald Mosley, born in 1896, had become

Photographed in September 1939, Leicester City Police headquarters is protected from bomb blast by 35,000 sandbags. Due to the excessive weight of this amount of sand, the pavement later collapsed and the sandbags had to be replaced with bricks.

government response to Mosley's activities was swift and positive. On 1 January 1936 the Public Order Act of that year imposed strict controls on political organizations and potential public disruption. It became an offence to wear uniforms relating to political affiliations in public, or to train any quasi-military organisation. The use of threatening behaviour or carrying of an offensive weapon in a public place became an immediately arrestable offence. Marches in public places required the specific consent of the local chief of police. At a stroke, police powers to deal with public order were codified and dramatically strengthened.

—oOo—

In April 1938 an increase in police numbers of one inspector (on the loss of one sergeants position) and 23 constables was granted by the Home Office. Additionally, the employment of a civilian to deal with garage maintenance released a further police officer. The response by men eager to fill the 23 newly-created vacancies was immediate. At the end of the first week of May a class of 12 men was receiving in-force training at Leicester, while a further six had been despatched to Birmingham on a 10-week induction course, at

versed in military lore at Sandhurst prior to serving in the Royal Flying Corps during World War One. Between 1918 and 1931 he held a seat at Westminster, first as a conservative, later as an independent and finally as a member of the Labour Party. Politically a loose cannon, in 1931 Mosley eschewed conventional politics and the following year formed the Union of British Fascists. Emulating Hitler's brownshirts, the British fascists affected a quasi-military uniform, and by means of ostentatious marches and general disruption attempted to preach the gospel of mobocracy. The general reaction throughout a country beset by unemployment and insecurity to Mosley's 'blackshirts' – as they liked to be known – was extreme, and wherever they went violence and civil disorder accompanied them.

Predictably, in the existing political climate,

Cell block at Charles Street police station. The figure in the background is Sergeant 16 Thomas Tallon.

Inspector Frederick George Shelvey (December 1928–October 1954).

a cost to the local authority of £10 per man. The overall training situation, with an increase in manpower and resources being diverted to preparations for war, became critical over the next 12 months. In September 1939, ex-superintendent Arthur (Gunner) Hall, who had retired six months previously, was recalled in order to redress the problem and organise an in-force training programme.

In 1920 the Home Office, drawing upon lessons learnt during World War One, had drawn up a set of guidelines for the creation of the First Police Reserve, to be employed in times of national emergency. It was envisaged that a small cadre of retired police officers would be employed as auxiliary policemen. Retired members of police forces and fire brigades were not eligible to join

PC 79 Cato, pictured in the sandbagged yard of Charles Street police station.

t h e

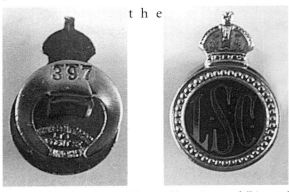

Lapel badges worn by special constables prior to a full issue of uniform becoming available.

Prepared for an air raid, PC 167 'Pat' Collins on point duty in the city centre. The legend on the box on which he is standing read 'Pedestrians wait for the Policeman's signal'.

newly-constituted Royal Defence Corps (the Local Defence Volunteers, later the 'Home Guard'), whose ranks were generally made up of men over 45 years of age or otherwise ineligible for military service. As the purpose of this particular corps was solely one of guard duties in time of war, it was felt that with their previous training, police and firemen possessed skills which could be better utilised.

In the early summer of 1936 Cole formed a unit of retired City Police officers. The 18 men were paid an annual retainer of £3, with the proviso that if called upon they would each be paid a wage equivalent to the lowest rate applicable to the rank which they had held on retirement.

It is perhaps relevant at this point to clarify the difference between the various voluntary police organisations which were in being, or planned.

The Special Constabulary was a long standing body of men who voluntarily performed unpaid duties as police officers in times of both peace and war.

The First Police Reserve was made up of police pensioners who undertook to serve as temporary police officers in times of emergency, whether during peacetime or wartime.

The Police War Reserve was to be a new auxiliary force, previously confined to the Metropolitan and City of London Police, formed with a view to providing full-time constables in time of war.

A Women's Auxiliary Police Corps was also formed, which was different and separate from the women's section of the police. Open to women between the ages of 18 and 55, this was an unpaid ancillary organisation with no police powers. The outdoor uniform was a blue peaked cap and belted rain coat, with an armlet or badge bearing the monogram 'WAPC' – a blue cotton overall with the same badge was worn indoors. Women who volunteered for this unit were employed driving and maintaining vehicles or working as telephonists and wireless operators. Those with other skills were engaged as clerical or canteen staff. Strictly regulated by the Home Office, no police force could recruit numbers to this corps which exceeded 10 per cent of its regular establishment. Although basically unpaid, there was a proviso that where a member of the WAPC was for any reason employed full-time, she could be remunerated at the rate of 40s per week.

Strenuous efforts were now being made to re-build the much-depleted Special Constabulary. Under the aegis of John Gabbitas, the deputy chief constable, by February 1937 150 new men had been recruited. Initially they were issued with a cap and buttonhole badge, a whistle and an instruction book. Later on, during 1938, great coats and jackets, along with trousers, gave the specials a complete set of uniform. At the beginning of April 1939 their ranks had been expanded to 314 men, with a regular inspector as their training officer. Additionally, 33 special

Special constables parading on the Cattle Market for the inspection of the force by His Majesty's Inspector of Constabulary, June 1945.

A view along bomb-damaged Charles Street during World War Two.

constables had volunteered to transfer to the Police War Reserve when the time came. In his Annual Report for 1939, published at the beginning of 1940, Cole stated that the Special Constabulary strength, split between six police stations, stood at: 6 inspectors, 22 sergeants and 432 constables. Of these, 310 had been issued with full uniform, while the remainder wore 'part uniform'.

At this stage of the war, the specials performed three hours of duty per week. Additionally, 200 of them worked an extra hour's duty once a week during the evenings.

Inevitably, different institutions were simultaneously competing for manpower. In addition to appeals for air raid wardens and Local

Defence Volunteers, the City Fire Brigade, as part of its fire precautions scheme, was endeavouring to obtain 1,250 auxiliary firemen. One of the difficulties under which all of those concerned laboured was that armed forces reservists and members of the Territorial Army and the Auxiliary Air Force were ineligible to join any of their causes.

As the summer of 1939 passed and war became imminent, the police headquarters itself needed to be rendered capable of withstanding enemy attack. Buildings needed to be made gas proof. Shower facilities costing £36 were built into the toilet area on the ground floor, for the benefit of men coming off of gas duty. Storage space for

Members of the Leicester City Police administration department, 1955. From left to right, back row: PC 175 Griffin, -?-, PC 135 Clarke, PC 142 Curtis, PC 250 Tebbutt, PC 229 Watchorn, PC 158 G. Smith, PC 176 Warrington, PC 224 Gordon, PC 239 Small, PC 161 Knight, PC 174 Morris. Middle row: PC 271 F. Walker, PC 187 Petcher, PC 146 Freear, PC 145 Welbourne, PC 179 Wolfe, PC 117 D. Smith, PC 100 Ditchfield, PC 234 Wright, PC 206 Hoy, PC 156 W. Gatward, -?-. Front row: Sgt 16 Aldridge, Sgt 4 H. Smith, Sgt 42 Goodman, Sgt 36 S.F. Smith, Insp. S.T. Branson, Supt T.P. Woolley, Ch. Cons O.J.B. Cole, Insp. J. Edwards, Insp. R. McCrory, Sgt 33 Broughton, Sgt 9 M. Woolley, Sgt 48 Walker, Sgt 7 Boyles.

protective clothing, respirators and air raid protection equipment was built on the flat roof of the main building. Protective steel shoring and steel window shutters were erected at a cost of £2,000. A further four exchange and eight new internal telephone lines were installed to accommodate the increased communications traffic that a war situation would engender. Five months before the declaration of war, direct telephone lines were laid between the police headquarters and the town hall, fire brigade headquarters, and the seven designated air raid warden's reporting stations.

The police stores were stocked with 25 'navvy' shovels and picks, bought from John Adams, a local ironmonger's, at 3s 10d and 3s 4d respectively, along with a batch of steel crowbars for lifting and removing fallen masonry and rubble. Seventy-five first aid haversacks were distributed around the police boxes.

A grateful thanks to the chief constable was noted from the Women's Voluntary Services for civil defence, for allowing them to purchase, for £5, a Morris Isis car which was of no further use to the constabulary.

Early in 1939 the Home Office, along with the other relevant departments, began to implement contingency plans for the safety of all public buildings falling within its remit.

In excess of 80,000 sandbags were allocated to the Leicester City Police force. Arthur Gooseman, the city surveyor, calculated that 35,000 of these would be required to sandbag the Charles Street headquarters complex. A further 50,000 would be needed to protect the city's police boxes. In July the waste land opposite the police station[10] was fenced off and 800 tons of sand, acquired from Sherriff's builders for £118, was deposited. The problem remained of how to transfer the sand into the bags and then move the bags to their designated place.

Originally the city surveyor was of the opinion that his workmen could perform the task. This was soon proven to be impracticable, given

[10] Later to be made into a traffic island.

Senior officers of the Special Constabulary c.1953. Special Commandant Andrew Philip Dugald Michael is in the centre of the front row.

the scale of the operation and the fact that he had responsibility for a large number of other similar public buildings. With the purchase of two sandbag fillers from a firm in Northampton, the problem was readily solved. An enthralled public were treated to the daily sight of a host of off-duty policemen in vests and braces, labouring in the summer sun to dispose of the bagged materials. Between 25 August and 1 September almost every constable and sergeant on the force spent their spare time (at a rate of 2s an hour for sergeants and 1s 6d for constables), filling bags and shifting sand. Having paid £50 for an additional 5,000 sandbags and £150 for police overtime, the end

result was achieved at a cost to the corporation of £200. Unfortunately, 14 months later, due to the weight imposed on the surrounding footways, the pavements started to collapse. All of the sandbags had to be removed at a cost of £130 and replaced with £750 worth of old bricks.

The Military Training and the Reserve and Military Services Acts of 1939 made various provisions in relation to reservists being recalled to the colours and to men who were called up into HM Forces. By virtue of these pieces of legislation,[11] any police officer serving at the outbreak of war, who was recalled as a reservist, would be deemed to be absent on leave. This

[11] Military Training (Consequential Provisions) Order, 1939.

meant that the relevant police authority could pay to him or his dependents the difference between his service pay and his salary as a constable. Also such an officer's time spent in the military would count as pensionable for police purposes.[12]

As an additional wartime measure, a unit of the First Police Reserve was initiated. This varied in numbers over a period of time. In 1936 it counted 18 members, in 1937, 21 and in 1938, 26. Wages for this unit appear to have equated roughly with those of the regular force. In September 1940, a PC's salary was between 70s and 72s a week, while a sergeant was paid £4 10s 0d. When the Home Office released special constables and war reserves from the prohibition to resign in July 1945, Leicester City Police had only two first reserve officers remaining – PC 22 Herbert Allcott and PC 11 Samuel Nichols.

The Police War Reserve establishment for Leicester City was, in June 1940, set at 187 men. At that time their wages as a constable were 64s a week plus 6s proficiency bonus after six months. This went up to 74s a week in 1942. The highest number of War Reserves attached to the force was 122 in 1941. Thereafter the strength varied from 96 in 1942 to 53 at the end of the war in 1945. In June 1947, only two of their number were still serving with the force when the Government declared that those men who had served in the Police War Reserve should be allowed to join the regular force, even if they were over the age limit of 30. Of the remaining two, only one elected to become a regular officer. Joining as PC 183, Charlie Downes was still a serving officer in 1967.

Leicester City Police, for whatever reason, do not appear to have fully exploited the facility during the war to enlist candidates for the Women's Auxiliary Police Corps.

Under the Government guidelines a unit of up to 10 per cent of the total force could be established, of which only those in full-time employment by the police authority were entitled

PC 259 Jack Briars on point duty in the mid-1940s.

to payment. This concessionary payment commenced in 1940 at £2 per week, and increased by 1942 to £2 12s 0d. In May 1940 the chief constable was given permission to engage 14 women as part of the corps to work as telephonists. They were to constitute the majority of the staff of the police duty room, which in readiness for air raids was manned on a 24-hour basis. The Auxiliary Corps personnel filled two shifts, while the third was made up of clerical workers taken from the Charles Street staff. These numbers of paid operators were scaled down over a period of time. In 1941 they had been reduced to five, and at the end of the war in 1945 only two remained.[13]

---

[12] This virtually mirrored the provisions made for constables away with the colours during World War One.

[13] A further four telephones were installed at the deputy police HQ at the town hall, which was intended as a fall-back in case Charles Street was destroyed. This facility was removed in March 1941 to the first floor of the Newarke Girls' School.

Charles Street police station sandbagged in preparation for aerial attack.

In the aftermath of the Battle of Britain (August 1940), Leicester suffered a series of air raids. As a precaution against a breakdown in communications in the event of the police headquarters being bombed (the City Police were responsible for training and co-ordinating the ARP service), the Police Auxiliary Messenger Service (PAMS)was formed late in 1940. Members of this group were primarily young men who were under age for, or exempt from, service in HM Forces.

Initially a volunteer organisation, in February 1941 the group was put onto a paid basis. Wages for those messengers employed full-time (as opposed to volunteers) varied according to age. A young lad under 17 was paid 23s a week,

thereafter a scale rose (after December 1941) to 70s a week for those over 20 years of age.[14] The uniform for this service comprised a set of overalls and a tin hat. For protection against adverse weather conditions they were supplied later in the war with capes from the special constables' stores.

One of the earliest members of the PAMS, prior to his joining the Royal Navy, was Clifford Robinson. After demobilisation from the services in July 1946, Cliff Robinson returned to join the Leicester City Police and, having served in the uniform and detective branches, was a patrol inspector by the time the force was amalgamated in April 1967.

It is worth noting that the PAMS was one of the

[14] The PAMS was a national service. A Watch Committee minute for December 1942, which gives the pay scales for full-time employees, carries the rider that 'in Leicester city we do not have anyone full time'. The implication is that until 1942–43, the service was conducted locally on a volunteer basis.

Det. Sgt 5 William 'Jock' Joiner came from Scotland to join the Leicester City Police in June 1935. He served in the CID during the war and was among the officers injured in the Highfields blast which killed three CID officers. In 1948 Sgt Joiner was involved in the arrest and trial of Josef Zawadski for the murder of Joan Henson. He was promoted to inspector in November 1958, and retired from the force in June 1965.

W. Sgt Hilda Mary Parkin with members of the policewomen's department, parading prior to the annual inspection of the force in 1953. (W. Sgt Parkin transferred to Leicester City Police from Halifax Borough Police in December 1951.)

forerunners of the Police Cadet Corps. When the PAMS was disbanded on 19 July 1945, Leicester City had 85 serving members, and 200 ex-members.[15] Apparently on the advice of the Home Office, it was decided that '…in it's place will be a Police Cadet Corp., open to youths between 16 and 20 yrs. They will be given training on one night per week in general education subjects, elements of police law, telephone switchboard, PT and Ju-Jitsu…'

One of the innovations introduced by the Home Office in the early months of 1940 was the combining together of police forces in geo-graphical areas to form 'regions' for the development of common functions.

It was proposed that in the East Midlands schemes should be established to co-ordinate forensic science work, the dissemination of criminal intelligence and the setting up of a more efficient wireless network.

The wireless and forensic science laboratory schemes were by this time already in place. With the criminal records offices at Wakefield and Scotland Yard acting as clearing houses for information, it was intended to open offices at Birmingham, Cardiff and Bristol.

—oOo—

As 1940 came to an end, the city became the subject of increased Luftwaffe attention. While the primary target in the area was the nearby city of Coventry, Leicester was by no means immune from attack.

Two daytime raids on 21 August, on the Cavendish Road and Gipsy Lane areas of the city, caused considerable damage. These were followed by a raid on 14 November, when a string of bombs dropped across the city.

---

[15]Responsibility for training and organisation of the PAMS was undertaken locally by Inspector Frederic Shelvey, and PC 186 Frank Brough, along with Special Sergeant Hector Jackson, and Special Constables Ward and Rogers.

The Special Constabulary Band was inaugurated in February 1945, with Special Inspector Anderson as band master. During the late 1940s and early 1950s the band entered and won various competitions throughout the region. It was dissolved at Easter in 1959.

The heaviest raid occurred on the night of Tuesday 19 November 1940. At about 7.30 in the evening bombers dropped flares over Leicester, soon to be followed by incendiaries which fell in the New Walk and South Albion Street area. Around 8 p.m. the initial wave of high-explosive bombs began to fall, the first of these hitting houses in Holmfield Road. One which failed to explode dropped through the roof of the town hall and lodged in the basement.

Soon after half past nine, the Highfields district was subjected to a particularly intense attack. Heavy bombs fell near to the junction of Highfield Street and Tichborne Street, causing extensive damage and killing 41 people. A bomb demolished the Sparkenhoe Street post office and killed two more, while explosions at Saxby Street, Sparkenhoe Street and Highfield Street accounted for a further 19 deaths.

Shortly after midnight a group of police officers who had been held at Charles Street police station in reserve were sent as reinforcements to the Highfields and Sparkenhoe Street area where the heavy bombing had occurred. About half past midnight, near to the junction of Sparkenhoe Street and Stoughton Street, a further explosion buried some of the men and injured others.

Detective Sergeant Leonard Thomas Norman and Detective Constable George Edwin Trump were killed outright by the blast. Detective Constable Brian Hawkes died a few hours later of his injuries. Detective Constable William 'Jock' Joiner was thrown some distance by the explosion and suffered severe shock. Constable 216 Horace 'Sandy' Burks was severely wounded by shrapnel.

One of the members of a mobile first aid unit which attended the scene, Miss Ivy Marsh, was later awarded a bravery certificate for the great

THE JOURNAL OF THE LEICESTER CITY POLICE FORCE

Vol. 2, No. 4   July 1948   Price 2d.

Typical advertisements for local firms carried in the Charles Street Clarion.

Continuing from an original news sheet which was distributed to men of the City Police away serving in the armed forces during World War Two, the Charles Street Clarion ran as the force magazine from March 1947 until October 1957. Selling for most of its existence at 2d a copy, it contained articles on many police-related subjects, as well as force sports news, home economics, gardening and short stories.

personal risks which she took in remaining with DC Hawkes and attempting to release him from fallen masonry.

For his part in the incident, the officer in charge at the scene, Inspector Jesse Weston, was later awarded the British Empire Medal.[16]

Two and a half years into the war, in May 1942, the reserved age limit for police officers was raised from 20 to 25 years, meaning that by August of that year 45 officers of the force would be liable for call-up. The manpower situation was now becoming critical. Although his establishment had been boosted by the addition of 96 War Reserve Officers, Cole had 56 regular police officers away in the armed forces. This was to rise to 70 the following year, while the War Reserve strength fell

[16] PC 'Sandy' Burks had been part of the original 'mobile patrol car' radio scheme as a morse code operator before the war. After several months sick leave due to his injuries, he returned to duties and retired in November 1950 having completed 25 years service. DC 'Jock' Joiner, who had joined the force in June 1935, retired from the force in 1965 as a patrol inspector. Inspector Jesse Weston, who was awarded the British Empire Medal for his part as officer in command at the scene, was already the holder of the Military Medal, awarded to him in World War One for attacking a machine gun post single-handed.

Members of the Leicester City Police force pictured outside Charles Street police station in December 1955.
(Courtesy N. Hull)

to 84. Although on a numbers basis the war reserves and special constables went a long way to redress the balance, the fact was that in wartime the calls upon the emergency services were such that it was still difficult for the force to fulfil its responsibilities. In 1939 the strength of the regular force was 312 men, but by 1944 it was 195.

During the summer of 1944 the Home Office circulated to chief constables the advice that, in areas where there was a concentration of British

In the years prior to 1967 every police force had its own distinctive type of helmet. Issued to PC 266 Hadley, this helmet shows the classic shape belonging to the Leicester City Police. (This particular helmet has a wicker work interior and may have been issued in 1938, or in the years immediately after 1945. *(Courtesy D. Chimley)*

A group of WPCs, photographed on the flat roof of Charles Street police station. From left to right: WPC Jean Valentine Garnett, W. Sgt Gwen Harvey, WPC Phyllis Edna Groom, WPC Joan Thirlby, WPC Jean Georgina Froude, WPC Mary Alice Borrett. *(Courtesy P. and J. Burt)*

and Allied servicemen, consideration should be given to increasing their establishment of policewomen, 'in order to deal with the problems caused by such concentrations…' The reasoning behind this bizarre advice is not given – nor apparently was it sought at the time. Oswald Cole informed the Watch Committee that in Leicester, the existing establishment of four women was

adequate. He would however look towards increasing the establishment of his Women's Auxiliary Police Corps by another two officers.

Cole's hand was, however, somewhat forced when, within weeks of the receipt of this circular, his only Woman Police Sergeant, Barbara Denis de Vitré, left the force on promotion to inspector in the Kent Police force. Having advertised for a replacement, the chief constable actually engaged two new supervisory officers. In June 1944, Women Police Sergeants Gwendoline Harvey, from Stoke-on-Trent, and Winifred Hope Winter, from Bristol, joined the Leicester City Police.

Post-war years

With the end of the war and an Allied victory in sight, in January 1945 Leicester, along with all of the other local authorities in the country, began to address the many questions raised by how to re-build the economy and its infra-structure once the war was ended.

The country was divided up into eight police districts, and district training centres were established. Leicester was in No.4 District.

Re-training courses for men returning from HM Forces began in the summer of 1945 at the

PC 102 Dick Markillie, photographed soon after joining the Leicester City Police in April 1953. Although Home Office approval was given in 1948 for police forces to wear the new style of open-neck tunic, availability of materials after the war meant that most forces continued to use the closed-neck seven-button tunic into the 1950s. (Courtesy W.R. Markillie)

Marching along Granville Road with the DeMontfort Hall in the background, this Battle of Britain day parade dates from 1952 or 1953. The contingent of policemen is passing (out of shot) the saluting point to the left of the picture. In the background the band of the Leicestershire Regiment is playing.

new district training centre at Ryton-on-Dunsmore in Warwickshire. The cost of an officer being billeted at the training centre was 30s a week per officer.

The first instructors from the Leicester City Police were Inspectors Clarence Kirkland and Frederic Shelvey, who had attended a six-week instructors training course in London.[17] Under its first commandant, Mr A. Bond, the chief constable of Rutland, training of new recruits for the different police forces in the district began at Ryton in November 1945.[18]

The centre remained at Ryton until 1948 when, due to the site being re-designated as the first police staff college, it was re-located to Mill Meece, near Cannock in Staffordshire. Training

for No.4 District remained at Mill Meece until late 1961, when it returned to Ryton.

One of the earliest instructors from Leicester city in the immediate post-war period was Sergeant Robert Meredith McCrory. After spending varying periods of time between the training centre and his home force, Robert McCrory, with the rank of superintendent, was appointed commandant at Mill Meece in January 1959. In May 1963, Superintendent McCrory left Leicester City Police to become the deputy chief constable of Bolton Police force.

Due to wartime conditions, men who were eligible for retirement had been retained in the police service. The gaps created by the exodus of these officers after 1945, both regulars and war

[17] Inspector Kirkland spent only six weeks at the district training centre. Inspector Shelvey was engaged in the re-training of officers from 30 July until 22 December 1945.

[18] The first post-war recruit to the Leicester City Police, in January 1946, was PC 66 Maurice Wells. At this time the initial training course was of 13 weeks duration.

reserves, caused an immediate problem nationally. Appreciating the need for a rapid recruitment drive, the Government decided to offer suitable applicants for the police service immediate disengagement from the armed forces. In order to facilitate this process, a police recruiting mission of three chief constables and an inspector was sent to India in January 1946. One of the chief constables selected was O.J.B. Cole.

The mission lasted four months. Initially, the members toured six centres in India and Ceylon. Owing to his companions becoming ill, Cole continued with the expedition alone, visiting Rangoon, Java and Singapore. During the trip over 1,200 servicemen were interviewed as candidates for various forces in England and Wales. As a result of the recruiting drive, 564 men were accepted into the British Police service.

Among these was Lieutenant Philip Burt, who was serving as a regular soldier in the ranks of the British Army at the outbreak of the war. Commissioned in the Devonshire Regiment and attached to the 12th Frontier Force Regiment of the Indian Army, Philip Burt was, at the time of the recruiting mission's arrival in India, serving with the Frontier Force in the Punjab. Having made a journey of some 800 miles across the Sind Desert from his regimental headquarters at Sialkot to Karachi for an interview, Lieutenant Burt was soon to become PC 74 (later Sergeant 54) Burt of the Leicester City Police.[19]

As an additional staff officer, Sergeant (later Superintendent) Cyril Waugh was given the rank of temporary inspector and posted to the mission. On Cole's return to England, Cyril Waugh was transferred to a second mission in Egypt and did not return to the United Kingdom until July 1946.

—oOo—

Operationally, with the return to duties of large numbers of experienced men, and the recruitment of others, the police began to resume

A group of post-war recruits to the Leicester City force at Ryton district training centre in July 1946. on the far right of the group is PC 152 Cliff Robinson, and PC 148 Norman Cox is in the centre. (Courtesy C.W. Robinson)

WPCs Froude and Thirlby, with W. Sgt Gwen Harvey, outside Charles Street police station in early 1947.

(Courtesy P. and J. Burt)

its peacetime responsibilities and activities. In January 1946, detective officers from the force attended the first post-war courses now being held at Wakefield. A new innovation, the 999 emergency telephone system, was initiated by the GPO to help members of the public making emergency calls through the national telephone system.

[19] The choice of Karachi as an interview venue may not have been accidental on Cole's part. In 1944 his son had been killed in a flying accident near to Karachi, and the chief constable may have taken the opportunity presented by the visit to deal with some personal matters.

The first recruits to the policewomen's department after the war, in December 1946. WPC 3 Jean Froude and WPC 4 Joan Thirlby are in class with instructor temporary Sergeant 'Bob' McCrory. (McCrory is seen wearing his PC warrant number, 215, and was not made a permanent sergeant until September 1947. He later became commandant of the training school.

(Courtesy P. and J. Burt)

As part of the reconstitution of the German social and economic structure, police officers were seconded to the Civil Control Commission in Germany. In February and March 1946, Inspector Charles Smith and PC 199 Norman Martyn were seconded to the commission for three years. Inspector Edwin Palmer, after a short-term secondment, returned from Germany in September 1946. On a longer attachment, Acting Inspector John May (who at the time was still serving in HM Forces), spent four years with the commission, returning to the force in June 1950 prior to spending a further 20 months in Greece.

In the early post-war years, a highly-successful Leicester City Police first aid team competed in and won several competitions locally. In a similar vein, with the standing down in February 1945 of the 1st Battalion of the Home Guard Band, the Special Constabulary were given permission to form a brass band of their own. Provided with bandsmen's uniforms, and under the leadership of their Band Master, Special Inspector Anderson, the band played for several years at public events and ceremonies. During the 14 years prior to its dissolution at Easter 1959, the Special Constabulary band won several trophies locally, in the Midlands and nationally for its playing and marching skills.

—oOo—

In September 1948 the Home Office approved a long-awaited change of uniform for the police

In February 1953 extensive flooding and damage to property along the east coast created a national emergency. Contingents of emergency services were drafted in to help from all over the country. A total of 83 Leicester City Police officers were sent to the Sutton-on-Sea district to assist Lincolnshire officers. The presence of senior officers and sergeants in this photograph indicates that this was probably the first group to be sent from Leicester. From left to right, back row: PC 224 J. Gordon, PC 166 R. Onions, PC 63 H. Dowell, PC 118 K. Saville, PC 79 R. Smith, PC 190 J. Briggs, PC 134 A. Bennett, PC 52 R. Allen, PC 164 L. Smith, PC 97 H. Botterill. Middle row: PC 162 R. Green, PC 244 A. Sheard, PC 198 R. Mould, PC 156 W. Gatward, PC 243 R. McFarlane, PC 59 K. Lockett, -?-, PC 262 J. Chambers, PC 74 P. Burt. Front row: PC 100 B. Ditchfield, Sgt 20 R. James, Sgt 43 J. Fisher, Sgt 25 C. Wren, Insp. R. McCrory, Insp. F. Wright, Sgt 45 T.F. Sandall, Sgt 21 A. Read, Sgt 40 J. Anstey, PC 81 Bingham.

(Courtesy P. and J. Burt)

service nationally. The old closed-neck tunics were to be phased out in favour of an open neck jacket, with a shirt, collar and tie. Due to the shortage of supplies (in common with most other forces), it was not for some time that the changeover took place in Leicester. From photographs it is most likely that the use of closed-neck tunics for day wear was phased out during 1953.

Another institution of the Cole era was an in-force magazine, which was published monthly. During the war Oswald Cole had arranged for a monthly news sheet to be sent out wherever possible to all members of the force who were serving in the armed forces. In March 1947 the newsletter was succeeded by the *Charles Street Clarion*, a magazine which carried news of events in the force, sport, short stories and other similar items. The first two editions were run off on a copying machine using loose sheets of paper and priced at 1d. After a few months, in July, once the magazine was established (by March 1948 it had a monthly circulation of 650 copies), the price was increased to 2d.

A group of recruits at Ryton district training centre, marching in file in February or March 1948. The officer acting as marker on the front rank (facing his front) is PC 154 'Charlie' Ralph. The medallion which the recruits are wearing is an identity disc.

(Courtesy N. Hull)

The *Clarion*'s final issue was produced in October 1957, when Cole's successor, Robert Mark, decided to discontinue it's publication on the grounds that the magazine, which by then was costing 2s a copy to produce, was still being sold for 2d, and that with a final circulation of 550 copies a month, less than 300 were being sold in-house. There is little doubt that apart from his concern over the losses being incurred in producing the periodical, Robert Mark was deeply worried about the amount of advertising subsidy which the magazine was accepting. In its latter years, the *Clarion* carried at least two advertisements for products which were being sold nationally, and depicted police officers who were clearly wearing the insignia of the Leicester City force. A sad irony was that the final copy of the *Clarion* contained an obituary for its recently deceased founder, Oswald Cole.

—oOo—

The end of the war did not necessarily signal an end to violence for those living in the city. As after World War One, it was not always an easy matter for men who had seen active service to re-adjust to a peace-time existence. One such was Squadron Leader Josef Smazyck Zawadski.

Born in Poland in 1909, Zawadski married a

This group photograph of recruits at Ryton in early 1948 gives a comprehensive display of the various badges and uniforms worn in the region in the immediate post-war years. The figure second from left in the middle row is PC 151 Norman Hull.

(*Courtesy N. Hull*)

woman of German extraction in 1938, prior to escaping from the Nazi invasion of Poland and fleeing to England, where he enlisted in the Free Polish Air Force. During the war Zawadski became a celebrated flyer, fighting in the Battle of Britain and later flying missions over Europe. Among his decorations were the Virtute Militari, the Cross of Valour and three bars and the Polish Air Force medal with three bars. In 1941 he received word that his wife in Poland had left him and was living with another man.

Considering himself to now be a single man, in 1942 Josef met and became involved with 21-year-old Frances Joan Minns. The couple set up

home together and in May 1945 had a son, André. Zawadski's first intimation that Minns was not all that she seemed was when, around this time, he was cited by her husband (of whom he claimed to be unaware), as correspondent in divorce proceedings. After her divorce Joan Minns reverted to her maiden name of Henson, and with Josef Zawadski stationed at an air base in Lincolnshire, she embarked upon a series of affairs with other men.

In August 1945, Zawadski and Henson split up, after which she and the child went to live with her mother, Kathryn Henson, at 51 Dersingham Road. This arrangement lasted for only a short

Leicester City CID officers, c.July 1955. From left to right, back row: DC 165 Tucker, DC 159 Haywood, DC233 White, DC241 R.B. Johnson, DC 162 R. Green. Middle row: DC 71 Broomfield, DC 136 R.A. Smith, Det. Sgt 8 Robinson, Det. Sgt 22 Hunt, DC 110 Bull. Front row: Det. Sgt 44 Saunders, Ms M. Dexter, WPC Atkins, Det. Sgt 29 Ward, Det. Insp. McMurdo.

Leicester City CID officers, c.July 1955. From left to right, back row: DC 123 B. Gannon, DC 265 Derry, DC 106 Dawkins, DC 56 Driver, DC 272 Holyoak, DC237 Price. Middle row: DC 116 Broughton, Det. Sgt 23 Corns, Det. Sgt Owen, DC 228 Hodge, DC 143 H. Green. Front row: Det. Insp. Beswick, Det. Insp. Sawford, WPC Rogers, WPC Turner, Det. Sgt 19 N. Cox.

Officers who represented the Leicester City Police force at the coronation of HM Elizabeth II in June 1953. From left to right, back row: PC 64 S. Berry, PC 115 L. Curtis, PC 48 F. Frost, PC 152 C.W. Robinson, PC 179 R. Wolfe, PC 62 C.H. Owen, PC 185 N. Peplow, PC 288 A. Glover, PC 240 L. Kirk, PC 248 F. Sutton, PC 127 D. Lusty, PC 128 H. Bradshaw. Middle row: Det. Sgt G.H.W. Bestwick, PC 109 C. Smith, PC 217 T. Chamberlain, PC 60 G. Abram, PC 249 R.M. House, PC 189 K. Greaseley, PC 149 C. Hilton, PC 290 W. Lewis, PC 86 L. James, PC 202 J. Glover, PC 57 H. Wardle. Front row: PC 146 W. Freear, PC 171 M. Davie, Sgt 33 H. Broughton, Sgt 34 K. Springthorpe, Insp. J. Bates, Sgt 22 T. Moorhouse, WPC D. Brailsford, PC 261 D. Carstairs, PC 69 J. Farley.

Inspector Harold Robert Toach (December 1920–December 1950).

while, until in January 1948 Joan moved out, refusing to tell her mother where she was living. She had in fact moved into rented accommodation at 200 Kitchener Road.

On the evening of 23 January, Zawadski visited Mrs Henson and his son at Dersingham Road. He told her that he had discovered where Joan was living, and telephoned her at Kitchener Road to arrange a meeting. The couple met the following day in the upstairs lounge of the Grand Hotel in Granby Street. Having gone downstairs for a drink in Simon's Bar, they left for Kitchener Road in a taxi driven by Frank Timson. On the journey, Zawadski and Joan Henson were arguing heatedly, and at one point Zawadski offered the taxi driver a pound note in payment for the taxi fare. (The defence would later make great play of this fact.) Turning to take the note, Timson saw that Zawadski was holding a Mauser automatic pistol in his right hand, which he was pointing at Henson. When Timson pulled up in Kitchener

Annual inspection of the force in the main yard at Charles Street between 1953 and 1955. The senior officers behind O.J.B. Cole are Chief Inspector William Meese and Assistant Chief Constable Bernard Ecob. The constable talking to Her Majesty's inspector is PC 214 Ron Singleton.

The lady in this posed photograph is seeking directions from PC 82 Cyril 'Tich' Leeson, with Inspector William Meese in the background. The presence of the military vehicle parked outside the police box near Victoria Park indicates that this is a publicity photograph taken during the war.

No.5 section of the Special Constabulary being inspected on the Magazine Barracks parade ground, June 1946.

Officers being paraded for special duty at the Leicester City Football Club ground at Filbert Street in February 1949. Detailing the men are Inspector William Meese and Sergeant 27 James 'Ike' Harrison. Harrison, who joined the force in December 1923, unfortunately died while still a serving officer in July 1951.

Road, Zawadski fired several shots at Joan Henson as she left the taxi, one of them entering through the heart and killing her.

The police were called and Sergeant Jock Joiner, accompanied by PC George Abram, arrived in a patrol car. Zawadski first fired a shot in the general direction of the police officers, then turned the pistol to point at his own head as if to shoot himself. As he fired the weapon again, the recoil deflected the shot away from his head, resulting in a minor scalp wound. At this point Zawadski was disarmed by Sergeant Joiner. Inspector Harold Toach had now arrived at the scene and Josef Zawadski was arrested. Having been taken into custody,

Officers marching out to their beats from force headquarters in Charles Street. Taken either during the war or immediately afterwards, this is probably a publicity photograph. It is obviously raining heavily, yet none of the officers is wearing a coat or carrying a cape. The sergeant leading the men out is Sgt 14 Cyril Withers. The officers, from the front to the back of the column, are: PC 217 Chamberlain, PC 180 Hackett, PC 225 Garfield, PC 49 Moore, PC 196 Johnson, PC 236 Newberry and PC 58 Swain.

he said to the officers 'alright, I killed her, and now I kill myself'. Later on, he said to them, 'I could have killed you, but I am an officer and a gentleman'.

At his trial at Birmingham Assizes on 15 March 1948, Josef Zawadski pleaded not guilty to the murder of Joan Henson on the grounds of insanity. Among other legal arguments, the defence attempted to show that the fact that he was unbalanced was indicated by his offering the taxi driver a pound for a fare which cost between 4s and 5s.

The prosecution, on the other hand, produced three letters which had been taken from his pocket when he was searched after his arrest.

The first was to the victim's mother, Mrs Henson:

Darling Mummy,
Sorry there cannot be another way. I shall kill her and myself and finish my tortures. As I expected she is not even coming to see me. Please arrange something for André's future. Cannot live any longer. Thanks for everything you were always so nice to me – Josef.

The second was to the police:

Dear Sirs,
Sorry to be trouble but it cannot be helped. I shall kill her, Mrs Zawadski for personal reasons. I shall kill myself. Yours faithfully.

Finally he had written to his Commanding Officer, Wing Commander D.A.Upton:

Oswald John Buxton Cole, chief constable January 1929–December 1955.

Senior officers of the Leicester City Police force, pictured on the flat roof of the force headquarters. From left to right, back row: Insp. W. Welch, Insp. S. Page, Insp. H. Clements, Insp. R. McCrory, Insp. F. Wright, Insp. G.H.W. Bestwick. Middle row: Det. Insp. E. Pym, Insp. D. Hackett, Insp. T. Kirk, Insp. J. Bates, Insp. J. Shipman, Insp. F. Shelvey, Insp. C. Dalby, Det. Insp. J. Woodward. Front row: Ch. Insp. T.P. Woolley, Supt C. Waugh, Asst Ch. Cons. B. Ecob, Ch. Cons O.J.B. Cole, Supt J. Critchlow, Ch. Insp. W. Meese, Insp. H. Poole.
At this time all the senior officers wore silver braiding around the peak of their caps. In later years this altered to black braiding for inspectors and chief inspectors, while ranks above chief inspector retained a silver braid.

Sorry I must write that letter, but cannot carry on as I told you. All my life I had very bad luck. Always met the wrong people and the result is death.

The jury found Josef Zawadski guilty but insane and he was sentenced to be detained at His Majesty's pleasure.[20]

—oOo—

As had happened in the aftermath of the previous war – although in less traumatic circumstances – a full review of police pay and conditions took place. In May 1948 a committee under the chairmanship of Lord Oaksey looked at and reported on pay, pensions, allowances, promotion and representation within the police service. As a result of the findings of the Oaksey Committee, in 1949 new improved pay scales were implemented.

A major post-war issue for the police service was the adequate housing of police officers and their families. At this time (January 1945), there were 47 vacancies in the Leicester City Police, with the prospect of a further 15 by the end of the year. This meant that 62 new recruits would be joining the force, in addition to a further 70 serving officers returning from active service in the armed forces.

Cole argued that the police should be given an allocation in existing council-owned housing areas, and especially in the present development of the New Parks Estate, which was being built on the edge of the city. Initially, in November 1945, the Housing Committee allocated nine such houses to the police authority. Over a period of time, more houses were secured for occupation by the police, but a new social phenomenon was now manifesting itself. Despite the improvements wrought by the Oaksey Committee, with a relative boom in the post-war economy, men joining the police were not remaining in the service. Having

Senior officers of the Leicester City Police force between July 1955 and October 1957. From left to right, back row: Det. Insp. G.H.W. Bestwick, Det. Insp. F. Sawford, Insp. R. Wigley, Insp. S. Branson, Insp. C. Dalby, Insp. H. Clements, Insp. R.G. Brobyn, Insp. D. Lusty, Det. Insp. D. McMurdo. Middle row: Insp. J. Shipman, Insp. S. Page, Insp. Edwards, Insp. C. Adkin, Insp. K. Springthorpe, Insp. T. Moorhouse, Insp. F. Wright, Insp. J. Todd, Insp. R. McCrory. Front row: Ch. Insp. D. Hackett, Supt C. Waugh, Asst Ch. Cons. B. Ecob, Ch. Cons O.J.B. Cole, Det. Supt E. Lacy, Supt P. Woolley, Ch. Insp. J. Woodward.

It is worth noting that up to the rank of superintendent the wide city coat of arms cap badge is worn. Superintendents and above wore the heavier senior officers' cap badge.

taken employment as police officers primarily to obtain housing, many left, but failed to quit their accommodation. In January 1950, when the Watch Committee, as part of an ongoing programme, authorised the building of more police houses, the Housing Committee refused to free up more council tenancies.

The financial wastage caused by high levels of manpower turnover caused concern nationally. When asked to comment on the situation locally, Oswald Cole attributed (correctly), the causes to: police work being uncongenial, the working of difficult and unsociable hours and work in industry paying better wages for less inconvenience.

Despite these difficulties, the council's budgets for dedicated police housing continued at an acceptable pace. In September 1951, the most recent phase of the building programme had

---

[20]After serving part of his sentence, Zawadski was deemed fit to be repatriated, and was returned to Poland.

produced 10 houses in the Fullhurst Avenue and Braunstone Avenue area costing £18,924; eight houses in Caledine Road and Frolesworth Road costing £15,399; and six in Saffron Lane and the Fairway for £11,436. In the 1952–3 estimates, a budget of £32,756 was provided for a further 24 houses to be built on the Eyres Monsell Estate. These, constructed by Messrs Laing and Son, were to be of an 'Easiform' design, as part of a local authority contract for a total of 400 council houses.

During the five years between 1945 and 1950, 2,904 houses and shops were built by the City Council – a large number of which were in the New Parks area of the city. Additionally an estimated 1,000 houses were built by private enterprise.

For a trial period, between 1948 and 1950, Cole established four self-contained police districts within the force area – Central, Western, Eastern and Southern. As a result of this experiment, it became apparent that there was a dire need for more police stations on the outskirts of the city.

Attempts to repossess part of the old Aylestone police station from the Library Committee were unsuccessful, and in December 1950 a suitable site for the building of a police station was identified at the junction of Welford Road and Houlditch Road. Purchased for £1,100 from the vicar and church wardens of St Michael's Church, at 1,198 square yards it was suitable for the erection of a police station, house and garage. The cost of building work was £7,250.

On the western side of the city (which centred upon Hinckley Road), there was only a hut, which had been erected on Wentworth Road 26 years earlier for the use of police officers working in the area. An available solution was the purchase of a disused medical dispensary at the corner of Hinckley Road and Tyndale Street. In March 1950, the property was bought from the Sheffield Regional Health Authority for £1,250, and work commenced on converting it into a police station.

In respect of the Eastern district, due to the increase in population in the area, it was proposed to build a completely new police station. Estimates showed that the work would cost around £4,000. The new police station on Uppingham Road was opened in June 1952.

Since November 1947 the Leicester City and County forces had been involved in talks aimed at combining to share a wireless scheme based on the use of two VHF transmitters. In January 1950, no working agreement had been reached between the two police authorities, and the scheme was not ready to proceed. Despite this situation, in March structural changes were made to the charge office at Charles Street, in order to accommodate the establishment of a wireless information room.

—oOo—

Gales on the night of 31 January–1 February 1953 caused extensive flooding along the east coast of England and created a situation requiring services throughout the country to send contingents of officers to assist the Lincolnshire emergency services. During the early part of February, immediately after the disaster, 83 officers from Leicester City Police were sent to the Sutton-on-Sea district to assist the Lincolnshire Police.[21]

On a lighter note, in June of that year a contingent of one inspector, four sergeants, one policewoman and 26 constables represented the force at the coronation of Queen Elizabeth II. This was followed in July 1954 by a further unit of officers participating in the Royal Review of Police Forces at Hyde Park in London.

—oOo—

In January 1953, the rank of assistant chief constable was instituted for the first time. Previously, the position of second in command of the force had been held by a superintendent

---

[21] In relays: 3 inspectors, 8 sergeants and 72 constables.

The opening of Uppingham Road police station, 30 June 1952.

designated deputy chief constable, paid (with Home Office approval) an allowance above his superintendent's salary in respect of the extra responsibilities. This function had been performed, since December 1945, by Superintendent Bernard Louis Ecob. He remained in the rank of assistant chief constable until his death in August 1960, when he was succeeded by Detective Superintendent Eric Ernest Lacy.

—oOo—

The early summer of 1953 saw the Leicester City Police engaged with county officers in the investigation of a particularly brutal murder. Soon after 5.15 p.m on Friday 22 May, 12-year-old Janet Warner left her home at 141 Leicester Road, Glenhills, to walk her black and white collie dog in nearby Blue Banks Spinney. Soon after she entered the spinney, two young boys playing nearby heard the sounds of screams and a violent

struggle. Running to where the noise was coming from they saw a man with what appeared to be a body near to some bushes. Frightened, the boys ran off to the house of a policeman who lived in nearby Dorothy Avenue. Finding no one at the house, they returned to Blue Banks Spinney at about a quarter past six, where they were joined by four other lads. Stopping a passer-by, they told him what they had seen, and the police were sent for. On the arrival of PC Harris, Janet Warner's body was discovered in nearby bushes. She had been strangled with a silk stocking and a school tie.

Detectives from the County and City Police forces set up an enquiry team, and descriptions of the man, supplied by the two boys (David Dryden from Hillsborough Road and Johnny Warren), were circulated to surrounding forces.

That same weekend, during the early hours of Monday morning,[22] PC 205 John 'Jack' Milner of

[22] This would be between 1 and 2 a.m.

the City Police, who was on night shift, was walking along Granby Street on his way to have his meal at Charles Street police station, when near to Rutland Street he saw a man behaving suspiciously in an alley way. When challenged by the constable, the man, who was Irish, gave his name as 'Cuthbert'. Not satisfied, and realising that the man answered the description of the killer, Jack Milner told him that he was taking him to the police station. Although the suspect agreed to go with him, after a short distance he broke away from the officer and tried to escape. A chase through the city streets ensued before PC Milner was able, after a struggle, to recapture the Irishman.

Once at the police station, Milner's prisoner quickly admitted to detectives that his real name was Joseph Christopher Reynolds, and that he was responsible for the murder of Janet Warner. Born in Dublin, he was 31 years of age and a devout Catholic. Educated first at a convent school and later by an order of the Christian Brothers, he had worked as a boot and shoe repairer before joining the army in Eire. For some unspecified reason, the army had discharged him after seven months, at which point he came to England and served for a while in the Royal Air Force in 1943. At the time of his arrest he was working as a labourer.

Reynolds told the detectives that for some time he had been subject to an overpowering desire to kill someone. Recently he had decided to murder a man who he had seen regularly walking through Blue Banks Spinney, and on the Friday afternoon had lain in wait for him. When the man (who was otherwise unknown to Reynolds) failed to appear, he decided that he would kill the young schoolgirl instead. Having engaged her in conversation, Reynolds took the girl to some bushes and after a struggle during which he received injuries to his face, strangled her with a silk stocking which he had found in an air raid shelter and taken.

There is no doubt that Joseph Reynolds – who lived in lodgings at 92 Uppingham Road, and

Executed at Welford Road Prison on Tuesday 17 November 1953, Joseph Reynolds was the last man to be hanged at Leicester prison.   (Courtesy Leicester Mercury)

was described by other lodgers as a quiet, unassuming man who spent most of his evenings listening to the radio – was criminally insane. The course of his subsequent trial and conviction are therefore somewhat strange. All of the evidence in relation to the police prosecution appears to have been presented to the magistrates on 22 June, when he was committed to Leicester Assizes for trial.

Reynolds's trial on 26 October, which was attended by the chief constables of both the City and the County, before Mr Justice Pilcher, must be almost unique in the annals of British justice. The entire trial lasted four minutes, at the end of which the judge, donning his black cap, sentenced the accused to be hanged. No evidence appears to have been offered by the defence counsel or sought by the judge as to Reynolds's mental state at the time of the killing.

Joseph Christopher Reynolds was executed at 9 a.m. on Tuesday 17 November 1953. He was the last man to be hanged at Leicester gaol.

In December 1955 Oswald John Buxton Cole

was 65 years of age. Under the police pensions regulations he had attained the age of compulsory retirement.

Next to Robert Charters, whose service with the Borough force had spanned 31 years, 'Jack' Cole was the force's second longest-serving chief constable. During his 27 years as head of the force, many things had happened, both nationally and locally. A policewomen's department had been inaugurated, the first radio patrol cars had taken to the roads, the policing of a major city in wartime had been effectively managed, and an housing project for the officers of his force had been accomplished.

Retiring on his 65th birthday, O.J.B. Cole continued to live at his home on the Fairway in Oadby, Leicester and took a post as the county director of the Leicestershire branch of the Red Cross. Sadly, his retirement was not to be a long one. On Monday 23 September 1957, while walking his dog, Cole collapsed and died three days later in Leicester Royal Infirmary.

His funeral was held at Leicester Cathedral and attended by his successor as chief constable, Robert Mark, Her Majesty's Inspector for Constabulary Commander Willis and chief constables from surrounding forces. A guard of honour was mounted by City Police officers and special constables.

CHAPTER NINE

Neil Galbraith
(January 1956–October 1956)

If Oswald Cole's period in office as chief constable of the Leicester City Police was one of the longest in its history, that of Neil Galbraith was indisputably the shortest.

Born a Scot, Galbraith, the son of a Burgh police officer, was at the time of his appointment at Leicester serving as the assistant chief constable of Monmouthshire Constabulary, a post which he had held since May 1951. Prior to that date he had served up to the rank of inspector in Lancashire, and then to chief superintendent in Hertfordshire.

Of the six applications for the chief constable's job, a shortlist of three was drawn up. Apart from Galbraith, the other two candidates were the assistant chief constable of Leicester, Bernard Louis Ecob, and Alexander James Paterson, the chief constable of Salford. Neil Galbraith, having been appointed, took up office on 17 January 1956.

—oOo—

During the summer of 1955, the first moves to improve working hours in the police service were begun. From July of that year, the working week for all ranks below superintendent was reduced from 48 hours to 44. In Leicester this was achieved by giving the force an extra rest day every fortnight. Where an officer was required for any reason to work that rest day, he or she had to either be paid, or allowed to have it re-allocated. Galbraith, eager to conduct a long overdue review of the running of the force, was, in view of this provision, hampered by having to project not only existing policing requirements, but the implications of potential overtime budgets.

—oOo—

One of the areas in which some progress was made at this time was in respect of training officers in the techniques of searching under water. Historically, the method employed for the recovery of dead bodies and items from areas of water such as the canal or River Soar had been by the use of drags. The 'drag' was a steel or iron multi-pronged hook, not dissimilar to a miniature ship's anchor, with an eye at the end of

Sgt 32 Norman 'Tam' Hadley served for four years in the Scots Guards prior to joining Leicester City Police as PC 266 in April 1938. Recalled as an army reservist in 1939, he served with the Small Arms school at Hythe in Kent before returning to the city force at the end of World War Two.

(Courtesy D. Chimley)

the shaft through which a length of rope was passed. The implement was employed by virtue of throwing it into the water and hooking one of the prongs into the object to be recovered, before hauling it to the side by means of the rope.[1]

In 1846, when making enquiries about the most suitable type of drag to purchase, the following information was sent to the Borough Police head-quarters by the Royal Humane Society in London:

...I beg to enclose an address card of the maker of said drags in which it shows an engraving of their shape and prices, [of] both pole and rope drags.

The firm there represented, has been found after many years experience to be the best, and the sharp iron prongs alluded to by

Superintendent Peter Wolley (September 1932 - July 1964) was promoted to superintendent in October 1953.

you are quite necessary in tidal rivers or where there is a strong and deep current. It is seldom or ever found that a body recovered by them is injured, owing to the great buoyancy given to all objects in the water and which when laid hold of rise to the surface with little or no hauling power...

In July 1955 Special Constable Park of the City Police attended an incident in the county (the location is not specified) to recover a body which could not be brought from the water using drags. Park recovered the body by diving in the water using a relatively new innovation, the aqualung. He was subsequently asked to make a presentation on underwater search procedures to the Watch Committee.

Relatively low priority seems to have been

Leicester City Police football team, 1954. From left to right, back row: PC S. Berry, PC J. Glover, PC C. Smith. Third row: PC G. Smith, PC J. White, PC A. Stevens, PC R. Wass, PC W. Mowl, PC P. Fawcett, PC D.O'Connell, PC R. Colledge, PC D. Weedon, PC G. Walton, PC A. Stevenson. Second row: Insp H. Clements, PC K. McDonald, PC A. Jacques, PC J. Jowitt, PC A. Chambers, PC B. Johnson, PC D. Smith, PC E. Bendell, PC J. Mann, Insp. F. Wright. Front row: PC D. Goggins, PC R. Hunt, PC C. Robinson, Asst Ch. Cons. B. Ecob, Ch. Cons. O.J.B. Cole, PC J. Broughton, PC B. Capon, PC A. Foster. (Courtesy C. Robinson)

[1] A set of drags was kept at the police box on Eastern Boulevard until the late 1960s.

PC 120 Norman Farrant (October 1933–October 1963)

Neil Galbraith, chief constable January 1956–October 1956.

attached to the subject thereafter, as no further discussion took place until October 1956, when the committee approved £130 to be spent on the purchase of 'under water swimming equipment'. There is, however, no record that the police did in fact purchase any such equipment. One possible explanation is that because at the time the force was between chief constables – Galbraith having resigned and Mark not yet appointed – the matter could have been held in abeyance.[2]

Subsequently, the Leicester City Fire Brigade appear to have taken a lead in the field of underwater search. In July 1957 Sub Officer Doore and Fireman Goodacre, using under water search equipment, recovered the body of a woman from the River Soar on behalf of the police. Later the same year, six members of the police swimming section were given training by

the fire service in the use of shallow diving equipment.

—oOo—

The continuing issue during the nine months of Neil Galbraith's incumbency was that of police housing and its effect on recruiting.

In September 1956, despite the efforts which had been made over recent years, there were still 17 married officers who were waiting for houses. This was perceived to be a factor in poor levels of recruitment. At that time over one fifth (22%), of the total force establishment was vacant, a figure which was only exceeded by the City of London Police.

The perspective, both locally and nationally, is worth examining as it gives an accurate snapshot of the social conditions surrounding post-war life in the police service.

Prior to the end of World War Two, the police authority had owned only two houses, both of which had come into the city area due to

---

[2] One other factor, in relation to which chief officers were powerless, was that in the post-war years, and into the 1960s, the turnover of officers was a real problem. A huge number of men joined the police service, remained for a matter of months and then left. The training and budgetary implications of this situation were to create a major problem.

Having been a policewoman first in Cairo and then for three years in Sheffield, Barbara Denis de Vitré joined Leicester City Police on 28 June 1933. Promoted to sergeant in November 1936, she left the force in May 1944 on promotion to inspector in the Kent Police. In later years, as an assistant to His Majesty's Inspectorate of Constabulary, Barbara Denis de Vitré was responsible for advising on matters relating to the women's branch of the service.

Assistant Chief Constable Bernard Louis Ecob. The son of a village post master (at Somerby), Bernard Ecob worked for a while as a railway man before joining the Leicester City Police in January 1923 as PC 86. Rising through the ranks during World War Two, he succeeded John Gabbitas as deputy chief constable in June 1945, a position which he held until his death. (The position of a superintendent being appointed deputy chief constable and paid an allowance was regularised in January 1953 when the rank of assistant chief constable was created.

boundary extensions. In the eight year period between 1948 and 1956, a total of 98 new houses were built, making a total of 100.

Throughout the country, and not only within the police service, there was a housing problem. Prior to World War Two it was easier to rent suitable houses, and a fair proportion of men could acquire accommodation at a reasonable price. By the mid-1950s rented houses were practically unobtainable and the terms under which houses could be purchased were beyond the average working man's means.

In 1956 approximately one fifth of the officers who had joined the Leicester City Police since 1946 were buying their own houses, which meant

that the remaining 80 per cent were seeking police houses – of which there were only 100 available. The housing problem was being exacerbated by the retirement of older men.[3]

Galbraith secured an undertaking from the Council in September 1956 that a further 20 houses should be built or acquired each year for the next five years, at which point the situation could be reviewed.

In October 1956, following the sudden death of the chief constable of Monmouthshire, Neil Galbraith was appointed as head of his old force and tendered his resignation as chief constable of Leicester City Police.

[3] Often on retirement an officer could apply to remain in his house and become a council tenant.

CHAPTER TEN

Robert Mark
(January 1957–March 1967)

Robert Mark is probably best remembered for his time spent as the commissioner of the Metropolitan Police. However, during the 10-year period between January 1957 and April 1967, he

Originally worn by senior officers, this cap badge in solid silver replaced the old wyvern and crown badge in 1957.

(Courtesy N. Haines)

was without question one of the outstanding chief constables in the history of the Leicester Borough and City Police force.

Born on 13 March 1917, Robert Mark joined the Manchester City Police force on 21 July 1937. In common with many other officers, he joined the army when recruiting restrictions were lifted in 1942, and saw wartime service in the Royal Armoured Corps and Phantom (GHQ Liaison) Regiment. Returning to his old force after

demobilisation, Mark was promoted through the ranks during the immediate post-war years and early 1950s, until he became chief superintendent, at which point he began to seek an appointment outside of Manchester.

Although the list of candidates for the post of chief constable of Leicester in December 1956 included three existing chief constables from other forces, the circuit was by now becoming noticeably smaller. Three of the seven applicants were among those whose names had appeared in the lists when Galbraith had been appointed. Mark himself had, 11 months earlier, applied for Galbraith's vacant position as assistant chief constable of Monmouthshire.

From the outset, Robert Mark established himself as a progressive and forward thinking chief officer. Although much had been achieved by his long term predecessor, Oswald John Buxton Cole's tendency had been, to a great extent, to react to events rather than create new situations. Mark, a natural administrator with 20 years policing experience behind him, favoured a different approach.

The Watch Committee, when presented with reports by the new chief constable, soon discovered that propositions put before them were usually prefaced with references to police regulations which basically outlined why his suggestions could not be refused. In April 1957 a consultant psychiatrist, having treated an officer for depression and instructed that the man be returned to 'light duties', wrote a letter of

PCs 334 Elliott and 102 Markillie assisting fire service officers at a fire at Pratt's Corn Merchants, St Nicholas Street, in around 1961. The patrol car is a Wolseley 6/90. (Courtesy W.R. Markillie)

complaint to the Watch Committee, demanding to know who had contravened his instructions by returning the officer to full-time duties. The chief constable's response was that he had personally overruled the consultant's recommendations, as, 'Police Regulations specify that a man is either fit for work, or not, and that he [and by implication, the Watch Committee], had no leeway in the matter'. The decision was not referred to again and the officer in question was allowed to retire a short time later.

When debating policing matters, Robert Mark developed a unique aptitude for prefacing a statement or report with a short comment intended (usually successfully) to focus the listener or reader's perceptions. An example of this occurs in 1958, when he was discussing an increase in the level of non-indictable offences in the city. Mark pointed out that '…crimes [indictable offences] are usually reported to the police and as such an increase is a cause for public concern. An increase in non-indictable offences, traffic matters etc., are an indication of police efficiency and activity…'

Not all of Robert Mark's logic would, in the context of later years, have been either valid or acceptable. In December 1959, as part of a management plan aimed at dealing with traffic problems in Leicester city centre, he ventured to secure an increase in the number of women police officers. His argument was that there were 23 vacancies in the male ranks, while on the other hand he had a full complement of women

The Ford Zephyr saloon car was an addition to the motor patrol fleet. Standing next to this 1964 model in Charles Street yard is PC 102 Dick Markillie. The two roller-shuttered doors behind the vehicle gave access to workshops where vehicles were maintained.

(Courtesy W.R. Markillie)

Leicester City Police football team, photographed between November 1961 and April 1962. From left to right, back row: PC 186 Bendell, PC 274 Blair, PC 90 Baines, PC 63 Parnham, PC 147 Walton, PC 349 Painter, PC 391 Coutts, Inspector R. Hunt. Front row: PC 381 Mottram, PC 335 Fletcher, PC 275 Barnett, PC 348 Campbell, PC 323 Struthers.

officers. Therefore it should not be difficult to continue recruiting into an increased female establishment; women officers would be less confrontational in dealing with motorists, and with an average service among policewomen of 3 years 145 days over the previous 10 years, the fact that it was unlikely that a female would serve long enough to qualify for a pension made their employment a sound financial measure.

—oOo—

In relation to the overall management of the force, Mark identified two main areas which required attention. The first related to the manpower available and the manner in which it was disposed. This he felt needed to be dealt with as a matter of urgency. As his opinion was shared by Her Majesty's Inspector of Constabulary Commander Willis, he was given a tacit undertaking that any changes he proposed were unlikely be challenged by the Home Office. The second concern was the question of traffic flow

through the congested streets of the city. A rather less pressing problem, this could in fact only be addressed when the first issue had been resolved.

While examining these matters Robert Mark began a programme of minor changes (many of which were long overdue), which would affect the force until the late 1960s.

Historically, young men who wanted to become constables were engaged as civilian clerks working on the telephone switchboard, or in an office, until they were old enough to join the force. The superceding of this process was commenced in 1956 by the inauguration of a Police Cadet Corps. The initial establishment was 12 cadets, which rose to 15 in 1957. The cadet scheme, which was being implemented throughout the country, allowed young school leavers to be trained in a more formal manner alongside regular police officers. As the system settled into place, a lower age limit for joining the Cadet Corps was set in 1957, at 17. In Leicester membership of the corps fluctuated over the

Officers of 'G' division police dog section, in the yard at Charles Street police station, presenting their dogs to members of the Watch Committee, c.1960. From left to right: PC 359 Barrie Swain, PC 115 David Simpson, PC 169 Keith Welsh, PC 124 Ben Farrar, PC 355 Alan Jackson.
(Courtesy D.W. Simpson)

coming years, on occasions dropping to as low as six. An example of the new chief constable's perspicacity is shown in his assertion that by sending a cadet away to the district training centre for 13 weeks initial training at the age of 18 years and 9 months (three months before he was eligible to join the police force), 13 weeks pensionable police service could be saved.

Another overdue reform of the system was the discontinuation, within the first 12 months of Mark's reign, of 'the key deposit system'. Almost half a century earlier, in 1908, the Borough Police force had begun a scheme which allowed the owners of business premises in the town centre to deposit the keys to their premises each night at the central police station. At that time an annual fee – which still stood – of one guinea was charged for

this service. In the intervening years, a further scheme had been implemented, whereby for a charge of 5s a year a depositor could leave their keys with the police against 'an emergency'. A tally showed that during 1957, 47 depositors were leaving and drawing keys on a daily basis and 107 keys were held on a 5s deposit. The implications were important. While having no power to enter any of these premises without the owner being present, the police could be in a highly compromising position should a burglary occur. All keys were returned forthwith to their owners and the scheme ended.

In the years between 1953 and 1957, the communications system between police boxes, sub-stations and the main headquarters had become overloaded. A new telephone network

PCs 170 Jowitt and 115 Curtis in Charles Street yard, with vehicles of the motor patrol fleet, between June 1955 and October 1957. *(Courtesy P. and J. Burt)*

An early example of a wireless-equipped patrol van. The distinctive cap badge worn by this officer – PC 330 Les Warner – was originally restricted to senior officers. It became the 'D' division badge between June and October 1957, replacing the old crown and wyvern.

Chief Constable Robert Mark (centre) and officers of 'B' division at Welford Road police station, during the summer of 1964.

was installed to route the telephones in police boxes outside the city centre directly to the sub-stations at Uppingham Road and Welford Road, instead of everything being passed to the Charles Street switchboard.

Re-organisation of the force both territorially and structurally presented a major challenge.

Geographically, at the beginning of 1957, the force comprised one centralised division with one territorial superintendent responsible for the entire area. The central division itself, which embraced the town centre and its environs, had a population of around 46,550 people. Eastern sub-division, covering Belgrave, Humberstone and Evington, had a population of approximately 117,750. On the other side of the city, the Southern sub-division, with responsibility for Stoneygate and Aylestone, along with the Western sub-division which covered Western Park, Braunstone and New Parks Estate, had a combined population of some 123,000 inhabitants. For each sub-division there was an inspector in charge, with the exception of Eastern, which was under the command of a chief inspector.

Overall the advantage of this arrangement was that it allowed for an economical deployment of supervisory officers, the weakness being that one superintendent could not efficiently manage such a large and unwieldy unit. With building developments taking place during the mid-1950s, it was now desirable that this structure be decentralised.

Mark's idea was to divide the force area into three geographic divisions. 'A' division, the city centre; 'B' division, the southern area and 'C' division, the eastern area. Each would be under the command of a superintendent. Home Office

Chief Constable Robert Mark with the officers and men of 'B' divison, photographed in 1958 in the yard of Welford Road police station.
(Courtesy D.B. Ralph)

consent for an increase in the establishment of superintendents from three to six was obtained, and by October 1957 the plan was put into operation.

A total overhaul of the management structure, essential to the success of the new territorial divisions, was also effected. The CID[1] and administration department were re-defined and a new traffic department introduced.

Members of the Watch Committee, photographed in the Watch Committee Room on the first floor of Charles Street police station, at the end of 1966. From left to right, back row: Alderman C.E.Worthington JP, Alderman Dr W.E. Howell, H.L. Milliard JP, Cllr W.B. Sercombe, C.W. Hadley JP, Town Clerk R.R. Thornton, Alderman W.H. Smith JP. Front row: Lady Oliver JP, Cllr Mrs L.R. Marriott JP, Ch. Cons. Robert Mark, Chairman Alderman C.H. Harris, Vice-Chairman Cllr P.C. Watts, Mrs F.M.Clark JP, Alderman Mrs C.E.Jackson. (Absent from the group are Cllr T.A. Harris, Cllr J. Alster and T.F.W. Pitchers JP.

[1] Crime figures at this time were low, at just under 3,000 a year, with a detection rate of around 63%.

Inspection of the policewomen's department in early 1958. From left to right, back row: WPC 7 B. Tovey, WPC 15 B. Pimp, WPC 14 I. Fox. Second row: WPC 5 P. Atkins, WPC 9 J. Knight, WPC 16 V. Gisborne, WPC 4 G. Hockey, -?-, WPC 10 J. Linsell, WPC 13 B. Watson. Front row: W. Sgt 1 M. 'Peggy' Glover, W. Sgt 2 D. Brailsford, Chief Constable Robert Mark, Her Majesty's Inspector, Miss Hill, W. Insp. H. Parkin, W. Sgt 3 D. Draycott.

The resultant structure, which provided a blueprint for the force until its amalgamation with the County Police in 1967, is shown overleaf:

PC 115 David Simpson and Rusty I. (Courtesy D.W. Simpson)

Proposed Structure of Leicester City Police Force 1957

(These figures are slightly in excess of the actual strength of the force at that time, and represent the target which the chief constable intended to achieve).

	Ch. Cons ACC	Supt	Ch. Insp	Insp	Sgts	PCs	Total
Ch. Officers	2						2
Administration ('F' Division)							
Ch. Cons Office		1	1	1	1		4
Training & Civil Defence				1	1		2
Prosecutions		1			1	6	8
Coroners Office					1		1
Central Stores					1		1
Entertainments Dept.,					1	1	2
Licensing					1	1	2
Traffic Department ('D' Division)							1
Motor Patrol		1	1	1	3	34	38
General Transport					1	2	3
Hackney Carriages					1		1
Criminal Investigation ('G' Division)							
Department		1					1
Detective Duties			1	2	8	25	36
Aliens Registration						1	1
Beat Patrol							
'A' Division		1	1	6	14	123	145
Charge Office & Information Room					6	11	17
'B' Division			1	3	9	74	87
'C' Division			1	3	8	64	76
TOTAL	2	6	3	17	57	343	428

Robert Mark was careful to emphasise to the police authority that this new structure, when implemented, would still not take into account the new 44 hour working week in respect of each officer of federated rank (below superintendent). This necessitated each officer being granted an extra rest day every fortnight.[2] Throughout the country, every force which did not have a sufficient strength to permit this- including Leicester – was having to pay officers to work that day.[3] The only financially sound solution was to seek a further increase in manpower.

PC 167 Tony Wain in Charles Street yard.

Another aspect to be considered was the number of officers per head of population. The estimated population of the city in 1957 was 281,200.[4] The authorised establishment of 428 male officers gave a ratio of 1:657, which was on a par with other forces in the Midlands. However, as the actual strength at the time was 356, the resultant figure of 1:790 was well below the average.[5]

---

[2] Since 1910 police officers had been entitled to two weekly rest days in each period of 14 days. The actual calculation at this juncture was to achieve a reduction from working 96 to 88 hours per fortnight. The problem was compounded when in 1964 the working week was again reduced from 44 to 42 hours.

[3] This was to continue for many years, and was known as 'ARD (Additional Rest Day) working'.

[4] Chief constable's Annual Report 1957.

[5] The average figure for England and Wales at this time was 1:567.

Officers manning the newly-opened control room, after it moved from the back of the charge office on the ground floor of Charles Street to the first floor of the building. From left to right: PC 369 Dick Bowditch (standing), PC 377 Ted Frank (in shirt sleeves), -?-, PC 277 Peter Graham.

The authorised female establishment of the force in 1957 (there were no vacancies), was one inspector, two sergeants and 12 constables. Under the new arrangements, by posting policewomen to the territorial divisions under the command of local superintendents,[6] the department was to a great extent decentralised.

In order to improve police response to

Officers of 'D' division in the yard at Charles Street police station between July 1955 and October 1957. Horseshoe from left to right: PC 74 Philip Burt, PC 118 Ken Saville, PC 157 John Thornelowe, -?-, PC 170 John Jowitt, PC 115 Les Curtis. Front row: Insp. Ronald Wigley, PC 242 Neil McLeod, PC 256 Trevor Hull, Sgt 28 Arthur Taylor. (Courtesy P. and J. Burt)

[6] After March 1958.

(Far left) PC 307 John Ivan Smith, awarded the British Empire Medal for gallantry in July 1964. PC Smith and PC 201 Michael John Clow, while on patrol in a wireless van, were sent to deal with a domestic dispute at 17 Schoolgate, on the Saffron Lane Estate. On arrival they found that Frederick George Buswell, an 18-year-old youth at that address, had recently left the house. He had been involved in an argument with his mother, Lucy Buswell, and threatened to shoot people. Outside, PC Smith found Buswell standing beside a parked van with a loaded shotgun. PC Smith ignored Buswell's threats to shoot him and stood his ground. PC Smith was joined by Mrs Buswell and PC Clow, and they tried to reason with Frederick Buswell. At one point Frederick Buswell swung the gun to point at his mother, and seizing the opportunity Ivan Smith jumped over the bonnet of the van to disarm him. During the ensuing struggle the breech of the gun came open and a live cartridge was ejected. For their bravery in the incident PC Smith was awarded the British Empire Medal, and PC Clow the Queen's Commendation for Brave Conduct. Frederick Buswell was later sentenced to detention in Borstal.

(Left) In May 1959, Leonard Thomas Shipman replaced Andrew Philip Dugald Michael as the commandant of the Special Constabulary.

incidents and deal more efficiently with traffic matters, the composition of the traffic department was modified. The force vehicle fleet was made up of eight patrol cars, two motor cycles, three CID cars and 10 cars and vans designated for general usage. While almost all of these vehicles were equipped with wireless, only three – Ford Popular motor cars – were allocated

The last recorded photograph of the senior officers of the Leicester City Police force, gathered together in the Watch Committee chamber at force headquarters prior to the amalgamation with the County Police in 1967.
Back row, from left to right: Supt R. G. Brobyn, 'C' div.; Det. Supt B. Saunders, 'G' div.; Supt G.H.W. Bestwick 'B' div.; Supt R. Wigley, 'D' div. Front row: Supt C. Adkin, 'A' div.; Ch. Cons. Robert Mark; Asst Ch. Cons. E. Lacy; Supt S. Page, 'F' div.

Chief Constable Robert Mark entering Leicester Cathedral. The presence behind him of the Lord Mayor, Monica Trotter, dates the picture to 1966.

to beat and patrol work. An increase of three new 10hp Ford Escort vans (£660 each), and four 500cc motorcycles (£230 each), was authorised, along with the hire of seven wireless sets at £34 2 0d each to create a fully-functioning vehicle fleet.[7]

With divisional headquarters located at Charles Street ('A' division), Welford Road ('B' division), and Uppingham Road ('C' division), it now became necessary to consider the need

DALMAS
Waterproof First-aid dressings stick fast – whatever the weather

Advertisements such as these, which clearly showed the insignia of the Leicester City Police, probably influenced Robert Mark's decision, at an early stage of his period in office, to close down the Charles Street Clarion.

STOP!
You'll stop sooner, go further and be safer on **JOHN BULL TYRES**

JOHN BULL

JOHN BULL RUBBER CO. LTD., EVINGTON VALLEY MILLS, LEICESTER

[7] In November 1958 the force vehicle fleet consisted of: 9 wireless equipped patrol cars; 6 motor cycles; 3 wireless equipped general purpose vans; 2 prison vans; 9 divisional and CID cars and 1 utility vehicle.

Probably one of the last photographs of its kind taken before the political situation in Ireland deteriorated. PC 151 Norman Hull,
on an International Police Association visit, takes point on a pedestrian crossing in Dublin.   *(Courtesy N.W. Hull)*

for these in their turn to be provided with sub-stations.

The most appropriate location for the 'B' division sub-station was on the Eyres Monsell Estate. Built by Messrs H. Sowden & Co. at a cost of £2,708, the sub-station was completed and opened on Glenhills Boulevard on 13 July 1959.

It was felt that on the eastern side of the city, 'C' division would benefit from two sub-stations. In common with the other outer division, a purpose built sub-station, costing £2,890 (also built by Sowden's), was opened on 2 June 1959 on Melton Road.

While plans for the Melton Road sub-station were being considered, it was decided to re-open the old police station at North Evington.

When in earlier years occupation of the other old police stations at Belgrave, Queens Road, Aylestone and Sanvey Gate had been relinquished the buildings had been sold – North Evington, because of it's joint tenancy with the fire brigade had been leased out. In April 1949, the occupant, Mr F.O. Dimblebee, was paying £60 a year rental as a lamp shade manufacturer. That same year, trading as Evington Food Products Ltd (still with the same tenant), 72 Asfordby Street became a potato crisp factory.

In March 1958, a notice to quit by September was served on the company and after refurbishment, the premises reverted to its original state as a police station.

Winners of the 1966 St John's Ambulance Brigade centre trophy, September 1966. From left to right: PC 390 Bruce Barker, Sgt 13 Bill Freear, PC 151 Norman Hull, PC 79 Ron Smith. (Courtesy N.W. Hull)

A relatively minor but significant innovation for the officers of the force (at the behest of the Home Office), was the introduction in 1959 of 'shirt sleeve' order. Shirts with breast pockets and epaulettes, known as 'bush pattern' shirts, were purchased to replace the wearing of tunics during the hot summer months.

—oOo—

At the same time that the regular force was being reorganised, the opportunity was taken to examine the ordering of the Special Constabulary. In 1945, at the end of the war, there were 204 serving special constables. By 1958 this had reduced to 146, and included three female officers.

During 1958, all members of the Special Constabulary were asked to opt for inclusion in either the 'active list', which involved ongoing periods of duty and training, or the 'reserve list', for call-out on ceremonial occasions and emergencies. Sixty-four chose to join the reserve list, while the remaining 82 signed on to the active list.[8] While the rank of commandant remained, his deputy now became a chief inspector. The remaining ranks from inspector down were not changed.[9] To accord with the organization of the regular force, the special constables were now posted to the various divisional headquarters.

In May 1959 the commandant of the Special Constabulary, Andrew Philip Dugald Michael,

[8] The Reserve List was allowed to reduce through natural wastage. By 1965 there were only six names left on it.
[9] The Special Constabulary Long Service Medal was awarded for nine years peace time service, with a bar for 10 years.

First Aid team 1949. From left to right, back row: PC 112 Eric Claridge, PC 120 Norman Farrant, PC 151 Norman Hull. Front row: PC 164 Len Smith, Sgt 13 Frank Brough, PC 185 Norman Peplow. (Courtesy N.W. Hull)

1930s – had been interrupted by the war, and was slow to recover during the post-war years. The first dog to be used by the Leicester City force was a Labrador, purchased in June 1938 for £12 and entrusted to PC 112 Charles Henry 'Harry' Clements. The dog was bought on the instructions of the Home Office, that 'as an experiment' it should be put out on an urban beat with a constable. In February 1939, it was announced that the dog was suitably trained and ready to commence work, and as such, PC Clements was in receipt of 7s 6d a week for its upkeep. In February 1940, with the increasing financial constraints imposed by the war, the Home Office announced that their training centre for police dogs was to be closed down due to lack of funding, and the police dog scheme was for the time being terminated. After the war, in late 1948 and again in 1950, there are vague references to the fact that Inspector Clarence Kirkland was responsible for maintaining first a dog called Monty, and later one named Silver.

In May 1956 two officers, PC 59 Swain and PC 295 Wass, attended a 13-week training course at the Metropolitan Police dog training centre at Keston in Kent. The cost to the force for this training amounted to two guineas a week training fee for the dog and handler, £1 10s 0d a week for dog food and £3 10s 0d for equipment and veterinary charges.

who had served at various levels since the war years, resigned. Michael, who had been commandant since February 1951, was replaced by his deputy, Leonard Thomas Shipman, a director and past chairman of Leicester City Football Club.

—oOo—

One further area which Mark wished to develop involved the use of dogs for police purposes. Police dog training – begun in the

A shift of officers being paraded for duty by Inspector George Brobyn, between May 1956 and October 1957. From left to right: Sgt 17 Norman Dolman, -?-, PC 236 Danny O'Connell, PC 310 John Stevenson, PC 134 Alan Bennett, PC 241 Barrie Johnson.

On their return to the force the dogs, known as Rusty I and Rusty II, were used on foot patrol for crime prevention and public order as well as for tracking criminals and searching buildings. In April 1959 PC Ronald Wass transferred to the County Police and his place with Rusty I was taken by PC 915 David Simpson.

At the beginning of 1963 it was decided to increase the dog section and four German Shepherd puppies were trained in-house by PC Simpson and PC Swain. Only one of these(a bitch named Alex who was replaced by an adult dog, Major), failed to become a trained police dog, and in late May the strength of the section was increased from two to six handlers. These four new officers were PC 355 Alan Jackson (Rowan); PC 124 Ben Farrar (Mayne); PC 347 Don Moore (Monty) and PC 169 Keith Welsh (Major).

Four years later, when the city and County Police dog sections were combined, the number of City Police dogs had risen to 10.

—oOo—

Robert Mark's first proposals in relation to improving traffic flow in Leicester city appeared in December 1959. The fact that new 'No Waiting' regulations were in the process of being ratified, with a view to their implementation the following year, was perceived by the chief constable to constitute a mixed blessing.

Charles Street police station. The two-storey building in the background, in Colton Street, housed garages on the ground floor and the police gymnasium above. Just visible on the roof in the top right-hand corner of the picture is the outline of a beacon. O.J.B. Cole was passionate about road safety and this beacon, which flashed red and green, was used to indicate to the public that a serious road traffic accident had occurred in the city. A green light meant that nothing had happened, while red indicated a fatality.

From a legislative standpoint, restrictions on parking in the city centre were to be welcomed. In 1947 there were 3.5 million motor vehicles in England and Wales, by 1958 this figure had risen to 7.5 million. In Leicester the number of vehicles licensed by the city authorities had risen from 18,000 at the outbreak of war, to 47,000 in 1958. This amounted to an increase locally of over 161%.

Mark had very strong views about the right of citizens to have free access to the roads of the city in which they lived – whether as motorists or pedestrians. He also had clear perceptions of the role of the police officer in the scheme of things. In his Annual Report for 1958 he made the point:

Many of the problems arising from the growth of vehicular traffic do not fall within the purview of the police – for example, the adequacy of highways and off-street parking, the provision of street car parks, the adequacy of traffic signals, &c... [however] It is the right of every citizen to pass freely along the highway, whether on foot or in a vehicle, and it is the inescapable duty of the police to see that this freedom is maintained. Whenever the problem of concentration of traffic is encountered in it's more severe form the enforcement of the law can generally be said to have two objectives, namely, the maintenance of free movement of traffic along essential routes and the sharing as fairly as possible of the space available for parking.

The other side of the coin was that any legislation was (and always will be) only as effective as the ability of the police to enforce it. Robert Mark felt that at this point, the time was not right for the enforcement of traffic regulations by civilians. Consequently implementation of the new regulations would have to be undertaken by police officers.

Overtime was already being paid to officers working the additional rest day. To impose an increased workload was not feasible. The national average per head of police to population at this time was 1:555. In Leicester it was 1:627. To remedy this factor alone would require an extra 57 officers, which would involve an additional annual cost in the region of £68,000 a year.

A further relevant factor in the equation was that current figures showed that, in England and Wales during the previous year (1958), indictable offences (crimes), stood at 626,509 – of which 45.6 per cent had been detected. In Leicester city the figure for this period was 3,276 crimes reported, with a detection rate of 56 per cent. One of the chief constable's reservations was that an abstraction of police officers to deal with traffic matters would most certainly have a detrimental impact upon his force's ability to solve crimes.

Having outlined his predicament to the Home

Sergeant 27 (later inspector) Fred Sutton, working in the first information room sometime between July 1955 and January 1958.

Office, Mark opted to bid for an increase in his establishment of policewomen, with a view to utilising female officers in the enforcement of the new regulations.[10] As the issue would generate a matter of national policy, the Home Office refused Mark's request.

At this stage, the chief constable was forced to revise his opinions about the suitability of civilians becoming involved in the enforcement of the law. There was a school of thought within the City Council which was in favour of the use of parking meters, and at one point an order for several hundred was placed, which subsequently had to be cancelled. The concept of meters was one to which Mark was particularly opposed, on the grounds that the ability to park should not be related to the ability to pay for the privilege.

As a consequence of his deliberations, in September 1960 Robert Mark gave notice to the Watch Committee that he was in the process of preparing a report on the viability of establishing a traffic wardens unit.

Just before Christmas 1960, the City Council were asked to authorise an establishment of 50 traffic wardens to be deployed in the city with effect from 1 April 1961. The initial salary proposed for newly-appointed wardens was £580 per annum, rising to £640 after three years. In

readiness for April 1961, a preliminary group of 20 wardens was inducted. This was increased to 31 during the following year.

The traffic wardens department, under Inspector Joiner, with a staff of one sergeant and a constable, was lodged in what was to become its permanent location, the old St George's School in Colton Street, at the rear of the police headquarters. The scheme was a success from the outset. One immediate effect was to remove from the police the time-consuming task of dealing with parked vehicles, while a longer term benefit was that the fixed penalty system considerably reduced the workload of the city magistrates

Two motor cyclists of the newly created 'D' division, outside the garages in the yard at force headquarters. Left: PC 256 Trevor Hull, right: PC 258 George McRae. The 'D' division letter is just visible on PC McRae's left shoulder.

courts. Following visits to the city by representatives from other local authorities, the traffic wardens scheme was quickly adopted nationwide.

—oOo—

While these major policy decisions were being implemented, other less notable but very relevant affairs were still being resolved.

A function which the Police Service had inherited during the war was the responsibility for

---

[10] Mark's reasoning was based on two factors. First, historically no policewoman had served long enough in the force to qualify for pension. Second, due to their hours, a woman's salary was slightly less than that of her male counterpart. (Police Regulations 1952 declared that a policewoman should work either a 7 or 7 ½ hour tour of duty, with a one hour meal break, as opposed to a male officer who worked 8 hours, with a 45 minute meal break. Leicester City Police had opted for the 7 ½ hour option.) Unless specifically required by the exigencies of duty, a policewoman did not usually work after 12 midnight.

Robert Mark, chief constable January 1957–April 1967.

civil defence training. As a part of this readiness, along with 11 other Midlands forces, Leicester City Police agreed to participate in the provision of a mobile column, to train annually, which could provide mutual assistance to areas in the surrounding region. The first of these exercises took place between 29 August and 6 September 1960. The overall column consisted of 115 men and 29 vehicles. Leicester's contribution was one inspector, one sergeant and eight constables, costing a total of £140, of which 75 per cent was absorbed by an exchequer grant. The yearly exercise continued until the mid-1960s. In 1964 one sergeant and 11 PCs spent three weeks during May and June with the column at Beckingham army camp in Lincolnshire. As an alternative to police patrol duties, a posting to the mobile column was hardly an exacting secondment.

Training of the warden section of the Civil Defence Corps remained the responsibility of the City Police, and the force training department staff continued to be civil defence instructors. In 1961 the warden strength for the city was: 8 sector wardens, 8 post wardens, 15 senior wardens and 20 other members under training.

Traditionally, the men and women of the force below the rank of inspector had been paid their salary on a weekly basis. By common consent it was agreed that from July 1961 everyone would be paid by cheque on a monthly basis.

One of the things which Robert Mark was keen to resolve was the situation whereby the city and County Police forces shared a radio scheme. From March 1962 the City Police instituted their own radio net, and the joint scheme with the County was discontinued.[11]

—oOo—

On 3 August 1960, the assistant chief constable, Bernard Louis Ecob, who had for some time been in poor health, died of a heart attack at the age of 56. Bernard Ecob had served with the Leicester City Police force since 1923, and had been the deputy chief constable from December 1945 until January 1953, when he became assistant chief constable. He was replaced on 1 September by Detective Superintendent Eric Ernest Lacy, another long-term city officer who had joined the force in January 1931.

—oOo—

The institution of a traffic warden scheme to deal with parking problems in Leicester city set Robert Mark on the road to becoming recognised as a radical among his fellow chief officers, a fact which on occasion did not endear him to many of them. An instance of this came in the early 1960s.

In August 1963 the hijacking of a train in the dead of night, on a lonely stretch of line in Buckinghamshire, and the subsequent theft of

11 The Leicester city radio call-sign was M2NT

Annual inspection of the force on the Magazine Barracks parade ground during the late 1950s. Standing behind Her Majesty's Inspector is Chief Constable Robert Mark, accompanied by the Lord Mayor. the first four officers in line from right to left are: PC 211 Peter Mason, PC 304 Brian 'Timber' Woods, PC 65 Albert Foster and PC 103 'Jack' Tingay.

£2,800,000 in used notes caused a furore which was to continue for many years.

Following the arrest and conviction of members of the gang responsible for the Great Train Robbery, serious questions began to be asked about the security of their prison accommodation. The criminals, who at the time were considered to be the most audacious in recorded history, were also regarded as being highly likely to escape from prison. One of the prisons in which they were serving sentence was HMP Leicester, the security for which was the responsibility of Leicester City Police. The other prison involved was HMP Durham.

At an early stage Robert Mark, along with the chief constable of Durham, was asked to discuss the matter of security with the Home Secretary, Sir Frank Soskice. Prior to their interview with the Secretary of State, they were summoned to a private discussion with the chief inspector of constabulary. At this preliminary conference Mark was asked to join with the other two in persuading the Home Secretary that the army and

not the police should be made responsible for ensuring that the train robbers did not escape from gaol. Mark did not subscribe to their view, and on the basis that any escape from prison constituted a criminal offence, he was emphatic that the police at Leicester would accept full responsibility for the security of HMP Leicester. What he did require prior to accepting the responsibility was that sufficient and suitable firearms be supplied to his men.

The resultant meeting with the Home Secretary was, in Robert Mark's own words, 'conducted in painful disharmony'. As far as Leicester City Police was concerned, the Home Office granted permission for firearms to be carried in certain vehicles under secure conditions, to be used as an armed response to any attempt at a break-out from the prison. The chief constable of Durham, taking a diametrically opposed position was (for a time at least) provided with troops to ensure the safekeeping of Durham prison.

Permission was given for the acquisition of a dozen Belgian FN self-loading rifles and ammunition by the Leicester City Police, which were thereafter carried in the rapid response traffic cars of 'D' division. Wireless vehicles made hourly checks of the perimeter of the Welford Road gaol, cryptically reporting that the check had been completed over the radio using code-words which were changed on a regular basis.

A consequence of this innovation was that it generated a training need. By September 1965 all CID, motor patrol and control room officers, along with senior officers, were being regularly trained and certified in the use of firearms. Due to financial constraints, the weapons used for training were mainly those which had been handed in over the years under amnesty conditions. This resulted in officers being instructed in the use of a range of weapons, from .303 rifles to a variety of handguns such as automatic pistols and .38 revolvers.

In late 1965, the chief constable reported that 'eight automatic pistols, six of which date back to 1940, are now unreliable…' To regularise the situation the Watch Committee agreed to purchase forthwith six Browning model 10/22 cal. 9mm automatic pistols at £16 16s 0d, each and two model B.22 rifles at £28 16s 0d, each.[12]

Two developments in 1964–5 were to have a lasting effect on operational policing in the city.

The possibility of organising criminal investigation on an inter-force basis had been under discussion for some time. In December 1964 Mark submitted a report to the Watch Committee asking that a sub-regional crime squad be established. He proposed that the new squad should be based in rented premises in Trafalgar House at 171-173 Charles Street.[13] City and county detective officers were to be assigned to the squad, and provisionally, when next a police house became vacant, it could be allocated for the use of an officer from Nottingham. The report was approved in February 1965 and the No.4 District Crime Squad came into being. Between April and June, Detective Inspector Norman Cox, along with Detective Sergeant William McGrory and Detective Constable Alan Beeston, was assigned to the new unit.

Between October 1964 and February 1965, at a cost of £845, 25 personal pocket wireless sets, five chargers, one base station and 75 batteries were acquired from the Home Office. Although these were initially used on an experimental basis, policing had moved into a new dimension. Later, in September 1965, a pilot scheme for the use of VHF pack sets carried by foot patrol officers was undertaken with a view to using the radios for crowd control and public order situations. Heavy and cumbersome, the radios greatly restricted an officers mobility and were not a success. Eventually, in July 1966 14 personal radio sets were purchased on approval and issued to officers in 'A' and 'B' divisions. As an adjunct to these moves toward giving foot patrol officers a means of radio communication, the force control room was removed from the rear of the charge office to a new location on the first floor of the building.

From then on, with a rapid increase in communications technology, the days of the old 'box system' were numbered. A decision was taken that the remaining 29 police boxes in the force area – most of which were now 35 years old – with the exception of the one at Upperton Road Bridge (Boulevard box), would be demolished as they fell into disrepair.

—oOo—

Although the compulsory amalgamations of police forces did not take place until April 1967, the spectre of amalgamation was beginning to loom as early as 1964. At this time there were in England and Wales approximately 125 separate police forces. By absorbing the smaller ones into the larger – which essentially meant that every Borough and City force was assimilated into the adjacent county force – the number could be reduced to less than half.

Early in 1964 the first inter-change of officers

---

[12] The first reference to the use of firearms by Leicester Borough Police is in February 1868, when an instruction was issued that sergeants and PCs in the 'A' division would be instructed in the use of revolvers. A further reference in January 1911 states that 'the Watch Committee have decided to train a number of officers in the use of firearms for use in extreme emergency'

[13] This was a building on the opposite side of Charles Street from the main police station.

Assistant Chief Constable Eric Earnest Lacy. Eric Lacy joined the Leicester force in January 1931 as PC 179, having previously worked as a traffic officer. He spent the larger part of his service in the detective department, rising to detective superintendent before succeeding the late Bernard Ecob as assistant chief constable. Eric Lacy was one of the last examples of an officer progressing through the ranks within the same force from constable to ACPO rank.

PC 179 Eric Lacy.

between the county and city forces began. At first, detective and motor patrol officers were seconded between the two forces for varying periods of time, usually a month, or two months. These exchanges extended in October of that year to include policewomen.

The Police Act 1964, which received Royal Assent on 10 June of that year, spelled out to police authorities the shape of things to come. The intentions of the Act were simply stated. Provisions were contained for the making of

schemes for the amalgamation of police areas, while further clauses dealt with the organisation of new police forces. The constitution of new police authorities was laid out, along with details relating to financial matters, the Special Constabulary, cadets, regulations and disciplinary matters.

Watch Committees were to be re-constituted as from 1 June 1965, and from that date were to be composed of a total number determined by the local Council. Two thirds of its membership was to be drawn from members of the local Council, and one third from the local magistracy.[14]

Because of reluctance by local authorities to accept what was essentially a political move by central government, in November 1965 a peremptory statement was issued by the

[14] It was decided that the body for the Leicester Police authority would be a total of 21 members.

government to the effect that '…amalgamations will take place under the authority of the Police Act 1964 which empowers the Home Office to make compulsory amalgamations'.

This reluctance was as evident in Leicester as in many other towns and cities throughout the land, none of whom wished to lose what had, for almost 130 years, been a dedicated police force. In May 1966 the Leicester Watch Committee received a letter from the Home Secretary 'suggesting', an amalgamation of the Leicester City Police and the Leicestershire and Rutland Police forces. The final sentence read '…The Secretary wishes to know by the 27 June 1966 whether the Authorities are prepared to enter into a voluntary amalgamation: if not he intends to promote a compulsory amalgamation…'

—oOo—

In the meantime, while various negotiations were taking place about who should be chief officer of the new force, Robert Mark had been busy elsewhere.

Maintaining his by now renowned radical stance on law enforcement, in October 1965 he drew considerable comment during a lecture to the 'Crime-a-Challenge Society' at Nuffield College. In this lecture Robert Mark proposed a series of controversial changes to criminal law. First he proposed that majority verdicts should be accepted in criminal trials, thus removing the problems of hung-juries and endless retrials. Next, he advocated the pre-trial disclosure by defence councils of any alibi on the part of an accused; this was to be accompanied by a requirement on the part of an accused to enter the witness box and be cross-examined. Finally, he proposed that the caution against self-incrimination given to a defendant during interview should be dispensed with.

The content of this lecture, while the basis for much debate, also served to establish Mark's independency as a chief constable. During the autumn of the following year, he was seconded to be a part of the Mountbatten Committee on prison reform.

When amalgamation between the City and County Police forces finally became a reality, it was the chief constable of the Leicestershire and Rutland Constabulary, John Albert Taylor, who became the new chief officer.

That Robert Mark was bitterly disappointed is not in doubt. However, politically there was a degree of inevitability in the decision. The county force was larger, and consequently had more seats in the new police authority. The county chief constable, although of retirement age, was in a more favourable position to secure the post.

After leaving the Leicester City Police as its last chief constable, Robert Mark moved on to become assistant commissioner, and later commissioner, of the Metropolitan Police, closing a 131-year circle.

In 1836, Frederick Goodyer had come from the Metropolitan Police to become head constable of Leicester Borough Police. In 1967, Robert Mark left Leicester to become commissioner of the Metropolitan Police.

Appendix I

Report of George Owston to the Watch Committee – 4 January 1836

At this meeting Mr George Owston was examined and made the following statement:

'Mr George Owston was chief constable and resigned the office on 22 December, which is now vacant. There were eight constables with salaries viz; Unwin, Hurst, Banks, Ross, Brooks, Hester, Jeffery, [......?].

Salary £10 a year. The ward constables had the fees for attending the sessions, the first day 5s as well as the second. The town servants who were constables were paid for the second day only. There are 15 Wards. The ward constables served different precepts under me – there was a Headborough in each Ward under the constables who performed the duty under the ward constable. The ward constables had no salaries, their remuneration depended on fees. [I] Think 78 were sworn in as constables last Holy Thursday. There were originally eight policemen with a salary of £10 and they attended the Exchange twice a week, ward constables and Headborough and Supernumaries. The town servants are mace bearers and constables. Five Black Gowns and 4 Red Coats. Situation of policeman may be worth £13 exclusive of fees received for executing warrants &c., and most, if not all of them in other business.

I reported to the magistrates as to the constables and I had the power to suspend but not put on. The Supernumaries had no salary, they were paid according to the time engaged 3s 6d to 5s a day. The night watch consist of four men and myself on Saturday night and fair and race times. The constable is only paid in one prosecution though he may be a witness in more. There are from 25 to 30 who may be considered in regular employ. I think there should not be less than 30 for a night police and 20 for the day and better for the night watch to be relieved every four or six hours. It would require 30 out at the same time. There should not be less than 7 or 8 to a Ward. At the present time, in case of constables being wanted application was made to the ward constable. I would certainly advise the police to wear livery – it is the most effective to prevent offences and at public times have part out of livery. Salary as chief constable – £50 a year. Fees about £20 more at the outside. One shilling for each precept and 5s for being out on Saturday nights.

I was keeper of the House of Correction, salary £120 a year – no fees. Should think 18s a week for salary, from that to a pound with a livery sufficient to ensure respectable young men. For salary for sergeants of police 25s to 28s about the sum paid in London. Some of the Leicester constables make regular trade of it, but some are respectable and efficient men. When reward given, the constable alone has had it – it has been paid into the general fund and the effect is injurious as it prevents one constable giving any information to another, in Cook's case the reward was distributed. Any rewards should go into a general fund. All the constables except police depend on fees. If the person apprehended be not committed for trial the constable is not paid so he has a strong interest in procuring commitments. No rewards for diligent discharge of duty. I should recommend a person from London decidedly to have an effective police.

The police is not so effective or extensive as it should have been.'

Appendix II
Comparison of the relative strengths of
Police Forces in England between 1874 and 1957

1874

Town	Population	Police Est	Ratio of Police officers per head of population
Newcastle-on-Tyne	128,160	180	1: 712
Salford	124,815	204	1: 611
Hull	121,598	182	1: 668
Sunderland	98,335	99	1: 993
Leicester Borough	95,084	105	1: 905
Nottingham	86,261	120	1: 718
Preston	85,428	97	1: 880
Oldham	82,619	82	1: 1,007
Norwich	80,390	94	1: 855
Blackburn	76,337	80	1: 954
Huddersfield	70,253	73	1: 962
Wolverhampton	68,279	69	1: 989
Halifax	65,124	66	1: 986
Rochdale	63,473	63	1: 1,007
Bath	52,557	87	1: 604
Middlesbrough	50,000	64	1: 781

1895

Town	Population	Ratio of Police officers per head of population
Liverpool	517,980	1: 400
Manchester	505,368	1: 490
Birmingham	478,113	1: 714
Leeds	367,505	1: 814
Sheffield	324,243	1: 796
Bristol	221,578	1: 564
Bradford	216,361	1: 845
Nottingham	213,877	1: 950
Hull	200,044	1: 722
Salford	198,139	1: 600
Newcastle-on-Tyne	186,300	1: 670
Leicester Borough	174,624	1: 1,027
Portsmouth	159,251	1: 816
Oldham	131,463	1: 925
Sunderland	131,015	1: 916
Blackburn	120,064	1: 945
Brighton	115,873	1: 662
Bolton	115,002	1: 942
Derby	94,146	1: 941
Northampton	61,012	1: 793

1952

Town	Population	Police Est	Ratio of Police officers per head of population
Nottingham	306,000	423	1: 723
Hull	302,000	457	1: 660
Newcastle-on Tyne	294,000	398	1: 38
Bradford	292,000	447	1: 653
Leicester	258,000	256	1: 1,007
Stoke-on-Trent	272,000	269	1: 1,011
Coventry	258,000	300	1: 860
Cardiff	243,000	329	1: 738
Portsmouth	240,000	309	1: 776
Plymouth	208,000	257	1: 809

* The figures shown are for constables, not the total force establishment

1957

Town	Population	Police Est	Ratio of Police officers per head of population
Hull	299,600	596	1: 502
Nottingham	312,500	572	1: 546
Bradford	286,500	534	1: 536
Newcastle-on-Tyne	281,000	487	1: 577
Cardiff	246,600	439	1: 561
Leicester	281,200	428*	1: 657
Portsmouth	240,020	388	1: 618
Coventry	267,300	370	1: 722
Stoke-on-Trent	274,000	368	1: 744

* 428 indicates the authorised establishment, actual male strength at this time was 356

Appendix III
Roll of Honour
Officers of the Leicester Borough Police force who died in World War One, 1914-18

PC 261	William Alfred Bailey	Royal Horse Artillery.	*Nov 1916
PC 48	John H.Briggs	Military Mounted Police.	*Dec 1917
PC 274	John Cobley	West Yorkshire Regt.	
PC 89	Richard Hazelwood	Grenadier Guards.	25 Jul 1917
PC 180	F.Hutson	Royal Marine Artillery	9 Nov 1917
PC 259	E.Maddock M.M	Royal Horse Artillery	3 Oct 1917
PC 232	Geo Arthur Manton	Coldstream Guards.	*Apr 1916
PC 199	Albert W.Osborn	Leicestershire Regt.	*Jul 1917
PC 276	T.Percival	Leicestershire Regt.	
PC 55	A.E.Reeves	Leicestershire Regt.	*Feb 1916
PC 183	W.Woodward	Royal Marine Artillery	9 Nov 1917

All dates are based upon the Watch Committee Notes. As such, those marked * are not the actual date of death but the date reported by the Watch Committee.

Details of the dates of death of PC 274 Cobley and PC 276 Percival no longer appear to exist.
PC Richard Hazelwood's warrant number is shown as '89', both at the time of his release to join the Colours in August 1914 and at the time of his death in 1917. An anomaly arises insomuch that this number was also allocated to PC 89 Fieldsend who joined the Leicester Borough Police in September 1914. Fieldsend is shown as holding this number in March 1915 when he was released to join the Colours, and in fact retained it until his retirement in October 1939. A possible explanation is that Hazlewood's number was for some reason reallocated immediately after he was released to the army on the basis that he would be given a new number on his return from the war – which his death prevented.

Appendix IV
Pay scales for Police Forces in England during World War One

Following figures are in respect of pay during 1915

Force	Strength of Force	Pay on appointment	After 20 yrs
Liverpool	2,261	30s	40s (after 15 years)
Glasgow	1,996	27s 5d	37s 4d (after 10 years)
Birmingham	1,431	29s	39s
Manchester	1,394	28s	40s
Leeds	720	28s 6d	37s 6d
Bristol	617	28s	40s
Sheffield	583	28s	39s
Hull	463	28s	38s
Bradford	448	28s	39s
Newcastle-on-Tyne	400	28s	39s
Nottingham	343	28s	39s (after 16 years)
Salford	330	27s	36s
Leicester	295	27s	36s
Cardiff	294	30s	40s (after 15 years)
Portsmouth	283	28s	38s
Dundee	256	27s	37s 4d (after 10 years)
Birkenhead	247	30s	40s (after 15years)
Stoke-on-Trent	233	28s	39s
Bolton	202	28s	38s
Aberdeen	200	27s 5d	37s 11d (after 15 years)
Oldham	172	28s	38s
Middlesbrough	168	28s	36s
Swansea	161	28s	37s (after 15 years)
Blackburn	158	27s	36s
Derby	153	28s	38s (after 18 years)
Huddersfield	138	29s	39s (after 15 years)
Coventry	137	29s	39s
Burnley	135	26s 6d	35s
Northampton	134	25s	35s (after 11 years)
St Helens	134	30s	41s
Stockport	133	27s	39s 2d
Preston	130	27s	35s (after 15 years)
Halifax	126	28s	38s

Appendix V
Location of Police Boxes 1930-31

Abbey Lane	–	Abbey Park Road
Abbey Lane	–	Thurcaston Road
Aylestone Road	–	Brazil Street
Aylestone Road	–	Middleton Street
Belgrave Road	–	LNER Railway Station
Braunstone Gate	–	Hinckley Road
Catherine Street	–	Railway Bridge
Charles Street	–	Belgrave Gate
Chesterfield Road	–	East Park Road
Church Gate	–	Burley's Lane
Cottesmore Road	–	Uppingham Road
Demontfort Street	–	London Road
Eastern Boulevard	–	Walnut Street
Evington Lane	–	Evington Valley Road
Fosse Road	–	Beatrice Road
Frog Island	–	Slater Street
Gipsy Lane	–	Harrison Road
Gipsy Lane	–	Victoria Road East
Haymarket	–	Wharf Street
Hinckley Road	–	Gimson Road
Humberstone Road	–	Cobden Street
London Road	–	Ratcliffe Road
Loughborough Road	–	Shaftesbury Avenue
Melbourne Road	–	Berners Street
Narborough Road	–	Railway Bridge
New Walk	–	Welford Road
Rendell Road	–	Recreation Ground
Richmond Road	–	Cavendish Road
Saffron Lane	–	Recreation Ground
Sparkenhoe Street	–	Swain Street
St Saviours Road	–	Charnwood Street
St Saviours Road	–	Copdale Road
Uppingham Road	–	New Park
The Newarkes	–	Oxford Street
Victoria Park	–	Victoria Park Road, London Road
Welford Road	–	Recreation Ground
Welford Road	–	Wordsworth Road
Wentworth Road	–	Recreation Ground
Woodboy Street	–	Police station

A small box was installed on a site owned by Montague Burton of Eastgates, at the Clock Tower in 1934.

Appendix VI
Officers of Leicester City Police who served in the Armed Forces ~ World War Two

Royal Navy and Royal Marines

Bentham, Reginald
Bingham, John
Freear, William
Lusty, Dennis
Mackenzie, Roderick*
Martyn, Norman
Munns, Leonard
Preston, Peter*
Robinson, Christopher
Woolley, Maurice
Wren, Christopher

HM Army

Adkin, Clement
Barnes, Albert
Beaumont, William
Bennett, Victor*
Berry, Stuart
Botterill, Hedley
Bush, Derek
Carstairs, Daniel
Cassie, John
Chambers, James
Davie, Maurice
Dawson, Clifford
Farley, Jack
Glover, Albert
Goodman, Winston
Green, Harry
Green, Leslie
Hadley, Norman
Hateley, Douglas
James, Alfred
Knox, William
Lott, Gwynne
McCrory, Robert
Martin, William
Milner, John
Ormerod, Jack
Orton, Douglas*
Owen, Christopher*
Pickles, Norman
Pinchbeck, Herbert
Pomfret, John
Salmon, Thomas
Sandall, Thomas
Sheldon, Geoffrey
Smith, Charles
Smithurst, Frank
Stamp, Arthur
Storey, Arthur
Sutton, Frederick
Taylor, Harry
Todd, John
Urquhart, Walter
Wells, Thomas
Wheatley, Charles
Wickham, Arthur
Wightman, George
Williams, Eric

Royal Air Force

Abram, George
Aldersley, John
Bestwick, George
Bird, Basil*
Bleackley, Charles
Briggs, John
Brobyn, Rowland
Chell, John
Fisher, James
Hackett, Derek
Hutchinson, John
Jones, John
Mathieson, Charles
Norris, John
Prentice, James
Roberts, William
Robinson, Septimus
Smith, Sydney
Suart, Robert
Watson, Frederick
Wigley, Ronald
Woodcock, Arthur

Industry

McMahon, Frank   O'Meara, Joseph

*Civilian Clerk

Appendix VII
Roll of Honour - World War Two

PC 72 Charles Bleackley	Sgt RAF	Killed whilst flying *October 1941.
Det Cons 140 Brian Hawkes	Leicester City Police	Killed by enemy action 20 November 1940.
PC 142 William Arthur Knox	Sgt Corps Military Police	Killed in action 23 March 1944.
Roderick Gimson Mackenzie MC (Civilian Clerk)	Captain Royal Marines	Died of wounds, Belgium, 2 November 1944
PC 291 Leonard Cyril Munns -	Royal Marine Commandos	Killed in action, Normandy, 10 June 1944.
Det Sgt 29 Leonard Thomas Norman	Leicester City Police	Killed by enemy action 20 November 1940.
PC 247 John Edward Norris	Pilot Officer RAF	Missing on operations, 12 December 1943 presumed killed in action.
PC 239 James McKinlay Prentice	Sgt Pilot RAF	Missing on operations 29 August 1943 presumed killed in action.
PC 277 Thomas William Salmon	Lieutenant Royal Army Tank Corps	Killed in action, Europe, 24 September 1944.
PC 94 Harry Taylor	Sgt Corps Military Police	Died in Japanese Prisoner of War camp, Malai, 31 August 1943.
Det. Cons. 118 George Edwin Trump	Leicester City Police	Killed by enemy action 20 November 1940.
PC 286 Frederick Donald Watson	Aircraftsman RAF	Killed whilst in training in South Africa * January 1943.

* This is the date reported to the Watch Committee and is not the actual date of death.

Appendix VIII
Special Constabulary Post World War Two

During the first six months of 1945 the average strength of the SC was 465.
When the 'freezing' order was removed, 261 resigned leaving a strength of 204.

Year	Comdnt	Dep Comdnt	Inspector	Sergeant	Constable	Total
1945	1		11	28	164	204
1946					200	
1947	1		11	24	160	196
1950	1	1	10	30	191	233
1951	1	1	8	29	189	228
1952	1	1	10	23	166	(inc 1 fem) 201
1953	1	1	10	21	160	(inc 4 fem) 193
1954	1	1	9	15	160	(inc 3 fem) 186
1955	1	1	8	16	146	(inc 3 fem) 172
1956						(inc 3 fem) 162
1957	1	1	7	15	139	(inc 3 fem) 163

(1958 Active List implemented)

Year	Comdnt	Ch Inspector	Inspector	Sergeant	Constable	Total
1959	1	3	6	13	62	85
1961	1	3	5	10	70	89
1962	1	3	7	9	68	88
1965	1	3	5	6	57	72

In 1958 the Special Constabulary was reorganized to conform to the pattern of the deployment of the regular force.

All members were asked to opt for inclusion in the Active List or the Reserve List.

64 Special Constables opted to serve on the reserve list, being available for ceremonial events and emergencies.

82 Special Constables opted to join the Active List and their subsequent distribution is shown below.

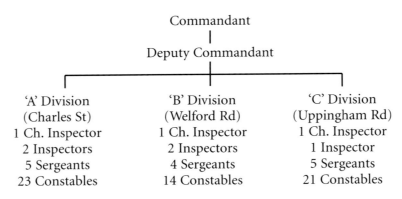

Commandant
|
Deputy Commandant

'A' Division
(Charles St)
1 Ch. Inspector
2 Inspectors
5 Sergeants
23 Constables

'B' Division
(Welford Rd)
1 Ch. Inspector
2 Inspectors
4 Sergeants
14 Constables

'C' Division
(Uppingham Rd)
1 Ch. Inspector
1 Inspector
5 Sergeants
21 Constables

Appendix IX
Traffic Warden Corps April 1960 - July 1961

Initial group appointed April 1961

1	Berry, Violet Mary
2	Bramwell, Jean Doreen
3	Dowthwaite, Kathleen May
4	Fairclough, Eva
5	Myles, Mary Helen
6	Smith, Mary Anne
7	Barson, Robert
8	Cunnington, Lionel
9	Dorgan, William Patrick
10	Lewis, Leslie Burfod
11	Maw, John William
12	
13	Trillo, Ronald Edward
14	Walmsley, John
15	Burnand, Thomas Albert
16	Cox, Maurice Raymond
17	Jones, Kenneth
18	Cockshaw, Irene
19	Collington, Pamela Ann
20	Poulton, Thomas William

Appointed in May 1961

21	Wykes, Harry Albert
22	Black, Winifred Jones
23	Carlyle, Mabel
24	Morris, Heather Jean

Appointed July 1961

25	Blockley, Margaret Elizabeth
26	Henderson, Eileen Mildred
27	Oakes, Ivy Annie
28	Solberg, Mary
29	Antill, George
30	Harris, Thomas Frederick
31	Key, Hedley

Appendix X
Dog Section on Amalgamation 31 March 1967

Officer	Dog
PC 115 D.W. Simpson	Trenchard
PC 124 A.R.B. Farrar	Luke
PC 137 T.A. Morris	Alexander
PC 169 S.K. Welsh	Major
PC 300 D.M. Stuart	Kim
PC 324 D.B. Ralph	King
PC 338 H.B.L. Fisher	Ricky
PC 347 S.D. Moore	Monty
PC 355 A.R.W. Jackson	Rowan
PC 407 D.K. Warsop	Steel

Leicester City Police Force
1 January 1929

Chief Constable
Cole, Oswald John Buxton

Deputy Chief Constable
Robertson, Dugard

Superintendents
Boon, Joseph
Choyce, Daniel
Gabbitas, John

Inspectors
Allen, Walter
Ashburner, Harry
Clowes, Roland
Cooper, Cecil William
Faulkner, George
Gray, Percy Edgar
Hall, Arthur
Kendall, Albert Edward
Newman, Ernest Henry
Shepherdson, Lancelot
Sims, Albert
Underwood, Henry Garford
Wicks, Shirley
Willis, Richard Braithwaite

Sergeants
1 Burton, Alexander
2 Parrott, Albert William
3 Wilson, Frank
4 Millward, Herbert
5 Newberry, George
6 Lyner, Walter
7 Porter, William
8 Thompson, Arthur
9 Bonnett, Samuel
10 Coleman, Albert
11 Whyman, William
12 Everitt, William
13 Allen, John
14 Wells, Walter Elliott
15 Crane, Ernest
16 Staines, George
17 Weston, Jesse Samuel
18 Hall, Harold E.
19 Hardesty, Herbert

20 Lucas, Albert James
21 Matthews, William
22 Root, Arthur Harry
23 Thornton, Herbert
24 Jenney, Harold George
25 Cross, Frank
26 Edwards, Alvin Gent
27 Hankinson, George
28 Crithclow, John Archibold
29 Hubbard, Arthur
30 Elton, Francis
31 Turner, Edward Charles
32 King, Charles

Constables
33
34 Holden, William
35 Mason, Ernest
36 Bateman, Charles
37 Matthews, William
38 Terry, George
39 Kirby, William
40 Tetstall, Albert
41 Lockwood, Arthur
42 Wilby, James
43 Gatward, William
44 Lovell, William
45 Garner, Walter
46 Cowley, William
47 Broadhurst, Joseph
48 Davis, Joseph
49 Moore, Albert
50 Lee
51 Rosevear, William
52 Preston, George
53 O'Leary, Francis Arthur James
54 Gill, Roy
55 Sheppard, James
56 Goodwin, Frank
57 Spencer, Egbert Augustine
58 Swain, Maurice
59 Simmonds, James
60 Beaver, Joseph
61 Watkins, Harry Lewis
62 Burley, Richard
63 Smith, Charles Alfred
64 Clowes, George

65 Conway, Thomas
66 Clarke, Ernest William
67 Jesson, Arthur
68 Goosey, William
69 Heywood, James
70 Moss, Percy
71 Brooksbank, Arthur
72 Adkinson, Matthew
73 Whitney, Samuel
74 Dawson, Edward Lawrence
75 Hakesley, George Thomas
76 Roper, Harry
77 Stretton, Samuel
78 Boyles, Ernest
79 Shaw, William
80 Reeve, Frank James
81 Merriken, John Thomas
82 Leeson, Cyril
83 Vines, Leonard Arthur
84 Scott, Francis, Edward
85 Eld, John
86 Ecob, Bernard Louis
87 Matthews, John
88 Fairey, W.
89 Fieldsend, William Henry Herbert
90 Goodman, Frank William
91 Pemberton, Herbert William
92 Kirkland, Clarence
93 Burton, Walter
94 Bassett, Albert
95 Attewell, Charles
96 Nichols, Herbert
97 Slater, Richard
98 Smith, Noel Herbert Dennis
99 Harbot, Horace
100 Haywood, Thomas William
101 Jelley, Francis
102 Shingler, Joseph Henry
103 Willett, George
104 Staniforth, Frederick, John
105 Billson, William Henry
106 Marshall, George Frederick
107 Benham, George
108 Draycott, Frederick
109 Norman, Leonard Thomas
110 Bull, David
111 Whittering, George

112	Clements, Charles Henry	165	Cox, Alfred	218	Moore, Samuel Vincent
113	Matthews, George	166		219	Medhurst, Arthur
114	Meese, William	167	Collins, Alfred Frederick	220	Hogg, Joseph
115	Seal, John Edward	168	Craxford, William	221	Fraser, Donald
116	Muir, James	169		222	Broadhurst, Walter
117	Harrison, James	170	Marriott, George Ronald	223	Foulds, Walter Edward
118	Palmer, Edwin	171	Southam, Charles	224	Burgess, Charles, Edward
119	Rouse, James	172	Withers, Cyril	225	Garfield, Frank
120	Geraghty Cyril	173	Jones, Frederick	226	King, Harold
121	Wilson, Frederick E	174	Pym, Eric George	227	Cox, Ernest
122	Godfrey, James	175	Griffin, Bernard Philip	228	Bailey, Frank Bernard
123	Webster, Isaac James	176	Rowell, Joseph	229	Kellett, Harry Arnold
124	Spicer, Arthur	177	Dalby, Charles John	230	Pratt, Willam S.F.
125	Anthony, Arthur	178	Neale, Ernest Edward	231	Robins, George
126	Lawson, John Leonard	179	Hallam, Augustus	232	Spencer, Leonard
127	Walker, James	180	Shelvey, Frederick George	233	Spencer, William Cyril
128	Bradshaw, David	181	Arnold, Walter Cyril	234	Coulson, Harold
129	Houghton, Samuel	182	Green, Leslie	235	Dilkes, Walter
130	Hawley, Sidney	183	Betts, Cyril James	236	Newberry, William Victor
131	Cook, James	184	York, J.	237	Hooke, Herbert Richard
132	McCartney, Frederick	185		238	Stead, Frederick William
133	Stokes, William	186	Ridley, Charles	239	Pinfold, Richard Cecil
134	Dickenson, William	187	Black, Ernest	240	Smith, George Harold
135	King, Charles	188	Smith, George Henry	241	Smith, Walter
136	Chesterton, James Frank	189	Bates, William	242	Warner, Harry
137	Harding, Thomas	190	Orton, Frank Edward	243	
138	Johnson, Bertie	191	Beaver, George	244	
139	Inwood, Charles	192	Graham, Edwin	245	Hubbard, A.
140	Ford, Frederick James	193	Southam, James Harold	246	Whittering
141		194	Capps, John Robert	247	
142	Middleton, William	195	Higgins, Arthur	248	
143	Jones, Samuel	196	Johnson, Frederick Joseph	249	
144	Smith, Charles	197	Francis, Sidney Bilney	250	
145	Tilley, Alfred	198	Woods, John William	251	
146	Hillman, Alfred	199	Shipman John H.	252	
147	Allcott, Samuel	200	Stainforth, George	253	Bateman, Charles
148	Brighty, Harry	201	Robertson, Frank Roy	254	
149	Gleed, Arthur	202	Nutting, James	255	Caunt, E.
150	Bates, James	203	Welch, William	256	
151	Preston, Harry	204	Pease, John William	257	
152	Tallon, Thomas	205	Auld, James	258	
153	Homan, George	206	Hoy, Edward	259	
154	Miller, Victor	207	Seaton, Lancelot Crown	260	
155	Thornton, Thomas	208	Stretton, Harry	261	
156	Vines, Charles	209	Bradley, Ernest James	262	
157	Perkins, Herbert Walter	210	Brooks, George	263	Gee
158	Poole, Harold	211	Larrad, Samuel	264	Jones, Samuel
159	Mowl, Frank Leslie	212	Edwards, Joseph	265	Porter, William
160	Bottrill, Edgar	213	Toach, Harold Robert		
161	Alborn, Cyril James	214	Adams, John Henry		
162	Wade, Wallace	215	Porter, George		
163	Foulds, Alfred	216	Burks, Horace		
164	Billson, Edward	217	Bennett, Frederick		

Officers of the Leicester City Police
1 January 1929 to 31 March 1967

All of the dates shown in the following section are taken from the original Watch Committee notes for the years 1929–67.

On an officer's retirement, it was customary to enter into the notes either, his/her length of service, or their exact date of engagement. From this it has been possible to arrive at a joining date for officers who served in the years prior to 1929 and retired in the period dealt with in this section.

Similarly, the effective dates of promotions are usually given very precisely.

In respect of the dates shown for officers joining the force, this is the date shown in the notes when the Watch Committee agreed to the individual's engagement. Consequently, there may, in a some cases, be a slight discrepancy (possibly of between two and four weeks), between the date when an officer joined and the date which is shown in the Watch Committee notes.

Name	No/Rank	Joined	Details	Resigned
Abram, George Robert	PC 60	Nov 1934	Sgt 47, Apr 1954	Nov 1959
Acton, Donald Frank	PC 208	Oct 1959		
Adams, Brian Arthur	PC 310	Jul 1965		
Adams, John Henry	PC 214	May 1920		Apr 1947
Adams, Peter Richard	PC 111	Apr 1946	Sgt, Oct 1957; Insp, Sep 1964	
Adcock, Philip Arthur	PC 409	Mar 1963		
Adkin, Clement Arthur	PC 273	Jun 1938	Sgt 7, Sep 1948; Insp, Nov 1954; Ch Insp, Nov 1958; Supt, Sep 1960	
Adkinson, Matthew	PC 72	1907		Jan 1932
Aitken, Robert Martin	PC 426	Mar 1965		Nov 1965
Alborn, Cyril	PC 161	Dec 1920		
Aldersley, John Anthony	PC 274	Jun 1938		Jul 1946
Aldridge, Robert Howard	PC 56	Dec 1937	Sgt 16	Jun 1964
Aldwinckle, Francis William	PC 99	Jul 1952		Mar 1953
Allcott, Samuel	PC 147	1905		Mar 1930
Allen, Brian	PC 182	Jan 1953		
Allen, John	Sgt 13	1906	Insp, Jun 1930	Sep 1934
Allen, Robert Arthur	PC 52	Jul 1946	resigned Jun 1955; rejoined Apr 1964 as PC 220; Sgt, Sep 1964	
Allen, Walter Henry	Inspector	May 1908	was PC71	Jul 1936
Allsop, Roy	PC 260	Aug 1965		
Alton, Terence Francis	PC 389	Sep 1959		
Amor, J.G.	PC 375	Mar 1959		Mar 1960
Anderson, David Gilmour	PC 51	Feb 1946		c.1950
Anstey, Walter Jack	PC 241	Sep 1932	Sgt 40, Sep 1940	Nov 1957
Anthony, Arthur	PC 125	Aug 1920		Feb 1946
Anthony, Michael James	PC 88	May 1966		
Armstrong, Darryl James	PC 406	Jan 1965		
Arnett, Adrian James	PC 296	Apr 1966		
Arnold, Walter Cyril	PC 181	Mar 1928		Mar 1953
Artless, Joseph	PC 246	Mar 1935		Oct 1935
Ashburner, Harry	Sgt	May 1912	was PC 267, Sgt, Dec 1922; Insp, Dec 1925; Det Supt, Sep 1935	Jan 1946
Ashcroft, Peter	PC 71	Apr 1964	later PC 458	Jul 1966
Atkin, Peter Roger	PC 378	Jul 1958		Aug 1961
Atkins, Matthew	PC	c.1930		
Atkins, Norman William	PC 270	Aug 1954	Sgt 67, Apr 1965	

Name	No/Rank	Joined	Details	Resigned
Atterbury, Cyril John	PC 295	May 1959		
Attewell, Charles	PC 95	Jan 1913		Feb 1939
Auld, James	PC 205	Nov 1927	Sgt 17, Mar 1939	Dec 1952
Bacon, William Robert Stuart	PC 421	Mar 1965		
Bailey, Cyril Stanley	PC 106	Sep 1936		Sep 1937
Bailey, Edward James	PC 150	Jun 1947		Apr 1948
Bailey, Frank Bernard	PC 228	Aug 1928		Jan 1946
Bailey, G.J.	PC 150	Sep/Oct 1947		*c.*1948
Bailey, John Francis	PC 184	Jul 1947		Apr 1951
Bainbrigge, John Eric Bernard	PC 264	May 1952	Sgt, Jul 1964	
Baines, Clive Barry	PC 90	Mar 1954		
Baker, Edward George	PC 96	Oct 1931		Feb 1935
Baker, Lewis	PC 213	Oct 1931		Feb 1946
Baldwin, Stephen Michael	PC 359	Oct 1964		
Banham, Anthony Leonard	PC 383	Jan 1964		
Barker, Bruce	PC 390	Sep 1959		
Barlow, David	PC 80	Jul 1962		
Barlow, William D.	PC 65	Sep 1938	Sgt, Aug 1951	
Barmby, Gerald William	PC 86	Apr 1937		Nov 1949
Barnes, Albert Edward	PC 98	Apr 1937		May 1948
Barnett, Thomas Alan	PC 275	Sep 1954	Sgt 26, Jul 1965	
Barratt, Geoffrey Arthur George	PC 192	Jan 1964		
Barrett, Anthony J.	PC 185	Sep 1955		
Barry, John Jeffery	PC278	Aug 1952		
Barston, Ronald Ernest	PC 328	Dec 1956		
Barton, Norman James	PC 64	Mar 1956	Sgt, Oct 1963	
Basford, Robert	PC 375	Aug 1961		*c.*Jan 1962
Bassett, Albert	PC 94	1906		Aug 1931
Batchelor, Ronald William	PC 195	Mar 1965		
Bateman Charles	PC 36	Dec 1924	later PC 253	Jun 1951
Bates, James Arthur	PC 150	Oct 1929	Sgt 37, Mar 1939; Insp, Dec 1941	Feb 1955
Bates, John Thomas	PC 290	Jan 1958		
Bates, William	PC 189	1904		Dec 1929
Batty, John	PC 245	Mar 1967		
Beaman, Ronald	PC 113	Oct 1935		Nov 1960
Beardsley, Roland	PC 270	Jul 1952		Jan 1954
Beaumont, William Richard	PC 245	Mar 1935		Mar 1965
Beaver, George	PC 191	May 1908	was PC 60, Sgt 29, Apr 31	
Beaver, Joseph	PC 60	May 1908		Nov 1934
Beazley, John Benjamin	PC 326	Sep 1965		
Bedford, Geoffrey Colin	PC 178	Nov 1949		Aug 1951
Beeby, Barry Royce	PC 217	Sep 1957		
Beeston, Alan Thomas	PC 321	Jun 1959		
Bell, James Kerr	PC 125	May 1946		
Bellamy, David Thomas	PC 272	Apr 1965		Dec 1965
Belton, Alan	PC 218	Jan 1958		
Bendell, Edward	PC 186	Jul 1948		
Benham, George	PC 107	Apr 1926		Apr 1951
Bennett, Alan John	PC 134	Jan 1951		
Bennett, Frederick	PC 217	1906		Sep 1932

Name	No/Rank	Joined	Details	Resigned
Bennett, Gerald	PC 210	May 1950		
Bennett, Victor	PC 53	Nov 1947		Aug 1955
Bent, William Dennis	PC 252	Jan 1952		Jan 1953
Bentham, Reginald	PC 84	Apr 1939		d. Jul 1946
Bentley, Fred William	PC 80	Sep 1936	Sgt 19, Oct 1957	Sep 1966
Berks, Harold	PC 52	Oct 1931	Sgt 31, Feb 1941	Aug 1963
Berridge, Graham Sydney	PC 207	Sep 1963		
Berry, Stuart	PC 64	Mar 1935	Sgt 18, Jul 1955	May 1960
Berry, Terence John	PC 168	Mar 1959		
Bestwick, George Hadyn Whitcroft	PC 43	Sep 1938	Sgt, Dec 1949; Insp, Jun 1953 Ch Insp, Sep 1960; Supt, Apr 1964	
Bestwick, Ivan	PC 201	Sep 1948		May 1959
Betts, Cyril	PC 183	Apr 1926		c.Jan 1941
Biggerstaff, Frederick J.	PC 131	Oct 1933	Sgt 18, Jan 1947	Apr 1953
Billings, Ronald Trevor	Pc 192	Feb 1955		Jan 1956
Billson, Edward Cecil	PC 164	Dec 1924	Det Sgt 30, Oct 1933	Mar 1947
Billson, William Henry	PC105	1904		Mar 1929
Bingham, John	PC 81	Sep 1939	Sgt 37, Dec 1953; Insp, Sep 1962	
Birch, Gerald John Francis	PC 64	Jul 1955		Mar 1956
Birnie, Alexander Edward	PC 200	Sep 1947		
Black, Eric	PC 72	Feb 1946		Mar 1954
Black, Ernest L.	PC 187	Oct 1926		Oct 1951
Blackburn, Ian	PC 150	Sep 1962		
Blackman, John Roger	PC 54	Dec 1946		Mar 1955
Blair, William John Matthew Mullen	PC 274	Nov 1961		Aug 1966
Blakemore, Donald Charles	PC 84	Dec 1947	Sgt 21, Apr 1966	
Blakesley, Peter Herrick	PC 292	Oct 1952		Oct 1953
Bleackley, Charles J.	PC 72	c.late 1930s		kia Oct 1941
Bocking, Geoffrey Oscar	PC 149	Nov 1954		Nov 1961
Boness, Laurence Frank	PC 133	Mar 1950	t/Sgt, Apr 1966	
Bonnett, Samuel	Sgt 9	Sep 1914	was PC158; Sgt, Jul 1925	Oct 1939
Boon, Joseph William	Det Supt	Sep 1904	PC 184 in 1906	Jun 1935
Booth, Robert Bernard	PC 245	Jun 1966		Mar 1967
Bosworth, Malcolm Phillip John	PC 226	Jan 1958		
Botterill, Hedley W.	PC 97	Apr 1939		Jul 1958
Botting, Frederick John	PC 154	Jul 1946		Dec 1946
Bottrill, Edgar	PC 160	1907		Jul 1933
Bowditch, Richard Henry	PC 369	May 1958		
Bowerman, Neville	PC 348	Feb 1958		Oct 1959
Boxall, Godfrey Winham	PC 192	Aug 1947		Jan 1949
Boyland, Harold William John	PC 50	Feb 1947		Feb 1955
Boyles, Ernest	PC 78	c.Nov 1926	Sgt 7, Nov 1954	Sep 1959
Bradford, Brian Mark	PC 412	Jan 1966		
Bradley, Alan Herbert	PC 226	Sep 1951		Nov 1955
Bradley, Ernest	PC 209	Dec 1920		Feb 1946
Bradley, Martin G.	PC 111	Sep 1964		
Bradshaw, Alan Frederick	PC 215	Apr 1964		Mar 1965
Bradshaw, David	PC 128	Apr 1905		Aug 1931
Bradshaw, Hedley	PC 128	Oct 1933	Sgt, Oct 1954	Oct 1963
Bradshaw, Walter	PC 450	Nov 1965		

Name	No/Rank	Joined	Details	Resigned
Braker, John Eric	PC 272	Sep 1964		Apr 1965
Bramley, Clifford Peter	PC 332	Aug 1957	Sgt 8, Apr 1965	
Brandreth, Ian Kenneth	PC 111	Jun 1959		Aug 1964
Branson, Sydney Thomas	PC 250	Mar 1935	Sgt 29, Nov 1946; Insp, Jul 1952	Sep 1960
Breeze, Douglas	PC 104	Mar 1964		May 1966
Bremner, George Sharpe	PC 297	Jun 1961		
Brennan, James Allen	PC 275	Jun 1953		Apr 1954
Brewin, Peter Edwin	PC	Jul 1965		
Briars, Jack	PC 259	Oct 1935		Aug 1947
Brice, J.	PC 237	*c.*1950		
Briggs, Jack	PC 172	Sep 1938		Sep 1939
Briggs, John William	PC 190	Sep 1939	Sgt 49, Nov 1954; Insp, Jul 1958	Jul 1965
Brighty, Harry	PC 148	1904		Jun 1930
Broadhurst, Joseph	PC 47	Nov 1925		Mar 1954
Broadhurst, Walter	PC 222	*c.*Dec 1936	Sgt 35, Apr 1935	Jun 1952
Brobyn, Rowland George	PC 109	Apr 1939	Sgt 23, Aug 1951; Insp, Jul 1955; Ch Insp, Apr 1964; Supt, Jul 1964	
Bromage, Jack Anthony	PC 297	Sep 1954		Jan 1961
Brooks, George	PC 210	Dec 1928		Mar 1930
Brooksbank, Arthur	PC 71	Sep 1905		Dec 1931
Broomfield, John Alfred	PC 71	May 1949	Sgt 44, Apr 1958; Insp, Apr 1964	
Brough, Frank Stanley	PC 186	Jan 1931	Sgt 13, Nov 1946	Jan 1956
Broughton, Henry Clarence	PC 194	Oct 1931	Sgt 33, Aug 1951	Dec 1958
Broughton, Jack Alan	PC 116	Feb 1949	Sgt 14, Mar 1958; Insp, Jun 1965	
Brown Frederick Henry	PC 54	Apr 1955		Oct 1955
Brown,	PC152	Aug 1966		
Brown, Alex	PC 312	Jun 1956	Sgt Apr 1966	
Brown, David Norman	PC 216	Dec 1965		Jan 1966
Brown, Frederick William	PC 350	Mar 1958		
Brown, George A.	PC 196	Oct 1955		Feb 1967
Brown, John S.	PC 132	Apr 1937		*c.*Jan 1964
Brown, Robert Anthony	PC 131	May 1946		Aug 1950
Brown, Robert Samuel	PC	Aug 1966		
Brownlow, James	PC 53	Feb 1947		Sep 1947
Bryan, Keith John	PC 117	Jul 1957		Sep 1957
Bugby, Brian Oliver	PC 345	Nov 1964		May 1965
Bugby, Gordon Patrick	PC 79	Jul 1948		Sep 1948
Bull, David	PC 110	Dec 1928		Dec 1958
Burgess, Charles Edward	PC 224	1927		d. Sep 1934
Burks, Horace N.	PC 216	Nov 1925		Nov 1950
Burley, Richard	PC 62	Feb 1914		Apr 1940
Burrows, Brian Edwin	PC 342	Aug 1961		
Burt, Philip	PC 74	Aug 1946	Sgt 54, Jun 1965	
Burton, Alexander	Sgt 1	Jan 1911		Apr 1937
Burton, Walter	PC 93	1909		Oct 1935
Bush, Derek Douglas	PC 44	Apr 1938	later PC 194; Sgt 9, Dec 1959	Apr 1965
Butcher, Frank Theophilus	PC 94	Oct 1931		Sep 1936
Butler Ronald Ernest	PC 80	Oct 1957		Jun 1962
Butler, A.	PC 372	mid 1950s		Jun 1963
Butler, Barry	PC 403	Jun 1962		

Name	No/Rank	Joined	Details	Resigned
Butler, James Graham	PC 69	Jun 1956		Feb 1958
Butler, Michael Frank	PC 320	Mar 1961		
Callington, Stuart James Vernon	PC 227	Oct 1964		
Cameron, Robert Angus	PC 246	Jan 1952		Apr 1966
Camp, John William	PC 319	Nov 1956		Apr 1957
Campbell, John Patrick	PC 151	Nov 1946		Nov 1947
Campbell, Robert George Mitchell	PC 348	Apr 1961		
Cannon, Barry Peter	PC 215	Dec 1950		Aug 1955
Cant, Malcolm	PC 168	Oct 1933		Dec 1958
Capon, Barry Peter	PC 215	Aug 1951		*c.*1955
Capps, John Robert	PC 194	Sep 1905	was PC 33; Sgt 5, Oct 1929	Jan 1935
Carden, Royden David George	PC 100	Oct 1958		Mar 1963
Carey, Robert Henry	PC 273	Apr 1964		
Carr, Donald Mclean	PC 71	Oct 1962		Feb 1964
Carr, Raymond Albert	PC 84	May 1966		
Carstairs, Daniel	PC 261	Oct 1935		Oct 1965
Carter, John	PC 33	Jan 1931	later PC 114; Sgt 24, Feb 47	Aug 1963
Cassie, John	PC 77	Dec 1937	Sgt 30, Oct 1950; Insp, Oct 1957; Ch Insp, Jul 1962	
Cato, Charles Frederick	PC 79	Oct 1929		Jun 1948
Cattell, Rodney Alan	PC 408	Jan 1963		
Cattermole, Owen James	PC 313	Jun 1956		
Cattle, Michael Arthur	PC 365	Apr 1958		
Cayless, Stephen David	PC 197	Dec 1958		Oct 1960
Chamberlain, Ronald	PC 305	Feb 1953		Jan 1954
Chamberlain, Thomas	PC 217	Sep 1932		Sep 1957
Chambers, Arthur Sidney	PC 112	Aug 1950		
Chambers, Fred Theodore	PC 274	Aug 1954	Sgt 7, Oct 1959	Sep 1966
Chambers, Gwynne Gregory	PC 120	Jan 1964		
Chambers, James Howell	PC 262	Sep 1938		Sep 1957
Chappell, Charles Stanley	PC158	Oct 1931		Jun 1932
Charles, Glyn Edward	PC 152	Oct 1964		Jun 1966
Chaston, Clive	PC 190	Mar 1966		
Cheadle, Geoffery William	PC	Nov 1947		Dec 1948
Chell, John G.A.	PC 119	Apr 1939		Dec 1947
Cherry, Michael John	PC 345	Feb 1958		May 1959
Chesterton, James Frank	PC 136	Dec 1928		Sep 1945
Choyce, Daniel	Supt	Jan 1895		Jun 1929
Clarke, Arthur	PC 166	Jan 1960		
Clarke, Ernest William	PC 66	Feb 1928		Sep 1944
Clarke, John Harold	PC 135	Jun 1946		
Clark-Monks, Eric Frank	PC 50	Mar 1930		Jan 1947
Clarridge, Eric	PC 112	Apr 1946		Jul 1949
Clements, Charles, Henry	PC 112	1928	Sgt 39, Nov 1939; Insp, Mar 1950	Sep 1957
Clitherow, John Paardeburg	PC 73	Jan 1952		Dec 1953
Clow, Michael John	PC 201	Feb 1961		
Clowes, George	PC 64	May 1909		Jan 1935
Clowes, Rowland	Inspector	Dec 1907	was PC 39, Sgt 28; Insp, Feb 29	Oct 1933
Cluer, Brian Frederick	PC 99	Sep 1960		Sep 1963
Coaton, John	PC 82	Oct 1962		

Name	No/Rank	Joined	Details	Resigned
Cole, Oswald John Buxton	Ch Constable	Jan 1929		Dec 1955
Coleman, Keith Herman	PC 280	Sep 1956		
Coles, John Morris	PC 119	Jan 1951		
Colledge, Raymond	PC 101	Jul 1948		
Collingwood, George Trevor	PC 154	Sep 1959		Nov 1960
Collins, Alfred Frederick	PC 167	Nov 1914		Jan 1946
Collyer, Eric William	PC 143	Dec 1957		
Conner, James	PC 294	Oct 1952		Nov 1952
Connor, Anthony Gerald	PC 249	May 1964		
Constable, John Brian	PC 192	Jan 1956		Oct 1957
Conway, Thomas	PC 65	prior 1929		d. *c.*1940
Cook, James Reginald	PC 131	1909		Jan 1934
Coombs, Alfred William Charles	PC 128	Oct 1954		
Cooper, Brian Charles	PC 206	Aug 1958		Aug 1962
Cooper, Cecil William	Inspector	1906	was Sgt 29	Apr 1933
Cooper, William Henry	PC 294	Dec 1952		Nov 1954
Cordon, Kenneth F.	PC 48	Apr 1938		May 1943
Corns, Edward	PC 219	Mar 1947	Sgt 23, Jul 1955; Insp, Oct 1959	
Cotterill, Neville Frederick	PC	Jun 1966		
Coulson, Garry	PC 288	Sep 1964		
Coupland, Thomas Kenneth	PC 274	Jul 1952		Dec 1953
Coutts, John Downie	PC 391	Sep 1959		
Cowley, Bruce Frederick Charles	PC 156	Oct 1957		
Cowley, William Henry	PC 46	1914		Mar 1941
Cox, Alfred	PC 165	1912		Jun 1937
Cox, David Brian	PC 155	Jan 1950		
Cox, Ernest	PC 227	Dec 1924		Dec 1950
Cox, Norman	PC 148	Jul 1946	Sgt 19, Jun 1953; Insp, Oct 1957; Ch Insp, Apr 1966	
Cox, Roger	PC 354	Sep 1962		Aug 1963
Coxon, Harry	PC 133	May 1948		Jan 1950
Coyle, Charles Gabriel	PC 383	Oct 1958		Apr 1963
Coyle, Michael Henry	PC 176	Nov 1946		Nov 1946
Crane, Ernest Reginald	Sgt 15	Sep 1914	was PC 218; Sgt, Apr 1925	Jan 1946
Crane, Peter Ronald	PC 363	Mar 1962		
Craven, Bernard	PC 296	Sep 1964		Mar 1966
Craxford, William	PC 168	1907		Sep 1933
Critchlow, John Archibold	Sgt 28	Feb 1920	Insp (Ch Clerk), Sep 1931; Supt, Mar 1939	Sep 1953
Crofts, Graham Leslie	PC 306	May 1961		Mar 1964
Crombie, Donald Graham	PC 133	Jun 1966		
Crooks, Clive Charles	PC 317	Nov 1956		Dec 1958
Cross, Frank	PC49	Sep 1914	Sgt 25, Feb 29	Sep 1939
Crossley, David	PC 309	May 1956		
Croxtall, Stanley Wilfred	PC 229	Jan 1958		Jun 1961
Cunningham, Robert	PC 362	May 1955	was PC 62	
Currall, Walter Harry	PC 232	Oct 1951		
Curtis, John Thomas	PC 142	Nov 1947	Sgt 1, Nov 1956	
Curtis, Leslie Edward	PC 115	Sep 1939	Sgt, Oct 1957	
Dakin, Brian Gordon	PC 420	Jan 1965		Jan 1965

Name	No/Rank	Joined	Details	Resigned
Dalby, Charles John	PC 177	Dec 1928	Sgt 9, Nov 1939; Insp, Oct 1951	d. Nov 1958
Dalgliesh, John Featherstone	PC 167	Aug 1964		
Daniels, John Oliver	PC 105	Mar 1930		Mar 1955
Davie, Maurice	PC 171	Mar 1935		Mar 1960
Davies, Eric Graham	PC 228	Jul 1958		
Davies, John	PC 392	Sep 1959		
Davies, William	PC 243	Aug 1958		
Davis, Joseph	PC 48	Mar 1913		Mar 1938
Davis, Ralph Ponting	PC 429	Mar 1966		
Dawe, Colin James	PC 401	Dec 1964		
Dawkins, Roy Charles	PC 106	Feb 1951		
Dawson, Brian	PC 339	Mar 1957		
Dawson, Clifford James	PC 151	Apr 1938		Oct 1946
Dawson, Edward	PC 74	Aug 1921		Aug 1946
Day, Michael John	PC 354	Mar 1961		Aug 1962
de Ville, Peter	PC 96	Jan 1949		
Deberex, John Edward	PC 341	Apr 1957		
Denton, Malcolm Frederick	PC 222	Jan 1967		
Derry, Douglas Raymond	PC 265	Jul 1952		
Dickenson, William	PC 134	1910		Aug 1936
Dilkes, Ronald S.	PC 173	Apr 1937	Sgt 51, Oct 1957	
Dilkes, Walter	PC 235	Dec 1920		Feb 1949
Dinsdale, Graham Spencer	PC 109	Feb 1963		
Ditchfield, Bryan	PC 100	Oct 1931		Sep 1958
Dolman, Norman Victor	PC 144	Sep 1939	Sgt 17, Dec 1952; Insp, Oct 1957	Oct 1964
Donnelly, Terence Stuart	PC 198	Jan 1961		
Double, Peter John	PC 75	Oct 1946		Oct 1954
Dowell, Howard Geoffrey	PC 63	Mar 1950		Apr 1956
Downes, Charlie	PC 183	Jun 1947		
Doyle, Patrick James	PC 188	May 1966		
Draycott, Frederick	PC 108	1928		
Drew, Stanley John	PC 87	Jan 1954		
Driver, Albert Edward	PC 56	Jul 1949	Sgt 50, Jun 1957; Insp, Mar 1961	
Duncan, George K.	PC 195	Apr 1937		Nov 1963
Dunham, Norman Leonard	PC 287	Sep 1953		
Durkin, Dennis Raymond	PC 170	Oct 1949		May 1950
Dutson, Horace Gilbert	PC 200	Sep 1939		Sep 1945
Eadie, Robert Morrison	PC 126	Mar 1930	Sgt 8, Dec 1952	Mar 1955
Easson, Alexander Wood	PC 106	Dec 1937	resigned Oct 1941; rejoined Oct 46 as PC 84	Sep 1947
Ecob, Bernard	PC 86	Jan 1923	Sgt 16, Sep 1934; Insp, Mar 1939; Supt-DCC, Jun 1945; ACC, Jan 1953	d. Aug 1960
Ecob, Douglas Arthur	PC 253	Apr 1959		Sep 1962
Edgar, Thomas	PC 316	Oct 1959		Jan 1960
Edgeley, Dennis John Nicholas	PC 448	Oct 1965		
Edwards Michael Staniforth	PC 278	Sep 1958		
Edwards, Alvin Gent	Sgt 26	Sep 1914	Insp, Jul 1936	Sep 1939
Edwards, Joseph	PC 212	1927	Sgt 13, Oct 1937; Insp, Feb 1946	Mar 1958
Edwards, Sidney	PC 400	Apr 1962		
Eld, John	PC 85	1909		Dec 1934

Name	No/Rank	Joined	Details	Resigned
Elliott, Roger John	PC 449	Oct 1965		
Elliott, Walter John	PC 334	Feb 1957		
Elliott, William Herbert	PC 129	Mar 1930	Sgt 32, Sep 1939	Jun 1955
Ellison, Davis James	PC 258	May 1961		Oct 1964
Elsworth, Montague	PC 144	Jun 1935		c.1940
Elton, Francis	Sgt 30	Sep 1914	was PC 199; Sgt, Oct 1925	Jan 1941
Elvin, Charles Frederick	PC 72	Sep 1932		c.1946
Elvin, Martin Charles	PC 431	Apr 1965		
Emerton, Barrie	PC 159	May 1961		
Evans, Ivor John maxwell	PC 372	Jan 1964		
Evans, Maurice Ramon	PC 107	May 1951		Mar 1953
Everitt, Wifred	Sgt 12	1907		Jul 1933
Fairey, W.	PC 88	Sep 1914		c.1945
Fairey, William Henry	PC 203	May 1950		Sep 1960
Farley, Jack	PC 69	Jan 1931		May 1956
Farmer, Peter Malcolm	PC 384	Mar 1959		Jan 1960
Farrant Norman H.	PC 120	Oct 1933		Oct 1963
Farrant, Bernard Keith	PC 398	Dec 1964		
Farrant, Robert Henry	PC 176	Feb 1960		Mar 1966
Farrar, Archibald Robert Benjamin	PC 124	Feb 1958		
Farrows, Dennis Arthur	PC 282	Jul 1959		
Faulkner, George	Inspector	1904	was Sgt 30	Feb 1929
Fawcett, Peter Gordon	PC 286	Oct 1952		
Felstead, David Robert	PC 316	Aug 1960		
Fieldsend, William Henry Herbert	PC 89	Sep 1914		Oct 1939
Fife, William	PC 201	Jul 1959		Sep 1960
Findlay, Bryan	PC 194	Aug 1961		
Finlayson, John Ross Mackenzie	PC 72	Mar 1954	later PC 459	
Fisher, Hugh Barry Loydall	PC 338	Mar 1957		
Fisher, James	PC 275	c.Jul 1938	Sgt 43, Jun 1952; Insp, Nov 1958	Oct 1963
Flannigan, Arthur	PC 178	Oct 1951		c.1955
Flattery, Lewis Ernest	PC 324	Dec 1956		May 1960
Fletcher, Ronald Arthur	PC 335	Feb 1957		
Flude, Keith	PC 291	Oct 1952		
Folkard, Brian Victor Neville	PC 231	Jan 1967		
Folker, Peter Gerald	PC 394	Jan 1962		
Ford, Donald Alan	PC 150	May 1948		
Ford, Frederick James	PC 140	1907		Dec 1932
Fosberry, Richard	PC 197	Oct 1962		
Foster, Albert James	PC 65	Nov 1950	later PC 413	
Foster, Wallace Gordon	PC 215	Nov 1955		Feb 1958
Foulds, Alfred	PC 163	Dec 1923		Jan 1951
Foulds, Walter Edward	PC 233	Nov 1925		d. Sep 1944
Fowkes, Ronald Walter	PC 199	Nov 1955		
Fowler, Graham Walter Nayland	PC 159	Nov 1959		Jun 1961
Fowler, Peter John	PC 111	Oct 1957		Jun 1952
Fox, John Gordon	PC 219	Jan 1956	Sgt 47, Dec 1959	
Fox, John Reginald	PC 376	Jun 1958	Sgt, Apr 1966	
Francis, David John	PC 219	Dec 1966		
Francis, Sidney Bilney	PC 197	Apr 1926		Apr 1951

Name	No/Rank	Joined	Details	Resigned
Frank, James Edward	PC 377	Nov 1964		
Fraser, Donald	PC 221	Aug 1920		Dec 1948
Fraser, Roger Cameron	PC 385	Aug 1959		
Freear, William	PC 146	Apr 1938	Sgt 13, Feb 1956	
French, Keith	PC 181	Jul 1954		Jan 1956
Frost, Frank	PC 132	Mar 1930		Dec 1936
Frost, Frank	PC 48	Sep 1936	later PC 357	Sep 1961
Frost, Terence Alfred	PC 257	Feb 1952		Feb 1960
Gabbitas, John	Superintendent	Feb 1909	was PC 244; Supt, Dec 28	
			DCC, Feb 1936	Jun 1945
Galbraith, Neil	Chief Constable	Jan 1956		Oct 1956
Gamble, Anthony John	PC 113	Dec 1960		
Gamble, Eric Leonard	PC 78	Nov 1954	Sgt, Jun 1964	
Gamble, Graham	PC 444	Sep 1965		
Gamble, Horace	PC 83	Feb 1946		Aug 1946
Gannon, Bernard	PC 123	Oct 1946	Sgt, Nov 1958	
Gannon, James Edwin	PC 130	Jun 1951	t/Sgt, Nov 1965	
Gardner, Robert	PC 164	Sep 1955		
Garfield, Frank	PC 225	Nov 1925		Dec 1958
Garlick, Peter John	PC 149	Dec 1961		Aug 1963
Garner, Walter	PC 45	Dec 1923		Jan 1948
Garside, Michael David	PC 380	Aug 1958		Jan 1963
Gascoyne, Raymond	PC 141	Mar 1930		May 1955
Gaskell, David James	PC 399	Apr 1962		
Gatward, Anthony Keith	PC 190	Dec 1954		Feb 1966
Gatward, William A.	PC 43	Aug 1929		
Gatward, William Albert	PC 156	Jul 1949	Sgt 52	
Gays, Richard Ernest	PC 86	Oct 1959		
Gee, Leonard	PC 263	Apr 1938		Feb 1947
Gee, Walter Frederick	PC 249	Mar 1935		Mar 1937
Gellatly, Alan Hamilton	PC 148	Feb 1967		
Geraghty, Cyril	PC 210	Dec 1924	Sgt 12, Oct 1933	Mar 1955
Gibson, Geoffrey Alan	PC 426	Dec 1965		
Gill, Leslie Grayson	PC 130	Dec 1965		
Gill, Roy	PC 54	1927	Sgt 8, Oct 1940	d. Oct 1952
Gillespie, Alastair Grant	PC 256	Dec 1966		
Gilmour	PC 71	1945–1946		Aug 1946
Glanville, John	PC 371	May 1958		
Glover, Albert Shirley	PC 288	Sep 1939		Jul 1953
Glover, Charles Barry	PC 71	Apr 1958		Sep 1962
Glover, John	PC 202	Mar 1950	t/Sgt, Jan 1967	
Godfrey, James	PC 122	Sep 1914		1944
Goggins, Douglas Robert Patrick	PC 227	Sep 1951	Sgt 3, Oct 1964	
Golland, Brian	PC 360	Dec 1963		
Goodman, Frank William	PC 90	1927		Nov 1952
Goodman, John Cornwall	PC 358	May 1962		
Goodman, Winston Charles	PC 276	Jun 1938	Sgt 42, Oct 1953; Insp, Jan 1958	
Goodwin, David Hugh	PC 303	Nov 1958		
Goodwin, Frank	PC 56	Dec 1923		c.1937
Goosey, Kenneth Maurice	PC 178	Feb 1955		Jan 1958

Name	No/Rank	Joined	Details	Resigned
Goosey, William	PC 68	Sep 1914		Oct 1939
Gordon, David John	PC 274	Nov 1959		Sep 1961
Gordon, James	PC 224	Jul 1952	Sgt, Apr 1958; Insp, Jan 1963	
Goulding, Graham James	PC 220	Sep 1956	Sgt 62, Apr 1964	Apr 1966
Graham, Edwin	PC 192	Apr 1914		Apr 1939
Graham, Peter	PC 277	Jul 1952		
Graham, William J.	PC 140	Jun 1946	Sgt 27, Jan 1958	
Grant, Peter	PC 344	Jun 1957		Sep 1958
Grantham, Ronald Edward	PC 221	Jun 1966		
Gratrix, James	PC 141	Jun 1955	Sgt, Apr 1966	
Gray, Geoffrey Stanhope	PC 88	Mar 1946		Aug 1949
Gray, Percy Edgar	Inspector	1911	was PC 207 or 106	Aug 1937
Greasley, Kenneth Harry	PC 189	Jul 1948	Sgt, Oct 1957	
Green, Alan Daniel	PC 326	Dec 1956		Aug 1965
Green, Brian Geoffrey	PC 318	Nov 1956		Feb 1959
Green, Harry	PC 143	Dec.1937	Sgt 40, Jan 1958; Insp, Mar 1961	
Green, Leslie	PC 138	Apr 1937		
Green, Leslie William	PC 182	Oct 1926		Sep 1939
Green, Piers Leslie	PC 213	Jun 1966		
Green, Raymond	PC 162	Jan 1950	Sgt, Jul 1960	
Greene, Robert A.	PC 178	Sep 1936		Mar 1939
Greet, Raymond	PC 255	Jul 1952		Apr 1953
Grey, Ian	PC 173	Jan 1961		
Griffin, Bernard Philip	PC 175	Dec 1928		Dec 1958
Groom, Ian David	PC 153	Nov 1965		
Grundy, JohnThomas	PC 235	Oct 1951		
Guiver, Christopher Dudley	PC 329	Jan 1958		
Gunby, Geoffrey Thomas	PC 278	Jan 1956		Jun 1956
Gunnell, Robert Allan	PC 74	Mar 1966		
Hackett, Derek Henry	PC 180	Nov 1934	Sgt 11, Apr 1948; Insp, Aug 1951; Ch Insp, Oct 1953; Supt, Dec 1959	Jun 1962
Hackett, Roy	PC 146	Mar 1956		
Hadfield, Alan Francis	PC 123	Nov 1960		
Hadley, Norman	PC 266	Apr 1938	Sgt 32, Nov 1955	
Haines, Palmer	PC 104	May 1948		Jul 1951
Hakesley, George Thomas	PC 75	Oct 1912		Feb 1943
Hale, Richard Alfred	PC 442	Sep 1965		
Halgarth, Terence G.	PC 366	Oct 1959		Jul 1960
Hall, Arthur Percy	Inspector	Apr 1910	was PC 253; Supt, Feb 1937	Feb 1939
Hall, Charles Jabez	PC 366	Nov 1958	Sgt, Jan 1967	
Hall, Harold	Sgt 18	May 1908	was PC 209	Jul 1935
Hall, Ian William	PC 149	Sep 1963		Mar 1964
Hall, John	PC 314	Aug 1959		Mar 1964
Hall, William Douglas	PC 292	Oct 1953		
Hallam, Augustus	PC 179	Aug 1920	Sgt 20, Sep 30	Aug 1949
Hallam, Peter David	PC 104	Jul 1951		Jan 1964
Hames, Lewis Geoffery	PC 387	Aug 1959		
Hamilton, Cyril Roy	PC 148	Mar 1954	Sgt, Oct 1966	
Hamilton, William George	PC 248	Mar 1935		Sep 1937
Hancock, Frank Roland	PC 142	Nov 1956		

Name	No/Rank	Joined	Details	Resigned
Hankinson, George	PC 92	Jun 1910	Sgt 27, Jul 1930	Jan 1936
Harbot, Horace	PC 99	Aug 1920	Sgt 32, Jan 1929; Insp, Sep 1939	Aug 1950
Hardesty, Herbert	Sgt 19	Sep 1914	was PC 33	Jan 1946
Harding, John Geoffrey	PC 149	Apr 1964		
Harding, Thomas	PC 137	1907		Mar 1932
Hardy, Dennis Wilfred Maurice	PC 267	May 1952		
Hardy, Robert	PC 306	Jul 1964		
Hare, George	PC 145	Feb 1947		Dec 1947
Hare, Roy Frederick	PC	Apr 1966		
Hargreaves, Noel	PC 71	Oct 1946		Apr 1949
Harley, George Henry	PC 222	Oct 1951		Sep 1953
Harris, Frederick	PC 160	Oct 1933		Jan 1939
Harris, Roy	PC 266	Mar 1956		
Harris, William Cyril	PC 134	May 1946		Nov 1946
Harrison, David George	PC 276	Nov 1953		
Harrison, James Henry	PC 117	Dec 1923	Sgt 27, Nov 1945	d. Jul 1951
Hassell, William Kenneth Gordon	PC 238	Nov 1951		Mar 1959
Hastings, Keith Arthur Aubrey	PC 333	Feb 1957		Dec 1958
Hateley, Douglas	PC 150	Apr 1939		Jun 1947
Hatton, Roy	PC 147	Sep 1966		
Hawkes, Brian	PC 140	Oct 1933		killed Nov 1940
Hawley, Sidney	PC 130	Dec 1922		Jan 1948
Haynes, David John Wilfred	PC 305	Apr 1956		
Haynes, Laurence Albert	PC 189	Sep 1932		Apr 1934
Haynes, Robert	PC 415	Jan 1966		
Hayward, Thomas William	PC 100	c.Jun 1921	Sgt 16, Sep 1931; Insp, Sep 1934; Supt, Jan 1946	Jul 1951
Haywood, Tony Michael	PC 246	Dec 1966		
Heath, John	PC 342	May 1957		Jun 1961
Hebdon, Raymond Thompson	PC 71	Sep 1932		c.1945
Hedworth, Francis James	PC 99	Apr 1953		Jun 1960
Henderson, John	PC 77	Sep 1955		c.1962
Hercock, Robert Stanley	PC 45	Jan 1948	later PC 218	Jan 1958
Hextall, Ian Leonard	PC 438	Aug 1965		
Heywood, George Leonard	PC 159	Jun 1951	Sgt, Oct 1959	
Heywood, James	PC 69	1905		Aug 1930
Hibbert, Phillip Terence	PC 60	Apr 1954	later PC 360; Sgt, Sep 1963	
Higgins, Arthur	PC 195	Apr 1926	Sgt 28, Feb 1937; Insp, Sep 1944	Jul 1951
Higgins, Patrick Robert	PC 195	Jan 1964		Mar 1965
Higgott, William Marshall	PC 155	Aug 1946		Sep 1947
Hill, Frank Western	PC 148	Jan 1931		Feb 1933
Hill, Harry	PC 192	Dec 1957		Jul 1963
Hill, Leonard	PC 83	May 1950		
Hill, Michael Edward John	PC 245	Mar 1965		Mar 1966
Hill, William	PC 169	Jan 1931	Sgt 2, Nov 1945	Jan 1956
Hillman, Alfred John	PC 146	Feb 1913		Feb 1938
Hilton, Cyril	PC 149	Mar 1930	Sgt 34, Nov 1954	Mar 1956
Hodby, Alan William	PC 269	May 1952		
Hodge, Roy	PC 228	Apr 1952	Sgt 49, Jun 1958	
Hodson, Alan James	PC 100	Jun 1963		Dec 1963

Name	No/Rank	Joined	Details	Resigned
Hogg, Joseph	PC 220	1928		Mar 1930
Hoggard, John Kenneth	PC	Nov 1951		
Holden, William	PC 34	Mar 1928	later PC 251	Mar 1953
Holehouse, Basil	PC 106	Mar 1946		Jan 1951
Holland, Edgar Thomas	PC 268	Mar 1961		
Holley, Michael	PC 351	Dec 1963		
Hollis, Hubert Elkin	PC 279	Aug 1952		
Holyland, Harold David	PC 153	May 1951		Jun 1955
Holyoak, Peter Michael	PC 272	Jul 1952	Sgt, Mar 1961	
Holyoake, David	PC 91	Nov 1958		
Holyoake, David Leslie Bean	PC 91	Nov 1958		
Homan, George	PC 153	1904		Apr 1929
Hooke, Herbert, Richard	PC 237	Dec 1920	Sgt 21, Jan 1931	Nov 1938
Hope, Thomas	PC 216	Dec 1955		
Horner, Anthony Louis	PC 272	Jan 1966		
Houghton, Samuel	PC 129	1904		Jul 1929
House, Richard Maurice	PC 249	Jan 1952	Sgt, Apr 1964	
House, Victor John	PC 363	Apr 1958		Feb 1959
Houston, Leslie	PC 241	Apr 1964		Apr 1966
Howard, Leonard W.	PC 203	Nov 1947		Nov 1948
Howes, Andrew Robert Maitland	PC 405	Oct 1962		
Hoy, Edward Alexander	PC 206	*c.*Jan 1928		Jun 1958
Hubbard, Arthur	Sgt 29		was PC 245; Sgt 29, Jan 1926; Insp, Sep 30	d. Jun 1940
Hubbard, Charles Robert	PC 255	Jun 1953		
Hughes, John	PC 169	Feb 1960		Jan 1961
Hughes, Michael Charles Max	PC 270	Jul 1965		
Hull, Norman Wilford	PC 151	Jan 1948		
Hull, Richard	PC 256	Jun 1965		d. Aug 1966
Hull, Trevor	PC 256	Feb 1952	Sgt, Jul 1964	
Hulme, Roy William	PC 129	May 1946		
Hunt, Brian Anthony	PC 357	Nov 1961		
Hunt, Wilfrid Roy James	PC 167	Aug 1946	Sgt 22, Oct 1954; Insp, Dec 1958	
Hutchinson, Arthur J.	PC 152	Apr 1939		Oct 1945
Hutchinson, Wilfred	PC 107	Apr 1953		Sep 1956
Illiff, Derek James	PC 229	Aug 1961		
Iliffe, Alan James Stapleton	PC 122	Mar 1948	Sgt, Nov 1958	
Illiffe, Graydon Cecil	PC 301	Aug 1953		Mar 1954
Illiffe, Michael	PC 308	Aug 1957		
Ingall, John Albert	PC 211	Oct 1950		Nov 1953
Ingham, Christopher John	PC 254	Jul 1965		Jan 1966
Ingham, Stanley Christopher	PC 212	Aug 1957		
Inwood, Charles	PC 139	1910		May 1935
Jack, Robert Anderson	PC 139	Jun 1946		Nov 1948
Jackson, Alan Ronald William	PC 355	Mar 1961		
Jacques, Colin Augustus	PC 77	Oct 1953		Aug 1955
Jacques, Ernest Alan	PC 253	Jan 1952		Apr 1959
James, Alfred Roland	PC 160	Apr 1939	Sgt 20, Jun 1953	Jan 1967
James, David	PC 422	Jan 1965		Feb 1966
James, Leslie	PC 86	Nov 1949	Sgt, Oct 1959	

Name	No/Rank	Joined	Details	Resigned
James, Oscar Harry	PC	Apr 1926		
Jarvis, William	PC 256	Jun 1935		Mar 1946
Jeffrey, Barry John	PC 278	Aug 1952		Nov 1955
Jelley, David Sidney	PC 388	Oct 1959		
Jelley, Francis William	PC 101	Feb 1920	Sgt 10, Nov 1945	Oct 1950
Jenney, Harold George	Sgt 24	Aug 1911	was PC 266; Sgt 24, 1919	Oct 1945
Jesson, Arthur	PC 67	Dec 1923		Dec 1949
Jewell, David Alfred	PC 131	Aug 1950		Sep 1958
Johnson, Bertie James	PC 138	Dec 1912		Dec 1938
Johnson, Frederick	PC 196	Oct 1926	Sgt 1, Nov 1946	Oct 1956
Johnson, Robert Barrie	PC 241	Jan 1952	Sgt 44, Apr 1964	
Johnson, Wilfred Arthur	PC 76	Nov 1950	Sgt, Jul 1960	
Joiner, William Jock	PC 139	Jun 1935	t/Sgt, Jan 1944; Sgt 5, Jan 1946; Insp, Nov 1958	Jun 1965
Jones, Carlton Harry	PC 447	Sep 1965		
Jones, Dennis Knill	PC 254	Jun 1935		Jun 1965
Jones, Fredrick	PC 173	1906		Jun 1931
Jones, John James Leslie	PC 289	Sep 1939	Sgt 34, Jun1956	Mar 1965
Jones, Kenneth Frederick	PC 248	Aug 1956		Jul 1961
Jones, Maurice	PC 127	Jul 1955	Sgt 19, Sept 1966	
Jones, Peter Donald	PC 293	Oct 1952		Mar 1955
Jones, Richard Ernest	Inspector	Apr 1966		
Jones, Robert Henry	PC 213	Apr 1952	Sgt 71, Apr 1966	
Jones, Samuel	PC 143	1911		Jul 1937
Jordan, Clifford Nelson	PC 189	Nov 1934		d. Oct 1945
Jordan, Malcolm	PC 233	May 1959		May 1960
Jowitt, Winston	PC 170	Jul 1948	was PC 119, left Dec 1950; rejoined Feb 1951	Apr 1965
Kayley, John Barnes	PC 321	Feb 1966		Dec 1966
Keeling, Peter John	PC 358	May 1961		Feb 1962
Kellett, Harry Arnold	PC 229	Aug 1920		Jan 1946
Kelly, Nelson Leo Mead	PC 114	Aug 1950		
Kemp, Michael William	PC 319	Feb 1959		Oct 1959
Kempin, Trevor Frederick	PC 423	Feb 1965		
Kendall, Albert Edward	Inspector	1900		Jan 1931
Kendrick, Clifford Arthur	PC 150	Jan 1955	Sgt, Jul 1962; Left Nov 1965; rejoined Sep 1966	
Kermode, Douglas Charles	PC 308	Apr 1956		Jun 1956
Kidd, Fred	PC 197	Mar 1962		Oct 1962
King, Charles	PC 135	1914		Nov 1940
King, Charles	Sgt 32	1903		Jan 1929
King, Harold	PC 226	Feb 1920	Sgt 26, Jul 1936	Apr 1940
King, Harold Edwin	PC 298	Dec 1952		Jun 1959
King, Peter	PC 419	Feb 1965		
King, Peter John	PC 429	Mar 1965		Mar 1966
Kinsman, Walter	PC 98	Jul 1948		Apr 1949
Kirby, William	PC 39	Sep 1912		Sep 1938
Kirk, John Thomas	PC 151	Oct 1929	Sgt 18, Oct 1937; Insp, Jan 1947	Oct 1954
Kirk, Laurence Ivan	PC 240	Nov 1951		Jul 1953
Kirk, Trevor Frank	PC 98	May 1949		

Name	No/Rank	Joined	Details	Resigned
Kirkland, Clarence	PC 92	Dec 1923	Sgt 4, 1932; Insp, Jun 1935	Aug 1951
Knight, Alexander	PC 263	Mar 1952		Jan 1967
Knight, Bernard Cecil Frank	PC 257	May 1960		Sep 1961
Knight, Brian Arthur	PC 457/456	Jan 1966		Jan 1967
Knight, Cecil Henry Frederick	PC 61	Sep 1932	later PC 161	Oct 1957
Knight, Gordon	PC 162	Oct 1960		Aug 1966
Knight, William Roberts	PC 113	Nov 1934		c.1935
Knott, Raymond John	PC 140	Jul 1958		
Knowles, Kenneth	PC	Jan 1946		
Knox, William Arthur	PC 142	Sep 1936		k.i.a. Mar 1944
Lacy, Eric Edward	PC 179	Jan 1931	Sgt 29, Dec 1941; Insp, Jan 1947; Supt, Jul 1951; ACC, Sep 1960	
Lamb, Kenneth	PC 255	Jan 1952		Jul 1952
Lambell, Ronald William	PC 82	Feb 1948		Dec 1953
Lambert John Keith	PC 187	Mar 1958		
Langton, Derek	PC 144	Jan 1953		
Larrad, Samuel	PC 211	Sep 1914	Sgt, Sep 1931; Inspector	Oct 1942
Lawson, John Leonard	PC 126	1904		Oct 1929
Lear, Clifford Roy Thomas	PC 282	Aug 1952		Jun 1959
Lee, Ian James	PC 242	Jul 1966		
Lee, John George William Arthur	PC 63	Apr 1956		Nov 1957
Lee, Lemuel	PC 104	Mar 1948		May 1948
Leeson, Alan		Aug 1949		
Leeson, Cyril	PC 82	Jan 1923		Jan 1948
Lenton, Donald Stanley	PC 152	Jul 1955		Jan 1956
Leverton, Peter	PC 298	Jul 1959		
Lewis, David Ivor Llewellyn	PC 116	Oct 1961		
Lewis, William Gordon	PC 290	Sep 1939	left Aug 1947; rejoined Jun 1948; Sgt 28, Jan 1958	
L'Homme, Thomas Peter	PC 203	Feb 1961		
Liggins, Keith Arthur	PC 327	Dec 1956		
Lillicrapp, Michael	PC 176	Jan 1959		Nov 1959
Lincoln, Keith Arthur	PC 181	May 1953		Jul 1953
Llewellyn, Frederick K.		Sep 1938		Jul 1940
Lockett, Keith Burton	PC 59	Aug 1950		May 1955
Lockton, David Michael	PC 165	Nov 1957		
Lockwood, Arthur	PC 41	Sep 1914	later PC 54	Jan 1946
Lockwood, Michael Andrew	PC 237	Mar 1964		
Long, Brian Cedric	PC 53	Aug 1955		Jun 1956
Looker, David John	PC 428	Mar 1965		
Lott, Gwynne S.	PC 281	Sep 1938		Mar 1946
Lovell, Dennis Charles Robert	PC 68	Feb 1946	later PC 416	Sep 1965
Lovell, William	PC 44	Feb 1913		Feb 1938
Lowe, George Noel	PC 89	Nov 1958		
Lowe, Gerald Walter	PC 374	May 1958		
Lucas, Albert James	Sgt 20	1901	was PC 123	Jul 1930
Ludlam, Michael Anthony	PC 85	Dec 1960		
Lusty, Dennis Frederick	PC 127	Sep 1936	Sgt 18, Jun 1953; Insp, Jul 1955; Ch Insp, Dec 1959	Sep 1966
Lynch, John Malcolm	PC 238	Apr 1959		Dec 1959

Name	No/Rank	Joined	Details	Resigned
Lyne, Anthony Trevor	PC 197	Jan 1961		Mar 1962
Lyner, David John	PC	Jan 1953		Oct 1954
Lyner, Walter	Sgt 6	1914		
McCartney, Frederick	PC 132	1904		May 1929
McCorkindale, John	PC 233	Oct 1964		
McCrory, Robert Meredith	PC 215	Apr 1937	Sgt 23, Sep 1947; Insp, Aug 1951; Supt, Oct 1957	Jul 1963
MacDiarmid, Alexander Archibald	PC 260	Mar 1952	Sgt 9, Apr 1965	
McDonald, Kenneth	PC 272	Jul 1952	Sgt, Jun 1964	
McElhinney, Michael Thomas	PC 317	Oct 1964		
McFarlane, Ronald	PC 243	Jan 1952		Sep 1958
McGeachy, Robert McLean	PC 294	Mar 1965		May 1966
McGeough, Noel Christopher	PC 320	Nov 1956		Oct 1960
McGrory, William	PC 139	Apr 1949	Sgt 54, Oct 1957; Insp, Jan 1966	
McIntosh, Andrew Donald	PC 425	Feb 1966		
MacIntosh, Angus James	PC 75	Oct 1954		
MacLeod, Angus Neil	PC 242	Jan 1952		Jun 1966
MacLeod, Duncan MacDonald	PC 158	Sep 1957		
McMahon, Frank A.	PC 267	Apr 1938		Jul 1947
McMillan, William	PC 451	Oct 1965		Jul 1966
McMurdo, Douglas Leslie	PC 43	Oct 1929	Sgt 27, Nov 1935; Insp, Nov 1945	Oct 1959
McRae, George	PC 258	Feb 1952	Sgt, Mar 1961	
McRitchie, John Henry	PC	Jan 1953		May 1953
McRobb, Alexander	PC 303	Feb 1953		Dec 1958
Main, Anthony	PC	Nov 1954		
Manger, David Charles	PC 192	Aug 1963		Dec 1963
Mann, Joseph	PC 288	Aug 1953	Sgt, Jul 1964; Insp	
Mann, Neil	PC 311	May 1956		
Mansell, Donald John	PC 209	Dec 1957		
Mark, Robert	Chief Constable	Jan 1957		Mar 1967
Markillie, Walter Richard	PC 102	Apr 1953		
Marlow, John Malcolm	PC 363	Mar 1959		Jan 1962
Marriott, George Ronald	PC 170	Oct 1929	Sgt 38, Feb 1947	Mar 1955
Marsh, Alan William	PC 346	Feb 1958		Mar 1959
Marshall, George Frederick	PC 106	Dec 1921	Sgt 23, Jul 1936	Dec 1946
Martin, Keith Cantrill	PC 375	Jul 1958		Jun 1965
Martin, Paul	PC 354	Nov 1964		
Martin, William George	PC 268	Apr 1938	Sgt 10, Oct 1953	May 1964
Martyn, Norman Montague	PC 199	Apr 1937		Jul 1955
Mason, Ernest	PC 35	Aug 1920	later PC 252	Nov 1945
Mason, John Alun Hubert	PC 345	Apr 1961		Mar 1964
Mason, Michael Edward	PC 248	Sep 1961		
Mason, Peter George Henry	PC 211	Nov 1953		
Mason, Roy	PC 370	May 1958		
Mathieson, Charles	PC 178	Apr 1939		Oct 1948
Matthews, George	PC113	1909		Mar 1934
Matthews, Norman	PC 241	Jun 1966		Jul 1966
Matthews, Norman	PC 427	Mar 1965		Sep 1965
Matthews, William	Sgt 21	1902		Oct 1930
Matthews, William	PC 37	Sep 1906		d. Jan 1932

Name	No/Rank	Joined	Details	Resigned
May, John	PC 201	Oct 1933	Sgt 42, Sep 1939	Oct 1953
Meadowcroft, Peter William	PC 109	Oct 1961		Mar 1963
Meadows, David Henry	PC 152	Jan 1956		Sep 1964
Measey, Allen Gort	PC 97	Jul 1958		
Measures, John Kenneth	PC 384	Dec 1964		
Measures, Kenneth Harold	PC 396	May 1962		
Medhurst, Arthur	PC 219	Nov 1925	Sgt 3, Apr 1935	Nov 1950
Meese, William	PC 114	Dec 1923	Sgt, Sep 1932; Insp, Nov 1935; Ch Insp, Aug 1951	Sep 1954
Meiring, John Frederick	PC 233	May 1960		Apr 1961
Merriken, John Thomas	PC 81	Apr 1926		Jul 1939
Merry, Robert Keith	PC 181	Jan 1961		
Messam, Michael John	PC 437	Jul 1965		
Middleton, William	PC 142	1911		Jun 1936
Miller, Victor John Walter	PC 154	Oct 1929	Sgt 6, Nov 1946	Feb 1955
Milligan, James	PC 259	Feb 1952	Sgt 66, Aug 1966	
Millington, Frank	PC 88	Oct 1949	Sgt, Apr 1965	
Millward, Herbert	Sgt 4	1907		Oct 1932
Milner, John A.C.	PC 205	Apr 1939	Sgt, Jun 1964	
Mitchell, Roy Lawrence	PC 78	Jul 1964		
Moffett, Ernest Alan	PC 333	Jul 1959		
Mogford, Alan Raymond	PC 192	Nov 1950		Feb 1955
Monk, James Covington	PC 318	Feb 1959		Mar 1964
Monk, Robert William	PC 237	Apr 1959		Dec 1962
Moody, Ivan David	PC 433	Apr 1965		
Moore, Albert William	PC 49	Oct 1929		Oct 1954
Moore, Barry	PC 123	Dec 1958		Jul 1960
Moore, Colin Gregory	PC 280	Aug 1952		Aug 1956
Moore, Robert Alfred	PC 305	Sep 1954		Apr 1955
Moore, Samuel Vincent	PC 218	Oct 1926		d. Mar 1946
Moore, Stanley Donald	PC 347	Feb 1958		
Moorhouse, Tom	PC 237	Oct 1931	Sgt 22, Nov 1945; Insp, Sep 1954; Ch Insp, Oct 1957; Supt, Oct 1959	Apr 1964
Morgan, Christopher John	PC 259	Jan 1967		
Morgan, Harold Lawton	PC 184	Jun 1951		
Morley, Terence William	PC 169	Aug 1956		Dec 1959
Morris Albert	PC 211	Oct 1931		Mar 1945
Morris, Thomas Alan	PC 137	Nov 1955		
Morris, Wilfred T.	PC 243	Apr 1939		Jul 1939
Morris, William Edward	PC 174	Jun 1935		Sep 1961
Morrison, Norman	PC 252	Jan 1953		
Morton, Thomas Edward	PC 148	Oct 1933		May 1944
Moss, Percy	PC 70	Nov 1927		Jan 1946
Mottershaw, Brian William	PC 268	Mar 1959		Jul 1960
Mottram, Roy	PC 381	Sep 1958		Apr 1962
Mould, Raymond	PC 198	Apr 1952	Sgt, Sep 1960	
Moulds, Francis Arthur	PC 116	Apr 1948		Dec 1948
Mowl, Ernest John	PC 243	Sep 1932		Nov 1938
Mowl, Frank Leslie	PC 159	Apr 1926		Apr 1951
Mowl, Joseph William	PC 285	Oct 1952		Dec 1955

Name	No/Rank	Joined	Details	Resigned
Moxey, Colin William	PC 160	Aug 1959		
Muir, James	PC 116	Aug 1921		Mar 1948
Mullett, Aidan Anthony	PC 331	Feb 1957	Sgt 3, Sep 1963; Insp, Oct 1964	Jan 1966
Munns, Leonard Cyril	PC 291	Sep 1939		k.i.a. Jun 1944
Musgrave, Anthony	PC 92	Sep 1958		
Naylor, Alan Frederick Stokes	PC 452	Oct 1965		
Naylor, Michael John	PC 264	Sep 1964		
Neale, Ernest Edward	PC 178	Aug 1921	Sgt 7, May 1936	Aug 1947
Needham, Terence	PC 294	Apr 1956		Jan 1965
Neilson, Leslie Peter	PC 207	May 1962		Aug 1963
New, Colin David	PC 205	Jul 1964		Sep 1966
Newberry, George	Sgt 5	Jun 1905		Jun 1930
Newberry, William Victor	PC 236	Dec 1924	Sgt 15, Jan 1947	Dec 1954
Newman, Ernest Henry	Inspector	1904	was Sgt 12	Oct 1929
Newman, William Alexander	PC 226	Jan 1956		Jun 1956
Newton, George Edward	PC 173	Oct 1931		Feb 1936
Nichols, David John	PC 424	Mar 1965		
Nichols, Herbert	PC 96	1905		Jun 1931
Nicol, James Terence	PC 319	Apr 1957		Feb 1959
Noble, George Angus	PC 89	Mar 1946	Sgt 43, Nov 1958	
Norman, Leonard Thomas	PC 109	1928	Sgt 29, Mar 1939	killed Nov 1940
Norris, Graham	PC 325	Sep 1957		Oct 1965
Norris, John Edward	PC 247	Mar 1935		m/k.i.a. Dec 1943
North, Malcolm Brian	PC 410	Nov 1958	Sgt 42, Jul 1964	
Nutting, James	PC 202	Aug 1921		Aug 1947
Nye, George Herbert Elliott	PC 70	May 1946		Dec 1946
O'Connell, Daniel	PC 236	Oct 1951		
O'Connor, Colin	PC 368	May 1958		
O'Dowd, David Joseph	PC 257	Nov 1961	t/Sgt, Jan 1967	
Ofield, Roy Albert	PC 148	Jul 1953		Jan 1954
O'Leary, Francis Arthur James	PC 53	Nov 1927		Mar 1945
Ollerenshaw, Fred	PC 398	Apr 1962		Nov 1963
O'Meara, Joseph Ambrose	PC 292	Sep 1939		Mar 1947
Onions, Richard	PC 166	Oct 1929		Oct 1959
Orchard, David Richard	PC 186	Jul 1947		Mar 1948
Ormerod, Jack	PC 269	Apr 1938		Jan 1946
Orton, Frank Edward	PC 190	1928		Jul 1939
Osborne, Eric David	PC 160	Jul 1953		Aug 1959
Osborne, Robert David	PC 322	Nov 1956		
Owen, Christopher Herbert	PC 62	Oct 1946	Sgt, Mar 1955; Insp, Jul 1962; Ch Insp, Aug 1966	
Owen, John Vernon	PC 216	Aug 1951		Jun 1955
Oxlade, Barry Norman	PC 440	Jul 1965		Sep 1965
Packer, Brian Albert	PC 153	Sep 1955		Sep 1965
Page, Sydney Leslie	PC 240	Jun 1935	Sgt 19, Jan 1947; Insp, Jun 1953; Ch Insp, Sep 1960; Supt, Jul 1962	
Painter, Anthony	PC 349	Feb 1958		
Palmer, Edwin	PC 118	Dec 1924	Sgt 18, Nov 1935; Insp, Oct 1937	Aug 1950
Palmer, Gordon	PC 131	Oct 1958		Apr 1960
Park, Clarence A.	PC 352	Apr 1956		Jan 1966

Name	No/Rank	Joined	Details	Resigned
Parker, David Sydney	PC 145	Jan 1959		Apr 1963
Parker, David Walter	PC 247	Apr 1961		
Parker, J.	PC 108	Jul 1950		
Parker, John Trevor	PC 240	Sep 1953		Mar 1954
Parker, Peter	PC 281	Aug 1952		
Parkins, Jeffrey	PC 337	Feb 1957		
Parkinson, John David	PC 319	Sep 1960		
Parnham, Ralph Edward	PC 63	Nov 1957	later PC 411	
Parrott, Albert William	Sgt 2	Sep 1914	was PC 34	Jan 1943
Parrott, George	PC 200	Jul 1939		
Paterson, David	PC 233	May 1961		Nov 1964
Payne, David	PC 141	May 1966		
Payne, Derek Ronald	PC 231	Feb 1955		Feb 1966
Payne, Michael John	PC 402	Apr 1962		
Payne, Roy Moore	PC 101	Mar 1946		May 1948
Payne, Walter	PC 273	Sep 1962		Jan 1964
Peacock, John Henry Groves	PC 395	Jan 1962	Sgt 48, Jan 1966	
Pearson, Ronald Arthur	PC 87	Feb 1946		Jan 1954
Pease, John William	PC 204	1928		c.1930
Peberdy, Walter Ernest	PC 134	Sep 1936		Jan 1946
Peet, John Harvey	PC 275	Aug 1965		
Pemberton, David Anthony James	PC 181	Aug 1953		May 1954
Pemberton, Herbert William	PC 91	Dec 1928	Sgt 26, Dec 1941	Jun 1954
Pender, John	PC 85	Jan 1960		Oct 1960
Peplow, Norman	PC 185	Mar 1930		Sep 1955
Perkins, David Frank	PC 174	Sep 1961		
Perkins, Herbert Walter	PC 157	Dec 1924		Dec 1947
Pert, Robert	PC 151	Dec 1937		Feb 1938
Petcher, Peter John	PC 187	Nov 1951	Sgt 48, Mar 1958; t/Insp, Jul 1965	Jan 1966
Petherick, Leonard Henry	PC 234	Feb 1961		
Pick, Wallace Raymond	PC 139	Oct 1957		
Pickles, Jack Granville	PC 96	Mar 1946		
Pickles, Norman	PC 96	Mar 1935		Oct 1945
Pickwick, Alan Joseph	PC 443	Sep 1965		
Pinchbeck, Anthony James	PC 225	Feb 1959		
Pinchbeck, Edwin Alfred	PC 343	May 1957		
Pinchbeck, Herbert J.	PC 85	Nov 1934		Nov 1959
Pinfold, Richard Cecil	PC 239	Dec 1920	Sgt 36, Nov 1935	Apr 1947
Pizzy, Michael	PC 215	Mar 1958		Mar 1964
Platts, Tony Robert	PC 223	Oct 1951		
Plowman, John	PC 172	Aug 1946		Jul 1952
Pomfret, Alexander John	PC 165	Dec 1937	Sgt 39, Mar 1950; Insp, Sep 1960	
Poole, Harold	PC 158	Nov 1925	Sgt 28, Sep 1931; Insp, Feb 1937	Nov 1954
Porter, George	PC 215	1910		Feb 1936
Porter, William	PC 265	1911	reduced from Sgt 7 to PC 265, Apr 1936	Nov 1936
Portsmouth, Brian G.	PC 364	Apr 1959		
Potter, Duncan Leonard	PC 420	Mar 1965		
Pratt, Dudley Charles	PC 83	Oct 1946		May 1950
Pratt, William S.F.	PC 230	Aug 1921		Aug 1951
Prentice, James McKinlay	PC 239	Sep 1939		k.i.a. Aug 1943

Name	No/Rank	Joined	Details	Resigned
Preston, George	PC 52	1906		Jun 1931
Preston, Harry	PC 151	1904		Jul 1929
Preston, Jack	PC 58	Feb 1951	Sgt 36, Sep 1960	
Preston, Roger Stuart	PC 440	Oct 1965		
Price, John Humphrey	PC 237	Oct 1951	Sgt 45, Nov 1958; Insp, Jul 1964	
Price, John James Cyril	PC 192	Nov 1949		Sep 1950
Pridmore, Kenneth	PC 70	Jan 1947	Sgt, Oct 1957	
Priest, Brian Howard	PC	Apr 1958		Nov 1958
Procter, Robert Kenneth	PC 154	Jan 1961		Nov 1965
Proudman, John Ernest	PC 373	May 1958		
Pryor, John Malcolm	PC 316	Nov 1956		Sep 1959
Purcell, Frederick Arthur	PC 119	Jan 1948		Jun 1948
Pyatt, Anthony John	PC	Apr 1965		
Pym, Eric G.	PC 174	Apr 1926	Sgt 34, Apr 1935; Insp, Feb 1946	Nov 1954
Quain, Robert Leonard	PC 91	Mar 1946		Nov 1946
Quinn, Thomas Fergus	PC 302	Jun 1956		Mar 1967
Ralph, Charles John	PC 154	Feb 1948	Sgt 29, Oct 1959	
Ralph, David Bernard	PC 324	Mar 1961		
Randell, Robert Ernest	PC 124	Feb 1951		Feb 1958
Ravenhill, James Allen	PC 314	Jan 1958		Jul 1959
Read, Albert William	PC 204	Mar 1930	Sgt 21, Sep 1951	Sep 1955
Reddell, John Anthony	PC 284	Sep 1952		
Redman, David Brian	PC 386	Aug 1959	Sgt 70, Apr 1966	
Reed, Graham Edwin	PC 93	Jul 1958		
Reeve, Frank James	PC 80	Sep 1905		Jan 1936
Reid, Ian	PC 315	Oct 1956		Sep 1966
Richardson, John Lindsay	PC 434	Apr 1965		
Ridley, Charles	PC 186	1928		Mar 1930
Rigby, Garry William	PC 329	Jan 1957		Oct 1957
Rigby, William	PC 99	Oct 1929	Sgt 35	Nov 1955
Riley, George Albert	PC 171	Mar 1960		
Ritchie, Alec McAra	PC 422	Mar 1966		
Roberts William	PC 282	1945–1946		Dec 1946
Roberts, Albert	PC 62	Jan 1946		Aug 1946
Roberts, Cyril	PC 163	Feb 1951		
Roberts, John Edward	PC 378	Jan 1962		
Roberts, William A.	PC 289	Sep 1938		prior to 1940
Robertson, Bob	PC 121	Dec 1950		
Robertson, Dugard	Superintendent	Sep 1905	was PC 87; Supt (Dep CC), Sep 1930	Jan 1936
Robertson, Frank Roy	PC 201	Feb 1920	Sgt 17, May 1933; Insp, Mar 1939	Feb 1950
Robins, David Stuart	PC 418	Oct 1957		
Robins, George	PC 231	Dec 1924		Dec 1954
Robinson, Christopher Thomas	PC 294	Sep 1939		Aug 1949
Robinson, Clifford Wilfrid	PC 152	Jul 1946	Sgt 8, Mar 1955; Insp, Dec 1964	
Robinson, Jack	PC 382	Oct 1958		
Robinson, Michael John	PC 228	Sep 1951		Mar 1952
Robinson, Septimus	PC 287	Apr 1939		Apr 1946
Rockingham, Colin	PC 201	Sep 1947		Feb 1948
Roe, Peter John	Inspector	Apr 1966		
Rogers, Ernest Travis	PC 380	Jan 1963	t/Sgt, Oct 1966	

Name	No/Rank	Joined	Details	Resigned
Rogers, Wilfred Scott Bohemia	PC 185			Jul 1929
Root, Arthur Harry	Sgt 22	1909	was PC 172	Dec 1931
Roper, Henry	PC 76	Nov 1925		Nov 1950
Rosevear, William James	PC 51	Sep 1914	Sgt 8, Dec 1931	Oct 1940
Roughton, Frank	PC 54	Jan 1946		Nov 1946
Rouse, James	PC 119	Jan 1917	was PC 249	Jan 1939
Rowell, Joseph	PC 176	1912		Feb 1941
Roy, Norman Florence	PC 299	Jan 1953		
Rudd, Francis	PC 86	Nov 1934		Jan 1936
Rushin, Alan	PC 410	Jan 1965		
Russell, Frederick Charles	PC 226	Apr 1937		Mar 1948
Russell, Gavin	PC 126	Dec 1952		
Russell, Kenneth	PC 99	Oct 1963		
Ryde-Rogers, John Anthony	PC 197	Sep 1956	Sgt 60, Nov 1958	
Rye, George Herbert Elliott	PC	May 1946		
Salmon, Thomas W.	PC 277	Jun 1938		k.i.a. Sep 1944
Samson, Arthur	PC 219	Jun 1935		Oct 1939
Sandall, Geoffey Francis	PC 261	Jan 1967		
Sandall, Gordon Stuart	PC 162	Sep 1966		
Sandall, Thomas Francis	PC 283	Sep 1938	Sgt 45, Dec 1952; Insp, Nov 1958	
Sandel, Ronald	PC 90	Dec 1952		Dec 1953
Sanders, Peter	PC 52	Jun 1955		Mar 1956
Sansome, Brian George Joseph	PC 344	May 1962		
Saunders, Basil Herbert	PC 182	May 1947	Sgt 44, Dec 1952; Insp, Jan 1958; Supt, Sep 1962	
Saunders, Hubert Frederick	PC 180	May 1948	Sgt 57, Oct 1957	Jun 1964
Savage, David Arthur	PC 122	Dec 1958		
Saville, Kenneth	PC 118	Apr 1946	t/Sgt, Jul 1966	
Sawford, Frederick William	PC 257	Oct 1935	Sgt, Apr 1951; Insp, Mar 1954; Ch Insp, Oct 1959; Supt, Sep 1960	Aug 1962
Saxton, Roy	PC 210	Jan 1931	Sgt 14, Apr 1947	Feb 1958
Schreder, James Barry	PC 53	Jul 1956	later PC 353	Jan 1958
Sciville, Robert Arthur	PC 67	Jan 1950		Jan 1966
Scott, David	PC 296	Nov 1952	Sgt 66, Jul 1964; Insp, Feb 1967	
Scott, Francis	PC 84	1906		Dec 1931
Scott, Gordon Haylett	PC 127	Nov 1966		
Scriven, Robert George	PC 191	Jul 1947		
Seal, John Edward	PC 115	Nov 1911		Sep 1939
Searston, William	PC 209	Nov 1947	Sgt 38, Jun 1957	
Seaton, Brian	PC 345	Aug 1965		
Seaton, Lancelot Crown	PC 207	Nov 1927	Sgt 13, Jun 1935 reduced to PC 55, Oct 1937	Feb 1940
Severn, James William McBean	PC 430	Mar 1965		
Sharman, David	PC 406	Dec 1962		Jan 1964
Sharp, John R.	PC 262	Oct 1935		
Sharpe, Alexander	PC 262	Dec 1937		Sep 1938
Sharples, Duncan Oliver Ernest	PC 289	May 1964		Nov 1966
Shatford, Ian	PC 379	Jun 1965		
Shaw, Ivan Roy	PC 69		Sgt 37, Sep 1962	
Shaw, Maurice William	PC 53	Oct 1946		Jan 1947

Name	No/Rank	Joined	Details	Resigned
Shaw, William	PC 79	Aug 1920	Sgt 5, Jan 30	Jan 1946
Sheard, Albert Edward	PC 244	Mar 1935		Mar 1960
Shearsby, Anthony George	PC 367	Aug 1959		
Sheldon, Geoffrey	PC 224	Nov 1934		Apr 1949
Shelvey, Frederic George	PC 180	Dec 1928	Sgt 23, Jul.1934; Insp, Apr 1938	Oct 1954
Shepherdson, Lancelot	Inspector	Dec 1912	was Sgt 17	Nov 1941
Sheppard, James	PC 55	Apr 1910		Jul 1937
Sherriff, Brian Alan	PC 367	Apr 1958		Jul 1959
Shevas, Albert	PC 314	Oct 1964		
Shevas, William	PC 301	Sep 1954		
Shewring, Albert	PC 306	Feb 1953		May 1961
Shingler, Joseph Henry	PC 102	Mar 1928		Mar 1953
Shipman, John	PC 199	Nov 1925	Sgt 33, Nov 1935; Insp, Aug 1951	Jun 1958
Shooter, Michael	PC 441	Oct 1965		
Simmonds, Eustace Latimer	PC 43	Apr 1950		Jul 1951
Simmonds, James L.	PC 59	Jan 1923		Aug 1950
Simmons, Roger John	PC 427	Sep 1965		
Simpson, David Walter	PC 115	Oct 1957		
Simpson, Robert Baxter	PC 247	Jan 1952		Oct 1952
Sims, Albert	Inspector	1904		Jun 1929
Sims, Donald	PC 131	May 1960		
Sims, Kenneth William	PC 61	Dec 1946	later PC 361	
Singleton, Alan Herbert	PC 130	Apr 1948		Jun 1951
Singleton, Ronald Edwin	PC 214	Feb 1951		
Skelly, Rodney Edward	PC 196	Mar 1967		
Slater, Richard Henry	PC 97	Jul 1920	Sgt 21, Dec 1938	Sep 1945
Slow, Clifford George	PC 95	Oct 1952		
Small, Wilfred Aubrey	PC 239	Apr 1937		
Smart, Peter Adrian	PC 454	Jan 1966		Nov 1966
Smith, Alfred Bedell	PC 220	Oct 1964		
Smith, Brian George	PC 325	Dec 1956		Sep 1957
Smith, Cecil	PC 53	Jan 1946		Aug 1946
Smith, Charles	PC 144	Dec 1923	Sgt 29, Apr1935; Insp, Mar 1939	d. May 1953
Smith, Charles Alfred	PC 63	1928		Feb 1950
Smith, Charles H.	PC 42	Sep 1936	later PC 109	Sep 1961
Smith, David Grindall	PC 107	Oct 1956		
Smith, Dennis Norman	PC 238	Mar 1960		
Smith, Derek Tyler	PC 177	Nov 1946		
Smith, Donald	PC 193	Aug 1947		d. c.1965
Smith, Eric George	PC 172	Aug 1952		
Smith, Frank	PC 453	Jan 1966		
Smith, Frederick	PC 137	Sep 1932	Sgt 21, Nov 1955	Sept 1962
Smith, Geoffrey	PC 100	Jun 1963		
Smith, Geoffrey George	PC 461	Mar 1966		
Smith, George	PC 158	Sep 1932		Sep 1957
Smith, George Brian	PC 289	Dec 1966		
Smith, George Henry	PC 240	Apr 1913	Sgt 14, Jun 1935	Apr 1938
Smith, George Henry	PC 188	c.Jan 1921	Sgt 36, Sep 30	May 1958
Smith, Harold	PC		Sgt 4	
Smith, Jack Eric	PC 168	Dec 1958		Feb 1959

Name	No/Rank	Joined	Details	Resigned
Smith, Jeffery Howard	PC	Jan 1964		
Smith, John Brian	PC 136	Feb 1956		
Smith, John Dennis	PC 117	Apr 1946	Sgt 41, Jun 1957; Insp, Oct 1959	
Smith, John Ivan	PC 307	Sep 1951		
Smith, John Maurice	PC 122	Apr 1946		Mar 1948
Smith, John Patrick	PC 197	Nov 1955		Sep 1956
Smith, John Richard Leslie	PC 455	Feb 1966		
Smith, Leonard Joseph	PC 164	Oct 1933	Sgt 12, Mar 1955	Dec 1958
Smith, Noel Herbert Dennis	PC 98	Dec 1928		Feb 1937
Smith, Norman	PC 344	Oct 1958		Mar 1962
Smith, Ronald	PC 79	Jan 1949		
Smith, Ronald Arthur	PC 136	Jun 1946	Sgt 2, Feb 1956; Insp, Jul 1964	
Smith, Silas Frank	PC 222	Jun 1935	Sgt 36, Apr 1947; Insp, Sep 1960; Ch Insp, Jul 1964	
Smith, Sydney	PC 284	Sep 1938		Jul 1948
Smith, Thomas	PC 462	Mar 1966		
Smith, Walter	PC 241			d. Nov 1931
Smithurst, Frank	PC 270	Apr 1938		Nov 1947
Snape, Donald	PC 260	Oct 1935		Jun 1948
Snell, Harold John	PC 212	Dec 1937	Sgt 35, Jun 1957	
Snell, Peter David	PC 154	Dec 1965		
Soden, Reginald Walter	PC 293	Feb 1956		
Southam, Charles	PC 171	1912		*c.*1935
Southam, James Harold	PC 193	Feb 1914		Mar 1942
Southgate, Frank William	PC	Jul 1948		Dec 1948
Spencer, Cyril	PC 233	Aug 1920		Jan 1946
Spencer, Egbert Augustine	PC 57	1904		Jun 1929
Spencer, John Watson	PC 105	Mar 1958		
Spencer, Leonard Arthur	PC 232	Aug 1920		Sep 1945
Spicer, Arthur	PC 124	Dec 1920		Jan 1951
Spiers, Peter Russell	PC 170	May 1947		Sep 1948
Spoors, David	PC 193	Dec 1965		Jan 1966
Springthorpe, Kenneth Gervaise	PC 208	Sep 1932	Sgt 34, Nov 1945; Insp, Nov 1954	Dec 1957
Stables, Stanley	PC 114	Mar 1949		Aug 1950
Stacey, Keith	PC 417	Oct 1962		
Staddon, Alfred Charles Harold	PC 77	Jul 1962		Oct 1966
Stafford, Alan T.	PC 219	Feb 1960		Oct 1966
Staines, George	Sgt 16	1905	was PC 241	Aug 1931
Stainforth, George	PC 200	1928		*c.*1939
Stamp, Arthur John	PC249	Apr 1937		Nov 1946
Stanger, Eric Edward	PC 278	Sep 1956		Sep 1958
Staniforth, Frederick John	PC 104	Dec 1922		Jan 1948
Staniland, William Arthur	PC 86	Sep 1936		Feb 1937
Start, Ralph William	PC 248	Jan 1956		Jul 1956
Statham, Sydney	PC 207	Jun 1935	Sgt 46	Jun 1960
Stead, Frederick William	PC 238	Dec 1924		Dec 1949
Stevens Michael Gordon	PC 251	May 1953		Jun 1957
Stevens, Harold Claude	PC 221	Apr 1965		Jun 1966
Stevens, Malcolm Charles	PC 88	Jun 1965		Apr 1966
Stevenson, Angus Ian	PC 188	Jan 1950	t/Sgt, Apr 1966	

Name	No/Rank	Joined	Details	Resigned
Stevenson, George	PC 169	Oct 1955		Aug 1956
Stevenson, John McOwen	PC 310	May 1956	Sgt, Jun 1965	
Stevenson, John William	PC 77	Nov 1950		Oct 1953
Stevenson, Michael	PC 425	Mar 1965		Jan 1966
Stevenson, Peter	PC 436	Oct 1965		
Stewart, George Robertson	PC 240	Mar 1954		
Stocks, Frederick	PC 289	Aug 1956		Jun 1963
Stokes, Geoffrey Walter	PC 110	Jan 1962		
Stokes, William	PC 133	Jan 1923		Jan 1948
Storey, Arthur	PC 279	Sep 1938	Sgt 27, Oct 1951	May 1955
Storry, John Guard	PC 43	Sep 1936		Jul 1938
Stretton, Harry	PC 208	1907		Jan 1932
Stretton, Samuel	PC 77	1912		Jun 1937
Strong, Henry James	PC 82	Jan 1954	Sgt 21, Sep 1962; Insp, Apr 1966	
Stroud, Alan George	PC 161	Nov 1957		
Struthers, Alexander McConaghy	PC 323	Nov 1956		
Stuart, Douglas McAllen	PC 300	Jan 1953		
Sturgess, Dennis	PC 397	Apr 1962		Dec 1962
Sturgess, William Hill	PC 204	Jan 1951		
Suart, Melvin	PC 263	Feb 1967		
Suart, Robert Lamb	PC 295	Sep 1939		Oct 1947
Summers, Brian David	PC 181	Jan 1956		Nov 1960
Summerson, John Charles	PC 155	Nov 1947		Dec 1949
Sutcliffe, Anthony	PC 206	Oct 1962		Feb 1963
Sutton, Frederick John	PC 248	Dec 1937	Sgt 27, Jul 1955; Insp, Jan 1958	Sep 1966
Swain, Barrie	PC 59	May 1955	later PC 359	Oct 1964
Swain, Jeremy Arthur	PC 254	Jan 1966		
Swain, Maurice	PC 58	Nov 1925		Feb 1951
Swift, Kingsley Pateman	PC 207	May 1953		Apr 1959
Swift, Sydney Edward	PC 51	Apr 1950	later PC 351; Sgt 31, Sep 1963	
Symmonds, George Thomas	PC 226	Aug 1956		Oct 1957
Tallon, Thomas	PC 152	Dec 1923	Sgt 16, Mar 1939	Mar 1949
Tarratt, Charles Anthony	PC 178	Jan 1958		
Taylor, Arthur	PC 51	Aug 1932	Sgt 28, Mar 1950	Oct 1957
Taylor, David Clarke	PC 241	Sep 1966		
Taylor, Harry	PC 94	Sep 1936		d. POW 1943
Taylor, Ronald Sydney	PC 205	Sep 1966		
Tebbutt, Alan	PC 250	Jan 1952		
Tebbutt, George William	PC 76	Aug 1960		
Tenniswood, John Edward	PC 234	Mar 1960		Sep 1960
Terry, George	PC 38	Oct 1926		Oct 1952
Tetstall, Albert	PC 40	1909		Mar 1934
Thirkell, Derek George	PC 180	Dec 1957		Jun 1960
Thomas, Donald L.	PC 377	Jun 1958		Aug 1964
Thomas, George	PC 384	Aug 1961		Oct 1964
Thomas, John Richard	PC 325	Nov 1965		
Thompson, Arthur	Sgt 8	1905		Dec 1931
Thompson, Maurice	PC 384	Feb 1951		c.1959
Thomson, James Ireland	PC 283	Jan 1953		
Thornelow, Albert Edward	PC 157	May 1948		

Name	No/Rank	Joined	Details	Resigned
Thornton, Herbert	Sgt 23	1909		Apr 1934
Thornton, Thomas	PC 155	Feb 1920		Jul 1942
Thorpe, Alan George	PC 145	Jun 1963		
Thorpe, Lot	PC 94	Mar 1946		
Thorpe, Robert James Edward	PC 110	Jan 1959		Jan 1962
Tidmarsh, Maurice Henry	PC 346	Mar 1959		
Tilley, Alfred	PC145	Dec 1923	Sgt 1, Apr 1937	Jan 1945
Timmins, Brian Arthur	PC 180	Aug 1960		
Tingay, John Harold	PC 103	Mar 1948		
Tipler John William Herbert	PC	Oct 1951		Jul 1952
Titterton, Frederick Charles	PC 354	Sep 1963		Mar 1964
Toach, Harold Robert	PC 213	Feb 1920	Sgt 13, Sep 1930; Insp, Jun 1935	Feb 1950
Todd, John	PC 258	Dec 1937	Sgt, Apr 1951; Insp; Ch Insp, Nov 1958	
Towers, Peter Cuthbert	PC 170	Aug 1950		Feb 1951
Treddell, Anthony David Rigby	PC 170	Apr 1964		
Trump,George Edwin	PC 118	Sep 1936		killed Nov 1940
Tucker, Clifford Derrick	PC 165	May 1950	Sgt, Oct 1957	
Tuckwood, Kenneth Edward	PC 404	May 1962		
Turner, Anthony Keith	PC 256	Aug 1964		May 1965
Turner, Edward Charles	Sgt 31	Feb 1920		May 1934
Turner, Laurence David	PC 289	Sep 1963		Jan 1964
Turner, Peter Leonard George	PC 318	Oct 1964		
Turrell, Brian Thomas	PC 397	Dec 1962		
Turrell, Paul Robert	PC 446	Sep 1965		
Underwood, Henry Garford	Inspector	1904		Jul 1930
Urquhart, Walter Jackson	PC 285	Sep 1938		Aug 1946
Vann, John William	PC439	Aug 1965		Mar 1967
Vaughan, John Alwyn	PC 197	Jun 1951		Aug 1955
Vesty, Trevor	PC 73	Dec 1953	later PC 460	
Vickerman, Michael	PC 175	Jan 1959		
Vines, Charles	PC 156	Dec 1923		Mar 1949
Vines, Leonard Arthur	PC 83	Dec 1928	Sgt 37, Dec 1941	Dec 1953
Waby, Michael	PC 432	Mar 1965		May 1966
Wade, Maurice Lancelot	PC 221	Aug 1951		May 1965
Wade, Robert Wallace	PC 162	Dec 1924		Dec 1949
Wadham, Alfred James	PC 46	Nov 1945		Mar 1947
Wain, Anthony	PC 167	Nov 1954	Sgt 2, Jul 1964	
Wakefield, Norman	PC 208	Nov 1947		Sep 1959
Walker, Phillip Joseph	PC 262	Jan 1958		
Walker, David	PC 194	Feb 1960		Aug 1961
Walker, Edward Arthur	PC 196	Aug 1947	Sgt 48, Oct 1954; Insp, Mar 1958; Ch Insp, Supt, Apr 1966	Feb 1967
Walker, Frederick	PC 271	Apr 1938		Feb 1964
Walker, James	PC 127	1910		Apr 1936
Walker, Michael John	PC 375	Jan 1962		
Walker, Phillip Joseph	PC 262	Jan 1958		
Walker, William Barry Alan	PC 356	Apr 1958		
Wallace, Philip John Millington	PC 271	Apr 1964		
Walters, Stephen Anthony	PC 77	Nov 1966		
Walton, Godfrey	PC 147	Aug 1952		Aug 1966

Name	No/Rank	Joined	Details	Resigned
Walton, John Robert	PC 353	Feb 1958		
Walton, William Bertram	PC 215	Jan 1965		
Wappat, Ralph	PC 366	Apr 1958		Dec 1958
Ward, Edward	PC 147	Jan 1931	Sgt 29, Jul 1952	Jul 1959
Ward, Raymond	PC 321	Nov 1956		Apr 1959
Ward, Victor Ernest Ellwood	PC 179	Dec 1954		
Wardle, Harry	PC 57	Oct 1929		Oct 1954
Wardle, Keith Trevelyan	PC 222	Oct 1953		Dec 1966
Wardle, Roger Neil	PC 331	Dec 1963		
Warner, Arthur Norman	PC 93	Sep 1932		Jul 1958
Warner, Harry	PC 242	Aug 1921		Sep 1946
Warner, Leslie	PC 330	Jan 1957		
Warren, Michael	PC 173	Nov 1957		Sep 1960
Warriner, Charles	PC 92	Sep 1932		Jun 1958
Warrington, Robert	PC 176	May 1947	Sgt, Jan 1959	
Warsop, David Keith	PC 407	Dec 1962		
Warsop, Trevor Ernest William	PC 189	Dec 1957		
Wass, Ronald Braithwaite	PC 295	Nov 1952		Apr 1959
Watchorn, Royce William	PC 229	Sep 1951	Sgt 42, Jan 1958; Insp, Jul 1964	
Waterton, Eric Gordon	PC 81	Dec 1953		
Watkins, Harry Lewis	PC 61	Nov 1927		Nov 1946
Watson Alwyne	PC 247	Oct 1952	Sgt 50, Mar 1961	
Watson, Frederick Donald	PC 286	Sep 1938		d. Sep 1941
Waugh, Cyril	PC 87	Oct 1929	Sgt 11, Nov 1945; Insp, Apr 1948; Supt, Jan 1953	Oct 1959
Waycott, Clifford	PC 116	Jul 1959		Sep 1961
Webster, Isaac James	PC 123	Aug 1921		Aug 1946
Webster, Kenneth John	PC 393	Oct 1959		
Weedon David Barrie	PC 268	Nov 1953		Mar 1959
Welbourne, John William Ashton	PC 145	Sep 1950	Sgt 33, Jan 1959	
Welch, William Edwin	PC 203	Dec 1926	Sgt 25, Sep 1939; Insp, Sep 1950	Mar 1954
Wells, Charles Henry	PC 336	Feb 1957		
Wells, Geoffrey Jack	PC 91	Dec 1946	Sgt, Nov 1958	
Wells, Maurice	PC 66	Jan 1946	later PC 414	
Wells, Thomas	PC 55	Nov 1934	later PC 355	Nov 1959
Wells, Walter Elliott	Sgt 14	1905		May 1930
Wells, Brian Trevor	PC 105	Jun 1955		Mar 1958
Welsh, Sidney Keith	PC 169	Feb 1961		
Weston, Jesse Samuel	Sgt 17	Apr 1919	was PC 66; Insp, May 1933	May 1949
Weston, Leslie George	PC 153	Jul 1946		Mar 1951
Wheatley, Charles Thomas	PC 278	Jun 1938		Jan 1946
Wheeler, Bryan John	PC 251	Aug 1957		
Wheelwright, Ian Thomas	PC 244	Apr 1964		
Whightman, Peter John	PC 237	Dec 1962		Mar 1963
White, Frederick Henry Samuel	PC 188	Jul 1947		Sep 1948
White, John Trevor	PC 233	Oct 1951	Sgt 22, Dec 1958	
White, Reginald Douglas	PC 75	Feb 1946		Jul 1946
Whitehead, Anthony F.	PC 253	Oct 1962		
Whitfield, Samuel	PC 263	Oct 1935		Jul 1937
Whitney, Samuel	PC 73	Nov 1926		Nov 1951

Name	No/Rank	Joined	Details	Resigned
Whittaker, Anthony William	PC 297	Dec 1952		May 1954
Whittaker, Edward Graham	PC 416	Sep 1965		May 1966
Whittering, George	PC 111	Apr 1909		Oct 1932
Whitworth, Roger	PC 224	Jul 1958		
Wholton, Harry	PC 275	Jul 1952		Apr 1953
Whybrow, Kenneth George	PC 114	Mar 1947		May 1948
Whyman, William	Sgt 11	1906		Sep 1931
Whyte, John Frederick	PC 116	Mar 1958		May 1959
Wickham, Arthur R.	PC 255	Jun 1935		Mar 1945
Wicks, Shirley Arthur	Inspector	Mar 1914	PC 104, Supt, Mar 1939	Jan 1946
Widdowson, Michael Ernest	PC 401	Apr 1962		Feb 1964
Wightman, George W.H.	PC 264	Oct 1935		Jul 1946
Wigley, Ronald	PC 272	Apr. 1938	Sgt 41, Aug 1951; Insp, Jul 1955; Supt, Oct 1957	
Wilby, James	PC 42	1911		May 1936
Wilkinson	PC 354	Nov 1955		Feb 1960
Wilkinson, David	PC 345	Sep 1959		
Wilkinson, John	PC 64	Nov 1963	later PC 412	Dec 1965
Willcox, Alan Murphy	PC 308	Oct 1956		Jun 1957
Willett, George	PC 103	Jan 1923		Jan 1948
Williams, Caryl Francis	PC 127	Jul 1953		Jun 1955
Williams, Eric Thomas	PC 265	Apr 1937		Oct 1949
Williams, Geoffrey Douglas	PC 176	Mar 1966		
Williams, Harold	PC 59	Aug 1950		Aug 1950
Williams, Roger Paul	PC 445	Sep 1965		
Williamson, John Swimburne	PC 398	Feb 1964		Oct 1964
Williamson, Terrence	PC 340	Mar 1957		
Willis, Richard Braithwaite	Inspector	Oct 1909	was PC 152; Sgt 5, Insp, Nov 1928	Oct 1935
Wilson, Bernard Anthony	PC 188	Jan 1931		d. Jan 1947
Wilson, Brian	PC 237	Aug 1959	left Apr 1960; rejoined Apr 1963	Feb 1964
Wilson, Donald	PC 134	Dec 1946		Dec 1950
Wilson, Frank	Sgt 3	Nov 1914	Insp, Apr 1935	Jan 1946
Wilson, Frederick E.	PC 121	Nov 1925		Nov 1950
Wilson, Geoffrey Laurie	PC 258	Oct 1964		
Winfield, William Roland	PC 169	Aug 1946	Sgt, Mar 1955	
Wing, Barry Hilton	PC 92	Jul 1958		Sep 1958
Winkless, David Samuel	PC 244	Apr 1960		Jul 1961
Withers, Cyril	PC 172	Dec 1920	Sgt 14, Apr 1938	Mar 1947
Withycombe, M.E.J.	PC 207	Apr 1959		Dec 1961
Wolfe, Robert	PC 179	May 1947	Sgt 26, Oct 1954; Insp, Jul 1965	
Wood, Adrian Allan	PC 381	Jun 1962		
Wood, David George	PC 117	Oct 1957		Aug 1960
Wood, James Arthur	PC 230	Oct 1951		
Wood, William John Neville	PC 189	Jul 1947		1948
Woodcock, Arthur	PC 111	Oct 1933		Mar 1945
Woodcock, David Bernard	PC 117	Nov 1960		
Woods, Brian Robert	PC 304	Feb 1953		
Woods, John William	PC 198	Feb 1928		Apr 1952
Woods, Keith Brian	PC 314	Oct 1956		Jan 1958
Woodward, Adrian, T.L.	PC 352	Jan 1966		

Name	No/Rank	Joined	Details	Resigned
Woodward, Joseph Albert	PC 153	Oct 1929	Sgt 28, Insp, Mar 1950; Ch Insp, Sep 1954; Supt, Oct 1957	Nov 1959
Woolley, John L.	PC 246	Oct 1935		Oct 1937
Woolley, Maurice John	PC 246	Dec 1937	Sgt 9, Oct 1951; Insp, Dec 1959	
Woolley, Thomas Peter	PC 84	Sep 1932	Sgt 38, Mar 1939; Insp, Nov 1946; Ch Insp, Aug 1951; Supt, Oct 1953	Jul 1964
Woolman, Alan	PC 206	Feb 1963		
Woolman, Brian Thomas	PC 332	Feb 1957		Sep 1957
Workman, Keith McLean	PC 216	Jan 1966		Sep 1966
Wortley, Percy Frederick	PC 142	Jun 1946		Dec 1947
Wren, Christopher G.	PC 145	Apr 1937	Sgt 25, Sep 1950	
Wright, Frederick	PC 191	Oct 1931	Sgt 21, Nov 1946; Insp, Sep 1950	Jan 1958
Wright, John Joseph	PC 234	Mar 1930		Mar 1960
Wright, Kevin Robert	PC 317	Aug 1960		Mar 1964
Wright, Michael George	PC 244	Sep 1961		Feb 1964
Yarwood, David Charles	PC 285	Feb 1956		
Yates, Geoffrey Alan	PC 287	Oct 1952		Aug 1953
York, J.	PC 184	Mar 1914		Jun 1942
Young, John Alexander	PC 193	Aug 1965	left Nov 1965; rejoined Jan 1966	
Zanker, Thomas Edward	PC 220			Sep 1956

Alterations to the establishment of Sergeants

Both the Leicester Borough and Leicester City Police had an establishment for sergeants in which the numbering commenced at 'Sergeant 1'. At the highest end of the establishment, sergeants numbers gave way to constables numbers. e.g. Sgt 58, PC 59 &c. This system had a rolling impact on the numbering of individual constables. Each time that an increase in the sergeants establishment occurred, a certain number of constables numbers were re-allocated to sergeants and the constables given a new number. e.g. an increase from 58 to 61 sergeants, results in constables '59', '60' and '61' being given new numbers. The table below gives the years in which an establishment increase caused such alterations.

Year	Existing establishment of Sergeants	Sergeant Establishment increased to	Resultant changes of Constables numbers
1932	32	33	33
1936	33	35	34, 35
1936	35	37	36, 37
1946	37	39	38, 39
1951	39	42	40, 41, 42
1952	42	45	43, 44, 45
1953	45	46	46
1954	46	48	47, 48
1957	48	57	49, 50, 51, 52, 53, 54, 55, 56, 57
1958	57	58	58
1959	58	61	59, 60, 61
1961	61	62	62
1962	62	63	63
1964	63	66	64, 65, 66
1965	66	69	67, 68, 69
1966	69	73	70, 71, 72, 73

Policewomen

Name	No/Rank	Joined	Details	Resigned
(m = married name; WAPC = Women's Auxiliary Police Corps)				
Atkins, Patricia Marjorie	WPC 5	Nov 1954	m = Holyoak	Apr 1959
Bates, Mary Eileen		Jul 1941		Jul 1945
Bell, Elizabeth Anne		Apr 1966		
Bentley, Elaine	WPC 21	Nov 1964		
Betts, Jean Annie	WPC 11	Jul 1954		Sep 1957
Betts, Jennifer Bridget	WPC 21	Oct 1959	m = Monk	Feb 1963
Booth, Janice Mary		Oct 1966		
Borrett, Mary Alice		Jan 1947		Jul 1947
Brailsford, Doreen Rosemary		Jul 1949	left Oct 1954; rejoined as Sgt 2, May 1955	Apr 1966
Brooks, Mary	WPC 12	Nov 1957	m = Woolley	Sep 1960
Buxton, Bettie	WPC 7	Feb 1965	Sgt, Feb 1967	
Calder, Lindsay Margaret	WPC 23	Jun 1965	also shown as, Lindsay, Margaret Calder	Dec 1966
Cheater, Sheila	WPC 17	Apr 1958	left Jul 1965, rejoined as Sgt May 1966	
Chesterton, Stella Vivien	WPC 11	Nov 1957	m = Garside	Aug 1960
Constable, Anne Briggs		Apr 1936		Mar 1941
Constable, Dora Hay		Sep 1936		Jan 1938
Conway, Margaret Christina Dympna	WPC 12	Jul 1955		Nov 1956
Cosier, Barbara		Oct 1966		Dec 1966
de Vitre, Barbara Denis		Jun 1933	Sgt, Nov 1936	May 1944
Donnelly, Brenda Mavis		Nov 1954	Sgt, Nov 1959	Nov 1965
Dow, Wanda		Oct 1966		
Draycott, Doreen Emily	WPC 8	Dec 1952	later Sgt 3	Apr 1966
Dunkley, Delia Mavis	WPC 1	Nov 1964		
Edginton, Frances Vera Ethel	WPC 12	Apr 1963		Jan 1965
Edwards, Doreen		Aug 1965		
Elder, Yvonne		Jun 1965		
Elvin, D.	WPC 26			Dec 1966
Farrell, Sandra Gail	WPC 20	Aug 1964	m = Green	Jun 1965
Fish, June Elizabeth	WPC 9	Mar 1960		Sep 1966
Forward, Katherine		Feb 1967		
Fox, Irene Doris	WPC 14	Oct 1955		Oct 1958
Froude, Jean Georgina	WPC 3	Dec 1946	m = Pratt	Nov 1948
Garner, Christine		Mar 1967		
Garnett, Jeanne Valentine		Jan 1947	m = Gannon	Jan 1948
Geary, Patricia Mary	WPC 7	Apr 1958	m = Spencer	Oct 1961
Gisborn, Valerie Ann	WPC 16	Jan 1958		
Gist, Jacqueline Ellen	WPC 18	Sep 1962	m = Cross	Jan 1965
Glover, Margaret Isabel		Dec 1948	left Sep 1954, rejoined as Sgt 1, Oct 1957	Nov 1958
Golder, Sheila Ann	WPC 13	Nov 1958	m = Goodwin	Aug 1960
Greaves, Cynthia Mary		Dec 1965		
Green, Diane Elizabeth		Jul 1965		
Groom, Phyllis Edna		May 1944		Apr 1951
Grove, Gwendolen Margaret	WPC 10	Feb 1955	m = Coombs	Nov 1956
Groves, Eileen Mary	WPC 4	Nov 1960		Dec 1963
Harvey, Gwendolen	Sgt	Jun 1944	joined as Sgt	Jul 1951
Herbert, Sylvia Jean	WPC 11	Nov 1960		
Hill, Janet	WPC 18	Jan 1959	m = Baker	Jul 1961
Hockey, Gillian	WPC 4	Aug 1956	m = Allen	
Holland, Joan Frances Marie	WPC 3	Jun 1966		Nov 1966

Name	No/Rank	Joined	Details	Resigned
Ingram, Patricia Anne	WPC 10	Nov 1960		
Jackson, Rita Marina	WPC 9	Feb 1955	m = MacDiarmid	Mar 1957
James, Maureen Sheila	WPC 12	Jan 1961		Feb 1963
King, Patricia	WPC 12	Dec 1964		
Knight, June	WPC 9	Aug 1957		Oct 1958
Laxton, Jane Elizabeth		Oct 1966		
Leese, Elaine Margaret		Nov 1962		Jul 1963
Lindsay, Margaret Calder	WPC 23	Jun 1965	also shown as Calder, Margaret Lindsay	Dec 1966
Linsell, Avril June	WPC 10	Jan 1957		Mar 1960
Low, Elizabeth Jean		Jul 1965		
McAleer, Patricia Anne	WPC 13	Mar 1962		Apr 1964
McIndeor, Shelagh	WPC 8	May 1957		Jun 1958
Mee, Jacqueline Rosemary	WPC 7			Jan 1965
Middleton, Sally Elizabeth	WPC 14	Jun 1959		Apr 1960
Mitchell, Betty		Aug 1947	m = Jones	Aug 1951
Molloy, Elizabeth Roseleen		Nov 1966		
Moran, Catherine Mary	WPC 5	Jun 1959		
Moss, Judith	WPC 20	Jun 1959		Nov 1960
Myles, Mary Helen	WPC 7	Nov 1961		Jan 1963
Newton, Sylvia Ann	WPC 4	Sep 1953	m = O'Connell	May 1956
Overton, Marjorie Anne		Apr 1964		
Overton, Marjorie Anne		Apr 1964		Sep 1964
Parker, Carole Anne	WPC 4	Apr 1964		Oct 1966
Parkin, Hilda Mary	Sgt 1	Dec 1951	joined as Sgt, Insp, Jan 1957	
Pimp, Barbara	WPC 15	Jan 1958	m = Rivington	Oct 1965
Potter, Edith Marjorie	WAPC	May 1944		
Pulsford, Susan		Jun 1965		
Reidy, Susan Rosalind	WPC 15	Nov 1965		Jul 1966
Rodwell, Mary		Apr 1948		Jun 1953
Rogers, Edith Irene May	WPC 3	Oct 1951	Sgt 1, Jan 1957	Jul 1957
Samson, Kathleen Florence	WPC 19	Oct 1958		Feb 1962
Sherriff, Barbara, Lucy	WPC 22	May 1965		Jul 1966
Shevas, Evelyn Boyles	WPC 8	Aug 1958	m = Proudman	Dec 1965
Sloane, Eileen St Claire		Nov 1929		May 1933
Squires, Sandra Yvonne		Jan 1967		
Stokes, Sheila Ann	WPC 14	May 1961	m = Ludlam	Sep 1965
Street, Frances Ann		Jan 1960		
Summers, Janet Edith	WPC 9	Feb 1959		Feb 1960
Tedder, Gladys		Jan 1941		Apr 1944
Thirlby, Joan	WPC 4	Dec 1946	m = Burt	Jan 1948
Thornelow Madeleine	WPC 22	Sep 1966		
Tovey, Barbara May	WPC 7	Sep 1956		Feb 1958
Turner, Jean Elizabeth	WPC 7	Jan 1952	m = Wood	May 1956
Vice, Christine Janet		Aug 1966		
Watson, Brenda	WPC 13	Jul 1955	m = Laight	Jan 1958
Weeks, Barbara Prinnett	WPC 20	Apr 1961		Feb 1963
West, Dianne M.	WPC 14	Oct 1965		Oct 1966
Winter, Winifred Hope	Sgt	Jun 1944	joined as Sgt, m = Joiner	Apr 1946
Wood, Olive		c.1950		
Woods, Jean Margaret		Oct 1951		Dec 1953
Yates, Mary	WPC 18	Mar 1965		Jun 1966
Yeates, Joan Gladys	WPC 13	Jun 1964		

Leicester City Police Force
31 March 1967

Chief Constable
Mark, Robert

Assistant Chief Constable
Lacy, Eric Ernest

Superintendents
Adkin, Clement	Jun 1938
Bestwick, George Hadyn Whitcroft	Sep 1938
Brobyn, Rowland George	Apr 1939
Page, Sidney	Jun 1935
Saunders, Basil	May 1947

Chief Inspectors
Cox, Norman	Jul 1946
Owen, Christopher Herbert	Oct 1946
Smith, Silas Frank	Jun 1935
Todd, John	Dec 1937

Inspectors
Adams, Peter Richard	Apr 1946
Bingham, John	Sep 1939
Broomfield, John Alfred	May 1949
Broughton, Jack Alan	Feb 1949
Corns, Edward	Mar 1947
Driver, Albert Edward	Jul 1949
Goodman, Winston Charles	Jun 1938
Gordon, James	Jul 1952
Green, Harry	Dec 1937
Hunt, Wilfrid Roy James	Sep 1946
Jones, Richard Ernest	Apr 1966
Kendrick, Clifford Arthur	Jan 1955
Mann, Joseph	Aug 1953
McGrory, William	Apr 1949
Pomfret, Alexander John	Dec 1937
Price, John Humphrey	Oct 1951
Robinson, Clifford Wilfrid	Jul 1946
Roe, Peter John	Apr 1966
Sandall, Thomas Francis	Sep 1938
Scott, David	Nov 1952
Smith, John Dennis	Apr 1946
Smith, Ronald Arthur	Jun 1946
Strong, Henry James	Jan 1954
Watchorn, Royce William	Sep 1951
Wolfe, Robert	May 1947
Woolley, Maurice John	Dec 1937

Sergeants

Allen, Robert Arthur		Apr 1964
Atkins, Norman William	Sgt 67	Aug 1954
Bainbrigge, John Eric Bernard	Sgt 64	May 1952
Barlow, William D.	Sgt 11	Sep 1938
Barnett, Thomas Alan	Sgt 26	Sep 1954
Barton, Norman James		Mar 1956
Blakemore, Donald Charles	Sgt 21	Dec 1947
Boness Laurence Frank (temp)		Mar 1950
Bramley, Peter Clifford	Sgt 8	Aug 1957
Brown, Alex		Jun 1956
Burt, Phillip	Sgt 54	Sep 1946
Curtis, John Thomas	Sgt 1	Nov 1947
Curtis, Leslie Edward		Sep 1939
Fox, John Gordon	Sgt 47	Jan 1956
Fox, John Reginald		Jun 1958
Freear, William	Sgt 13	Apr 1938
Gamble, Eric Leonard	Sgt 10	Nov 1954
Gannon, Bernard	Sgt 58	Oct 1946
Gannon, James Edwin	Sgt 6	Jun 1951
Gatward, William Albert	Sgt 52	Jul 1949
Glover, John (temp)		Mar 1950
Goggins, Douglas Robert Patrick	Sgt 3	Sep 1951
Goulding, Graham James	Sgt 62	Sep 1956
Graham, William	Sgt 27	Jun 1946
Gratrix, James	Sgt 72	Jun 1955
Greasley, Kenneth Harry	Sgt 53	Jul 1948
Green, Raymond		Jan 1950
Green, Raymond	Sgt 18	Jan 1950
Hadley, Norman	Sgt 32	Apr 1938
Hall, Charles Jabez	Sgt 20	Nov 1958
Hamilton, Cyril Roy	Sgt 7	Mar 1954
Haywood, George Leonard		Jun 1951
Hibbert, Phillip Terence		Apr 1954
Hodge, Roy	Sgt 49	Apr 1952
House, Richard Maurice		Jan 1952
Hull, Trevor	Sgt 45	Feb 1952
Illiffe, Alan James Stapleton	Sgt 5	Mar 1948
James, Leslie	Sgt 23	Nov 1949
Johnson, Barrie	Sgt 44	Jan 1952
Johnson, Wilfred Arthur		Nov 1950
Jones, Maurice	Sgt 19	Jul 1955
Jones, Robert Henry	Sgt 71	Apr 1952
Lewis, William Gordon	Sgt 28	Jun 1948
MacDiarmid, Alexander Archibald	Sgt 9	Mar 1952
McDonald, Kenneth	Sgt 57	Jul 1952
McRae, George		Feb 1952
Milligan, James	Sgt 66	Feb 1952
Millington, Frank		Oct 1949

Milner, John		Apr 1939	
Mould, Raymond		Apr 1952	
Noble, George Angus	Sgt 43	Mar 1946	
North, Malcolm Brian	Sgt 42	Nov 1958	
O'Dowd David (temp)		Nov 1961	
Peacock, John Henry Groves	Sgt 48	Jan 1962	
Preston, Jack	Sgt 36	Feb 1951	
Pridmore, Kenneth		Jan 1947	
Ralph, Charles John	Sgt 29	Feb 1948	
Redman, David Brian	Sgt 70	Aug 1959	
Rogers, Ernest Travis(temp)		Jan 1963	
Ryde-Rogers, John Anthony	Sgt 60	Sep 1956	
Saville, Kenneth (temp)		Apr 1946	
Searston, William	Sgt 38	Nov 1947	
Shaw, Ivan Roy	Sgt 37		
Snell, Harold John	Sgt 35	Dec 1937	
Stevenson, John McOwen		May 1956	
Stevenson, Angus Ian	t/Sgt 68	Jan 1950	
Stevenson, Angus Ian (temp)		Jan 1950	
Swift, Sydney Edward	Sgt 31	Apr 1950	
Tucker, Clifford Derrick	Sgt 56	May 1950	
Wain, Tony	Sgt 2	Nov 1954	
Warrington, Robert	Sgt 12	May 1947	
Watson, Alwyne	Sgt 50	Oct 1952	
Welborne, John William Ashton	Sgt 33	Sep 1950	
Wells, Geoffrey Jack	Sgt 59	Dec 1946	
White, John Trevor	Sgt 22	Oct 1951	
Winfield, William Roland	Sgt 15	Sep 1946	
Wren, Christopher G.	Sgt 25	Apr 1937	

74	Gunnell, Robert Allan		Mar 1966
75	MacIntosh, Angus James		Oct 1954
76	Tebbutt, George William		Aug 1960
77	Walters, Stephen Anthony		Nov 1966
78	Mitchell, Roy Lawrence		Jul 1964
79	Smith, Ronald		Jan 1949
80	Barlow, David		Jul 1962
81	Waterton, Eric Gordon		Dec 1953
82	Coaton, John		Oct 1962
83	Hill, Leonard		May 1950
84	Carr, Raymond Albert		May 1966
85	Ludlam, Michael Anthony		Dec 1960
86	Gays, Richard		Oct 1959
87	Drew, Stanley		Jan 1954
88	Anthony, Michael James		May 1966
89	Lowe, George Noel		Nov 1958
90	Baines, Clive Barry		Mar 1954
91	Holyoake, David		Nov 1958
92	Musgrave, Anthony		Sep 1958
93	Reed, Graham Edwin		Jul 1958
94	Thorpe, Lot		Mar 1946
95	Slow, Clifford George		Oct 1952
96	de Ville, Peter		Jan 1949

97	Measey, Allen Gort	Jul 1958
98	Kirk, Trevor Frank	May 1949
99	Russell, Kenneth	Oct 1963
100	Smith, Geoffrey	Jun 1963
101	Colledge, Raymond	Jul 1948
102	Markillie, Walter Richard	Apr 1953
103	Tingay, John Harold	Mar 1948
104		
105	Spencer, John Watson	Mar 1958
106	Dawkins, Roy Charles	Feb 1951
107	Smith, David Grindall	Oct 1956
108	Parker, J.	Jul 1950
109	Dinsdale, Graham Spencer	Feb 1963
110	Stokes, Geoffrey Walter	Jan 1962
111	Bradley, Martin G.	Sep 1964
112	Chambers, Arthur Sidney	Aug 1950
113	Gamble, Anthony John	Dec 1960
114	Kelly, Nelson Leo Mead	Aug 1950
115	Simpson, David Walter	Oct 1957
116	Lewis, David Ivor llewellyn	Oct 1961
117	Woodcock, David	Nov 1960
118	Saville, Kenneth (t/Sgt, Jul 1966)	Apr 1946
119	Coles, John Morris	Jan 1951
120	Chambers, Gwynne	Jan 1964
121	Robertson, Robert	Dec 1950
122	Savage, David Arthur	Dec 1958
123	Hadfield, Alan Francis	Nov 1960
124	Farrar, Archibald Robert Benjamin	Feb 1958
125	Bell, James Kerr	May 1946
126	Russell, Gavin	Dec 1952
127	Scott, Gordon Haylett	Nov 1966
128	Coombs, Alfred William Charles	Oct 1954
129	Hulme, Roy William	May 1946
130	Gill, Leslie Grayson	Dec 1965
131	Sims, Donald	May 1960
132		
133	Crombie, Donald Graham	Jun 1966
134	Bennett, Alan John	Jan 1951
135	Clarke, John Harold	Jun 1946
136	Smith, Brian	Feb 1956
137	Morris, Thomas Alan	Nov 1955
138	Green, Leslie	Apr 1937
139	Pick, Wallace Raymond	Oct 1957
140	Knott, Raymond John	Jul 1958
141	Payne, David	May 1966
142	Hancock, Frank Roland	Nov 1956
143	Collyer, Eric William	Dec 1957
144	Langton, Derek	Jan 1953
145	Thorpe, Alan George	Jun 1963
146	Hackett, Roy	Mar 1956
147	Hatton, Roy	Sep 1966
148	Gellatly, Alan Hamilton	Feb 1967
149	Harding, John Geoffrey	Apr 1964

150	Blackburn, Ian	Sep 1962		203	L'Homme, Thomas Peter	Feb 1961
151	Hull, Norman Wilford	Jan 1948		204	Sturgess, William Hill	Jan 1951
152	Brown	Aug 1966		205	Taylor, Ronald Sydney	Sep 1966
153	Groom, I.D.	Nov 1965		206	Woolman, Alan W.	Feb 1963
154	Snell, Peter David	Dec 1965		207	Berridge, Graham Sydney	Sep 1963
155	Cox, David Brian	Jan 1950		208	Acton Donald Frank	Oct 1959
156	Cowley, Bruce Frederick Charles	Oct 1957		209	Mansell, Donald John	Dec 1957
157	Thornelow, Albert Edward	May 1948		210	Bennett, Gerald	May 1950
158	McLeod, Duncan	Sep 1957		211	Mason, Peter George Henry	Nov 1953
159	Emerton, Barrie	May 1961		212	Ingham, Stanley Christopher	Aug 1957
160	Moxey, Colin	Aug 1959		213	Green, Piers Leslie	Jun 1966
161	Stroud, Alan George	Nov 1957		214	Singleton, Ronald	Feb 1951
162	Sandall, Gordon Stuart	Sep 1966		215	Walton, William Bertram	Jan 1965
163	Roberts, Cyril	Feb 1951		216	Hope, Thomas	Dec 1955
164	Gardner, Robert	Sep 1955		217	Beeby, Barry Royce	Sep 1957
165	Lockton, David Michael	Nov 1957		218	Belton, Alan	Jan 1958
166	Clarke, Arthur	Jan 1960		219	Francis, David John	Dec 1966
167	Dalgliesh, John Featherstone	Aug 1964		220	Smith, Alfred Bedell	Oct 1964
168	Berry, Terence John	May 1959		221	Grantham, Ronald Edward	Jun 1966
169	Welsh, Sidney Keith	Feb 1961		222	Denton, Malcolm Frederick	Jan 1967
170	Treddell, Anthony David Rigby	Apr 1964		223	Platts, Tony	Oct 1951
171	Riley, George Albert	Mar 1960		224	Whitworth, Roger	Jul 1958
172	Smith, Eric George	Aug 1952		225	Pinchbeck, Anthony James	Feb 1959
173	Grey, Ian	Jan 1961		226	Bosworth, Malcolm Phillip John	Jan 1958
174	Perkins, David Frank	Sep 1961		227	Callington, Stewart James Vernon	Oct 1964
175	Vickerman, Michael	Jan 1959		228	Davies, Eric Graham	Jul 1958
176	Williams, Geoffrey Douglas	Mar 1966		229	Illiff, Derek	Aug 1961
177	Smith, Derek Tyler	Nov 1946		230	Wood, James Arthur	Oct 1951
178	Tarratt, Charles Anthony	Jan 1958		231	Folkard, Brian Victor Neville	Jan 1967
179	Ward, Victor Ernest Ellwood	Dec 1954		232	Currall, Walter Harry	Oct 1951
180	Timmins, Brian A.	Aug 1960		233	McCorkindale, John	Oct 1964
181	Merry, Robert Keith	Jan 1961		234	Petherick, Leonard Henry	Feb 1961
182	Allen, Brian	Jan 1953		235	Grundy, JohnThomas	Oct 1951
183	Downes, Charlie	Jun 1947		236	O'Connell, Daniel	Oct 1951
184	Morgan, Harold Lawton	Jun 1951		237	Lockwood, Michael	Mar 1964
185	Barrett, Anthony J.	Sep 1955		238	Smith, Dennis Norman	Mar 1960
186	Bendell, Edward	Jul 1948		239	Small, Aubrey	Apr 1937
187	Lambert, John Keith	Mar 1958		240	Stewart, George Robertson	Mar 1954
188	Doyle, Patrick James	May 1966		241	Taylor, David Clarke	Sep 1966
189	Warsop, Trevor Ernest William	Dec 1957		242	Lee, Ian James	Jul 1966
190	Chaston, Clive	Mar 1966		243	Davies, William	Jun 1956
191	Scriven, Robert George	Jul 1947		244	Wheelwright, Ian Thomas	Apr 1964
192	Barratt, Geoffrey Arthur George	Jan 1964		245	Batty, John	Mar 1967
193	Young, John Alexander	Aug 1965		246	Haywood, Tony Michael	Dec 1966
194	Findlay, Bryan	Aug 1961		247	Parker, David Walter	Apr 1961
195	Batchelor, Ronald	Mar 1965		248	Mason, Michael Edward	Sep 1961
196	Skelly, Rodney Edward	Mar 1967		249	Connor, Anthony Gerald	May 1964
197	Fosberry, Richard	Oct 1962		250	Tebbutt, Alan	Jan 1952
198	Donelly, Terence Stuart	Jan 1961		251	Wheeler, Bryan John	Aug 1957
199	Fowkes, Ronald Walter	Nov 1955		252	Morrison, Norman	Jan 1953
200	Birnie, Alexander Edward	Sep 1947		253	Whitehead, Anthony F.	Oct 1962
201	Clow, Michael John	Feb 1961		254	Swain, Jeremy Arthur	Jan 1966
202	Glover, John (t/Sgt, Jan 1967)	Mar 1950		255	Hubbard, Charles Robert	Jun 1953

256	Gillespie, Alastair Grant	Dec 1966		309	Crossley, David	May 1956
257	O'Dowd, David Joseph (t/Sgt, Jan 1967)	Nov 1961		310	Adams, Brian	Jul 1965
258	Wilson, Geoffrey Laurie	Oct 1964		311	Mann, Neil	May 1956
259	Morgan, Christopher John	Jan 1967		312	Brown, Alex	Jun 1956
260	Allsop, Roy	Aug 1965		313	Cattermole, Owen James	Jun 1956
261	Sandall, Geoffey Francis	Jan 1967		314	Shevas, Albert	Oct 1964
262	Walker, Phillip Joseph	Jan 1958		315		
263	Suart, Melvin	Feb 1967		316	Felstead, David Robert	Aug 1960
264	Naylor, Michael John	Sep 1964		317	McElhinney, Michael Thomas	Oct 1964
265	Derry, Douglas Raymond	Jul 1952		318	Turner, Peter	Oct 1964
266	Harris, Roy	Mar 1956		319	Parkinson, John David	Sep 1960
267	Hardy, Dennis Wilfred Maurice	May 1952		320	Butler, Michael Frank	Mar 1961
268	Holland, Edgar Thomas	Mar 1961		321	Beeston, Alan Thomas	Jun 1959
269	Hodby, Alan	May 1952		322	Osborne, Robert David	Nov 1956
270	Hughes, Michael	Jul 1965		323	Struthers, Alexander McConaghy	Nov 1956
271	Wallace, Philip John Millington	Apr 1964		324	Ralph, David Bernard	Mar 1961
272	Horner, Anthony Louis	Jan 1966		325	Thomas, John Richard	Nov 1965
273	Carey, Robert Henry	Apr 1964		326	Beazley, John Benjamin	Sep 1965
274				327	Liggins, Keith Arthur	Dec 1956
275	Peet, John Harvey	Aug 1965		328	Barston, Ronald	Dec 1956
276	Harrison, David George	Nov 1953		329	Guiver, Christopher Dudley	Jan 1958
277	Graham, Peter	Jul 1952		330	Warner, Leslie	Jan 1957
278	Edwards, Michael S	Sep 1958		331	Wardle, Roger Neil	Dec 1963
279	Hollis, Hubert Elkin	Aug 1952		332		
280	Coleman, Keith Herman	Sep 1956		333	Moffett, Ernest Alan	Jul 1959
281	Parker, Peter	Aug 1952		334	Elliott, John	Feb 1957
282	Farrows, Dennis Arthur	Jul 1959		335	Fletcher, Ronald Arthur	Feb 1957
283	Thomson, James Ireland	Jan 1953		336	Wells, Charles Henry	Feb 1957
284	Reddell, John Anthony	Sep 1952		337	Parkins, Jeffrey	Feb 1957
285	Yarwood, David	Feb 1956		338	Fisher, Hugh Barry Loydall	Mar 1957
286	Fawcett, Peter Gordon	Oct 1952		339	Dawson, Brian	Mar 1957
287	Dunham, Norman	Sep 1953		340	Williamson, Terrence	Mar 1957
288	Coulson, Garry	Sep 1964		341	Deberex, John Edward	Apr 1957
289	Smith, George Brian	Dec 1966		342	Burrows, Brian	Aug 1961
290	Bates, John Thomas	Jan 1958		343	Pinchbeck, Edwin Alfred	May 1957
291	Flude, Keith	Oct 1952		344	Sansome, Brian George Joseph	May 1962
292	Hall, William Douglas	Oct 1953		345	Seaton, Brian	Aug 1965
293	Soden, Reginald Walter	Feb 1956		346	Tidmarsh, Maurice Henry	Mar 1959
294				347	Moore, Stanley Donald	Feb 1958
295	Atterbury, Cyril John	May 1959		348	Campbell, Robert George Mitchell	Apr 1961
296	Arnett, Adrian James	Apr 1966		349	Painter, Anthony	Feb 1958
297	Bremner, George Sharpe	Jun 1961		350	Brown, Frederick William	Mar 1958
298	Leverton, Peter	Jul 1959		351	Holley, Michael	Dec 1963
299	Roy, Norman Florence	Jan 1953		352	Woodward, Adrian T.L.	Jan 1966
300	Stuart, Douglas McAllan	Jan 1953		353	Walton, John Robert	Feb 1958
301	Shevas, William	Sep 1954		354	Martin, Paul	Nov 1964
302	Quinn, Thomas Fergus	Jun 1956		355	Jackson, Alan Ronald William	Mar 1961
303	Goodwin, David Hugh	Nov 1958		356	Walker, William Barry Alan	Apr 1958
304	Woods, Brian Robert	Feb 1953		357	Hunt, Brian Anthony	Nov 1961
305	Haynes, David John	Apr 1956		358	Goodman, John Cornwall	May 1962
306	Hardy, Robert	Jul 1964		359	Baldwin, Stephen Michael	Oct 1964
307	Smith, John Ivan	Sep 1951		360	Golland, Brian	Dec 1963
308	Illiffe, Michael	Aug 1957		361	Sims, Kenneth William	Dec 1946

362	Cunningham, Robert	May 1955		413	Foster, Albert	Nov 1950
363	Crane, Peter Ronald	Mar 1962		414	Wells, Maurice	Jan 1946
364	Portsmouth, Brian G.	Apr 1959		415	Haynes, Robert	Jan 1966
365	Cattle, Michael Arthur	Apr 1958		416		
366				417	Stacey, Keith	Oct 1962
367	Shearsby, Anthony George	Aug 1959		418	Robins, David Stuart	Oct 1957
368	O'Connor, Colin	May 1958		419	King, Peter	Feb 1965
369	Bowditch, Richard Henry	May 1958		420	Potter, Duncan Leonard	Mar 1965
370	Mason, Roy	May 1958		421	Bacon, William Robert Stuart	Mar 1965
371	Glanville, John	May 1958		422	Ritchie, Alec McAra	Mar 1966
372	Evans, Ivor John Maxwell	Jan 1964		423	Kempin, Trevor Frederick	Feb 1965
373	Proudman, John Ernest	May 1958		424	Nichols, David John	Mar 1965
374	Lowe, Gerald Walter	May 1958		425	McIntosh, Andrew Donald	Feb 1966
375	Walker, Michael	Jan 1962		426	Gibson, Geoffrey Alan	Dec 1965
376				427	Simmons, Roger John	Sep 1965
377	Frank, James Edward	Nov 1964		428	Looker, David John	Mar 1965
378	Roberts, John Edward	Jan 1962		429	Davis, Ralph Ponting	Mar 1966
379	Shatford, Ian	Jun 1965		430	Severn, James William McBean	Mar 1965
380	Rogers, Ernest Travis (t/Sgt, Oct 1966)	Jan 1963		431	Elvin, Martin Charles	Apr 1965
381	Wood, Adrian Allan	Jun 1962		432		
382	Robinson, Jack	Oct 1958		433	Moody, Ivan David	Apr 1965
383	Banham, Anthony Leonard	Jan 1962		434	Richardson, John Lindsay	Apr 1965
384	Measures, John Kenneth	Dec 1964		435		
385	Fraser, Roger Cameron	Aug 1959		436	Stevenson, Peter	Oct 1965
386				437	Messam, Michael John	Jul 1965
387	Hames, Lewis Geoffery	Aug 1959		438	Hextall, Ian Leonard	Aug 1965
388	Jelley, David Sidney	Oct 1959		439		
389	Alton, Terence Francis	Sep 1959		440	Preston, Roger Stuart	Oct 1965
390	Barker, Bruce	Sep 1959		441	Shooter, Michael	Oct 1965
391	Coutts, John Downie	Sep 1959		442	Hale, Richard Alfred	Sep 1965
392	Davies, John	Sep 1959		443	Pickwick, Allan Joseph	Sep 1965
393	Webster, Kenneth John	Oct 1959		444	Gamble, Graham Richard	Sep 1965
394	Folker, Peter Gerald	Jan 1962		445	Williams, Roger Paul	Sep 1965
395				446	Turrell, Paul	Sep 1965
396	Measures, Kenneth	May 1962		447	Jones, Carlton Harry	Sep 1965
397	Turrell, Brian Thomas	Dec 1962		448	Edgeley, Dennis John Nicholas	Oct 1965
398	Farrant, Bernard Keith	Dec 1964		449	Elliott, Roger John	Oct 1965
399	Gaskell, David James	Apr 1962		450	Bradshaw, Walter	Nov 1965
400	Edwards, Sidney	Apr 1962		451		
401	Dawe, Colin James	Dec 1964		452	Naylor, Alan Frederick Stokes	Oct 1965
402	Payne, Michael John	Apr 1962		453	Smith, Frank	Jan 1966
403	Butler, Barry	Jun 1962		454		
404	Tuckwood, Kenneth Edward	May 1962		455	Smith, John Richard Leslie	Feb 1966
405	Howes, Andrew Robert Maitland	Oct 1962		456		
406	Armstrong, Darryl	Jan 1965		457		
407	Warsop, David	Dec 1962		458		
408	Cattell, Rodney Alan	Jan 1963		459	Finlayson, John Ross Mackenzie	Mar 1954
409	Adcock, Philip Arthur	Mar 1963		460	Vesty, Trevor	Dec 1953
410	Rushin, Alan	Jan 1965		461	Smith, Geoffrey George	Mar 1966
411	Parnham, Ralph Edward	Nov 1957		462	Smith, Thomas	Mar 1966
412	Bradford, Brian Mark	Jan 1966				

Policewomen

Inspector
Parkin, Hilda Mary — Dec 1951

Sergeants
Buxton, Bettie — Feb 1965
Cheater, Sheila — Apr 1958

Constables
Bell, Elizabeth Anne — Apr 1966
Bentley, Elaine — WPC 21 — Nov 1964
Booth, Janice Mary — Oct 1966
Dow, Wanda — Oct 1966
Dunkley, Delia Mavis — Nov 1964
Edwards, Doreen — Aug 1965
Elder, Yvonne — Jun 1965
Forward, Katherine — Feb 1967
Garner, Christine — Mar 1967

Name	WPC	Date
Gisborn, Valerie Ann	WPC 16	Jan 1958
Greaves, Cynthia Mary		Dec 1965
Green, Diane Elizabeth		Jul 1965
Herbert, Sylvia Jean	WPC 11	Nov 1960
Hockey, Gillian	poss left prior to 1967	Aug 1956
Ingram, Patricia Anne	WPC 10	Nov 1960
King, Patricia	WPC 12	Dec 1964
Laxton, Jane Elizabeth		Oct 1966
Low, Elizabeth Jean		Jul 1965
Molloy, Elizabeth Roseleen		Nov 1966
Moran, Catherine Mary	WPC 5	Jun 1959
Pulsford, Susan		Jun 1965
Squires, Sandra Yvonne		Jan 1967
Street, Frances Ann		Jan 1960
Thornelow Madeleine	WPC 22	Sep 1966
Vice, Christine Janet		Aug 1966
Yeates, Joan Gladys	WPC 13	Jun 1964

Bibliography

Hewitt, Eric J. *A History of Policing in Manchester* Morton, 1979.

Smith, Gordon *Bradford's Police* Northway Printing.

Sillitoe, Sir Percy *Cloak Without Dagger* Cassell & Co. Ltd, 1955.

Mark, Sir Robert *In the Office of Constable* Collins, 1978.

Research & Planning Dept, Leeds City Police *The Leeds Police 1836-1974* Leeds Police, 1974.

Grant, Douglas *The Thin Blue Line The Story of Glasgow City Police* John Long Ltd, 1973.

Veranov, Michael *The Third Reich At War* Siena Books, 1998.

Simmons, Jack *Leicester Past and Present Volumes I & II* Eyre Methuen London, 1974.

Tovey, Malcolm *Leicester's Battle Against Fire*

Opening of Charles Street Unpublished Programme.

The Oxford Interactive Encyclopeadia TLC Properties Inc., 1997.

Elliott, Malcolm *Victorian Leicester* Phillimore & Co., 1979.

Watch Committee Minutes 1836-1967.

Haynes, Barry *Working Class Life in Victorian Leicester. The Joseph Dare Reports* Leicestershire Libraries & Information Service, 1991.

Index

home
sanctuary

home
sanctuary

josephine collins

RYLAND
PETERS
& SMALL
LONDON NEW YORK

Designer *Sarah Fraser*
Editor *Miriam Hyslop*
Picture Research *Claire Hector and Tracy Ogino*
Production Manager *Patricia Harrington*
Art Director *Gabriella Le Grazie*
Publishing Director *Alison Starling*

Editorial Consultant *Christina Rodenbeck*

First published in
the United Kingdom in 2004 by
Ryland Peters & Small
Kirkman House
12–14 Whitfield Street
London W1T 2RP
www.rylandpeters.com

10 9 8 7 6 5 4 3 2 1

ISBN 1 84172 694 X

A CIP record for this book is available from the
British Library.

Printed and bound in China.

contents

you and
your home

what your home means to you

You and the other people you live with are the most important elements in your home. The way you behave, your habits and routines, your likes and dislikes, all have an influence on your living environment. To create a home that is a sanctuary and a haven, you need to decide what it is that makes your ideal home and how that could realistically fit in with your personality. Your home sanctuary is a place for your spirit to rest as well as your taste to be expressed.

Your home is your territory, your personal space, somewhere that you and everyone who lives with you should feel free to be yourselves. It is the one place where you are completely at liberty to express yourself, your hopes and your dreams. It's also a showcase for who you are, and where your guests can feel at ease and see the best you in your own environment.

The place in which you live should be supportive and nurturing, enabling all of its occupants to deal with the demands of everyday life. It should have an atmosphere that encourages the pursuit of heartfelt ambitions and desires. It is where you go to sleep and where you begin and end each day, so it should be safe, relaxing and rejuvenating. It should provide a positive platform from which to go out into the world.

Home should not be static though – it should be flexible enough to be lived in, used and loved. As taste, technology and the needs of its inhabitants grow and change, your environment should evolve, too. Think of your home as a living thing, an organic whole that develops with you.

But is your home currently all those things? When you think about your home, do you conjure up images of relaxation and enjoyment, or stress and conflict?

keeping a home notebook

To use this book effectively, you should start keeping a notebook. Use it to jot down ideas, take note of colours or patterns that you like, track your own habits, keep a check on prices and work through some of the exercises in this book. Keeping a notebook should be something you enjoy because it will show the steady progress you make, turning the place you live into a real home sanctuary.

read your home

Someone walking into your home for the first time gets an immediate impression of the kind of person you are and the way you live. The general ambience, the décor and your sense of organization all create an atmosphere.

In many ways the outside of your home represents the image you give to the outside world. Take a good look at your house from the outside. What do you notice? Does it look well kept and well loved?

As you open the door and come in, what is the first impression you get? Does it smell nice? Does it feel welcoming? Take in the detail and imagine that you are a stranger looking at your home for the first time. What sort of person do you think would be living here? Does it match up with the image you have of yourself?

Take a look around your home right now and think about what it says about you. Does your home reflect who you really are? Or has it somehow ended up saying something quite different? As you move through your house, take in the atmosphere. If you look at your home from a new perspective it is much easier to see how it relates to who you are and to decide what aspects of it you would like to change. Is the place messy or tidy? How does that make you feel? An overly tidy home carries with it a certain tension, but too much chaos is just plain stressful.

The furniture and décor you choose for your home are an important part of the atmosphere you create. Consider your chairs and sofa. Are they more about function or style? Are you attracted to old pine and the comfortable, sociable image that goes with it or to dark, polished wood and the sense of authority and traditional values it represents? Perhaps you have a penchant for antique pieces and you feel an association with a particular period in history, or you have inherited furniture that has a sentimental connection. Maybe you like designer items because they show that you have your finger 'on the pulse' or perhaps you prefer to indulge in your own creations and put your own stamp on your home.

Look, too, at the colours you have chosen for your walls, carpets and furnishings. Are they dark and seductive, bright and uplifting or cool and soothing? Maybe you've chosen white or cream to give a sense of purity and space. Are the colours you've chosen practical or did you make your decision because they were visually appealing alone? Everything in your home represents you and the other occupants in some way. Is your home giving you the image and the feelings that you want it to?

what does my house say?

In your notebook, answer these questions:

1 What kind of person (or people) lives in this place? Make a list of positive and negative adjectives describing this person.

2 Do I like him or her? Be honest but also be kind. There's no point beating yourself up!

3 What is it about this home that makes me reach these conclusions? Be as specific as you can (for example the books in the living room are in alphabetical order, so he must have a lot of time on his hands; the collection of kitchen knives is in top condition, so this person must love to cook…)

4 Do I feel comfortable in this home? Consider this question carefully and if the answer is no, ask yourself why.

a home for you

Take a look at what you wrote about your home in your notebook under 'What Does My House Say?' (page 11). Does the person described there resemble you? In most home decorating books, a lot of emphasis is put on the practical and the aesthetic, but there is another dimension to your home – the spiritual. Your home is a space for your soul as well as your body and your mind. It's a place to house your dreams as well as your old hiking boots and teddy bear. As such, you need to create a comfortable space for your mind, body and soul, which means getting to know yourself well, and your own strengths and weaknesses as a housekeeper.

How tidy am I? Most people like to live in an organized environment because it makes life less complicated and gives them a greater sense of control. Ideally, your home should be organized enough to function well, but also be a place where you can kick off your shoes and relax.

Do I like housework? Some people will never be able to lift a dustpan without experiencing a strange sinking feeling, others have discovered the Zen joy of ironing. You should simply acknowledge how you feel, and try to organize your home accordingly. If you live with others, split the chores between you and plan to make sure that everyone does their fair share. Once you have followed the steps in 'Purify Your Home' (pages 46–79) housework may be less of a bore.

Do I own too much stuff? You may find that somehow your possessions have become more powerful than you. You make way for the umbrella stand in the hall and you all squeeze into the living room to watch a giant TV. Your home sanctuary will benefit from less rather than more stuff. Once you have created the right space for yourself, you may find the need to shop less urgent.

What are my habits? Do you like to entertain or spend hours in the bath? Are you an early bird while others in your household are night owls? Do you snack at the refrigerator door or do you sit down to a three-course meal most nights? Go through your household's daily and weekly routines and decide which of your domestic habits is good and which could be changed.

How do I express myself at home? If you haven't got a place at home where you can express who you are – cooking in the kitchen, labelling the shelves in the wardrobe, dancing in the dining room, yoga on the bathmat – your frustration will come out somehow. You and everyone else in your household need to be able to feel free to do their thing. This does not necessarily mean hobbies. Think about this idea laterally. When are you at your best? When are you most relaxed?

the best me

List ten things you like about yourself.

List three things you would like to change.

List ten things you love to do.

List three things you loathe (but have to do).

Do the same for each member of the household.

Now think, how can you organize your home so that you make the most of your qualities and change what you want to change; and so that you get to do the things you like more often?

castles in the air

Close your eyes for a few minutes and try to visualize the home you would love to have. Let your imagination roam. So it's a beach house in Malibu with a jacuzzi overlooking the Pacific Ocean – add a solid pine deck and a little etching by Picasso over the guest bed. Maybe it's a little hand-built hut by a Norwegian fjord with a bearskin rug, an open fire and Sibelius on the CD player. Be open to any image that comes to you and revel in your own fantasy for a while.

In your notebook, describe your fantasy home. If you like, draw a floorplan. Go into as much detail as you can. This is not reality, so don't let a tight budget or a lousy climate hold you back. You are allowed to live anywhere you want. When you have indulged yourself to the full, look at what you have written. What are the most important features of your fantasy? Is it the open fireplace? Is it the view? Try to put them in order of importance. Are any of these ideas achievable now? Could you adapt them to the place in which you currently live?

your ideal home

To create a home sanctuary, you need to exercise your imagination. This is more important than any amount of money or any number of style magazines. You need to imagine transforming the space you live in now into what you would like it to be. So the first step is to figure out exactly what it is you want. You may surprise yourself. Often our desires are far less extravagant and far more achievable than we think. The only thing that's stopping us is ourselves.

Take a look at the following list of words and, with your home in mind, put them into the order of their importance to you: *comfortable, practical, beautiful, stylish, original, spacious, tranquil, social, safe, relaxing, fun*. The first three words you have chosen in the list are most likely to be the three elements you base many of your choices and decisions on when it comes to setting up and altering your home. But what else is important to you?

Answering the questions below will help you become clearer about what you need for your home sanctuary. In your notebook, write down your answers in as much detail as you like.

- What impressions would I like to experience when I walk through my front door?
- How would I like others to feel when they come into my home?
- Is a sense of organization important to me?
- Is cleanliness a priority?
- Do I like to invite friends or neighbours over?
- Do I want a home that shows off my originality or creativity?
- Is fashion and style important to me?
- Is having somewhere comfortable to relax important?
- Does my home have to be family or flatmate friendly?
- Is privacy a priority?
- Do I need somewhere quiet to meditate/relax/study?
- If I could choose five words to describe my home, what would they be?

one step at a time

You've assessed yourself and your home. You've worked out what your ideal home sanctuary is. So now it's time to take some positive steps towards achieving your household goals.

In your notebook, make two columns. In column A, list all the things you love, or even just like, about the place you live now. These are the things you want to keep, for example, the sofa, the colour scheme, the view. In column B, list all the things you want to change, including you and your family's habits and behaviour, for example, the pile of post left on the stairs, the dirt on the kitchen floor, the left-over cooking smells.

Is column A compatible with the home sanctuary that you've written about so far in your notebook? How can you bridge the gap between what you have and what you would like your home to be? If column A is almost empty, that's great, you're starting with a blank slate. If it's full, then you're practically living the dream already.

Put the items in column B in order by priority and affordability. If most of column B is about cleaning and organizing what you already have, you may want to move straight on to 'Purify Your Home' (pages 46–79). If there seems to be an overwhelming amount to do, cut the list down to what is realistic. There is nothing more off-putting than a seemingly unachievable list of chores.

Now, read what you've written in your notebook so far, starting right at the beginning. It's time to describe a new fantasy house, but this time one that you can start creating right now. Describe the home you live in (or the home you are moving to) as if it were your ideal home. Make a floorplan and write comments and descriptions.

See what you need to change; it may be very little. Try to keep changes to the actual fabric of your home to a minimum and see what you can improve simply by breaking a habit or doing some dusting or by the addition of some colour or a picture.

make a style board

Taking into account all the things you've written in your notebook so far, it's time to create some style boards. These are a great way to focus your ideas. You'll need one or several pieces of hardboard and a handful of pins. Don't stick anything down permanently. The whole idea of a style board is that you can move things around to see how different colours, textures and patterns work together.

Start by gathering together pictures of houses, rooms and gardens that really inspire you. Look for ideas in magazines and books and cut out or colour photocopy any pictures that you feel strongly attracted to. Think in terms of colours that work together and colours that you love. Go into your local furnishing, DIY or fabrics shop and pick out samples that you really like. Think about textures, colours and patterns. Initially, don't be held back by considerations like cost or space. That will come all too soon.

When you've collected your pictures and samples, stick them onto the boards. Use one for each room that you intend to tackle. Try arranging your pictures and samples in the general order of the room. For example, position the carpet or flooring you've chosen at the bottom, soft furnishing samples and furniture in the middle, and curtain material or paint colours near the top of the board. This will give you a clearer idea of how the style of the whole room will come together.

Try lining up your style boards in room order and seeing how they work together. Imagine what you see in the picture becoming part of your home and think about whether it would suit the use of the room and would go with the belongings you already have and intend to keep.

get started

Unless you have lots of money and plenty of people to help you, transformation takes time and patience, but if you want to get started right now try one or more of the following:

1 Think about what your ideal home means to you and decide on three things you can do immediately to make your living environment closer to your ideal. This might be hanging a new picture on the wall or painting your bathroom a different colour – do anything that makes you feel positive.

2 Think of just one regular habit or pattern of behaviour that prevents you from obtaining your ideal home and make a commitment today to change it. This could be anything from bad money management, which prevents you from buying what you want for your home, to smoking in the living room.

3 Think of one way in which you could give yourself a bit more time to either enjoy or work on your home. You might want to consider getting home earlier from work, for example, cutting down on your social activities or giving less time to a hobby.

4 If you live with other people, take time today or this week to talk to them about your intentions for your home. See how they feel about it and ask for ideas. If they are positive, find ways in which they can be part of your plan. Maybe you could delegate some of the tasks to them or ask them to help you decorate.

behaviour patterns

If you find yourself repeating behaviour that seems
to hold you back from improving your home, like
making your house a mess just after tidying it up or
always leaving a DIY job half finished, you could be
stuck in a pattern. We adopt certain patterns
throughout our life, picking them up from our
parents and friends or taking them on because they
suited us at a particular time, but which may not
work for us now. The problem with patterns is that
they become so ingrained in our everyday
behaviour that they begin to subtly run areas of our
lives and this is especially recognizable at home.
The good news is that patterns are learned
behaviours and can therefore be changed. So if you
find yourself consistently tripping yourself up at
home, spend a day studying your behaviour, observe
its effects and take action to change it.

what's stopping you?

If you find yourself making excuses as to why you can't get on with creating your home sanctuary, take a look at the pointers below and see if any of them are holding you back.

Not knowing what you want It is very difficult to get anywhere unless you know what you want to achieve. Without a clear vision of what you want your ideal home to be, you cannot work steadily towards your target.

Procrastination Even when we know what we want from our home, it can take time for us to start moving towards our goal. Maybe you're waiting until you feel differently, have more money or a new job or relationship – but how long is it going to take? The longer you wait for something to happen, the longer it will take to accomplish your goal. Don't let procrastination get the better of you, start now by doing just one thing in the 'Get Started' panel (page 19).

Taking on too much at once Sometimes when we look at where we are now and where we want to be, our goal seems almost impossible to reach. If this is the way you're feeling, break down what you need to do into achievable steps.

Comparing yourself with others When you're looking to improve your home, it's a waste of time comparing yourself with others. No one is the same as you and no one lives life as you do, so adopting someone else's home style is unrealistic. Admiring what they have or how they run their home is something different. If this is the case, put your finger on what it is that you like and see whether it suits you and your household.

Not managing your time and energy One of the biggest problems in our busy lives is trying to fit too much into a limited number of hours. Time management is essential for good housekeeping. If you haven't got a cleaning, cooking and tidying routine, start one now. Having enough energy is also important, so make sure you allocate time to do tasks when you're not too tired.

Lack of money Not having enough money is something that holds many people back from achieving their dreams. This is often just an excuse, because you may well be able to transform your living space simply by instituting a new cleaning regime and moving the furniture. Not everything you need to do with your house will need money, but if you want to buy expensive fixtures and fittings, make a plan and create a budget. This way you will be working towards your goal and even though it may be slow, you will be making progress.

Lack of commitment It is no good just having a desire to create a better home, you also need to have the commitment. This means making a promise to yourself that you will work steadily towards your goal.

enhance
your space

living space

Whether it's a tiny flat or a Venetian palazzo, your home is basically a space to put things in. The shape and design of that space are factors that you have to take into consideration when you are creating a home sanctuary. Your possessions affect the general dynamic of the space in your home, too. Unless you want to replace any of these items with something more suitable, they should be taken as the basic materials you have to work with when creating your sanctuary. After assessing the current state of your home, there are some simple steps that you can take to make the whole house work better as a unified space.

There's no point pretending your home is a cosy, little miner's cottage in the Yorkshire Dales when it's really a spacious Georgian townhouse in Edinburgh – or vice versa. You need to work with what you have available. Your home sanctuary is a marriage of your ideal home and the real space that you have to work with. A cool, clear assessment of your home – what you like about it and what you hate; what you can change and what's best left alone – is required.

You also need to think about how long you plan to stay in your current home. If you're going to move next year, why waste time and money putting a skylight in the bathroom? A coat of light-coloured paint may do a similar job. You should consider what will attract prospective buyers. Their taste might not be the same as yours. However, if this is the home you want to spend a few more years in, then it's worth creating a long-term strategy.

You may well be able to create your home sanctuary by spending little or no money at all. Before you go out shopping you need to look at the furniture and accessories that you already have – you may throw away more than you buy.

efficiency assessment exercise

The purpose of this exercise is to assess how efficiently your home works. The more smoothly it functions, the more harmonious it will feel. Keep the results of this exercise in mind as you organize the space in each room of your home.

1 Begin by walking around your home and as you look at each area or room, ask yourself the following questions. Can I move comfortably around this area/room or am I navigating an obstacle course? Are there any items on the floor or furniture that could be put on shelves or in cupboards? Are there any items or pieces of furniture that I no longer need or like? Are there any spaces that could be used for storage? Am I making the most of the natural daylight or is something obstructing the windows? Do I have adequate lighting for my needs? Is it too bright? Is this room arranged in the most practical way? Are the items I use most often within easy reach? Does the furniture do its job well?

2 As you move from room to room, ask yourself how easy it is to do so. Pay special attention to the 'in-between' spaces in your home. Are they blocked or used as a dumping ground? Is there room for extra storage? Is the style you've chosen in keeping with the style of your house? You don't want to live in a museum, but completely disregarding a building's original features can sometimes damage the spirit of the home. You should be working in sympathy with the fabric of the place.

3 Write the names of each member of your household in your notebook along the top of the page. Under each name write down the activities each person likes to do, how and where they use the house the most. Ask each person how they feel the home could look better and function more efficiently. If the members of your household are old enough you can ask them to do the list themselves. Take into consideration your lifestyle, your daily routines and those of the other members of your household. Think about how and where you all cook, eat, communicate, recreate and relax. How does your home serve your needs? Do you have adequate space to fulfil all of these activities or do some areas need addressing? For example, you might want to consider creating more counter space in the kitchen for a family member who likes to cook or put aside a quiet area for someone in the household who needs to study. If you have children maybe you want to find a safe, comfortable place where they can play and toys can be stored away with ease.

common energy stoppers

Mess

Dirt

Stale air

Bad odours

Décor that needs updating

Broken objects

Uncomfortable furniture

Unwelcoming colours and designs

create flow

Our homes are an extension of ourselves and, like us, they need to have a healthy energy flow. Another way to describe this energy is to call it the 'spirit' or 'vitality' of your home. The people and pets in your home, the quality of the air, the smell, light and sounds, the shapes, colours and textures and the way you use space all affect the spirit of your home and the way its vital energy flows.

Improving and working with the energy flow is not a new idea and has been recognized by various ancient cultures throughout the world for centuries. European pagans, for example, understood the process of space clearing and working with the elements and seasons, while the West African and Mayan shamans made transformations possible by creating sacred space through ritual. More recently, the Chinese practice of feng shui and the Indian practice of vastu shastra have come back into fashion. Both traditions focus on the importance of energy flow and keeping the equilibrium and both are based on the laws of nature, offering precise methods for manipulating your environment to improve all areas of your life.

However, it isn't necessary to follow a specific school of thought to understand how to improve the flow of energy in your home. Many of the actions you can take, like opening the windows or clearing the clutter are common sense. Other changes you might want to make should come down to your personal taste and how you feel about your environment. Your home is such a unique space that the improvements you make should be connected to your feelings and instincts. If you want to set about improving the spirit of your home right now, try working your way through the following list of actions:

Tidy up The minute your home looks tidy, you should notice a greater feeling of ease.

Clean up Cleaning the surfaces and vacuuming the floor shows that you care about yourself and your environment.

Open the windows Doing this fairly regularly will let stale air out and fresh air in. It not only lifts the atmosphere, but it is also better for your health.

Clear away anything that stops you moving around your home with ease If you find yourself always tripping over shoes or a piece of furniture, do something about it. Part of having a good atmosphere in your home is being able to move around freely.

Take time to get to know your favourite colours and styles and bring them into your home If you choose décor that makes you feel good, you will naturally lift the atmosphere.

Make sure your furniture is comfortable If you have comfortable beds, dining chairs and living room furniture, you will find it much easier to rest, eat and relax, creating a more satisfying environment.

Add something living to the atmosphere like a plant or fresh flowers Plants and flowers will add their own positive energy to your home. Plants are beneficial because they can improve the quality of the air.

Create an aroma you love Make some fresh coffee, buy a bunch of flowers or spray your home with your favourite essential oil. You will find that the right aroma gives your home an instant lift.

Do something in your home that makes you feel happy Watch your favourite movie, invite a group of friends round or have a luxury bath. Do something that anchors good feelings to your home.

rules for room arrangement

Figuring out the best way to arrange a room is tricky – even the professionals usually have to try a few ways before getting it right. But if you have a lot of furniture or possessions, a limited amount of space or an unevenly shaped room, finding just the right disposition of objects can seem almost impossible. Sometimes, the problem is that you bought your furniture for one home and now that you have moved, it just doesn't fit. If you move your furniture around and find it still doesn't work, try again. You will eventually find the best way or you could opt to exchange it for something different.

Always keep in mind the smooth flow of energy when you're arranging a room. Feng shui practitioners suggest that you don't want energy to move too quickly through an empty space, or too slowly in an overcrowded room. There are a number of basic rules you can follow which will help.

Know the traffic patterns One of the most important elements to laying out a room well is understanding the traffic patterns. These are the spaces where people need to move through the room. Starting at the door, look at where people are most likely to walk through the room. Take into consideration the need to access bookshelves, drawers, the stereo and television, windows and exits. You don't want too much traffic right through the main seating area of your sitting room for instance.

Find the focus Most rooms have at least one focal point. This could be a fireplace, a work of art, an attractive window or a special piece of furniture, say a double bed. Arrange the room around the focal point. Think how your eye travels around the room. Does the arrangement flow in an aesthetically pleasing way? You may want to use colour to create points of interest that connect the space – for example bright cushions along a pale sofa leading to a colourful painting, then over to a vase on the mantelpiece, and down to a strongly coloured armchair.

Create balance Often rooms are easier on the eye when they give the impression of being balanced. You can achieve this quite simply by having two matching objects in the room, for example two lamps, or two candlesticks. You can also achieve this more subtly by using objects of a similar size and/or colour – say, a red armchair and a blue one.

Cluster furniture Furniture, especially in the living and dining rooms should be placed close enough together to allow people to see each other and hold a conversation with ease. People often make the mistake of pushing furniture up against a wall when it would be better to allow traffic to flow behind the piece.

questions to ask yourself when arranging a room

1 What are the functions of this room?

2 How often do I plan to use this room?

3 How many people will be using the room?

4 Who is going to be using the room?

5 What do I want to display and store in this room?

6 What is my ideal floor covering?

7 What kind of lighting do I need in this room?

8 Is there any furniture I need to add to this room?

9 What electrical equipment do I need in this room?

10 How can I arrange this room so that it pleases me?

enhance your space

create space

If your house or flat is feeling overwhelmed and claustrophobic, use these ideas to create a feeling of spaciousness. Even the biggest area can sometimes feel cramped simply because of the way things are arranged. These ideas also help with the general flow of energy and allow your home to 'breathe'.

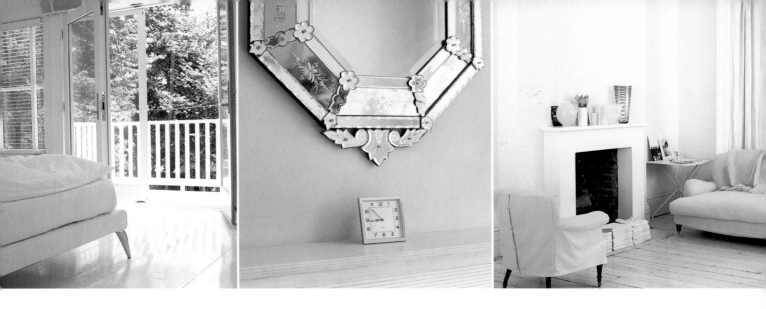

Eliminate obstructions The further you can see through a space, the larger and more open it will seem. Whenever possible, arrange your furniture so that it leaves plenty of floor exposed and avoid blocking views to windows and doors.

Use lighter colours Lighter colours make a room look bigger and, if you want to keep the space uncomplicated, opt for matching or complementary furnishings.

Bring in more light Expand the size of your space by allowing in as much natural light as possible and adding additional light fittings.

Use mirrors Mirrors reflect light and add space to a room. Make sure you place them opposite something attractive like a window, a painting or your favourite piece of furniture.

Go for open plan If you live in a small space and have the option, knocking down walls and opening up rooms will give you a greater feeling of space and light. If you have an open plan room but need some temporary privacy between spaces, folding doors or screens can be useful.

Build in furniture where you can You will save space if you can build in furniture like bookshelves, desks and cupboards to fit the precise dimensions of the space available.

Choose furniture with care A few carefully chosen pieces of furniture rather than lots of smaller pieces of furniture make a room look bigger. If you don't have room for full-scale arm-chairs or sofas, an upholstered armless style will still provide the comfort but allow more space.

Opt for multifunction furniture In small spaces, choosing furniture that can multitask will save you space. Settees that can fold into beds are great space savers and high beds that have enough room for a desk or wardrobe beneath them double your usable space.

Keep décor simple Complicated designs overwhelm, so keep fabrics and furnishings like curtains, carpets, wallpaper and furniture coverings simple. Emphasize a sense of space by covering sofas and chairs with plain or textured upholstery rather than complex patterns.

Keep flooring continuous Keeping the same flooring material throughout the house gives a sense of continuity and space.

Take advantage of outdoor space Stretch your living space by making the views from windows, balconies or patios more accessible.

a tour of your home

Now it's time to take a serious tour of your house, thinking about how it works as a unified whole and how the rooms work individually. Think about the blocks of space created by walls and furniture in each room. Are they awkwardly shaped? Apply all the ideas you have already learned in this chapter to each room. As you walk around, make notes in your book.

the outside

Estate agents know better than anyone the importance of the front of a dwelling – most people make up their mind about a potential buy within 15–30 seconds of seeing it. The entrance to your home – front door, steps, garden or driveway – is like an introduction into your world, and it is the means by which you and others make a transition from the public realm into your personal space.

We often assume that everyone wants the front of their house to be welcoming – but this is not necessarily the case. If you live in a bad neighbourhood, it might be quite a good idea to put people off. Alternatively, you may be a very private person. You must decide how you want your entrance to work.

You already have some idea of your ideal home – how does the front of your house or apartment show this? Is there any correspondence between your ideal and the reality? If you live in a small flat with a scruffy front door but your ideal home is rather grand, ask yourself what you can do to bridge the gap between reality and fantasy. What about painting the front door a shiny black and replacing the door furniture?

Feng shui experts also consider the front of the house to be of great importance, believing that the front door is where the majority of 'chi', or energy, enters your home. Keeping the entrance clear and well presented is said to welcome in new opportunities and money. If you feel your front door is dreary, polish the door furniture and clean the front steps. You may want to consider fixing a good outside light. Also make sure that your doorbell works.

colours

The colour you choose for your front door makes a statement about who you are.

Natural wood A no-nonsense approach to life.

Dark blue Practical and authoritative.

Black Serious and aloof.

White A desire for perfection.

Yellow Sociable and lively.

Pink Nurturing and welcoming.

Purple An individualist.

numbers

The number of your home is said to have an influence on your life. Pythagoras, one of the great philosophers and mathematicians of Ancient Greece is understood to be the founder of numerology. He believed that the whole universe was ordered mathematically and that each number, especially the numbers from one to nine, exerted a particular influence over our lives. If your home number is more than one digit, you will need to add the digits together until you get a single number. For example, if your house number is 356, you need to add together 3+5+6=14, then add together 1+4=5. So your house number would be 5.

if your house number is:	
1	*Expect to live an independent and individual existence in this home. You may find yourself called on to be a leader in some way.*
2	*This is a home best shared with someone else. You should find it easy to express your feelings, but may feel lost if you don't have a partner.*
3	*This is an ideal house in which to work on a creative project, study or enjoy a good social life. Romance should thrive in this location as long as you treat it with respect.*
4	*This home should provide a good solid foundation for a family home. It is an excellent number if you want to bring a sense of order and structure into your life.*
5	*This is a great home for people who don't like to be pinned down to a routine. It's particularly good if you are impulsive or like variety.*
6	*This is a wonderful house for love and harmony, especially if you have children or pets. However, too much importance placed on possessions could create discord.*
7	*This is a house with a feeling of privacy, which is good for spending time alone to learn and study. There may be a desire for perfection and elegance.*
8	*This is a wonderful home for working towards a goal. A feeling of authority and respect for the community influences this home.*
9	*This is a house for learning about humanity. It may create a number of changes and experiences for the inhabitants.*

public spaces

Unless you live in a studio flat, your home probably divides naturally into public and private spaces – and for most of us it's important to keep the atmosphere and ambience of these two parts of the home different. Conversation pieces that we happily display in the living room may be wasted in the bedroom – and a loving portrait of your granny may be lost in the living room but just right on a dressing table.

Your public spaces are not only where you are on show but also where you have to share with the rest of the household. Public spaces also tend to be high-traffic areas. You need to be able to move around them easily and you need to take into account wear and tear.

Naturally, these are the areas where most compromise is necessary, but there's no reason why they have to end up an aimless mishmash of things. You can make people's differing needs work together.

the front entrance

The entrance of your home should be given special care and attention since it's the first place seen by you and other people on entering your home. Most people want their entrance to be warm and welcoming and the right lighting, attractive pictures and well-chosen colours will all encourage this. Bear in mind that some callers may see only this part of your living environment, so it should give the right impression.

Always remember that the main function of the front entrance is to allow people to enter and leave your home, so it should be free of obstacles and the décor ought to be easy to look after. A good door mat inside and outside the front door cuts down on grime.

There are other functions of the front entrance that you need to consider, too. The front door is usually the place where the post comes in, so you need somewhere to put your unopened mail. You'll also need a place to hang hats and coats, and maybe leave shoes and umbrellas.

halls, landings and staircases

In-between spaces can be a challenge to use well. First and foremost they are designed as traffic routes to allow people to move from one area of the house to another, so this must always remain the priority. As with all high-traffic areas, halls, landings and stairs need to be furnished with materials that are durable and easy to clean. Safety is always a priority here so make sure these areas are well lit and clear of clutter. If you often find toys, magazines or other items on the stairs, get a stair basket that is shaped to fit steps and can be used as short-term storage.

However, your in-between spaces do not have to be uninteresting or left as wasted space. With careful consideration they can be used for other purposes too – whether it's storing books in the hall, putting up shelves above doors or finding space for a hidden bathroom under the stairs. Even small halls and landings can be used as miniature picture galleries or compact libraries. Paperbacks can be stored on wall-hung bookshelves in any of these areas if space allows, since they don't demand particularly deep shelves. If you want to make the space appear larger, painting the walls a lighter colour or using a well-placed mirror will help.

living room

The living room is one of the most important rooms in the house. It's the place to spend time relaxing, talking and entertaining, so you should spend time and effort getting it just right. Often we have too much or too little furniture in here, making it feel squashed or uncomfortable. Check to see whether your arrangement follows the guidelines in 'Rules for Room Arrangement' (pages 30–31). Is your furniture comfortable? Try sitting in each seat and see how it feels. Does your furniture work well together? Choosing colours that complement each other or opting for matching cushions and throws will help create a sense of harmony.

Does your living room have a focal point – other than the television? It should be something beautiful, fascinating or soothing – perhaps a fireplace, a work of art or a view. Check to see whether your lighting is doing its job. It should be warm and intimate but at the same time there should be some seats with light that is good enough to read by.

dining room

Dining rooms are often reserved for eating, although with a shortage of space in many homes, dining rooms often double up as an office or a hobby room. Is your dining room table clear of clutter? Can you have your meals here efficiently and comfortably?

kitchen

Whether your taste is trendy stainless steel or cosy farmhouse, your kitchen is often the heart of your home. It is probably somewhere we congregate for a chat. However, for most of us, the first function of the kitchen is cooking and storing food. This is the moment to think about just how you use this space. Is everything stored in the most sensible place? Are the things you use easy to access? Are your cupboards well organized? Is there any wasted space? If you're thinking of completely revamping the kitchen, think about your pattern of movement between sink, stove, storage and worksurface.

kitchen tips

There are some simple steps you can take to make your kitchen work more efficiently. Arrange your utensils, such as chopping boards, knives and mixing bowls near to where you use them. Be clever about finding new storage space. Putting a hinge on kickboards (the boards at the base of floor units) creates a whole new storage area for baking trays. To keep your kitchen surfaces clear, find new ways to store your equipment – such as ceiling hangers for saucepans or hooks for cups. Make sure your kitchen is well lit without being harshly bright. Make sure your bin is handy to get to and, lastly, have flooring that's easy to clean.

private spaces

The private rooms in your home are
where your imagination can work freely –
somewhere you can nurture your dreams.
Check to see whether you have taken full
advantage of your private spaces. You
should feel completely relaxed here and
totally at peace with your surroundings.

bedroom – your personal sanctuary

One of the greatest gifts you can give yourself is a bedroom where you can totally relax and shut out the world. Unless you have a dressing room, you are likely to keep your clothes, shoes and other personal belongings in the bedroom, so good storage that is easy to access is a top priority for a bedroom.

It's worth spending money on a decent bed – adults spend almost one-third of their lives in bed. Lie on it and see whether it's really comfortable. Your bed should be a focal point of your bedroom, so choose attractive covers.

children's bedrooms

For children the bedroom is not only a place to sleep, but also a playpen and a study. They easily create a sea of toys so storage that is simple to get to and will encourage your children to tidy up is key.

study or workroom

If you are lucky enough to have your own room in which to work or pursue
your hobby, you should make absolutely sure that it is laid out in a way that
optimizes its functions. The same applies to any study areas within other
rooms in your home. The chair should support your back. The desk should
be at the right height to support your wrists if you work on a computer.
Books, computer equipment, tools and any other accessories should be
easily accessible and neatly stored. This may be only the tiniest of spaces,
so you need to keep it shipshape, and that means a place for everything and
everything in its place. It's worth getting specific storage for specialist hobbies
and if space is tight, consider wall-mounted drawers and small shelves.

bathroom

Bathrooms can be both public and private spaces. Consider what it's like from a guest's point of view. Is it clean and inviting? If you share your home, your bathroom may be something of a crossroads with traffic jams in the morning and evening. Is there any way you can ease the congestion? You should allocate space for each person's belongings, so that they know just what should be kept tidy.

10 things you can do right now

Enhancing the space in your home is not just a matter of tidying up and reshuffling your furniture. It's about taking a look at where and how you live and making time to think about how you can arrange your living space to enhance the quality of your life. Start by improving the space that you live in right now by trying one or more of the following.

1   Brighten up the front of your home by giving your door and the surrounding area a good clean. Create a more attractive exterior by adding a large potted plant, a hanging basket or a window box filled with flowering plants.

2   Part of having a relaxing atmosphere in your home is being able to move around with ease. So have a look at the high-traffic areas in your home and clear away anything that creates an obstacle.

3   Take a look at and try out the furniture that you, your family and your guests use the most. How comfortable is it? Pay particular attention to your chairs, sofas and beds. Is there anything you can add to them to make them more comfortable, for example cushions or new upholstery?

4   Connect your home to positive feelings and memories by choosing a symbol that represents your favourite place to be. This could be a shell from a beach you love to visit, a painting of your favourite woodlands or a holiday photograph of yourself having fun. Place it somewhere that you will see it often.

5   Give your home a breath of fresh air by opening the windows to let the air circulate for a while. Place house plants around your home to improve the quality of air and add life to the atmosphere.

6 Take a look around your home and think of three ways in which you can improve the way your home functions. For example would it help to clear a bigger space for cooking? Maybe you could arrange your bedroom so that the clothes and possessions you use most often are the handiest, or perhaps you could improve the quality of the lighting in one of the rooms to better suit your needs.

7 Choose two rooms that you use frequently like the living room and bedroom and decide on the focal point of each room, for example an attractive window, a fireplace, a bed or a picture. Once you've chosen your focus, arrange the furniture accordingly.

8 Get rid of or replace one possession that you really don't like or use very often. If you can choose something that you have to look at every day, the improvement will be more obvious.

9 Think of different ways of creating an environment that better represents the personalities of everyone who lives in your home. You might want to choose particular colours, pictures or ornaments that mean something special to each of you.

10 Bring pleasant feelings into your home by doing something that makes you feel happy. This could be watching a favourite film, holding a dinner party or enjoying a good soak in the bath.

purify your home

good housekeeping

Your home may already be perfectly decorated and ideally designed, but in order to create a real sanctuary, you also need to keep the place running smoothly. This means doing three things: tidying, cleaning and organizing.

Having a good clear out, letting go of what you don't want and finding a place for those items you want to keep is a good place to start if you want to improve the state of your home. It will not only help to cut down on the time you spend searching for things you have mislaid, but also reduce the time you spend cleaning and tidying. Giving your home a thorough clean will give you a fresh start and help you keep up the good work you've already achieved. Finally, you will need to give your habits an overhaul and adopt a method of organization that will allow you to stay in control of your wonderful revamped home.

Before you embark on any home transformation, devote some thought to what makes you happy and puts you at ease when it comes to your home. Create a vision of the end result you would like to achieve. Imagine what it would be like to have a home that functions well and runs smoothly. If you haven't already done so, you may want to write down your ideas in your notebook. Make your vision compelling and exciting. What will you have room for in your life when you are free of the clutter that is holding you back? What will it be like to be able to find things when you want them? How will it feel to have a perfectly clean home? Will it feel good to make a favourable impression on others when they enter your home? Make your vision as real as you can – it is this image of a wonderful home that will drive you on to achieve your goals and keep you motivated.

As with any big task it's best to take an overall view of the job ahead, then break it down into small assignments that are easy to achieve, so that you are heartened by each result and feel inspired to keep going. So take your notebook and using a different page for each room, head three columns: Tidying, Cleaning and Organizing. Write the name of the room you are dealing with above the headings. Then walk around your home making a note under each column of where your clutter, cleaning and disorganization problems lie in each room. Take a particular note of whether you feel nourished or drained by what you see, which rooms need the most attention and where in the house your biggest clutter hotspots and neglected cleaning duties lie.

This is now your task list, but don't feel you have to complete it all at once. As you clean, tidy and reorganize each area on your list, tick it off and give yourself a reward commensurate with the effort involved. So for an easy task, for example, you could allow yourself a chocolate eclair and for a really time-consuming, emotionally draining one, buy some tickets to the theatre. Giving yourself a treat will help you to keep up the good work.

confront yourself

Most people find it a challenge to stay on top of their household chores, but if you find yourself consistently amassing clutter without effort or never quite managing to conquer the housework, your problem could be rooted at a deeper level. Take a look at the following personality types and see whether any of them strike a chord with you.

the hoarder

Hoarders tend to keep most things, with the belief that they may be useful one day. Cupboards, shelves, attics and garages are full of old stuff that the hoarder has never felt able to let go of – 'just in case'.

The sad thing is that many of the items a hoarder holds on to never actually get used and instead their home becomes more and more bogged down with stuff. This behaviour is often rooted in insecurity – hoarders hold on to things because they fear they may not have what they need when the time comes. This can be a very practical view in times of scarcity, but nowadays material possessions, packaging and junk mail come into our lives with such ease that a clearing out strategy is essential if any home is to function well.

If hoarding is your problem, you need to remind yourself that if you let go of what you don't need, you make space for what you do need and want. Life will become simpler, you'll have more time and less stuff to get in your way. If you find it difficult to let go of things because you hate waste, think about your unwanted items going to good homes where they will be used. You can also look at ways of recycling, whether it's cardboard, packaging or old electrical items, instead of letting clutter clog up your life.

the deferrer

Deferrers often have piles of paperwork, videos, photographs and all sorts of other possessions just waiting to be sorted and organized. Guilty of putting off today what they can do tomorrow, deferrers come in two guises: the 'perfectionist deferrer' and the 'lazy deferrer'. The former puts off jobs until they have time to do it properly and if they tend to be short of time, the task never gets done. 'Lazy deferrers' just can't get themselves motivated and so ignore the situation until it gets out of hand. Bills that need paying, letters that need answering, items that need cleaning or repairing, ironing and other household chores are all set aside to be dealt with another day.

If this is you, you need to remind yourself that action does pay off and the sooner you get your chores done, the quicker you'll create guilt-free time to do those things you really enjoy. Since this behaviour is grounded in procrastination, the answer is to take action. For some deferrers, simply making a start creates the energy and motivation they need to keep going, but for most deferrers, they need a bit more of a push and could do with a friend to help.

the rebel

Rebels are often surrounded by mess – clothes strewn around the house, old food packaging in the kitchen and a bath that's never cleaned. Rebels find it hard to get themselves to do such boring activities as putting their clothes away, doing the washing up or the vacuuming. Even if they would like to live in a presentable home, they see tidying, cleaning and organizing as conforming to rules and regulations that just don't appeal to them. Sometimes rebels come from equally rebellious families where they learnt to question and rebel against authority and rules, and sometimes they come from families where they were forced to tidy up and keep clean as children, and they still resent it.

If this is you, you need to think about how your rebelliousness is interfering with what you want in your life. Remind yourself that you are not carrying out chores because you want to conform to someone else's rules, but because it helps you achieve your goals, by allowing your life to run more smoothly. If you come from a rebellious family, look at how you could improve on the habits you were taught. If your problem stems from being bossed around as a child, tell yourself that you are the adult now and acknowledge that you decide what you want to do and what you need to do – then do it.

the sentimentalist

Sentimentalists often have a home full of knick-knacks, ornaments, soft toys, letters, cards and all sorts of other mementoes. Like the hoarder, the sentimentalist suffers from insecurity. At the root of most sentimentalism is the desire or need to hold onto the past, with each memento treasured for its connection to a particular period in their life. Sentimentalists often fear that if they let go of a particular item or possession the memory will disappear with it and so everything is kept – from old school papers, to out-of-date greetings cards – even if they are never looked at again.

If this is you, you need to remind yourself that whether or not you keep your mementoes, the memory still remains. If you want something to connect you to a particular memory or person, keep the special items that have the strongest connections like a favourite photograph or an important letter or write down the events in a special diary. There is no need to keep everything. If you have a pile of your children's drawings, or loads of soft toys, keep a selection of the best and let the rest go, so that you have room for the new things to come in. Remind yourself that the past is gone, that your life right now is more important and that you have a future ahead with more good times and positive memories to come.

half-finished tasks

You may have a raft of reasons for not finishing a task that you have set out to do – but most of these reasons come down to bad planning. Take a look at this list and see whether any of these ring a bell.

1 Attempting to do too much at once.

2 Lack of setting clear goals and deadlines.

3 Running out of time.

4 Changing priorities halfway through a task.

5 Not having the right organizational tools available, for example bags, boxes and storage facilities.

6 Loss of interest in the task.

tidy up

Living a tidy, organized life must be a conscious decision. Keeping your home in the best state possible requires you to stay aware of what is going on around you and to be mindful of how your actions affect your surroundings. Take note of any habits that create clutter, for example leaving your coffee mug beside the bed in the morning, not cleaning the bath when you've finished, and leaving the top off the toothpaste.

In your notebook, you have a list of the most untidy areas of your home. Start by tackling the easiest. Keep mess to a minimum by following these guidelines.

Learn to recognize clutter Whether it's junk mail, a bad purchase or a present that you dislike, learn to recognize clutter as soon as it enters your house and you will soon cut your clutter down to size.

Be aware that most material items can be replaced, but your time can't Your time is precious and far more important than your possessions. When you feel hesitant or guilty about letting go of possessions, think how often you waste your time buying, tidying up and being concerned about possessions that don't really matter in the bigger scheme of life.

Attack the worst hotspots in your home first Stuff like books, videos, clothes and paperwork tends to pile up in particular areas. If you choose the worst hotspots to clear first, you will notice the results immediately and the smaller muddles around your home will be a breeze to conquer.

Be prepared before starting a task Before you start clearing clutter gather together everything you'll need to complete the task. For example make sure you have the right boxes and bags. Maybe you'll need labels and pens or a basket to put things in. Being prepared will stop you having to wander off to look for things while you work, which could lead you to being distracted and never finishing the job.

Keep motivated by working in short bursts
If you find it difficult to stay motivated, work for 15 minutes at a time, then give yourself a break. It may take longer overall to get your task done but you'll be more likely to complete the task.

Learn to stay on top of your clutter Once you have cleared the backlog of mess, set aside 5–10 minutes a day to put things back in their place and sort out any new clutter. This will save you time, space and energy in the long run and help you to stay organized.

Fix things Instead of leaving broken china to gather dust on a shelf or shirts with missing buttons in your wardrobe, get them mended – or do it yourself.

sentimental clutter

To make our house a home we need some sentimental belongings, but the problem comes when we have too many. Out of all the clutter we own, the hardest to part with is probably the sentimental stuff. These are items that we keep because they allow us to connect to people or situations in the past. Letting go of personal memorabilia can be hard, especially if the situation to which it is connected was emotionally important.

Sometimes we hang onto things after a trauma and find it difficult to move on. On other occasions clutter provides a useful distraction from thinking about the deeper issues in our lives. Hoarding sentimental items often leads us to become stuck in the past, which prevents us from moving on and making the most of our lives.

If you feel that sentimental clutter is one of your biggest problems try the suggestions from the list below. If, after you've tried these guidelines, you still feel stuck it may be healing to seek professional help and find out how to get to the core of the problem.

Sift out the sentimental items Gather together all the things you think you're keeping for sentimental reasons.

The choice is yours Don't feel obliged to get rid of anything that you don't want to. Ultimately the choice is yours, so don't bother to justify your choices or make excuses. Just let go of those things you feel ready to relinquish.

Save the best If you have a choice of items with a similar sentimental connection, choose the best to keep and let the rest go. Sort out those items that have a real personal connection and history from those that don't.

Enlist the support of close friends and family If you feel unsure about which items to keep or let go, get someone you trust to help you decide.

Make space for your mementoes Make sure your mementoes have somewhere to live. Save only those you have space for.

Keep the mementoes that make you happy Go through your mementoes and ask yourself how you feel about each one. If any of them make you feel sad or bad in any way, ask yourself why you are keeping them.

Organize and cut down on your mementoes by arranging them in a scrapbook or journal or by placing them in a specially chosen box If you want to let something go, but still want a connection to it, make a record of it in your journal – it will help you keep the memories fresh, but let go of the clutter.

Give yourself time Don't let go of sentimental clutter until you're ready to or you may worry about whether you've done the right thing. Have a 'decisions box' in which to keep your undecided sentimental clutter and review it every now and again when you're in the mood. If items sit in your 'decision box' for a long time without you noticing or thinking about them, ask yourself whether you really need the items or would miss them if you let them go.

tackle the paper mountain

One of the most time-consuming and common clutter hotspots in many homes are paper piles. Letters, bills, bank statements, catalogues and junk mail land on the doormat almost daily, workbags explode with papers and children come home from school armed with artwork and notices. It's no wonder that keeping control of paperwork is a challenge in most homes. A useful tip is to have a special notebook or pad for notes, messages and lists to prevent writing on scraps of paper all over the house. Once the book is full, you can transfer any useful information into address books, calendars or scrapbooks and throw it out if you choose.

Paper clutter costs time, energy and sometimes money and without an organized plan, a household can drown in a rising inflow of paper. So if you're struggling, take control. Set aside some time every day to do your paperwork. Have a wastepaper basket beside you as you work, and your diary or calendar and address book handy. Put paperwork that needs action, such as bills, letters and any other post that needs a response in a special tabletop file or folder. Have another file for material that you intend to read. Anything that should be kept ought to be filed immediately.

To stop accumulating drifts of paper, you should decide what to do with each piece of paper as soon as it lands in your hands.

- Set aside some time each day to keep your paperwork and files organized.
- When the post arrives, immediately get rid of anything you don't want or need. In addition to the obvious junk mail, get rid of the ads that accompany bills and magazines as well as the envelope. Sort the remaining post into categories like letters, bills, magazines, newspapers and catalogues, ready to be put in the right place.
- When the latest issue of a magazine comes in, recycle the previous issue. If you want to save them for a while, have a basket or magazine holder to put them in. Create a rule that you will only save as many magazines as will fit in the basket or holder.
- Keep any important schedules on a pin board.
- Read your newspapers daily and recycle afterwards. If there is an article that you don't have time to read, cut or tear it out and put it into a reading file. If you have a great pile of these to read through, break them down into small sections. You can then read these smaller piles each day – on the bus or train to work, in the bath, in bed in the evening or at any other time that is convenient to you.

paper clutter-busters

A filing cabinet This is where you should file everything that needs to be kept in the long term. Each drawer should be equipped with labelled hanging folders. You can organize your folders alphabetically, but it is often better to make sure that you place the most frequently used files near the front of the drawer and the less frequently used ones near the back.

Storage boxes These are essential for bulky paperwork like old tax information, which you don't want to put or can't fit into your filing cabinet, but you still need to keep.

your wardrobe

Arranging your clothes well can make a significant difference to how you look and feel. Typically, we tend to wear 20 per cent of our clothes 80 per cent of the time, so it's the other 80 per cent of your clothes that need to undergo careful scrutiny. Before you get started, it's important that you decide how much uninterrupted time you can spare. To clear out your wardrobe and clothes drawers, a large chunk of time is better than small sessions if you can manage it, since it's better to complete the task in one go. If you have a lot of clothes you may decide to take three sessions: wardrobe, drawers and then shoes. You'll need bags or boxes ready to pack the clothes for the charity shop, reselling or recycling.

- Take everything out of your wardrobe and drawers and put it on your bed.
- Give your wardrobe and drawers a thorough clean.
- Put back those clothes, shoes and bags that you love and wear or use.
- Let go of anything that doesn't suit you in either style or colour or that is made from fabric you don't like.
- If anything that you want to keep needs mending or sending to the dry cleaners, vow to sort it out when you've finished.
- Try on the items that are left, deciding whether they look and feel good. Ask yourself whether you can imagine yourself wearing these clothes or shoes again, whether they suit you and whether you really want them. If you haven't worn these items over the last couple of years, will you wear them again?
- If you have clothes or shoes that you are not sure about, put them to one side and give yourself a few weeks to think about them. If you can, wear them during this time to see how they feel.
- When you've finished, group similar items together. Then put them in order of seasons and colours. For example winter dresses should be grouped together and then similar colours put together within these groupings.
- Make sure each item of clothing has a place and make sure the clothes you wear most often are handiest.

be clothes conscious

There are three reasons why you could be hanging onto clothes unnecessarily: guilt, a change in your size or sentimentality.

You feel guilty about letting them go Guilt often crops up when we've spent a lot of money on an outfit that is inappropriate in some way or we were given clothes as a present. Either way, if you are not going to wear them it's not worth keeping them. Get over your guilt by giving them to someone who will appreciate them.

You're waiting until you lose weight Be realistic, are you really going to lose enough weight to get into this outfit or is it just going to clog up your wardrobe? If you do seriously intend to lose enough weight to get into it, set yourself a deadline and do it.

You feel this outfit has sentimental connections Outfits you wore on special occasions will usually hold memories for you, in which case you might want to keep them, but be selective. Know why you are keeping the outfit and what you intend to do with it. For example, do you intend to save your wedding dress for your daughter when she gets married or would you be better off making an evening dress out of the material, so that your wedding dress is still being worn and not wasted. Keep only those clothes that have strong sentimental connections and let the others go.

practical cleaning

Household cleaning can feel like a
never-ending chore, but with planning
and a regular routine the effort you
need to stay on top of the housework
can be greatly reduced.

Some people are natural cleaners, who can't go to bed or leave the house until every chore is done and others just can't seem to get themselves motivated to accomplish even the smallest task. If you recognize yourself in the latter, you need to take yourself in hand and start introducing some helpful habits.

Part of staying on top of housework is also about preventing build up. This means that you should clean up after yourself, tidy the kitchen after each meal, clean the bath after you've used it and generally restore your home back to its clean and orderly state as you go through the day.

Having a routine may sound boring, but it is the successful way to achieve a clean and tidy house. You may choose to do all your cleaning on the same day, but it's probably easier to do a few chores every day. Try having a weekly schedule, for example Monday is laundry day, Tuesday is cleaning the kitchen day and so on. If you share your home with others, instigate a rota. This may not be popular at first, but once everyone gets used to it, having a rota means everyone knows what they're doing so there's less room for argument.

daily tasks

Open the windows to let fresh air circulate This will create a healthier environment, cut down on humidity and reduce the number of dust mites.

Clean surfaces In the kitchen leave your cleaning product to soak up the grime on the cooker top while you wipe down the surfaces, tiles, sink and taps, then go back to the cooker afterwards to make the job easier.

Air the beds Allowing air to get to your mattress will cool the bed down and discourage dust mites.

weekly tasks

Tidy up Having clear floors, seats and surfaces is essential if you want to do a fast and full clean up. If you don't have time to put things away before you start cleaning, have a box or basket ready to put everything in from each room.

Clean toilets, bath, shower and basins and wash down the tiles Spray your toilet cleaner around the bowl and let it soak in while you clean the bath, shower and basin. Then go back to the toilet and give it a good clean.

A cup of bicarbonate of soda poured down the toilet once a week is great for neutralizing odours and preventing blockages.

Change the towels Wash your towels at 60°C.

Put out the rubbish and sort out the recycling Make sure that the rubbish always goes out before the rubbish collectors come, otherwise you may have bags of rubbish hanging around for up to a week outside your house. When it comes to recycling, it helps to have somewhere to store your recycling during the week.

Wipe down doors, cupboard handles and appliances Everyone in the house tends to use the doors, handles and appliances leaving dirty hand marks and germs, so make sure you use hot soapy water and a clean cloth to prevent bacteria being spread around.

Change the bedding Wash your bed linen at 60°C to kill dust mites.

Sort out your laundry If you want to feel the full benefits of your clean clothes and linen, make sure you hang out the laundry or put it in the dryer the same day that you wash it.

Shake out and rearrange your cushions and throws Plumping up the seats and cushions and straightening the throws is a speedy way to give your living room a fresh look.

Dust Start with the higher shelves and surfaces and move downwards. Make sure you do the dusting before cleaning the floors so that the dust gets cleaned up. A slightly damp duster will

help you collect dust instead of dispersing it, but make sure you rinse it out thoroughly as you go. If you are really short of time, leave the dusting. As long as you do it regularly enough you should notice the benefits.

Vacuum the floors Vacuuming should always be done after most of the dirty jobs have been finished, so that you can vacuum up any dirt or dust left over. Once you have clear floors it is often easier to vacuum the whole house doing one room after the other, instead of stopping and starting.

Clean the floors If you have wooden, tiled or laminate floors you need to sweep up or vacuum the crumbs and dirt before cleaning the floor. Make sure you have a mop for the bathroom and a mop for the kitchen.

monthly tasks

If you've been following your daily and weekly routine your home should be looking good. But there are some chores that need to be done only once a month or so. Nevertheless these are real essentials. As with the weekly chores, it's best if you have a schedule and a rota. Don't be frightened off because that sounds like work. Being organized means less work in the long run – and more time for fun.

Turn the mattresses This will help to air the mattresses and encourage them to recover their shapes. If your mattress smells musty, sprinkle bicarbonate of soda on top, leave for at least an hour, then vacuum off.

Clean the windows and mirrors You may not need to or have time to clean all of your windows every month, so choose a couple of windows to do at a time. Mirrors are more likely to benefit from a monthly clean especially the bathroom mirror, which often gets sprayed with toothpaste. A little distilled white vinegar buffed with kitchen paper or newspaper gives a good shine.

Clean cushion covers and throws Keep your chairs and settees looking good by cleaning the cushion covers regularly.

Clean the oven Keeping a sheet of aluminium foil at the bottom of the oven will help to keep the oven clean by catching any crumbs or spillages and can be changed regularly. If your oven has a lot of grime you may decide to use a professional oven cleaning product, which can be toxic so make sure you follow the manufacturer's instructions. For a natural cleaner sprinkle bicarbonate of soda on the oven surfaces and rub with a wet wire or nylon pad. Then rinse by wiping down with a clean damp cloth.

Dust the areas you normally neglect You will find it much easier to stay on top of cobwebs and the dust that collects on top of curtain rails, blinds, pictures, lights and lamps if you dust them regularly. Lambswool dusters help to collect dust instead of dispersing it.

Polish wood and brassware When it comes to polishing wood, furniture polish will do, or beeswax for unpolished woods, but make sure you don't put too much on or you could end up with a polish build up. Depending on use, furniture should be polished once a year. Brass and copper can be cleaned with distilled white vinegar mixed with salt or bicarbonate of soda, or lemon juice mixed with salt, but do not use on anything plated.

Vacuum the areas you normally neglect It's surprising how much dirt, hair and crumbs seems to accumulate in places that we rarely see, like under the beds, cupboards and sofas. Vacuuming these areas regularly helps to keep control of dust mites and textile pests.

Clean the porch or steps outside the front door This makes a huge difference to the first impression of your home. Make sure you sweep up old leaves or dirt first. Then wash down with warm soapy water or a cream cleanser for difficult stains and dry with an old towel or a cloth.

teamwork

Everyone in the household should get into the habit of tidying up after themselves. It should be the responsibility of each member of the household to tidy their own room, put their clothes in the washing basket and put their clean clothes away after washing. Just carrying out a few tasks like this will give you a head start.

When it comes to weekly and monthly chores, hold a meeting with everyone who lives in your house and decide how you are going to divide up the tasks between you. Bear in mind the capabilities and available time of each member of the household when delegating. For jobs that are more difficult or boring than others and that no one really wants to do, a rota is probably the answer. Having the agreement of everyone about how the responsibilities are divided is far more likely to lead to a successful workforce.

If you want your home to be a beautiful and functional sanctuary, cleaning is just one of those tasks that you have to get on with, but this doesn't mean that it has to be boring.

Make it fun Keep your spirits up while cleaning by playing your favourite music or by listening to a book on tape.

Enlist some help Get your family or flatmates to help you. Have a race (but make sure the jobs are done properly). If you have children, turn cleaning into a game and give rewards for tasks well done (but don't expect a perfect job from young children).

Give the right impression If you're short of time focus only on those areas that guests will see, like the hallway, living room and bathroom.

Chill out While your intention should be to create a clean and organized home, if cleaning tasks fall by the wayside from time to time, don't let it bother you. Sometimes other things take priority, so go easy on yourself.

get the family to help

If you have a family, encourage them to keep tidy by following these pointers.

Encourage your family to put their dirty clothes in the right place and save on laundry time by having double compartment washing baskets, with one section for light clothes and one for dark clothes. Position the baskets in a place where each member usually gets undressed.

To encourage everyone to put their things away leave a basket at the top and the bottom of the stairs to deposit items that need to be brought up or down stairs. Make it a rule that everyone in the household checks the basket for items before they go up or down stairs empty-handed.

When requesting someone to carry out a task, be specific. For example, instead of asking that your children tidy up the mess in the living room, ask specifically for the toys or the books to be put away – you're much more likely to get the right job done.

Make tidying up easy. Create easily accessible storage containers like baskets, plastic boxes, trunks or cupboards to make tidying up a simple task.

the right equipment

One way to make cleaning speedier is to have the right tools ready to use. Keeping a cleaning kit in the kitchen and bathroom will encourage you to use them whenever you need to. For the rest of the house, get yourself a light, open, plastic tool box or bucket. This holds your cleaning essentials and can be carried with you as you go around the house. Also make sure that you can easily access the other tools you need, like the vacuum cleaner, mop and dustpan and brush. In your bucket you should have dusters, a rubber sponge, rubber gloves, a multipurpose cleaner and anything else that you feel is especially useful.

A stroll down the cleaning aisle at the supermarket could leave you feeling confused. There are so many choices, each product claiming to do a different job – but are they really necessary? There is no doubt that some cleaning products do their job superbly, but the problem of using manufactured products is that they often contain so many chemicals and can have an unhealthy impact both on people and on the environment. If this is something that concerns you, why not try some of the time-honoured natural alternatives, which are easy to come by and simple to use (see opposite).

essential cleaning kit

Washing-up liquid For dishes, floors, walls and clothes stains.

Cream cleaner For grease and grime in the kitchen and bathroom.

A multipurpose surface cleaner For all other surfaces.

Bleach For stained sinks, some kitchen surfaces and toilets.

Oven cleaner For tackling the inside of your oven.

Furniture polish or beeswax For wooden furniture and banisters.

Window cleaner For cleaning windows.

Rubber gloves For protecting your hands.

Dishcloth Good for wiping down surfaces, but must be washed often.

Sponge with scouring pad Good for getting rid of grime and stains, but should be cleaned thoroughly after use.

Wire or nylon pads For some hobs, ovens and baking tins.

Dusters and towels For dusting and drying surfaces.

Chamois leather or linen scrim Good for polishing windows and mirrors, although newspaper or kitchen paper will do.

Old clean toothbrush For cleaning the edges of taps and hobs.

Spray bottles For making your cleaning work easier.

Broom, dustpan and brush Start at the far end of the room and sweep the dirt into a pile. Sweep the pile into your dustpan and brush and pour the debris into the rubbish bin.

Vacuum Essential for cleaning carpets and useful for freshening upholstery.

Mop and bucket Useful for washing floors.

the natural selection

Soapflakes Plain soapflakes mixed with hot water and a little washing soda will accomplish most cleaning tasks.

Washing soda crystals Also known as sodium carbonate, washing soda naturally softens the water and cuts through grease and grime with ease. It can be used for cleaning kitchen surfaces, walls and hard floors and is also good for clearing plugholes and drains.

Bicarbonate of soda Also known as baking soda, this is wonderful for most types of cleaning. Mixed with a little water it is particularly good for cleaning stainless steel and can be used with hot water to soak burnt casserole dishes. As a dry powder it can be sprinkled onto carpets and rugs to soak up odours before vacuuming.

Distilled white vinegar The acid in white vinegar helps to cut through dirt and limescale in an instant. It gives amazing results when used for cleaning glass and tiles, and can also be used to remove tea stains from cups and teapots. When mixed with bicarbonate of soda or salt, it can be used to polish brass and copper. It is also useful for dealing with pet urine stains.

Lemon juice Lemon juice is not only a great cleaner, but it gives off a wonderfully fresh fragrance, too. It can be used to remove stains and to bleach chopping boards and kitchen surfaces. When mixed with a little salt it can also be used to clean copper and brass.

Table salt Salt makes an excellent mild disinfectant and can be used as a gentle scouring abrasive.

Essential oils Eucalyptus, grapefruit, lavender, lemon and pine all make wonderful room disinfectants. Any of these oils can be added to water in a spray bottle to create a lovely, fragrant air freshener (see pages 96–97).

get organized

Once you've cleared your clutter and given your home a thorough clean, you should be feeling good about what you've achieved. The question is – how long will it take until your home is back to the same state it was in before you started? For most of us it's very likely that if we carry on as usual without creating a new system to help us stay in control of our home, it won't be long before we're back to square one.

Your ability to stay on top of the clutter and cleaning in your home comes down to having good storage, being choosy about what comes into your home and having an organized routine.

Creating a routine that becomes second nature is the easiest way to stay on top of your household chores. Your routine needs to be realistic, something that you have time to fit into your lifestyle and are willing to stick with.

The best way to organize your routine is to make a list of the household chores you need to carry out to create the home you desire. Next to each chore write down how often the chore needs to be done, whether this is every day, week, or month. Then next to each chore write down how much time you are going to need to complete it. If you're not sure, time yourself next time you do the task. Now go down your list and add up how much time you need to spend on your everyday chores, your weekly chores and your monthly chores. This will give you a good idea of how much time you need to keep your home looking good.

Think now of how much time you have available each day and each week to devote to your home. If you don't have enough time available to complete all the tasks you've chosen, you may have to lower your aims. You could also consider hiring a cleaner. Either way you need to bear in mind that if you create a routine that is practical, easily achieved and takes into consideration your personal quirks, lifestyle and the sort of people who live in your home, you are far more likely to make your routine a success.

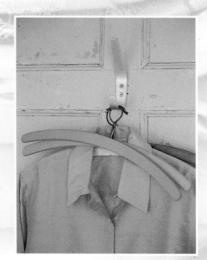

Allocating a schedule for your household chores is only a part of creating a home that runs smoothly – other areas of your life need to be organized, too. The everyday demands on time and energy can create a juggling act for most people. Whether these demands come from jobs, the needs of children, getting the housework done, keeping finances on track or allowing ourselves time to indulge in a social life, we need to be good time managers if we want our home to function efficiently.

a diary

Procrastination often paralyses people when it comes to organizing their households, especially if they don't know where to begin. So the best place to start is with a diary. When you purchase a diary make sure you put into it any important dates that you know about. These could be holidays, birthdays, events like parties or weddings and deadlines like tax returns or car insurance that you know will be coming up.

Look at the month ahead. Are there any events or deadlines that you need to put into your diary for this month? A coffee morning, someone's leaving do or perhaps bills that need to be paid? If you've worked out your cleaning routine, you can allocate the time you need to get your chores done both weekly and monthly. Now look at the week ahead. Is there anything you need to get done this week?

Using a diary will immediately give you a greater sense of organization. You no longer need to carry dates around in your head and if you refer to your diary every day you will find it much easier to keep track of everything.

plan your day

Last thing at night or first thing in the morning, put aside at least ten minutes to plan your day ahead. The most effective way to do this is to write a 'to do' list. Make sure you put your most important tasks at the top of the list and be realistic. If you really don't have much time, limit yourself and put only about three to five things on your list.

stress-free housekeeping

Be realistic It's no good adopting someone else's housekeeping standards if they don't suit your household and your lifestyle. Be realistic and tailor your schedule to suit you and those you live with.

Make it manageable When faced with a daunting task or a chore you don't have enough time to complete in one go, break it down into smaller, more manageable pieces that can be achieved a bit at a time.

Be willing to delegate Partners, flatmates and children are all capable of doing certain tasks, so delegate those that are suitable.

Use your most productive time Recognize when during the day you work most productively and schedule any important activities for this time.

Do the tasks that bring the most rewards When you have a long 'to do' list, think about which tasks will make the biggest difference. Doing these tasks first will not only keep you motivated, but will also bring the greatest achievements.

create a household file

Whether you live on your own or with other people, it's a good idea to keep a record of all your household information in one central location. This should include any important numbers and addresses, details of important events, take-away menus, shopping lists, video hiring cards or anything that you or your household use regularly. This information can be kept in a folder, a concertina file or on a pin board – whatever you feel is most useful.

If you have a family you might also want to keep a family diary in the same spot, so that important information, dates and deadlines are shared.

10 things you can do right now

Clearing and cleaning your home from top to bottom can take time, especially if you have let things slide. Commitment and patience are essential, but the finished result will be worth it. Getting started is the first hurdle, so if you want to make an immediate improvement to your home try one or more of the following.

1 Choose a clutter hotspot and give away, throw away or recycle five items. This could be from a pile of paperwork, a shelf overloaded with books, a mantelpiece with too many ornaments or anywhere that you seem to accumulate items. Letting go is one of the first steps towards purifying your home.

2 Create more space instantly by clearing the floors and surfaces of anything that shouldn't be there. Take a couple of cardboard boxes or plastic bags and fill them with all the bits and pieces that need sorting out. This helps you gain an immediate feeling of being in control and allows you to start cleaning up – but do allocate time to go through each box or bag and sort it out.

3 Add a sparkle to your windows and mirrors. Symbolically, windows represent your view of the world and mirrors represent your view of yourself, so it's not good to leave them dusty and dirty. To get a super clean shine, mix 25 ml (1 oz) vinegar with 275 ml (9 oz) of water in a spray mist bottle. Shake and spray onto the windows and mirrors sparingly then wipe off with kitchen paper or linen scrim.

4 Purify your carpets by sprinkling them liberally with salt or bicarbonate of soda. Leave for a couple of hours before vacuuming. To make vacuuming more pleasant, add a few drops of a cleansing essential oil like lavender, lemon or orange to the filter or place a cotton wool ball that has been dipped in an essential oil in the vacuum bag.

5 Add new life to white kitchen appliances that have turned yellow. Mix 4 tablespoons bleach, with 25 g (1 oz) bicarbonate of soda and 300 ml (½ pint) of warm water. Spread on with a sponge and leave for 10 minutes. Then rinse off with clean water and dry.

6   Choose a habit that negatively influences your home and change it today. This could be making sure you put things away after you've used them, dealing with your post as soon as it arrives or doing the washing up after each meal. Keeping your home clear and clean will only come from adopting good habits, so make these new habits part of your usual routine.

7   Choose something that needs mending – this could be an ornament that needs gluing, a jacket that needs a button or a toaster that needs repairing. Doing your mending while watching the television or listening to your favourite music will make it less like work. If you need to send something off to be repaired – do it today.

8   Add some hooks to create more space. Look around your home and see whether there are any places where you can add a hook or two. They are great for instantly getting things like keys, aprons, coffee cups and shopping bags off floors and surfaces, allowing you to concentrate on purifying the space.

9   Freshen your wardrobe and clothes drawers with sachets of dried lavender, particularly where you have items made of natural fibres like wool, linen, cotton and silk. This will not only keep your clothes smelling fresh, but also discourage moths.

10   Light some incense. If you don't have time to carry out an incense cleansing ritual (see page 123), choose an incense stick like lemon or pine, which is naturally cleansing, and place it in a holder in the middle of the room while you tidy and clean. When you've finished in one room take it with you to the next room and let it burn while you work again.

create harmony

add that extra something

By now your home should be clean and
tidy, it should be functioning smoothly and
at least on the way to having the kind of
character that makes you feel good. But
that's just the start of creating a home
sanctuary. To feel completely at home, you
need to add something far more personal
and uplifting. You need to create an
atmosphere that is uniquely your own.

To turn your home into a sanctuary you need to embrace a feeling of serenity and harmony. Not only will this turn your living environment into somewhere soothing, it will also boost your health and lift your spirits. Clinical studies have demonstrated that views of nature, natural light, harmonious colours and therapeutic sounds all have the power to enhance our health and feelings of wellbeing. And there are many other ways to boost our environment, too, such as using crystals, herbs, plants and beautiful fragrances. Use this chapter as a stimulus to your imagination, and see it as a starting point to pursuing your own ideas. Don't forget to jot down any thoughts in your notebook. You may feel inspired in the most surprising ways, so be sensitive to how you respond to different environments as you build your home sanctuary.

finishing touches

To turn a house into a home you need to evoke feelings
of warmth, comfort, nurture and protection.

Familiar items These can be any objects that give you a
feeling of security and comfort. For some people this might
be a favourite mug or blanket. For others it could be a well-
loved teddy bear or even a video that conjures up positive
memories. These objects will make you feel as though your
home belongs to you.

Photographs Placing photographs of you, your partner, your
family and your friends around your home, which conjure up
happy memories will tap you into those feelings again. It
may also be nice to hang pictures (if you have any) of your
ancestors on your walls or place them on other surfaces to
create a feeling of security and support.

Evocative pictures What sort of scenery inspires you? A
town house? A cottage in the country? A beautiful garden?
Boats on the sea? Think about the sort of buildings, natural
surroundings and places that make you feel good and choose
drawings, paintings or photographs that portray these scenes
to hang around your home and inspire positive feelings.

Cushions and soft fabrics Cushions in attractive fabrics are
wonderful for giving your sofas and chairs an inviting feeling.
They help to soften the shape of the furniture, but a few well-
chosen cushions are better than too many, which prevent you
from sitting comfortably. Curtains, sofas, chairs and throws
made of fabrics that are attractive to touch make a home
more intimate. Velvet, wool and cotton are particularly nice to
feel and, when combined with warm colours or patterns, give
an instant glow to a room.

Rugs A few well-chosen rugs will warm up wooden or tiled
floors and add a splash of colour to carpeting. If you plan to
sit on your rug or have children who would like to play on it,
make sure you opt for something soft and welcoming rather
than hard-wearing materials such as sisal and jute.

Plants and flowers Having a plant or vase of flowers in a
room adds a feeling that your home is being nurtured and
appreciated. Flowering plants or flowers are particularly nice if
you want to add colour and warmth to a room.

Table lamps Table lamps are one of the fastest ways, next to candles, to create a cosy atmosphere. One or two table lamps in the living room will produce a soothing, relaxing light. Choose lampshades with slight yellow, orange or pink tones to create a warming glow.

An open fire An open fire is unequalled when it comes to conjuring up a feeling of warmth and intimacy. In ancient times, the hearth was regarded as a magical place, somewhere that provided heat and nourishment. Nowadays, gas open fires have made the hearth more convenient, since they can be automatically lit and don't require cleaning out. If an open fire is not practical for you, candles – although a lot smaller – can create the same atmosphere.

find your colours

Changing the colour of your walls, floors or furnishings is one of the quickest ways to alter the environment in which you live. When we begin to appreciate the far-reaching effects of colour on ourselves and those around us, we can incorporate those that suit us best into our home. This will not only cut down on the stress we experience, but enhance our confidence and wellbeing, too.

We each experience colour in a very personal way and, while some colours create a feeling of harmony, others drain our energy. Changing the colours around you can have a dramatic effect so before you do anything drastic, experiment with swatches of colour and sample pots of paint. Refer to the style boards that you made earlier and any notes you've made about colour in your notebook. Remember that colours can also look quite different in the shop from how they look when you get them home. This is to do with light and also with how colours work together. For example, a rich red carpet may look delightfully vibrant in the shop but when you get it home and place it next to some orange, it may just clash. Think about the purpose of each room and how colours complement each other as you devise your colour scheme.

Warm and cool colours Colours can be divided into warm and cool, depending on the visual warmth they give off. Warm colours – essentially those colours based on red and orange – tend to advance visually, which means they appear to come closer. Warm

colours should be used in rooms that feel or appear cold, are large or don't receive much sunlight. Cool colours, on the other hand, are based on blue and are described as receding because they give a feeling of distance. They are useful for decorating small rooms or rooms that feel too hot or sunny. Cool colours can be warmed by the addition of a small amount of red, while warm colours can be cooled by the addition of a small amount of blue. Generally, the warm colours like red, orange and yellow are best used in areas in your home where there is lots of activity like kitchens, playrooms or recreation areas. The cool colours, which help us relax or think, are best suited for bedrooms, bathrooms and home offices.

Light and dark colours Light colours make a room look larger and lighter, while dark colours reduce the amount of light reflected. If you have a large room, a high ceiling or want to create more intimacy opt for darker, warmer colours. If you have a small room or a room that receives little natural light opt for lighter, brighter colours to give the illusion of more space and light.

Neutral colours Neutral colours such as cream, beige, grey and white or off-white are also good for expanding smaller rooms and bringing in light. They are equally excellent for providing a neutral background for colourful pictures and furnishings. Depending on the undertone a neutral colour can be either warm or cool. For example, white mixed with a little blue will be cool, while white mixed with a little red, to give it a pink tint, will be warm.

colour codes

Colours have the power to make us feel happy or sad, calm or excited and each colour has an influence and symbolism of its own.

Red is invigorating with its associations of warmth, daring and passion. It's linked with carnal love and intimacy, the hearth, fire and action.

Purple is the colour of royalty and also of mysticism. It is good for encouraging psychic ability and spiritual guidance.

Blue is restful, encourages serenity and helps meditation. It's one of the healing colours, and deep blue is associated with good communications.

Yellow is vivid and cheerful, the colour of hope. It's also associated with mental work and helps to lift the mood.

Green is calming and balancing, symbolizing nature and healing. In yogic teaching, love is associated with green and pink. Green has been found to help concentration and calm nerves.

Orange is vivid, sociable and exciting. It's believed to stimulate the appetite and is associated with creativity.

Brown is warm, natural and robust, symbolizing the earth.

Black is a dramatic, mysterious and protecting colour, conveying a sense of the unknown. Too much black can be negative but a small amount is grounding.

White conveys light and purity. It provides an uncomplicated background for other colours and patterns, but can also appear clinical and austere.

lovely lighting

When thinking about lighting for a particular room you must first analyse the function of the room and then decide what is required. Most rooms need an acceptable level of general lighting, which can be provided by a central pendant or chandelier, and controlled by dimmer switches allowing you to alter the level of illumination. Areas where you work or relax, however, will need something extra. There are three distinct types of lighting in the home – general, task and specific lighting. The type of lighting you choose will depend on what you want the lighting to achieve and the type of atmosphere you would like to create.

- General lighting delivers light throughout a room and does not concentrate on any particular area. This can be in the form of central pendants, downlighters, uplighters (which bounce reflected light from the ceiling), standard lamps or table lamps.
- Task lighting provides a suitable light for tasks such as reading, writing and sewing. Task lighting is required when the level of general lighting is inadequate and more local light is needed. Examples of task lights are desk lights, reading lights and the light in a cooker hood.
- Specific lighting highlights special features in a room without allowing too much light to spill over into areas where it is not wanted. All spotlights fall into this category because they project a tightly controlled beam of bright light.

coloured lights

When you are investing in lampshades for your home, remember that coloured light is said to have a therapeutic effect. You may even want to invest in tinted lightbulbs.

Blue light is soothing and cooling. Use it to cool hot rooms or to calm yourself when you are feeling angry.

Green light is good for relaxing, unwinding and balancing the emotions.

Orange light is warming and stimulating; it helps to lift the mood and combat depression.

Pink light encourages a warm, loving and nurturing environment.

Red light creates a warming, exotic and emotionally arousing atmosphere.

Violet light calms and lifts the spirit, helps to harmonize your mental and emotional state.

bring light into your home

No form of artificial lighting can match the beauty of sunlight, so try to allow as much natural light into your home as possible. Here are some ways to bring more light into your home:

- Keep your windows clean.
- Keep your windows free from obstructions.
- Draw curtains back as far as possible and keep blinds up during the day.
- Opt for curtains or blinds that are lighter in colour so that they don't absorb the light.
- If you have net curtains, consider opting for half nets that cover only half of the window.
- Open your windows frequently to allow the light to come into your home.
- Hang mirrors where they can reflect natural light from windows.
- Consider installing full-spectrum lighting if you feel that you are suffering from a lack of light.
- Paint your walls a light colour and choose lighter, brighter fabrics for your furnishings.

the air you breathe

Air is the primary source of our life energy, so it is important to pay attention to the quality of the air in our homes. For many of us indoor pollution can be a serious health concern, especially since most of us now spend so much time indoors. We are surrounded by man-made substances and materials, all of which can create a build-up of toxins in our environment. There are many ways to improve the quality of air in your home, most of which are inexpensive. Below are a few suggestions:

- Decorate and furnish your home with as many natural materials as possible.
- Make your household a no-smoking zone.
- Open doors and windows to encourage fresh air to circulate.
- Hang dry-cleaned garments outside to let them air before hanging them in the wardrobe.
- Cut down on the amount of plastic you use in your home.
- Limit your use of chemical household products.
- Use an aromatherapy burner with an essential oil like eucalyptus or lavender to scent and disinfect the air naturally.

Some people are more sensitive to polluted environments than others and as a consequence suffer from physical ailments like allergies, headaches and asthma. For many people plants help to alleviate this, not only because they absorb toxins and give out oxygen, but also because many plants emit moisture, which counteracts the dryness caused by central heating and air conditioning. Plants also have a symbolism of their own, which is used by feng shui practitioners today (see opposite).

detox plants

These plants are especially good for improving air quality:

Aloe vera *(Aloe barbadensis)*

Bamboo palm *(Chamaedorea seifrizii)*

English ivy *(Hedera helix)*

Peace lily *(Spathiphyllum)*

Rubber plant *(Ficus robusta)*

Spider plant *(Chlorophytum comosum)*

Boston fern *(Nephrolepis bostoniensis)*

Chinese evergreen *(Aglaonema crispum)*

Chrysanthemum *(Chrysanthemum morifolium)*

Dracaena *(Dracaena deremensis)*

plant symbolism

Feng shui practitioners believe that plants can be used to increase the 'chi' or energy in the home, bringing more luck into the environment.

Wax begonia *(Begonia semperflorens)*: Stability.

Boston fern *(Nephrolepis bostoniensis)*: Vitality.

Cyclamen *(Cyclamen persicum)*: Interest.

Ivy *(Hedera helix)*: Loyalty.

Money plant *(Crassula ovata)*: Money.

Peace lily *(Spathiphyllum)*: Peace.

Poinsettia *(Euphorbia pulcherrima)*: Glory.

Spider plant *(Chlorophytum comosum)*: Variety.

herbal magic

In days gone by, herbs were an essential part of every household. As well as being used to flavour and preserve food and to make medicine for both people and animals, herbs were also used to keep pests at bay and to purify and add fragrance to the air inside the home.

In fact, before the days of carpets and other permanent floorcoverings, dried herbs were often spread over the floor to absorb dirt and give off a pleasant fragrance when trodden on. Some herbs such as lavender, catmint and tansy also had medicinal properties and were used to help prevent pest infestations, deterring unwanted guests like fleas and rats. When the herbs had passed their best, they were simply swept up and replaced with fresh ones. These were known as 'strewing herbs'.

Placing herb-filled sachets, such as lavender bags, in wardrobes or drawers was also done, not just to perfume clothes and linens but also to keep moths at bay. Herbs like lavender and rue were burnt as air cleansers, too, to purify and freshen the air, particularly after someone had been ill. In a similar way, herbs, leaves, petals and flower buds were used in scented mixtures known as pot pourri. The name pot pourri comes from the French language and is directly translated as 'rotted pot' because the original method of making pot pourri was to place semi-dried herbs with salt in a bowl, causing them to give off their fragrance by fermenting. Nowadays, most pot pourri is made by a dry method, which is easier to create and more attractive to look at.

Herbs are still as useful today as they were centuries ago. They can provide a healthier alternative to many manufactured household products and can still be used in a variety of different ways around the home. One way to combine both the sensual and practical uses of herbs is to make a herb cushion filled with dried hops to use as an aid to sleep. The weight and warmth of your head will release the fragrance of the herbs, helping dissolve feelings of stress and tension.

uplifting herb potpourri

450 ml (2 cups) dried lemon peel
450 ml (2 cups) dried orange peel
450 ml (2 cups) dried rose petals
225 ml (1 cup) dried basil leaves
225 ml (1 cup) dried lavender flowers
2 drops grapefruit essential oil
2 drops geranium essential oil
2 drops orange essential oil

Mix the above ingredients together and display the pot pourri in an attractive bowl or container that allows the scent to escape. Stir the contents every now and again to release the scent. Pot pourri should remain fragrant for several months, although both the colour and scent will gradually fade. You can refresh the mixture by adding a few more drops of essential oil when the fragrance has faded.

herbs and their protective properties

Aloe vera Guards against negative influences and prevents household accidents.

Camomile Scatter around the house boundary to protect property.

Dill Tie with red cotton and hang from the ceiling next to the front door to keep away harmful predators.

Fennel Hang in windows to deter any unwanted visitors.

Rosemary Burn as incense, hang around the house or place in pot pourri to repel thieves.

scent sense

You may not realize it, but your house has a particular aroma. To you it just smells like home, to guests, the aroma of your house communicates a powerful – and often subconscious – message about the kind of person you are. Our sense of smell is closely connected to our feelings, our memory and our psychological wellbeing.

We tend to block out unpleasant odours in our own homes. We find we can ignore that slight odour of carpet underlay or the smell of wet dog that hangs around the hall cupboard. But bad smells insidiously create a gloomy atmosphere. Go around your house and take some deep sniffs. Does it smell good? Are you secretly proud of the delicious aroma of your home? Or slightly ashamed? Letting unwanted scents take over your home is letting the side down.

By now, you should have cleaned your home from top to bottom and it should smell of furniture polish and fresh air, so it's time to introduce some new, delicious scents. Think of some aromas that you love and see whether you can introduce any of these into your home right away. Think of percolating coffee, freesias, roses, freshly baked bread or cut grass.

If you want to achieve a specific emotional reaction like a feeling of tranquillity or joy, try using essential oils. Each oil has its own unique fragrance, which is said to subtly influence your brainwave patterns and alter your feelings and the atmosphere of your home. You may need to experiment to find the right fragrance or the right mixture of fragrances to suit your home or your mood. Some fragrances will soothe and relax, while others will lift your spirits or even act as an aphrodisiac. Some essential oils also have natural disinfecting properties, so offer the added bonus of cleaning the atmosphere as well as altering the ambience. Use a diffuser or a ceramic ring that fits on a lightbulb – or try making your own air freshener. All you need is a mist spray bottle, then add 25 drops of essential oil to 25 ml (1 oz.) of water and shake before spraying.

essential oils for lifting the atmosphere	
Bergamot	Healing and cleansing. Good for balancing the atmosphere and the emotions.
Camomile	Soothing, calming and healing. Good for balancing the atmosphere and the emotions.
Clove	Good room disinfectant. Helps to stimulate and warm the atmosphere.
Eucalyptus	Good room disinfectant. Helps with clear thinking and soothes heated emotions.
Frankincense	Helps with psychic cleansing and purifying, enhances meditation and soothes grief.
Geranium	Helps to boost self-esteem. Soothes fear, discontentment and heartache.
Grapefruit	Good room disinfectant. Helps to relieve self-doubt, dependency, frustration and grief.
Jasmine	Helps to lift depression and create a more joyful atmosphere.
Lavender	Good room disinfectant. Healing and balancing. Helps with fears, trauma, worry and burnout.
Lemon	Good room disinfectant. Helps with mental clarity and optimism.
Neroli	Helps to lift depression and create a more joyful atmosphere. Energizes and protects the emotions.
Orange	Helps with worry, burnout, lethargy, depression and emotional balance.
Pine	Good room disinfectant. Helps with transforming regrets, self-blame and feelings of inadequacy.
Rose	Aphrodisiac. Lifting and harmonizing. Helps to heal a broken heart and create strong boundaries.
Rosemary	Purifying and stimulating. Helps to attract positive energies and mental clarity.
Vetiver	Good for balancing, energizing, grounding and stabilizing the atmosphere.
Ylang Ylang	Aphrodisiac. Helps with relaxing, releasing anger, anxiety and irritability.

Important: Essential oils are potent and should never be applied directly to the skin or put anywhere near the eyes.

sweet sounds

As with all the senses, some people are more sensitive to sounds than others, but if you want to create a home that acts like a sanctuary, having peace and quiet or harmonious sounds around you is important. Sounds such as traffic noise, slamming doors and certain types of music can produce a variety of stress-related responses – including raised blood pressure and increased heart rate.

Music has been recognized as an essential part of healing, meditation and religious experience in many cultures. Most people have listened to their favourite music at one time or another and felt an instant change of mood. In Eastern traditions sacred sounds like chants were used in healing rituals and to enhance spiritual awareness. Shamans have long used music combined with chants and rhythmic movement to induce an altered state of consciousness. The ancient Chinese believed that music was the basis of all things and Confucius suggested that if the music of a kingdom changed, then the attitude of its people would change, too.

For the Ancient Greeks the healing power of music was applied to help digestion, aid sleep and treat mental problems. Plato, Aristotle and Pythagoras all had a keen interest in music and offered many ideas on music in healing, education and culture.

Studies have shown that music affects the pulse rate, skin temperature, blood pressure, muscle tension and brainwave activity. It can help alleviate pain, speed post-operative recovery and bring temporary relief to people suffering from debilitating illnesses. But the wrong type of music can also have harmful effects, encouraging aggression and a sense of unease. If you share your home with others whose musical taste conflicts, investing in a set of headphones could well change your life.

It's impossible to generalize too much about the effects of different kinds of music, but in general, pop music, rock and roll, gospel and Latino tend to lift the spirits and speed

everything up. Classical music calms things down and creates a sense of harmony. New Age music is said to expand consciousness and encourage a feeling of wellbeing, as does chanting. Another way to create a sense of harmony and balance in your home is to listen to the sounds of nature – either by having something like a water feature nearby or by playing nature sounds on the stereo. Waves lapping on the seashore, flowing streams or bird song can help to lower blood pressure and pulse rate, reduce anxiety levels and promote a feeling of calmness and wellbeing – choose whatever feels good to you.

Total silence will sometimes help you to relax, concentrate and sleep, but if you live in an urban area it may be difficult to get rid of background noise. If this is a problem for you look at ways of cutting down incoming noise. Double-glazing may do the trick.

Finally, think about the noise you create. Do you have the TV or the radio on all the time? Do you shout from room to room? Allowing silence into your home can be a little bit scary because it forces you to listen to what's going on inside your own mind. But that listening is one of the first steps to achieving tranquillity.

crystal energy

Precious and semi-precious stones have long been valued for their beauty and supposed healing properties. Like many alternative therapies, the true power of crystals still remains unknown, however it is believed that crystals can be used to rebalance energy in the home. Heating, electrical appliances and man-made furnishings are all said to generate negative energy, which can be neutralized by crystals. However, too many crystals in the home can have an overpowering effect that may make the occupants feel uncomfortable, so it's important to experiment.

There are no rules as to where to place crystals, but here are some suggestions:

- An obsidian sphere or an amethyst facing or near the doors in your home will enhance the feeling of protection.
- A rose quartz opposite the front door to greet visitors will feel welcoming.
- A rose quartz and amethyst in the centre or to one side of the room will encourage a positive environment.
- A clear quartz or citrine in the area where you read, work or study will enhance studying, working or reading at home.
- To absorb the energy of electrical equipment like computers and televisions, place a large amethyst, obsidian or unakite, or a bowl of smaller stones, near the equipment.
- Arrange a bowl of smaller citrines or one large citrine by the telephone to enhance your conversations.
- A clear quartz, a fluorite or a malachite in the room in which you choose to meditate will enhance the energy around you.
- Place three small amethysts or rose quartz under your bed – one under the top centre of the bed, the other two under each corner at the foot of the bed. Some people find that large crystals in the bedroom can disturb their sleep so see what suits you best.

cleanse your crystal

When you bring a new crystal home the first thing you need to do is cleanse it of negative energy. There are a number of ways to do this:

Running water Place your crystal under the cold water tap to cleanse away old energy. You can also place your crystal in a bowl of water containing sea salt for a couple of hours, but make sure that the crystal is not water soluble or easily scratched.

Sunlight Revitalize your crystal by placing it outside in the sun for a day. You can also do this after you have cleansed your crystal in running water.

Sound You can purify your crystal by placing it near beautiful music or ringing a bell with a clear tone next to it.

crystal sensitivity

Many crystals are sensitive to light, heat or water, which means that they may fracture, dissolve or lose their colour if cleansed in the wrong way.

Water-sensitive crystals	*Halite, selenite, lapis lazuli, malachite, turquoise.*
Light-sensitive crystals	*Amethyst, rose quartz, turquoise.*
Heat-sensitive crystals	*Amethyst, quartz, lapis lazuli, malachite, tourmaline, turquoise.*
Scratch-sensitive crystals	*Metallic crystals, celestite, malachite, rhodochrosite, fluorite, apatite, lapis lazuli, sodalite, turquoise, hematite, moonstone.*

common crystals and their properties	
Agate	Calms, stabilizes and helps with challenges.
Amethyst	Cleanses, protects, absorbs atmospheric pollution and aids sleep.
Aquamarine	Reduces fear and stress, encourages creativity, protects against pollutants.
Aventurine quartz	Promotes overall wellbeing, enhances creativity and soothes stress.
Bloodstone	Purifies, strengthens and improves decision-making.
Celestite	Revitalizes, regenerates and helps dream recall.
Citrine	Dispels fear, encourages openness and positivity and helps with absorbing information.
Clear quartz	Helps with balance, purity, concentration and meditation.
Fluorite	Protects, energizes, calms and is good for meditation.
Hematite	Protects, grounds and helps to transform negativity.
Jade	Encourages harmony, prolongs life, protects and aids dreams and sleep.
Lapis lazuli	Helps with mental clarity, protects against depression and boosts the immune system.
Moonstone	Calms and balances the emotions and helps with intuition.
Malachite	Lifts the spirits, calms and harmonizes the environment, good for meditation.
Obsidian	Adds strength and protection and absorbs negative influences.
Rose quartz	Encourages a loving and peaceful atmosphere and heightens self-esteem.
Sodalite	Creates harmony, increases spiritual awareness and aids sleep.
Turquoise	Helps with communication, encourages self-awareness.
Tiger's eye	Helps with inner strength, optimism and challenges.
Unakite	Calms the environment and negates the effects of electromagnetic pollution.

your spiritual home

Your home should be a place that refreshes the soul and revives the spirit. Within your sanctuary you can create a still, calm space where you can centre yourself and listen to your own inner voice, and where you can remind yourself of just what it means to be you.

One of the most important elements in creating a home is making it a welcoming space where you feel a sense of belonging. The fastest way to do this is to add those things that are familiar to you, that give you a sense of reassurance and security, whether these are childhood toys, photographs or a favourite chair. Also important is incorporating a feeling of your family, your history or your culture – all these things will help you feel as though your space belongs to you.

But as well as connecting to your own roots, your home should allow you to express yourself as a spiritual being. If you are religious, you may want to display icons or religious artefacts or create a place for prayer. If your spiritual instincts are more eclectic, you will probably choose to express yourself in other ways. By letting your creativity flourish you are connecting with your spirit, which is a deeply personal act. This could be as simple as arranging a vase of flowers or a bowl of stones, or as profound as playing a beloved musical instrument or meditating. According to Zen Buddhist teaching, it is the intention with which we do things that is important.

an altar

Your home should be a place that not only provides a safe refuge from the outside world, but also encourages and inspires you to be all that you can be. For this reason you should have in your home reminders of the symbols, images and objects that connect you to the people, situations and qualities in your life that are important to you.

One way of doing this is to create an altar in your home where you can display the treasures that tune you into positive and harmonious feelings. This should be a part of your home that acts as a manifestation area, a focus point or a dream space where you enjoy, attract and celebrate those things that are most important to you. There is no need to build an altar specially – a mantelpiece, dressing table, window sill or shelf will do or you can choose more than one spot to place your precious symbols and artefacts. Just make sure the location you choose is somewhere that makes you feel calm, and somewhere that you see often, so that you are reminded and uplifted by your positive treasures throughout the day.

The purpose of an altar is to help you get in touch with your positive feelings and your potential. Whatever you place on your altar should have a meaningful

association for you and be pleasing to look at. Some of the items should act as 'power tools' or symbols, which help you to affirm and attract those qualities and situations into your life that you desire, for example a picture of someone who has qualities you admire or a symbol that represents a goal you are working on. Of course the objects and symbols you place on your altar will change and evolve over time as you develop and grow, and only you can determine what works for you, but below are some suggestions:

- Photographs of family, friends, pets or special places
- Religious/spiritual images
- Crystals
- Fresh flowers or plants
- Symbols that have a meaning for you (see pages 108–109)
- Objects that have special significance
- Colourful fabric
- Pot pourri or an essential oil burner that creates an attractive fragrance

a treasure box

You may find an altar unappealing or you may want to keep some of your most precious objects private. If so, why not make yourself a treasure box. Any box will do – a shoe box is ideal. You can place inside your box anything that is important to you, be it pictures or objects. If you want to make your box look a little more special, you could cover it in pictures that are important to you or attractive wrapping paper.

create harmony

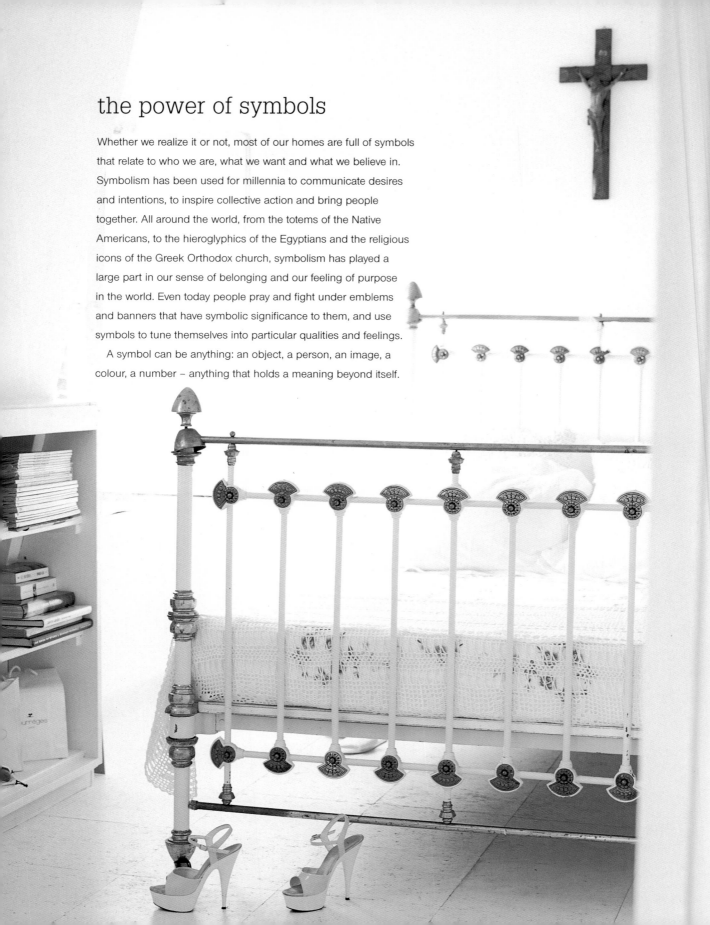

the power of symbols

Whether we realize it or not, most of our homes are full of symbols
that relate to who we are, what we want and what we believe in.
Symbolism has been used for millennia to communicate desires
and intentions, to inspire collective action and bring people
together. All around the world, from the totems of the Native
Americans, to the hieroglyphics of the Egyptians and the religious
icons of the Greek Orthodox church, symbolism has played a
large part in our sense of belonging and our feeling of purpose
in the world. Even today people pray and fight under emblems
and banners that have symbolic significance to them, and use
symbols to tune themselves into particular qualities and feelings.

A symbol can be anything: an object, a person, an image, a
colour, a number – anything that holds a meaning beyond itself.

For example the Chinese symbol of yin and yang represents the complementary forces of life – positive and negative and male and female – while the crucifix represents eternal life, faith, forgiveness and redemption.

It may be that symbols hold their power not only because of their historic connotations, but also because we respond to them almost instinctively. In more recent times the symbols we have adopted have often been connected to our lifestyle, our aspirations and our goals.

Symbols can inspire us to adopt particular qualities, feelings and actions and can be wonderful tools to have around us to encourage a positive and harmonious living environment. Although certain symbols have specific meanings, how you relate to a symbol is personal to you and you should choose a symbolic object or image based on your own instincts.

When it comes to our homes there are many symbols that can encourage the kinds of feelings and qualities we need to create a positive atmosphere around us. Below are some of the best-known symbols:

balance and harmony

The scales Balance, equality and justice.
The harp Spiritual harmony.
The colour green Balancing and soothing.
Yin and yang symbol Balance and equality.
Buddha Balance, joy and spiritual growth.

peace and tranquillity

Calm water Calm emotions, purity and tranquillity.
The colour blue Calming and tranquil.
Blue sky Tranquillity and freedom.
A dove Peace.

healing

Archangel Raphael Physical and emotional healing.
Archangel Uriel Wisdom, healing and recovery.
An apple Youth, health and healing.
The snake Potency and strength.

protection

Archangel Michael Overcoming obstacles, protection, wisdom.
The lion Courage and protection.
The dragon Strength, endurance and power.
A sword Protection.

uplifting atmosphere

Archangel Gabriel Truth, hope and purpose.
The sun Warmth and positivity.
The colour yellow Positivity, lifts the spirits.
A rainbow Luck and spiritual guidance.
A star Hope and good fortune.

honour your history

Part of creating an atmosphere of security and stability in your home is honouring who you really are. Although you are creating yourself from moment to moment you also have a history and a powerful pathway that you have followed to become who you are now.

Honouring your past puts you in touch with the greater wheel of life and your importance in the chain of history. Even people who dislike much of their past can find times that created a feeling of joy or success. To bring these feelings into your home, find something that symbolizes the positive times, such as a photograph or a toy, and place it somewhere special – perhaps on a mantelpiece, a dressing table or a special shelf – where you will be reminded of those happy times.

Many cultures and religions around the world still celebrate and revere their connection to their ancestors. The Celts viewed ancestral worship as a continuation of the Celtic spirit and believed their ancestors were watching over them and would strengthen the Tribal Soul. Some Chinese believed that the successes of the previous generations could be aligned with their own energy and added to their own successes, and in some forms of feng shui there is still a part of the home that is put aside to pay homage to the elders and ancestors.

Another way to bring a sense of history into your home is by honouring the power of myths, legends and traditions. Mythical or legendary tales and characters can hold a symbolic feeling of belonging for some people, particularly if those myths or legends come from your culture.

five ways to bring your history into your home

1 Lay out your family tree.

2 Research the meaning of your family name or something
that represents your family, like a tartan or a coat of arms.

3 Display photographs of you as a child and those you love.

4 Display inherited possessions.

5 Display symbols that represent your culture or a family tradition.

space clearing

Our homes are our sacred space, a place where we should feel safe and comfortable, where we can shut out the world and feel free to be ourselves. However the tension and stresses that we endure in our day-to-day lives can build up, leaving a negative impression on the atmosphere of our homes.

The best way to combat this tense atmosphere and turn your home back into your sanctuary is to carry out a space clearing ritual (see opposite). Most houses could do with a space clearing ritual to refresh the atmosphere, particularly if you notice stress in the air, if you've had an argument, if someone has been ill or if you are having trouble sleeping.

efficient space clearing

1 Carry out the space clearing ritual after you have tidied and cleaned your home.

2 Carry out the ritual during the day between the time of a New and Full Moon.

3 Make sure that you are in a positive frame of mind when you carry out the ritual.

4 Try to put aside time to do your ritual when you won't be interrupted.

5 If you feel the atmosphere in your home is particularly muggy, use more salt in the ritual (see opposite).

space clearing ritual

You will need:

A bowl of salt
A bowl of water
A lavender joss stick
A long white candle

1 Open all the doors and windows in the house.

2 Gather together your equipment and bless the salt, water, joss stick and candle with your good intentions, stating that you would like them to help you clear and renew the energy of your home.

3 Starting at the front door, hold your bowl of salt and walk around the house in a clockwise pattern. Also follow a clockwise direction within each room. Sprinkle the salt with your dominant hand (the hand that you write with) as you slowly walk through the house. As you do this imagine the salt neutralizing any negative energy in the house. Say out loud or to yourself: 'May this salt of the earth absorb all negative and unwanted energies from this place and replace them with love, peace and joy for everyone who lives in this home.' Go through the whole house until you have covered all the areas.

4 Go back to the front door. This time walk slowly through the house in a clockwise direction with your lighted candle, saying: 'May this candle of fire burn up all negative and unwanted energies from this place and replace them with love, peace and joy for everyone who lives in this home.'

5 Start again at the front door, this time with the lighted lavender joss stick. Go through the house again as before, this time stating: 'May this joss stick of air dissolve all negative and unwanted energies from this place and replace them with love, peace and joy for everyone who lives in this home.' Extinguish your joss stick and go back to the front door.

6 Finally, take your bowl of water and walk slowly around your home in a clockwise direction, sprinkling water as you go and saying: 'May this water purify all negative and unwanted energies from this place and replace them with love, peace and joy for everyone who lives in this home.'

7 Finish the ritual by giving thanks to the elements for cleaning your house.

create harmony

year-round purity

keep up the momentum

If you've worked through the book; decided what you want to achieve, cleared your clutter, given your home a good clean, set yourself a workable routine and added those finishing touches that make your home into a place that you love – give yourself a pat on the back!

Creating the perfect place to live is a dynamic process and takes time, energy and dedication. Adopting new habits and changing routines takes persistence and it's easy to fall back into old ways, to get swept up with current distractions or just lose your drive. If you live a busy life, have a demanding career, children or both, there are bound to be times when your harmonious home reverts to chaos – so take this in your stride. With a little patience and hard work you'll have your home sanctuary back in no time.

However, if you find yourself constantly unable to cope, feeling tired or overstretched just trying to keep up, then you need to look at where your life is not in balance. Being out of balance will ultimately result in feeling stressed and stress doesn't just make us ill by undermining our natural defences, it also encourages unhealthy behaviour and unhappiness. For example, when we're tired we often drink too much caffeine to get us going and then drink too much alcohol to wind ourselves down. We graze on convenience food instead of feeding ourselves nutritious meals and flop in front of the television like a couch potato in an attempt to relax. Our quality of life goes out of the window and this has a negative influence on ourselves, our relationships and our home.

Of course some stress is essential to keep us feeling motivated and interested in life, but if you're feeling overly challenged and tired, trying to keep up with a schedule that really doesn't seem to be working, then you need to stand back and see what needs to be changed. Being happy is far more important than trying to achieve a perfect home, so don't punish yourself if you don't manage to stay on top of everything all the time. Find your own balance and settle for what best suits you and those you live with.

find your own balance

We all have our own personal sense of balance. For some of us this means being active most of the time, for others it means having plenty of time to sit, think and relax. If you're a morning person, you'll prefer to do most of your hard work before lunch, but if you're a night owl you might not get going until the evening. Whatever your body's natural rhythm, if you try to work with it, you'll find your own sense of balance much easier to achieve.

Not so long ago people's lives were dictated by the phases of the Moon and the changing of the seasons, but with the advent of developments like electric lighting and central heating the rhythm of our lives has become more and more artificial. Although we often forget that we are part of nature, our bodies still have their own natural body clock, which is affected by the Moon, the Sun and the seasons.

If you are having trouble finding a sense of balance, it may be worth looking at ways you can work with these natural rhythms. Reminding yourself of the season by bringing the natural world into your home is a great way of staying grounded, as is keeping in touch with the cycles of the Moon. Most people know about the Moon's powerful influence over the tides of the earth and since the physical body is mainly composed of water, it is not illogical to conclude that the waxing and waning of the Moon is likely to affect human beings too.

It has long been believed that the Moon has a powerful influence over all living things. Gardeners still plant and reap by the Moon's phases and, until recently, Moon madness or lunacy – which comes from the Latin word Luna meaning Moon – was taken seriously.

The Moon's cycle is roughly 29 and a half days and begins at the New Moon, which is usually invisible. The Moon then gradually waxes (gets bigger) until it becomes a Full Moon. After this point, the Moon wanes (gets smaller) until it becomes an invisible New Moon again. When it comes to using the rhythms of the Moon to improve your life or your home, the phases below are a useful guideline:

New Moon This is the best time to start something new, like a new habit or routine.

Waxing Moon This is the time for doing anything that you would like to increase in size or would like to give extra energy to.

Full Moon This is an excellent time to find a solution to a problem or protect or purify your home.

Waning Moon Now is the time to give up bad habits, clear out your clutter and rest.

the great spring clean

Of all the Pagan festivals, Imbolc, the celebration of spring (also known as Groundhog Day in America) is probably the most important when it comes to our homes. Imbolc, which takes place at the beginning of February, was always celebrated as the time for spring cleaning. Later, the grease and grime left by the use of oil, gas and candles for heating and lighting made spring cleaning even more essential. Sometimes winter curtains and covers would be changed for something more summery. The winter furnishings would be cleaned thoroughly and then put back in autumn, when another big house clean took place.

The best way to get your spring cleaning done is to make a list of all the jobs you want to do, set aside a long weekend or a week and make a commitment to keep going until the tasks are done. The whole point of a spring or autumn clean is to scrub those furnishings and areas in your home that don't usually get done during the year. In your home notebook, you should keep a record of what you need to do for each big clean and, gradually, you will evolve your own list of spring cleaning jobs.

There are some tasks listed opposite that you will probably need to do, but your own home will have some unique features, for example floors that need waxing or an Aga to clean and service. Before you start, make sure you have all your equipment to hand.

Clear the ceilings of cobwebs and wash down the walls You need to start at the top so that you can vacuum afterwards anything that falls to the floor. Pollution, cigarette smoke, fingerprints and daily bumps and scrapes often leave stains and marks on the walls. Don't forget to wash behind pictures and mirrors and dust the tops of frames.

Clean and tidy your cupboards, wardrobes and drawers Take everything out of your cupboards, wardrobes and drawers and give things a thorough clean before putting them back. This is a major job, so do it one cupboard at a time. Kitchen cupboards should really get this treatment at least twice a year; this is a good time to throw out any out-of-date food.

Clean rugs and mats Take rugs and mats outside and beat them with a carpet broom or a normal broom to get the dust out. Hand-made carpets benefit from some time airing in the sun. You may want to have them cleaned professionally.

Shampoo your carpets This makes a world of difference to the freshness of your home. You may want to hire a machine to do this effectively.

Clean under your furniture and appliances Clean and vacuum under any furniture that you don't usually manage to get to, like beds, chests of drawers and sofas.

Clean pillows, duvets and cushions If you can't fit these into your washing machine, take them to the launderette where they have much larger machines.

Air mattresses Stand them up, beat them and if possible put them in the sun.

Clean your curtains If you have the storage space and the money, you can put up summer curtains and swap them back to your winter curtains in autumn.

spiritual spring clean

Certain places fill us with a feeling of peace and tranquillity. We feel good just being there. That is what you want your home to feel like. You've cleaned it, maybe you've redecorated, you've thrown away your clutter and displayed a few choice pieces to perfection – but still something isn't quite right. It's time to try some spiritual purification.

Walk around your home to see whether there are any particular areas that feel uncomfortable to you. It's hard to be precise about what constitutes a 'bad atmosphere', but it's likely to give you a feeling of being cold, tense or generally unhappy. When you come across feelings like this in your home, you may find that all you need to do is add warmer, lighter colours to the décor, open the windows or change the lighting. But if an uncomfortable atmosphere persists, cleansing the air with incense could be the answer. This is a particularly good technique to use if you think the atmosphere has been caused by an unhappy event or an area of your home has gone unloved. Whatever the cause of a bad feeling in any part of your home, it's essential that you deal with it so concentrate on any specific trouble spots first and then continue with a general atmospheric clean.

Cleansing the atmosphere with incense is one of the fastest ways to clear the energy in your home. The practice dates back thousands of years. In the early Egyptian and Indian civilizations incense was used to drive away bad spirits and manifest the presence of gods. Native Americans burnt sage to release negative thoughts, feelings and entities and both the Hindu and Buddhist traditions still use incense to create an atmosphere conducive to meditation. For Roman Catholics incense is used in many of their ceremonies to symbolize the sacredness of a person or an occasion and to create an atmosphere that is more receptive to prayer.

With such sacred and ancient roots, the act of burning incense should be treated with respect. The Annual Spiritual Cleansing (opposite) can be a powerful cleanser and great to do after you've had a big clearout and a good clean. It can be particularly beneficial if you've moved into a new house and want to release the energy of the previous owners or if you want to create a calm and tranquil atmosphere.

annual spiritual cleansing

You will need:

Incense (see below) and a holder
A bowl of pebbles or sand
A fan, a large feather or a piece of card
Matches

1 Decide whether you are going to do a specific room or the whole house.

2 Place your incense in the holder. Light the incense so that it smoulders.

3 Take your incense to the middle of the room you've chosen and say: 'I call upon the sacred powers of sage (or whatever incense you are using) to cleanse (or whatever actions they will be doing) my home. I give thanks for this help.'

4 Walk around your room going into each corner with your incense. You might want to carry your bowl of pebbles or sand underneath it to prevent any bits falling onto your carpet. Or, you can stay in the centre of the room and waft the smoke with your fan, feather or piece of card in the different directions. Make sure you move the smoke above you and below you to cover all areas.

5 When you've finished thank the herbs once again and extinguish the incense.

herbal incense for cleansing		
There are many different types of incense to choose from, but these are some of the best:		
	Basil	*Helpful for maintaining concentration, overcoming fatigue and attracting love and wealth.*
	Bay	*Boosts energy, good for healing, protection and attracting success.*
	Lavender	*Good for cleansing, restoring balance and creating a peaceful atmosphere. Lavender also attracts loving energy and spirits and is good for housewarming.*
	Rosemary	*Use for stimulating, healing and protecting. Wards off thieves, repels negativity and brings clarity to problems. Good for love and friendship.*
	Rose geranium	*Protects the home and family, helps to restore harmony.*
	Sage	*Good for calming, healing and cleansing, helps to bring wisdom.*
	Thyme	*Helpful for stimulating, purifying and protecting. Good for boosting courage.*

year-round purity

123

10 things you can do right now

Keeping your home at its best can take time and energy, especially if you have just begun to adopt new habits. Commitment and patience are essential if you want to maintain your hard work, but trying one or more of the following should help you to keep up the momentum.

1   If you find that your motivation to keep on top of your household is flagging, remind yourself as to why you wanted to create a wonderful home in the first place. If it helps, you could keep pictures of homes that you admire handy to keep you in touch with what you want from your home.

2   If you're not sure when your peak times are (those times when you are most alert and energetic) keep a diary for a week. Take into account that you may be altering your energy levels by drinking caffeine or alcohol.

3   If you find that your home often reverts back to chaos, note the events that lead up to it. Is there something in your habit patterns or routine that could be altered to make it happen less often?

4   Think of something you would like to begin. This could be a new habit or routine or it could be a job, like painting a room you would like decorated. During the next New Moon (many ordinary diaries provide the New and Full Moon dates), begin your chosen task.

5   At the next Full Moon have a look around your home and see whether there is anything you would like to get rid of. Make sure you get it out of your home before the next New Moon. The weeks between Full and New Moons are also ideal for kicking bad habits.

6 Since our natural rhythms change with the seasons, you may find that you need to alter your routine to stay in harmony with your energy levels. Think about how your lifestyle and your home function during the four seasons, then decide whether there are any changes you need to make as you enter a new season.

7 To keep in touch with the year's natural cycles, bring the season into your home. For example, in spring you could bring a bowl of bulbs into the living room, in summer fresh flowers, in autumn a bowl of shiny apples and in winter an arrangement of pine cones.

8 Use incense to cleanse the atmosphere of the room in your home that you feel most needs it. Take a note of whether you think it has worked. Do one room each week until you have cleansed your whole home.

9 If you don't have time for a thorough spring or autumn clean in one time block, create a checklist in your notebook. Do one major task, for example washing the curtains, every week until you have completed them all. Each time you've checked off a task in your notebook, give yourself a reward.

10 Throw out three things that you don't need.

picture credits

Key: a=above, b=below, r=right, l=left, c=centre.

UK Jacket **bc** ph Debi Treloar

Front endpapers ph Polly Wreford; **Back endpapers** ph Debi Treloar/Robert Elms and Christina Wilson's family home in London; **1** ph Debi Treloar/Susan Cropper's family home in London, www.63hlg.com; **2** ph Polly Wreford; **3** ph James Merrell/Janie Jackson stylist & designer; **4** ph Polly Wreford; **5, 5al,ac** ph Polly Wreford; **5ar** ph Debi Treloar; **6al** ph David Brittain; **6l** ph Jan Baldwin; **6bl** ph Debi Treloar; **6bl** below ph Dan Duchars; **6r–7** ph Jan Baldwin/The Meiré family home, designed by Marc Meiré; **8** ph Polly Wreford/Ros Fairman's house in London; **9** ph Catherine Gratwicke; **9al** ph Polly Wreford; **9ac** ph Debi Treloar; **9ar** ph Dan Duchars; **10al** ph Polly Wreford; **10ar&b** Christopher Drake/John Minshaw's house in London; **11** ph Polly Wreford; **11a** ph Jan Baldwin/Christopher Leach's apartment in London; **11b** ph Jan Baldwin/Interior Designer Didier Gomez's apartment in Paris; **12** ph Jan Baldwin/Mona Nerenberg and Lisa Bynon's house in Sag Harbor; **13l** ph David Montgomery; **13r** ph Tom Leighton/Roger & Fay Oates' house in Herefordshire; **14al** ph Jan Baldwin; **14cl** ph Jan Baldwin/Philip Cox's house in Palm Beach designed by The Cox Group; **14cr** ph Jan Baldwin; **14bl** ph Debi Treloar; **14r** ph Chris Tubbs; **15** ph Jan Baldwin; **15ar** ph Jan Baldwin/David Davies' house in East Sussex, England; **15br** ph Jan Baldwin; **16** ph Debi Treloar/Nicky Phillips' apartment in London; **17** inset ph Dan Duchars; **17** ph Debi Treloar/Clare and David Mannix-Andrews' house, Hove, East Sussex; **18a & c** ph Tom Leighton; **18b–19al** ph Debi Treloar/Kristiina Ratia and Jeff Gocke's family home in Norwalk, Connecticut; **19ac** ph Jan Baldwin/The Meiré family home, designed by Marc Meiré; **19ar** ph Catherine Gratwicke/Francesca Mills' house in London; **19bl** ph Richard Learoyd/Morag Myerscough's home in Clerkenwell, London; **19bc** ph Polly Wreford/Ros Fairman's house in London; **19br** ph Debi Treloar/Susan Cropper's family home in London, www.63hlg.com; **20** ph James Merrell/Janie Jackson stylist & designer; **21a** ph Dan Duchars; **21b** ph Andrew Wood/Ian Bartlett and Christine Walsh's house in London; **22al & cl** ph Polly Wreford; **22cl** below ph Jan Baldwin; **22bl** ph David Montgomery; **22r–23** ph Jan Baldwin/The Meiré family home, designed by Marc Meiré; **24c** ph Polly Wreford/Francesca Mills' house in London; **25l** ph Polly Wreford/House Stylist Clare Nash's house in London; **25r** ph Polly Wreford/Glen Carwithen and Sue Miller's house in London; **26** ph Debi Treloar/Robert Elms and Christina Wilson's family home in London; **27a** ph Christopher Drake/Roger & Fay Oates' house in Herefordshire; **27c** ph Polly Wreford/Mary Foley's house in Connecticut; **27b** ph Debi Treloar/Sarah Munro and Brian Ayling's home in London; **28al** ph Polly Wreford; **28bl** ph Andrew Wood/Gabriele Sanders' apartment in New York; **28r** ph Tom Leighton; **29a** ph Sandra Lane; **29b** ph Andrew Wood/Mikko Puotila's apartment in Espoo, Finland/Interior design by Ulla Koskinen; **30** ph Andrew Wood/Alastair Hendy and John Clinch's apartment in London, designed by Alastair Hendy; **31a** ph Polly Wreford/Carol Reid's apartment in Paris; **31b** ph Andrew Wood/Gabriele Sanders' apartment in New York; **32–33l** ph Jan Baldwin/The Meiré family home, designed by Marc Meiré; **33c** ph Polly Wreford; **33r** ph James Merrell/Janie Jackson stylist & designer; **34a** ph Jan Baldwin/Mark Smith's home in the Cotswolds; **34b** ph Melanie Eclare/Elspeth Thompson's garden in south London; **35** inset ph Chris Tubbs/Jonathan Adler and Simon Doonan's house on Shelter Island near New York/designed by Schefer Design; **35** ph Jan Baldwin; **36** ph Simon Upton/Zara Colchester's house in London; **37a** ph Christopher Drake/Vivien Lawrence, Interior Designer in London; **37b** ph Debi Treloar/Family home in London of Paul Balland and Jane Wadham of jwflowers.com; **38** ph Andrew Wood/Mikko Puotila's apartment in Espoo, Finland/Interior design by Ulla Koskinen; **39a** ph Chris Everard/Interior Designer Ann Boyd's own apartment in London; **39b** ph Debi Treloar/Nicky Phillips' apartment in London; **40** ph Debi Treloar/Robert Elms and Christina Wilson's family home in London; **41a** ph Debi Treloar/ Susan Cropper's family home in London, www.63hlg.com; **41bl**

ph Caroline Arber/Emma Bowman Interior Design/All work by Caroline Zoob; **41bc** ph Debi Treloar/An apartment in London by Malin Iovino Design; **41br** ph Debi Treloar/Ben Johns and Deb Waterman Johns' house in Georgetown; **42al & ac** ph Polly Wreford; **42r** ph Polly Wreford/Lena Proudlock's house in Gloucestershire; **42b** ph Dan Duchars; **43l** ph Jan Baldwin/Sophie Eadie's family home in London; **43ar** ph Henry Bourne; **43cr** ph Debi Treloar/ Robert Elms and Christina Wilson's family home in London; **43br** ph Chris Everard; **44** ph Debi Treloar; **45l** ph Jan Baldwin; **45ar** ph Polly Wreford; **45cr** ph Andrew Wood/Gabriele Sanders' apartment in New York; **45br** ph Debi Treloar; **46al** ph Alan Williams; **46cl & bcl** ph Polly Wreford; **46bl** ph Andrew Wood/Gabriele Sanders' apartment in New York; **46r–47** ph Andrew Wood/Mikko Puotila's apartment in Espoo, Finland/Interior design by Ulla Koskinen; **48** ph Dan Duchars; **49a** ph Andrew Wood; **49c** ph Dan Duchars; **49b** ph Tom Leighton; **50** ph Polly Wreford; **51bl** ph Debi Treloar; **51bc** ph Jan Baldwin; **51br** ph Polly Wreford; **52al** ph Polly Wreford/Francesca Mills' house in London; **52c** ph David Brittain; **52br** ph Polly Wreford/Karen Nicol and Peter Clark's home in London; **53al** ph Catherine Gratwicke; **53c & br** ph Caroline Arber; **54** ph Debi Treloar/Nicky Phillips' apartment in London; **55a** ph Caroline Arber; **55b** ph Dan Duchars; **56a** ph Catherine Gratwicke; **56b** ph Catherine Gratwicke/Rose Hammick's home in London; **57a** ph Tom Leighton; **57b** ph Caroline Arber; **58ar** ph Andrew Wood; **58br** ph Andrew Wood; **58b** ph Polly Wreford; **59** ph Catherine Gratwicke/House Stylist Clare Nash's home in London; **60** ph Debi Treloar/Mark and Sally of Baileys Home & Garden's house in Herefordshire; **61a** ph Polly Wreford; **61b** ph Catherine Gratwicke; **62l** ph Debi Treloar; **62ar** ph Catherine Gratwicke/Francesca Mills' house in London; **62br** ph Andrew Wood; **63** ph Polly Wreford; **64** ph Debi Treloar/Imogen Chappel's home in Suffolk; **65** ph Debi Treloar/Robert Elms and Christina Wilson's family home in London; **65** inset ph James Merrell; **66ar** ph David Brittain; **66br** ph Andrew Wood; **66c** ph Tom Leighton; **67** ph Dan Duchars; **68** ph Debi Treloar/Family home in Bankside, London; **69a** ph Sandra Lane; **69c** ph James Merrell; **69b** ph Caroline Arber; **70r** ph Debi Treloar/ Family home in London of Paul Balland and Jane Wadham of jwflowers.com; **70l** ph Debi Treloar/ Kristiina Ratia and Jeff Gocke's family home in Norwalk, Connecticut; **71** ph Jan Baldwin/ Sophie Eadie's family home in London; **72ar** ph David Brittain; **72c** ph Jan Baldwin; **72b** ph James Merrell; **73l** ph David Montgomery; **73ar–br** ph Caroline Arber; **74** ph Andrew Wood/House in London designed by Guy Stansfeld; **75a & c** ph Polly Wreford; **75b** ph Debi Treloar; **76** ph Jan Baldwin/Peter and Nicole Dawes' apartment/Designed by Mullman Seidman Architects; **77a** ph Peter Cassidy; **77b** ph Chris Tubbs/Nickerson-Wakefield house in upstate New York/Designed by anderson architects; **78** ph Ray Main; **79l** ph Andrew Wood; **79ar & br** ph Debi Treloar; **79cr** ph David Montgomery; **80al** ph Polly Wreford; **80cl** ph Debi Treloar/Dominique Coughlin's apartment in London; **80cl** below ph David Brittain; **80bl** ph Debi Treloar; **80r & 81** ph Polly Wreford/Kimberley Watson's house in London; **82** ph Jan Baldwin/Family home in Parsons Green London/Architecture by Nicholas Helm and Yasuyuki Fukuda (architectural assistant) of Helm Architects; **83** ph Polly Wreford; **84r** ph Polly Wreford; **84l** ph Jan Baldwin; **85** ph David Montgomery; **86** ph James Merrell; **86** inset ph Tom Leighton; **87a** ph Polly Wreford; **87c** ph Jan Baldwin; **87b** ph Chris Everard/Jonathan Wilson's apartment in London; **88al & ar, cl** ph Polly Wreford; **88acl & r** ph Debi Treloar/Home of Studio Aandacht/Designed by Ben Lambers; **88bl** ph Debi Treloar/Debi Treloar's family home in northwest London; **88br** ph Polly Wreford/Louise Jackson's house in London; **89** ph Debi Treloar/Debi Treloar's family home in northwest London; **90** ph Ray Main; **90al** ph Ray Main/Loft in London designed by Nico Rensch; **90ar** ph Andrew Wood/Christer Wallensteen's apartment in Stockholm, Sweden; **91** ph Jan Baldwin/Interior Designer Didier Gomez's apartment in Paris; **92** ph Jan Baldwin; **92ar** ph Ray Main/The contemplative space of Greville Worthington; **92br** ph Polly Wreford/Kimberley Watson's house in London; **93–93ar** ph Polly Wreford; **93br** ph Debi Treloar; **94a** ph Caroline Arber; **94b** ph David Montgomery; **95** ph William Lingwood; **95a** ph Caroline Arber/Rosanna Dickinson's home in London; **95b** ph David Montgomery; **96a** ph Polly

Wreford; **97** ph Dan Duchars; **98** ph Chris Tubbs; **98a** ph Polly Wreford; **98b** ph Dan Duchars; **99** ph Polly Wreford; **100** ph Debi Treloar/Susan Cropper's family home in London, www.63hlg.com; **101** ph Daniel Farmer; **101l** ph Emma Lee; **101r–102** ph Polly Wreford; **103** ph Simon Upton/Residence in Highlands, North Carolina/Designed by Nancy Braithwaite Interiors; **104** ph Jan Baldwin/Claire Haithwaite and Dean Maryon's home in Amsterdam; **105a** ph Dan Duchars; **105b** ph Debi Treloar/Catherine Chermayeff and Jonathan David's family home in New York/Designed by Asfour Guzy Architects; **106–107** ph Polly Wreford; **107l** Louise Jackson's house in London; **108** ph Tom Leighton; **109** ph Jan Baldwin/Michael D'Souza of Mufti; **109 inset** ph James Merrell; **110a** ph Debi Treloar; **110b** ph Caroline Arber; **111** ph Polly Wreford/Kimberley Watson's house in London; **112** ph Debi Treloar/Clare and David Mannix-Andrews' house; **113a** ph David Montgomery; **113b** ph Polly Wreford; **114al** ph James Merrell; **114cl** ph Debi Treloar; **114cl below** ph Christopher Drake; **114bl** ph Andrew Wood/Alastair Hendy and John Clinch's apartment in London, designed by Alastair Hendy; **114r–115** ph Polly Wreford/Marie-Hélène de Taillac's pied-à-terre in Paris; **116** ph Debi Treloar/Susan Cropper's family home in London, www.63hlg.com; **116 inset** ph James Merrell; **117** ph Polly Wreford; **118** ph Debi Treloar; **118a** ph Chris Tubbs; **118b** ph Henry Bourne; **119a** ph Jan Baldwin/Camp Kent/Designed by Alexandra Champalimaud; **119b** ph Andrew Wood/Gabriele Sanders' apartment in New York; **120** ph Debi Treloar/Robert Elms and Christina Wilson's family home in London; **121a** ph Andrew Wood/Apartment in London designed by Hogarth Architects (previously Littman Goddard Hogarth Architects); **121bl** ph Debi Treloar; **121bc** ph David Brittain; **121br** ph Chris Everard/Programmable house in London designed by d-squared; **122–123** ph Polly Wreford; **122a** ph David Montgomery; **122b–123 chart** ph Caroline Arber; **124** ph Debi Treloar; **125l** ph Chris Tubbs; **125ar** ph Polly Wreford; **125cr & br** ph James Merrell; **126–127** ph Tom Leighton; **128** ph Debi Treloar.

business credits

Alexandra Champalimaud & Associates Inc
One Union Square West, #603
New York, NY 10003, USA
t. +1 212 807 8869
f. +1 212 807 1742
www.alexchamp.com
Pages 119a

anderson architects
555 West 25th Street
New York, NY 10001, USA
t. +1 212 620 0996
f. +1 212 620 5299
e.info@andersonarch.com
www.andersonarch.com
Pages 77b

Baileys Home & Garden
The Engine Shed
Station Approach
Ross-on-Wye
Herefordshire HR9 7BW
t. +44 1989 563015
sales@baileys-home-garden.co.uk
www.baileyshomeandgarden.com
Pages 60

Emma Bowman Interior Design
t. +44 20 7622 2592
emmabowman@yahoo.co.uk
Pages 41bl

Ann Boyd Design Ltd
33 Elystan Place
London SW3 3NT
t. +44 20 7591 0202
f. +44 20 7591 0404
Pages 39a

Nancy Braithwaite Interiors
2300 Peachtree Road
Suite C101
Atlanta, Georgia 30309, USA
Pages 103

Lisa Bynon Garden Design
PO Box 897
Sag Harbor
New York 11963, USA
t. +1 631 725 4680
Pages 12

Imogen Chappel
t. +44 7803 156 081
Pages 64

Zara Colchester
Writer
20 Frewen Road
London SW18 3LP
Pages 36

The Cox Group
Architects and Planners
204 Clarence Street
Sydney 2000, Australia
t. +61 2 9267 9599
f. +61 2 9264 5844
www.cox.com.au
Pages 14cl

Susan Cropper
www.63hlg.com
Pages 1, 19br, 41a, 100, 116

d-squared design
6b Blackbird Yard
Ravenscroft Street
London E2 7RP

t. +44 20 7739 2632
f. +44 20 7739 2633
dsquared@globalnet.co.uk
Pages 121br

Ory Gomez, Didier Gomez
Interior Designer
15 rue Henri Heine
75016 Paris, France
t. +33 01 44 30 8823
f. +33 01 45 25 1816
orygomez@free.fr
Pages 11b, 91

Asfour Guzy Architects
594 Broadway
New York, NY 10012, USA
t. +1 212 334 9350
Pages 104b

Helm Architects
2 Montagu Row
London W1U 6DX
t. +44 20 7224 1884
f. +44 20 7224 1885
nh@helmarchitects.com
Pages 82

Alastair Hendy
Food Writer, Art Director
& Designer
f. +44 20 739 6040
Pages 30, 114bl

Hogarth Architects
61 Courtfield Gardens
London SW5 0NQ
t. +44 20 7565 8366
www.hogartharchitects.co.uk
Pages 121a

Vivien Lawrence Interior Design
Interior Designer of private homes – any project from start to finish, small or large.
London
t. +44 20 8209 0058/0562
vl-interiordesign@cwcom.net
Pages 37a

Malin Iovino Design
t/f. +44 20 7252 3542
m. +44 7956 326122
iovino@btconnect.com
Pages 41bc

Janie Jackson/Parma Lilac
+ 44 20 7912 0882
Children's nursery furnishings and accessories
Pages 3, 20, 33r

Jacksons
5 All Saints Road
London W11 1HA
t. +44 20 7792 8336
Pages 88br, 107l

jwflowers.com
Unit E8 & 9
1–45 Durham Street
London SE11 5JH
t. +44 20 7735 7771
f. +44 20 7735 2011
jane@jwflowers.com
www.jwflowers.com
Pages 37b, 70r

Christopher Leach Design Ltd
Interior Designer
m. +44 7765 255566
mail@christopherleach.com
Pages 11a

Francesca Mills
Designer/Stylist
t. +44 20 7733 9193
Pages 19ar, 24c, 52al, 62ar

John Minshaw Designs Ltd
17 Upper Wimpole Street
London W1H 6LU
t. +44 20 7258 5777
f. +44 20 7486 6777
enquiries@johnminshawdesigns.com
Pages 10ar–b

Mufti
789 Fulham Road
London SW6 5HA
t. +44 20 7610 9123
f. +44 20 7384 2050
www.mufti.co.uk
Pages 109

Mona Nerenberg
Bloom
43 Madison Street
Sag Harbor
New York 11963, USA
t. +1 631 725 4680
Pages 12

Roger & Fay Oates
The Long Barn
Eastnor, Ledbury
Herefordshire HR8 1EL
t. +44 1531 632718
www.rogeroates.co.uk
Flooring, plates, place mats & glassware by Roger Oates
Pages 13r, 27a

Kristiina Ratia Designs
t. +1 203 852 0027
Pages 18b–19al, 70l

Nico Rensch Architeam
t. +44 7711 412898
Pages 90al

Schefer Design
David Schefer & Eve-Lynn Schoenstein
41 Union Square West, No 1427
New York, NY 10003, USA
t. +1 212 691 9097
f. +1 212 691 9520
scheferdesign@mindspring.com
www.scheferdesign.com
Pages 35 inset

Guy Stansfeld
t. +44 20 8962 8666
Pages 74

Studio Aandacht
Art direction & interior production
ben.lambers@studioaandacht.nl
www.studioaandacht.nl
Pages 88acl–r

Wallensteen & Co ab
Architect & Design Consultants
Floragatan 11
114 31 Stockholm, Sweden
t/f. +46 8 210151
m. +46 70 7203117
wallensteen@chello.se
Pages 90ar

Christina Wilson
Interiors Stylist
christinawilson@btopenworld.com
Pages 26, 40, 43cr, 65, 120, back endpapers

Caroline Zoob
Textile Artist and interior design
For commissions:
t. +44 1273 479274
Pages 41bl

127

index